Prima Games
An Imprint of Random House, Inc.
3000 Lava Ridge Court, Suite 100
Roseville, CA 95661

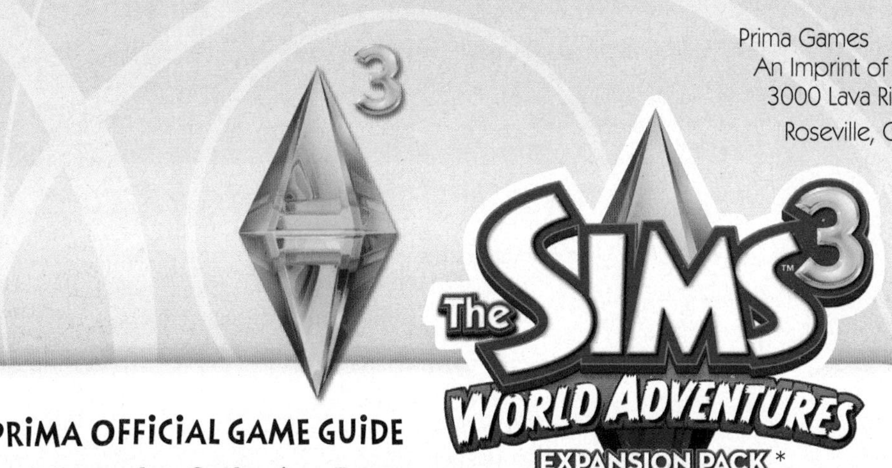

* Requires *The Sims 3* or *The Sims 3 Collector's Edition* game to play *The Sims 3 World Adventures*

PRIMA OFFICIAL GAME GUIDE

Written by Catherine Browne

Product Manager: Todd Manning

Associate Product Manager: Sean Scheuble

Copyeditor: Asha Johnson

Design & Layout: In Color Design

Manufacturing: Suzanne Goodwin & Stephanie Sanchez

eProduction: Cody Zimmer

Catherine Browne

Catherine grew up in a small town, loving the proverbial "great outdoors." While she still enjoys hiking, camping, and just getting out under the big sky, Catherine also appreciates the fine art of blasting the Covenant in *Halo* as well as arranging a perfect little village in *Animal Crossing*. (Seriously, you cannot just plant apple trees all willy-nilly. Neat rows, people!)

We want to hear from you! E-mail comments and feedback to

cbrowne@primagames.com

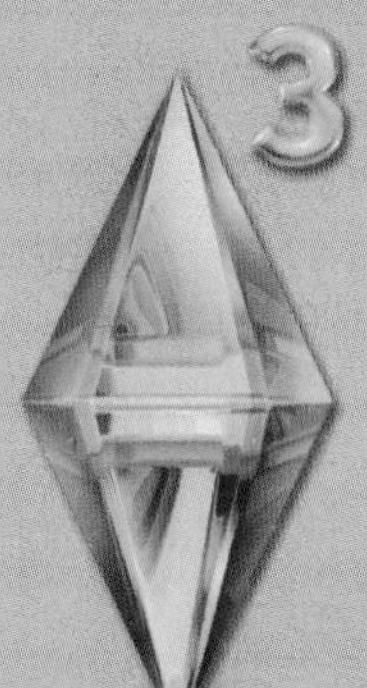

ISBN: 978-0-3074-6659-4
Library of Congress Catalog Card Number: 2009911153
Printed in the United States of America

09 10 11 12 LL 10 9 8 7 6 5 4 3 2 1

Contents

How to Use This Guide

The Sims™ 3 World Adventures is the very first expansion pack for *The Sims™ 3*. It offers three incredible destinations for your Sims to explore, from the mountains of Shang Simla to the burning dunes of Al Simhara. Each new destination offers thrilling adventures to undertake. As Sims rub elbows with locals, they learn of exciting (and dangerous) tombs just under their feet. Raiding tombs, collecting treasures, and living to tell the tale is all part of the excitement in *World Adventures*.

This book is your tour guide to the three new destinations—China, France, and Egypt. It also details how to develop the brand-new skills learned at these destinations, how to use the new social interactions, and what new objects are available. And just in case this is your first time playing *The Sims 3*, we've included an entire chapter to get you acquainted with the basics of the game before heading off on one of your many adventures.

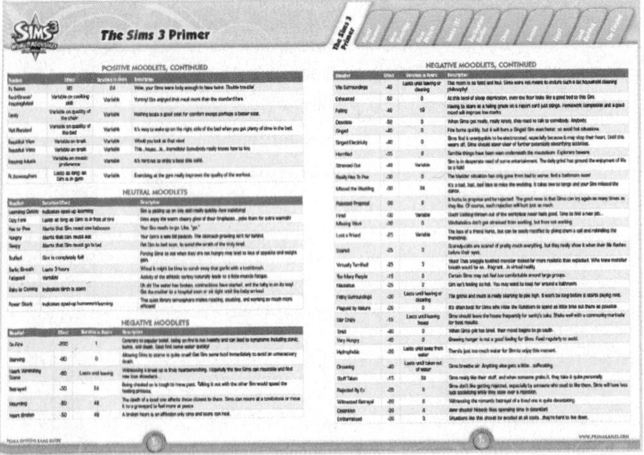

***The Sims 3* Primer:** Are you just getting started with *The Sims 3*? Our primer explains everything you need to know about defining your Sims' lives. How to build a house. Tips for falling in love. The best way to develop skills and get career promotions.

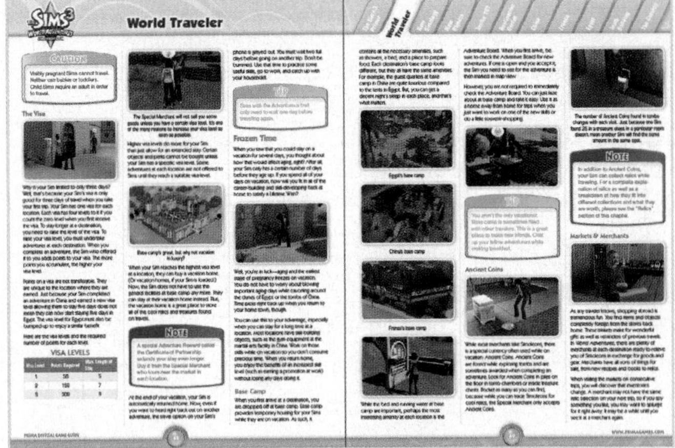

World Traveler: *World Adventures* lets your Sims travel to exciting new destinations. This chapter covers the basics of travel, like how to increase your visa and enjoy longer trips, how to find new adventures from locals, and what kinds of treasures are waiting for you.

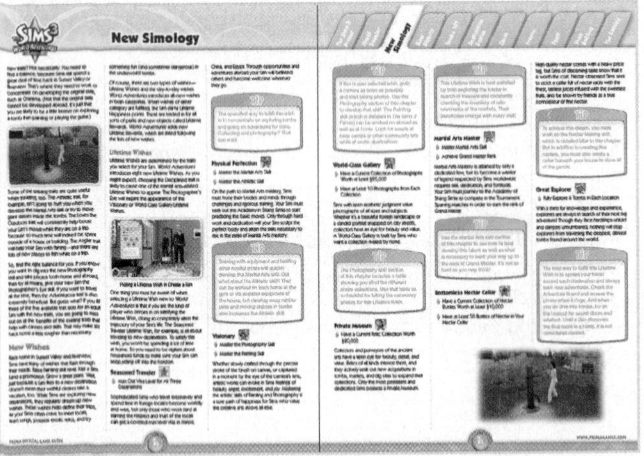

New Simology: This chapter covers the three new skills in *World Adventures:* Nectar Making, Martial Arts, and Photography. All of the new moodlets and wishes (both regular and Lifetime Wishes) are also detailed here so you can keep your Sims just as happy abroad as they are at home.

New Objects: All of the new Buy Mode objects for *World Adventures* are cataloged here along with all pertinent stats, such as environment and fun ratings.

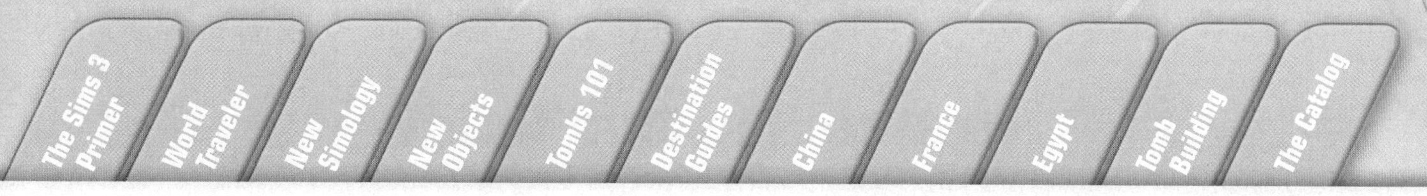

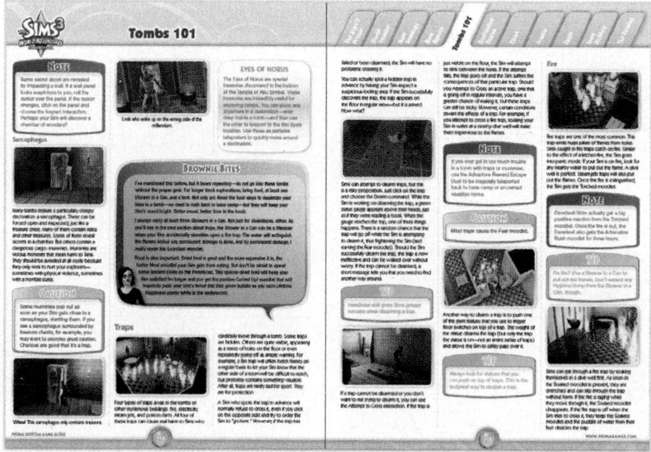

Tombs 101: Exploring tombs is a major part of travel. Before stepping into the underworld, read up on traps, puzzles, mummies, and how to effectively explore a tomb.

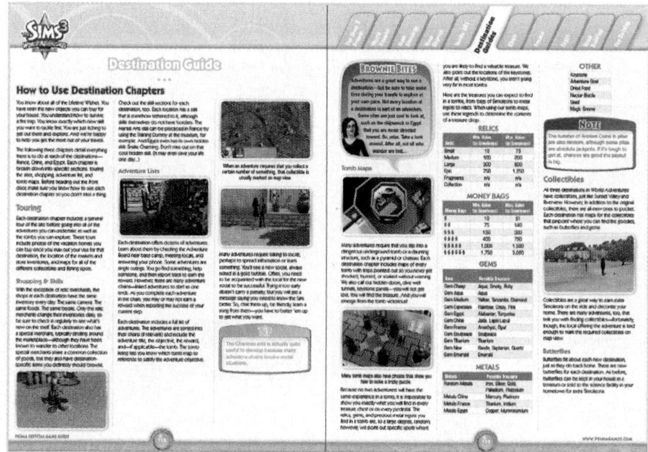

Destination Guide: This chapter explains how each of our destination guides works, from shopping to the value of the collectibles at each location.

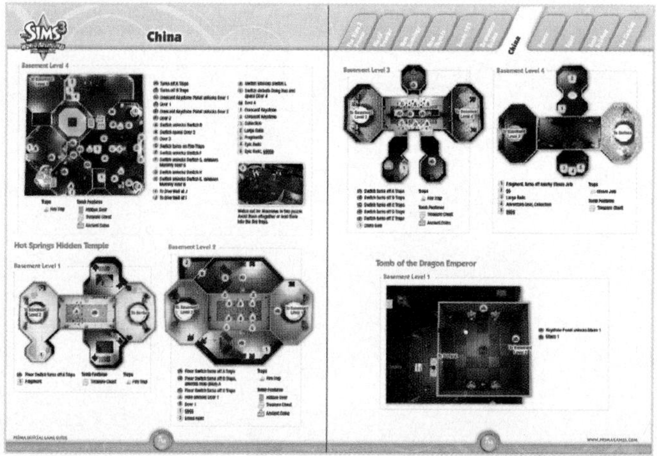

China: Welcome to Shang Simla! Our tour guide details everything from store inventories to complete lists of all adventures to undertake while in China. This chapter, as well as the France and Egypt chapters, includes maps for all collectibles, too.

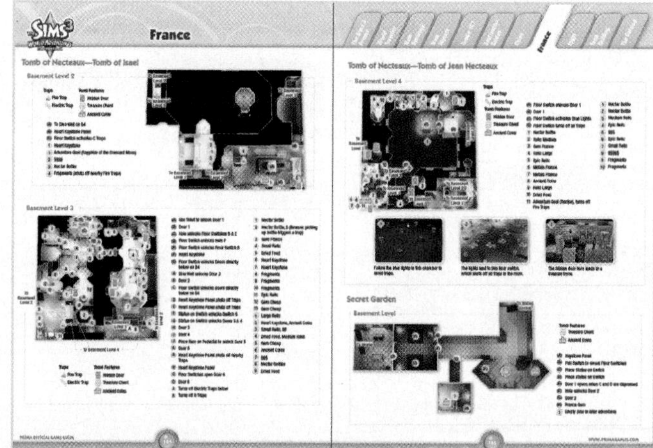

France: Your Sim is sure to love touring Champs Les Sims in France. This chapter details France's adventures, top sights, and all tomb maps.

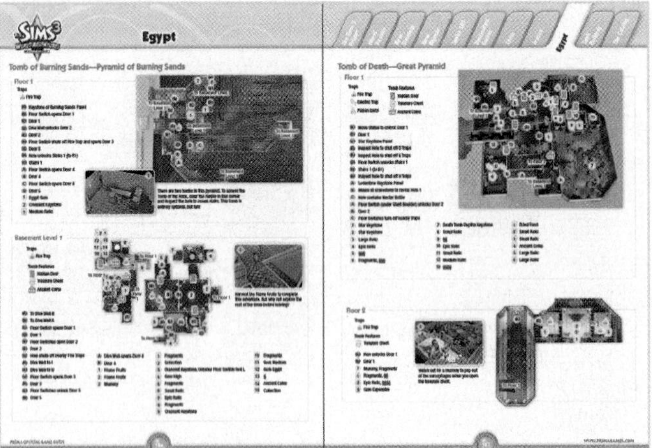

Egypt: Al Simhara is a popular destination for thrill-seeking Sims. This chapter explains all adventures to undertake in Egypt, and provides a map of every tomb.

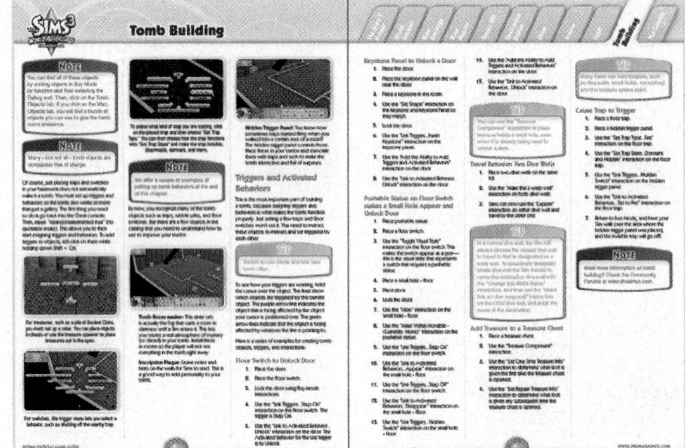

Tomb Building: You've scoured a world's worth of tombs. Now it's time to build one right at home. This chapter explains the special debug commands and menus that let you create basements full of traps and treasures.

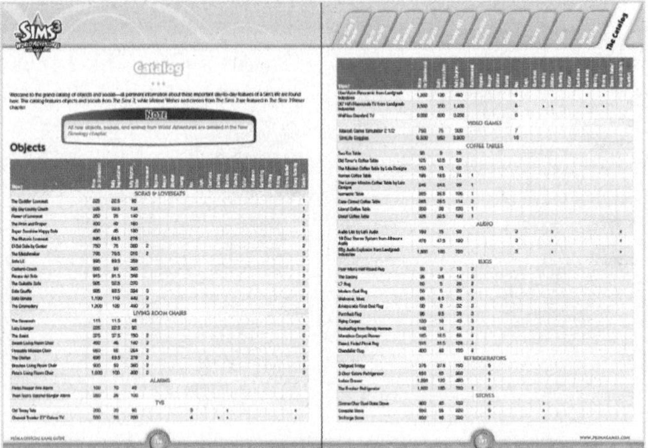

The Catalog: This chapter includes complete tables for objects and social interactions from *The Sims 3*.

The Sims 3 Primer

Before jetsetting off into the horizon to undertake a World Adventure, you need to make sure your affairs back home are in order. As thrilling as it is to see new lands and explore underground cities, there is plenty of excitement to be had back in Sunset Valley or Riverview. Plus, understanding how to get the most out of your Sims' regular lives in *The Sims 3* is important in order to get the most out of *World Adventures*. So, before you book that ticket for Egypt, France, or China, let us take you through all the essentials of *The Sims 3* such as how to create a Sim, how to develop skills and careers, and how to manage your many relationships with the fellow citizens of your selected hometown.

What's New in *The Sims 3*

Is this your first time diving into *The Sims 3*? If you are entirely new to the bestselling series of games (well over 100 million Sims games have been sold around the world), then everything in *The Sims 3* is brand new. But if you are just checking into the game after experiencing *The Sims* or *The Sims 2*, then you will be surprised at how much the game has changed. Yes, you are still in control of your Sims as they embark on individual narratives created from the houses you build, the relationships you forge, and the dreams you pursue.

However, *The Sims 3* gives you even greater control over your Sims' destinies—even though life does tend to hurl a curveball (or five) while you play. There are more enhanced options for creating new Sims—both on the inside and outside. A new mood system uses hundreds of little moodlets to help you steer Sims toward happiness whenever possible by letting you know exactly what the Sim is feeling at that exact second. New social interactions help you guide matters of the heart. And finally, a new Lifetime Wish system gives your Sims overarching dreams to achieve, giving their lives a sense of structure.

This is not to say that everything you do with your Sims has to be in pursuit of this big dream. No contract says you must be 100 percent benevolent. No enforcement mechanism prevents you from charting a new course. The whole point of the changes in *The Sims 3* is that you have a new level of interaction and control to make your game experience—the life experiences of your Sims—as unique as a snowflake.

Create a Sim

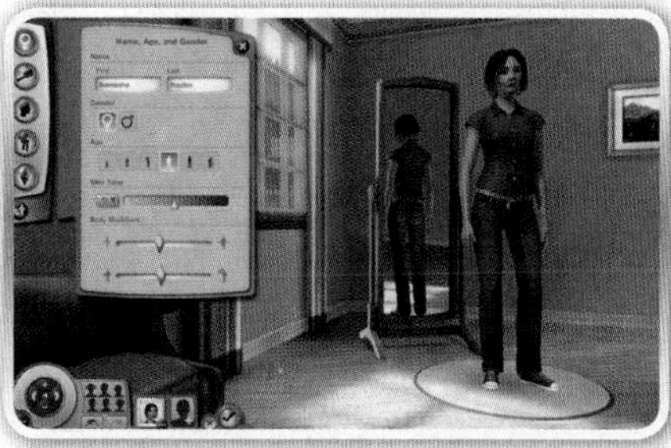

If you have already played a *The Sims* game, then you are familiar with Create a Sim, the toolbox that allows you to conjure up brand new Sims either from scratch or by modifying a selection of pre-made Sims. In *The Sims 3*, Create a Sim is boosted with an even more powerful set of visual enhancements and improvements. Sims now look more real than ever and you have an unparalleled set of options for giving them faces and features just as individual as the people you see walking down the street.

There are not just hundreds of eyes, ears, and noses to choose from. You can also modify cheekbones, eye shapes, height, weight, muscle mass, and those lovable curves that make us human in the shadow of near-unattainable perfection.

But in addition to all of the cosmetic surgery you can perform on your Sims, the Create a Sim mode lets you build an entire personality out of an advanced selection of traits. Traits include everything from Great Kisser to Green Thumb, from Bookworm to No Sense of Humor. With more than 60 different traits to select from (and even more if you include the new personality traits added to the Create a Sim tool when you install *World Adventures*), you have the means to craft a robust personality. Depending on the age of the Sim you create, you can have up to five traits.

These traits are responsible for more than just a general personality. Traits affect the lifelong goals of your Sim, the way certain skills are developed, and even mood swings. (The Over-Emotional trait lets your Sim feel true highs...but also some crashing lows.) For example, a Sim with the Green Thumb trait will be a better gardener out of the gate than a Sim without the trait. A Natural Cook Sim will have a predilection for cooking and excel at the Culinary career.

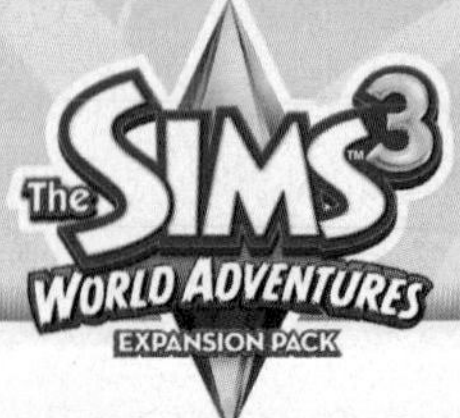

The Sims 3 Primer

Building and Buying

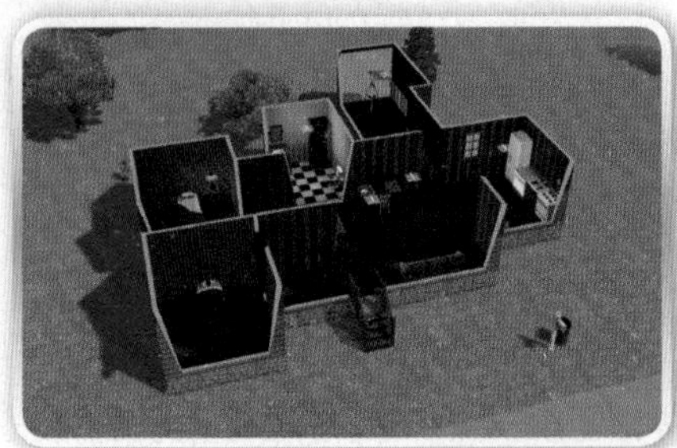

The outward appearance of your Sims and their individual personalities are not the only way to express yourself in *The Sims 3*. You can show off your sense of style with the home you build for your Sims. You can either move your Sim into a pre-built (and even pre-furnished) house, or build a house from the foundation up with the revised Build Mode toolkit. When you initially move in, your options are only limited by the number of Simoleons in your pocket, but as you bank more and more cash, that inner architect can really blossom.

It's not just where and how you put up those four walls that completes your Sim's house. There are hundreds of objects to fill the house with, from couches to computers. Sims cannot live without certain objects, such as a toilet or shower. But other objects, such as an easel, telescope, television, or globe are optional. We're taught that material things do not always equal happiness, but the arrival of new stuff in a Sim's house typically results in a smile.

Many objects are important for developing skills that give your Sims extra definition. In the case of the weight set, that definition comes with increased muscle via development of the Athletic skill. The arrival of a guitar allows your Sim to practice the Guitar skill.

Moods, Needs, and Wishes

The Sims 3 introduces a whole new way to get a snapshot of what your Sims are thinking and feeling. The new mood system encapsulates the entire need system from previous Sims games. Instead of constantly watching over individual needs, your Sim now expresses needs through moodlets.

Moodlets are like slivers of overall mood. Taken separately, they key you into a specific feeling, such as a Sim being happy about being outdoors or frustrated over a messy house. The sum of these moodlets is then reflected as the overall mood. Maintaining your Sims' happiness by alleviating the stresses that lead to negative moodlets and doing things to elicit positive moodlets lets you really get into the skin of your Sims more than just monitoring a handful of need gauges.

Wishes are the things that drive Sims. There are two kinds of wishes in *The Sims 3* now: Lifetime Wishes and normal wishes. Lifetime Wishes are the big dreams that give purpose to a Sim's existence. The smaller wishes are day-to-day wants and desires that we all experience such as wanting to take a class, get a promotion, or start a new relationship.

Skills and Careers

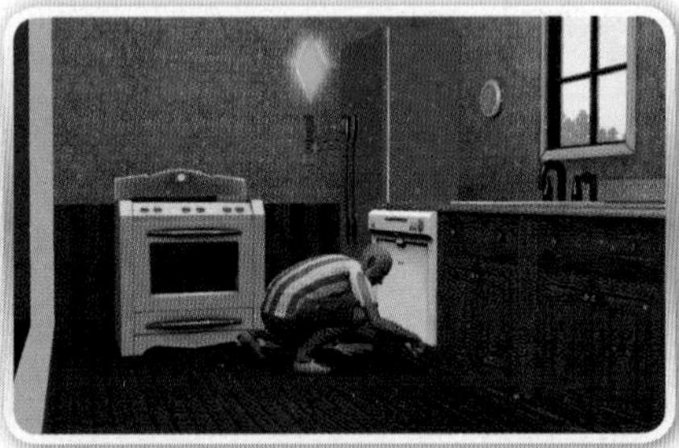

Wishes, traits, moods—that's a lot of different ways to define a Sim, right? But wait, there's more. Your Sims can embark on rewarding careers in many different fields, such as science, music, politics, and even crime. Careers are not just the means for earning Simoleons; they are also a good way to meet other Sims, close in on a Lifetime Wish, and also give direction to skill-building.

Sims love to develop skills. There are many skills in *The Sims 3*, including Athletics, Charisma, Writing, and Cooking. As skills are learned and developed, they not only help out with certain careers, but they also give Sims even more ways to express themselves and fill their days. The Gardening skill, for example, lets Sims grow harvestables that they can sell to the supermarket for Simoleons. And if Sims get really good at Gardening, they can even start growing special harvestables that have wonderful properties, such as the Money Tree and Flame Fruit.

Skills and careers also present your Sim with opportunities. Opportunities are special offers and challenges that can help your Sim with work, skill-building, social interactions, and even the ol' bank account. Your Sims will encounter dozens upon dozens of different opportunities throughout their lives. You are not required to undertake every opportunity, but the rewards of completing as many as possible make the effort worth the time spent.

Social Life

There is a whole lot of living to do between the house and the work site. The cities your Sims live in—either Sunset Valley or Riverview—are not empty places. Each city is alive with other Sims, each on their own personal trajectories. How you bump into and interact with these other Sims changes not only your own narrative, but also the course of these other lives.

To get the most out of *The Sims 3*, do not just keep your Sim holed up at home with a book, leaving only to hustle down to the bistro or science facility for their shift. Get out there and mingle. Meet strangers and turn them into friends. Maybe one of those friends will end up being the love of your Sim's life. Maybe one will be a bitter rival. That's right—you will not win over every Sim out there, not even if you max out the Charisma skill and can schmooze with the best of them. But that's life.

Show the World

What would be the point of giving you all of these new ways of interacting with your Sims and creating amazing narratives without

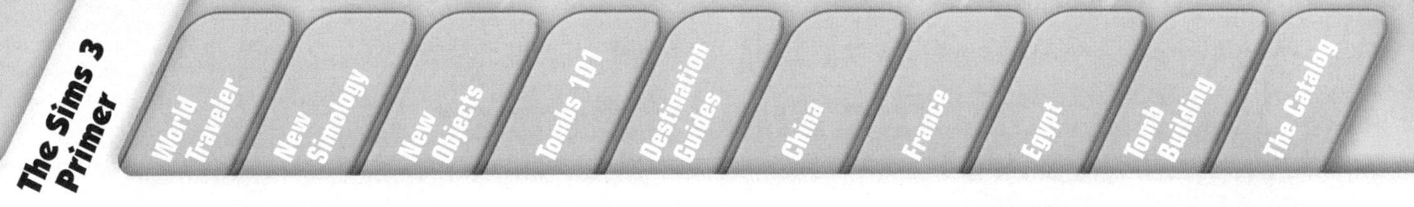

offering the means to share these stories? *The Sims 3* includes a full set of tools for capturing screenshots and video so you can construct movies and slideshows of your Sims. Share these stories with *The Sims 3* community, right from your game. You can also share custom content, such as clothing and furniture patterns created with the different tool sets. And when you spot objects, patterns, clothes, and other good stuff online at The Sim Exchange (the central location for all of the things you can upload and download—all right from The Game Launcher), you can import it into your game and further customize your Sims and their experiences.

What stories will you share with the world?

Create a Sim

Your Sim starts as a spark of imagination—an idea. With Create a Sim, you can turn that idea into a life. How will you fashion your Sim? Will you make them handsome and perfect? Or will you embrace the foibles of the human condition and include one or two unfortunate or undesirable wrinkles into your Sim's appearance and personality? That is what the Create a Sim took is all about: navigating a full field of choices and options as you take an empty vessel and build something as wonderful and unique as you.

Appearances

When you first enter the Create a Sim tool, you meet a pre-built Sim, just waiting for you. You can choose this pre-set Sim and dig right into the personality or you can use this Sim like modeling clay. You can also play around with the Sim Bin, a collection of pre-made Sims that can be called into the Create a Sim "dressing room" and changed to your liking. Perhaps you dig that Sim's hairstyle but want a different color. Or you are struck by the face of a Sim but just aren't sold on a certain aspect, like the chin.

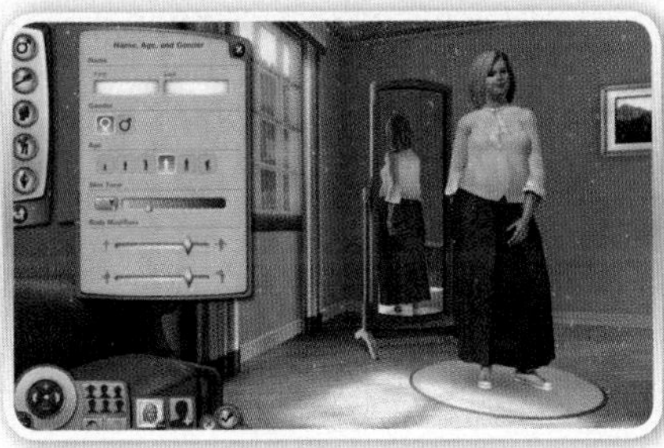

Chances are, though, that you will want to make more than just one or two small tweaks. You will want to design a Sim from the toes up (or the hair down). From the first screen of the Create a Sim toolkit, you have five tabs of options and potential changes. Here are the five tabs and their functions:

- **Basics:** This tab lets you name your Sim and change its gender, skin tone, and age.
- **Hair:** Use this tab to change your Sim's hairstyle, which includes adding headgear.
- **Looks:** Go here to change the general appearance of your Sim's head and face, including making adjustments to chin, nose, eyes, and cheeks.
- **Clothes:** Select your Sim's basic wardrobe from this tab, including everyday wear, athletic garb, and formal clothes.
- **Personality:** This tab lets you assign specific traits to your Sim, choose personal favorites (food, music, and color), and select a Lifetime Wish.

Basics

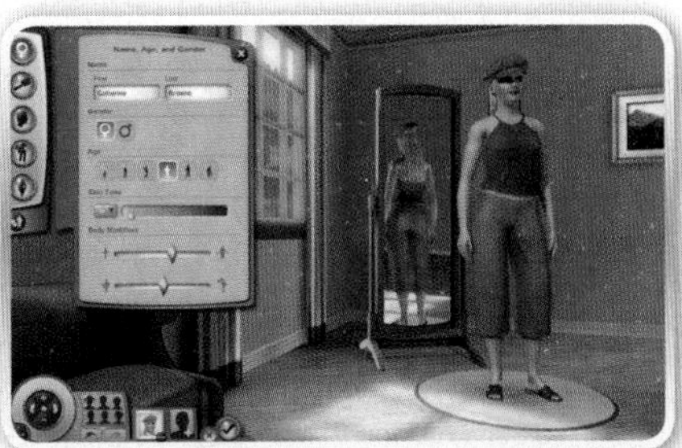

Should you decide to make a completely new Sim, you will likely start tinkering with the Basics tab right away. The Basics tab lets you give your Sim a new name, assign a specific age, and decide the gender. You do not need to settle on a name right away (after all, the Sasha you see at the beginning of the process may not look like a Sasha by the time you are all finished), but the age does affect a lot of other things in the Create a Sim process. For example, Sims from young adult up get five traits. Children have only three traits—as they advance into teen and then into young adult do they gain additional traits, just as your own life experiences shape your personality.

NOTE

Gender does not make a difference in *The Sims 3* in regards to skills, traits, careers, or wishes.

The basics tab also allows you to alter the size, shape, and skin tone of your Sim. Skin tone is pretty self-explanatory. The body modifiers let you change the general shape of your Sim, from tall to short or somewhere in between. You can add muscle mass to tone them up or add a few curves.

Hair

For many, no physical feature defines them more than hair. As such, hair is highly customizable inside the Create a Sim toolkit. There are many different hairstyles to choose from for either gender and each 'do can be further personalized by adjusting hair color and adding highlights. You can add hair accessories too, such as berets and flowers.

Once you've settled on a hairstyle—and you can actually choose a different hairstyle for each of your Sim's different outfits, such as formal and everyday wear—you can make changes to your Sim's eyebrows and eyelashes. You can select from a number of brows and make adjustments to each. A slider bar determines the length of the eyelashes.

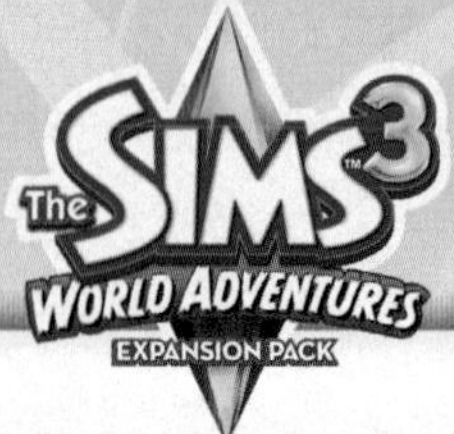

Looks

The Looks tab of Create a Sim is where you select facial features, such as eyes and a nose. This is basically a painless plastic surgery tab, as you can adjust each feature. Want fuller lips? Use the mouth sub-tab and then click into the deeper adjustment tool to use slider bars. Here, you can make all sorts of changes such as the fullness of the bottom lip or the thinness of the upper lip. You can also make changes to the head shape, add freckles, and even apply a little make-up. (Or a lot, if that's your thing.)

Clothes

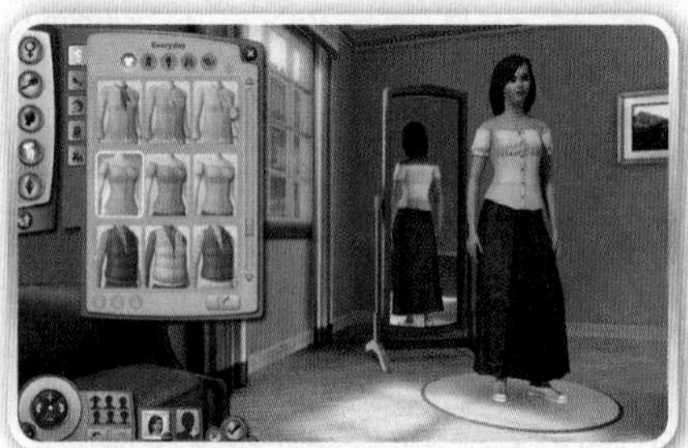

The Clothing tab of the Create a Sim toolkit lets you throw open a virtual closet and select five different outfits for your adult Sim: everyday, formal, sleepwear, athletic, and swimwear. (Younger Sims have fewer outfits.) Depending on the selected gender of your Sim, the clothing options in each sub-tab change.

Everyday clothing is what your Sim commonly wears when at home during normal waking hours or while out and about the town. The formal wear is donned for special events or going out for a nice meal. When it is bedtime, Sims slip into their comfy sleepwear. Before heading to the gym, Sims put on athletic clothes. Finally, swimwear is what your Sim puts on when they, well, swim.

Many categories have entire ensembles to choose from, but you can also mix-and-match different pieces to make a complete outfit, as well as add accessories such as glasses, watches, and rings. Each article of clothing has a default color, but that can be adjusted with the Create a Style toolkit, which is basically Create a Sim for clothes.

Here's how the Create a Style tool works:

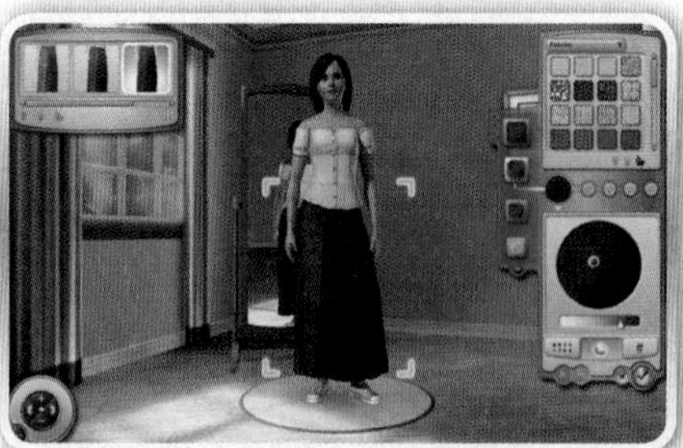

1. **Patterns:** Use the pull-down menu to select from different pattern categories, such as abstract and geometric.
2. **Elements of Pattern:** These color circles are individual parts of the pattern. Click a circle to change the color of that part of the pattern or texture.
3. **Colors:** Depending on how you choose to look at colors, they appear here. Clicking on the different colors changes the selected element.
4. **Color Palette:** View individual colors in small boxes.
5. **Color Wheel:** View colors on a wheel to see how they blend together.
6. **Color Numbers:** Use hex values to assign colors to elements of your outfits.

Let's turn this regular summer dress into a houndstooth classic.

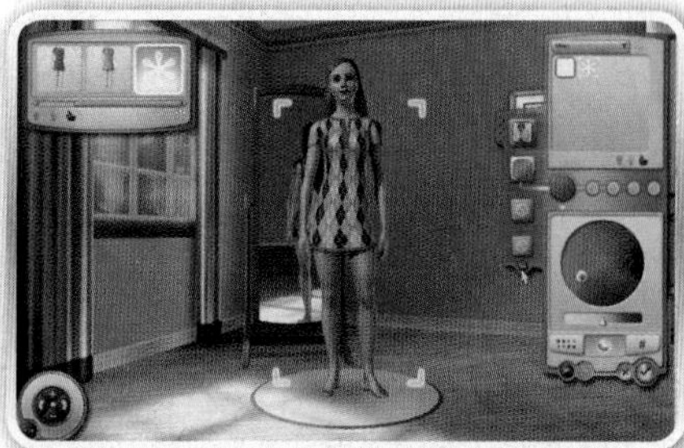

A plain nightie becomes a unique piece of sleepwear if you choose a pattern for the main body and then use the color wheel to make some matching trim.

Personality

The fifth tab of the Create a Sim tool is where you determine your Sim's personality. If the Sim is a young adult or older, you may assign five traits that define their personality. There are more than 60 traits to choose from in the Create a Sim tool—and not all of them are positive. For every Ambitious trait, there is the Loser trait.

Traits affect your Sim's lifelong wishes and goals as well as their core personality. The selections you make here stick with your Sims for the remainder of their lives (well, there is actually a way around this...but more on that later). Choose carefully because these traits have far-reaching effects on all aspects of life, from how the Sim functions in a social situation to how they like to spend quiet time at home—if at all.

Note

Selecting certain traits removes others from the available list. For example, if you select Technophobe, then the Computer Whiz trait is no longer available.

Your trait choices also affect your Sim's Lifetime Wish. The Lifetime Wish is the big dream your Sim hopes to grab. Depending on the combination of your traits, you have

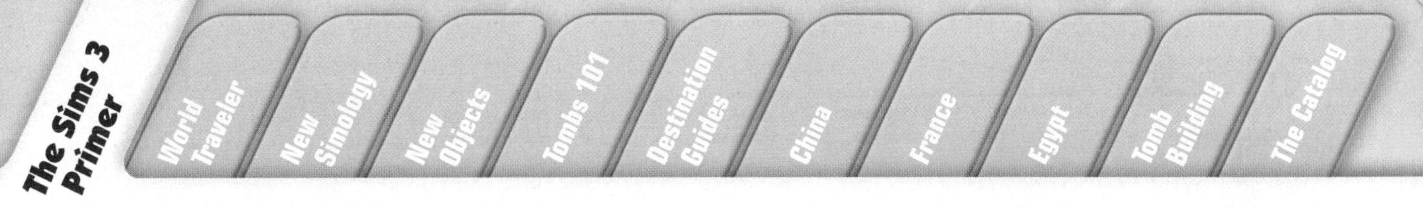

five different Lifetime Wishes to choose from. There is no obvious mathematical formula for determining which traits combinations result in which Lifetime Wishes you are offered, but common sense plays into it. Selecting the Bookworm trait makes it more likely your Sim will be offered the Illustrious Author Lifetime Wish.

NOTE

Look for full definitions of the 31 Lifetime Wishes after the trait list.

We have compiled a list of all of the available traits in the *The Sims 3* here so you can make informed decisions when determining your Sim's personality.

Traits

There are 63 possible traits to choose from in *The Sims 3*. Traits include personality triggers such as Brave, Frugal, Loner, and Unlucky. They range from positive to negative with a handful of relatively neutral traits somewhere in the middle. Because these five traits not only make up the core of your Sims' personality but also affect what Lifetime Wishes are available to them, consider how they might factor into the kind of life you'd like to live inside *The Sims 3*.

This is a full list of all of the currently available traits:

Absent-Minded 

Description: Absent-Minded Sims get lost in their thoughts and occasionally forget what they are doing or where they are going.

Benefits: None

Shortcomings: Sim will often stop in mid-action, disrupting progress and losing valuable time.

Unique Features: Absent-Minded Sims sometimes turn off the television when they finish watching—even if other Sims are still watching.

Ambitious 

Description: Ambitious Sims dream big and are more rewarded when their wishes are satisfied in life. They are driven to move up the corporate ladder more quickly, but fall prey to low mood if they don't quickly receive the promotion they desire.

Benefits: Ambitious Sims enjoy improved performance at work. Fulfilled wishes are worth more Lifetime Happiness points.

Shortcomings: Sim gets the Anxious to Advance negative moodlet if promotions or skill level advancements dont come at a regular pace.

Unique Features: To keep Ambitious Sims happy, make time to advance skills. Stay on top of goals at work, too.

Angler 

Description: Anglers catch fish better than any other Sims. They also enjoy fishing more than anyone else.

Benefits: Anglers catch more fish and gain Fishing skill faster than normal Sims.

Shortcomings: None

Unique Features: Anglers start their lives with a Fishing skill book in their personal inventories. Fishing lowers their stress and decreases the need for Fun.

Artistic 

Description: Artistic Sims are naturally gifted artists with a paint brush. They make pretty good writers or musicians.

Benefits: Artistic Sims gain the Painting skill faster than normals Sims. They also gain the Writing and Guitar skills faster, too, but not as fast as the Painting skill.

Shortcomings: None

Unique Features: Artistic Sims automatically interact with guitars and easels more often. Trait introduces Talk About Art social.

Athletic 

Description: Athletic Sims are the best athletes in town. They can push themselves harder and longer than others, and will do so to feel the burn.

Benefits: Athletic Sims earn the Athletic skill faster than normal Sims. Athletic Sims also take longer to get the Fatigued moodlet.

Shortcomings: Do not like to listen to other Sims complain about exercise or athletic activities.

Unique Features: Athletic Sims cannot possess the Couch Potato trait. Athletic Sims get the Talk About Exercise social.

Bookworm 

Description: Bookworms have a passion for reading that surpasses their other desires. They also tend to become good writers.

Benefits: Bookworm Sims read faster. Bookworm Sims also write faster whether working on the Writing skill, writing novels, or doing homework. They get increased Fun from reading, which helps dispel the Stressed Out moodlet.

Shortcomings: None

Unique Features: Bookworm Sims get an increased environmental bonus from a room with a bookcase. They receive a Talk About Books social.

Brave 

Description: Brave Sims are fearless individuals who will fight fires, wrangle Burglars, and work to protect those around them.

Benefits: Brave Sims will fight and defeat Burglars. If a fire breaks out on the lot with the Brave Sim, the Brave Sim will not panic. He/she will immediately grab a fire extinguisher and put out the flames. Brave Sims do better in the Military and Law Enforcement careers. (Brave Sims also won't be scared by bugs in *World Adventures*.)

Shortcomings: None

Unique Features: Brave Sims can sometimes demand a raise from their boss with success. Brave Sims are not scared by ghosts. Brave Sims cannot pick the Loser or Coward traits.

Can't Stand Art 

Description: Sims who Can't Stand Art will never appreciate the latest masterpiece or expensive home decor. They are the anti-connoisseur.

Benefits: None

Shortcomings: Sims with this trait have a negative reaction to all art. They do not like to talk about art either.

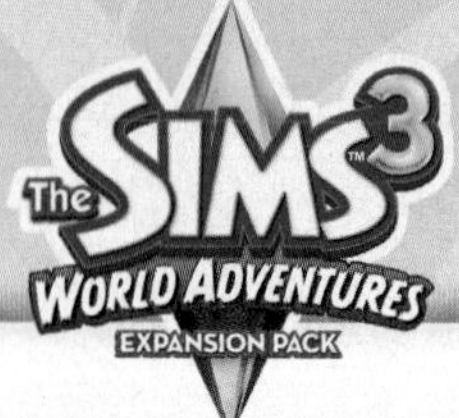

Unique Features: Sims get the negative Can't Stand Art moodlet whenever they are around art.

Charismatic 

Description: Charismatic Sims love to socialize and often know the perfect thing to say. They also like to throw parties.

Benefits: Charismatic Sims start with a Charisma skill building book and gain the Charisma skill faster than other Sims. Charismatic Sims fare well in almost all conversations. It's a useful trait for the Political career because it boosts the chances of contributions. Social-oriented tones in career have greater effect on performance.

Shortcomings: None

Unique Features: Charismatic Sims are great in conversations, which makes it easier to make friends. They're good at everything from Debate Politics to Boast About Fishing. Cannot have the Loser trait at the same time.

Childish 

Description: Childish Sims find it difficult to "act their age." They love playing with children's toys, see things through the eyes of a child, and need to be constantly entertained.

Benefits: Childish Sims get benefits from having children's toys around, such as environmental boosts. They can also play with toys.

Shortcomings: Childish Sims are easily bored in conversations. They are particularly sensitive to repeated socials.

Unique Features: Childish Sims are not afraid of ghosts. Childish Sims can fish in swimming pools.

Clumsy 

Description: Clumsy Sims muck up life with shoddy footwork and poor planning.

Benefits: None

Shortcomings: Clumsy Sims drop food, trip, and lose fish while reeling them in from the water.

Unique Features: Clumsy Sims drop engagement rings when proposing. It's actually cute...

Commitment Issues 

Description: Sims with Commitment issues don't really want to settle down into a long-term relationship or lifelong career. Marriage is out of the question.

Benefits: None

Shortcomings: This Sim reacts poorly to many relationship-oriented socials, like proposing marriage.

Unique Features: Commitment Issues Sims must have a high romantic relationship with another Sim to accept marriage proposal. This Sim will desire to change careers just when things are getting good at work.

Computer Whiz 

Description: Computer Whizzes love spending time on the computer. They are great at tinkering with computers, and can even make money as hackers if they choose.

Benefits: If the Sim has the Handiness skill, they almost instantly repair computers without fail. Unlocks the Hack interaction, which offers a new revenue stream. Sim gets greater pleasure out of Play Computer Games interaction.

Shortcomings: None

Unique Features: Unlocks Talk About Computers social.

Couch Potato 

Description: Couch Potatoes are perfectly happy sitting on the couch to watch TV and eat junk food. They'll need additional prodding to lead active lives.

Benefits: Comfy moodlet is 50 percent stronger. Watching TV improves Fun need quicker than other Sims.

Shortcomings: Couch Potatos need to sleep longer.

Unique Features: Couch Potato Sims cannot have Athletic trait. Will not workout unless in a very good mood.

Coward 

Description: Cowards are terrified of everything that can and will go bump in the night. They are scared of the dark and frequently faint in "dire" situations.

Benefits: None

Shortcomings: Gets the Scared moodlet when seeing any of the following—Burglar, ghost, fire, Grim Reaper. Runs from these things most times, but will occasionally faint.

Unique Features: The trait unlocks the Run Away interaction. Cowardly Sims cannot have the Brave or Daredevil traits.

Daredevil 

Description: Daredevils seek the extreme side of life, even if it means making an everyday chore extreme. They also love fire.

Benefits: Quickly puts out fire when on the same lot. Daredevils never burn to death if on fire.

Shortcomings: None

Unique Features: Many interactions now have the word "extreme" in them. Adds the Watch This social, which asks others to watch as the Sim does something crazy. After being crazy, Sim enjoys the Adrenaline Rush moodlet. Cannot have Daredevil and Coward trait at same time.

Dislikes Children 

Description: Sims who Dislike Children do not want to have anything to do with children. No talking, no playing, and certainly no reproduction.

Benefits: None

Shortcomings: Sims reacts poorly to Sims with children or on a lot with children.

Unique Features: Dislikes Children Sims are in a bad mood any time they are around young Sims.

Easily Impressed 

Description: Easily Impressed Sims are easily astounded by everyday stories and are always pleased with the smallest of accomplishments.

Benefits: Easily Impressed Sims are always receptive to boasting socials.

Shortcomings: None

Unique Features: Discovering an Easily Impressed Sim is a goldmine for adulation. These Sims hang on every boastful word, whether it's about fishing or dancing.

Evil 

Description: Evil Sims love the dark, take great delight in the misfortune of others, and prefer to lead a life as far away from goodness as possible.

Benefits: Evil Sims are not discouraged by a lack of light. These Sims also get positive moodlets from other Sims' misery, like Very Hungry or Smelly. Natural advanced performance in the Criminal career track.

Shortcomings: Other Sims are naturally wary of the Evil Sim once this trait is discovered, especially Good Sims or Sims in the Law Enforcement career.

Unique Features: Evil Sims cannot have the Good trait.

Excitable 

Description: Excitable Sims get excited about everything. They enjoy an extra dose of self-satisfaction when good things happen.

Benefits: Excitable Sims get positive moodlets from many activities, such going on dates, eating a favorite food, getting a promotion, or catching a fish.

Shortcomings: None

Unique Features: Excitable Sims cannot have Grumpy trait.

Family Oriented 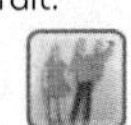

Description: Family Oriented Sims make great parents. They love big families and being surrounded by their children.

Benefits: Family Oriented Sims can help children with walking and talking better than other Sims. These Sims also start out with even better familial relationships than other Sims.

Shortcomings: None

Unique Features: Family Oriented Sims have the Talk About Family social.

Flirty 

Description: Flirty Sims are constantly looking for romance and are most often quite successful in this endeavor.

Benefits: Flirty Sims do exceptionally well with romantic socials and have more available right away. Massages from Flirty Sims have extra positive effects.

Shortcomings: None

Unique Features: Flirty Sims naturally drift toward flirting unless it would negatively affect a current relationship.

Friendly 

Description: Friendly Sims smile frequently at other Sims and are quick to make friends.

Benefits: Friendly Sims default to friendly socials and develop friendships faster. Friendly Sims have an easier time becoming friends with other Sims.

Shortcomings: None

Unique Features: Friendly Sims cannot have the Mean trait.

Frugal 

Description: Frugal Sims love to clip coupons to save money, relish a good deal, and hate being wasteful.

Benefits: Frugal Sims get coupon-related interactions with newspapers and computers and enjoy the Got a Good Deal moodlet whenever a discounted object/service is purchased.

Shortcomings: Frugal Sims react poorly to purchasing expensive objects, even if they are beneficial to household or Sim.

Unique Features: Frugal Sims give less in campaign donations.

Genius 

Description: Geniuses are brilliant logical thinkers, masters of chess, and excellent hackers. They savor pursuits of the mind.

Benefits: Genius Sims generally have accelerated learning with brain-related skills and activities, such as the Logic skill or using a telescope. Genius Sims do well in the Science, Law Enforement, and Medical careers and are naturals at chess.

Shortcomings: None

Unique Features: Genius Sims often automatically use the Contemplate interaction.

Good 

Description: Good Sims go out of their way to help friends and family in need, are charitable with their money, and frequently comfort those around them.

Benefits: Good Sims don't react negatively to socials or interactions as often and try to see everything in a positive light. When Good Sims "help" another Sim in a negative mood, that Sim gets the Comforted moodlet.

Shortcomings: None

Unique Features: Good Sims cannot have the Evil trait. Good Sims get the Donate to Charity interaction with the mailbox. Donating results in the Charitable moodlet. Good Sims can only donate once per day.

Good Sense of Humor 

Description: Sims with a Good Sense of Humor tell the best jokes.

Benefits: Sims with this trait have an easier time starting relationships with other Sims, even those with No Sense of Humor. Jokes have a greater impact on relationships with other Sims.

Shortcomings: None

Unique Features: Sims with a Good Sense of Humor also respond well to jokes.

Great Kisser 

Description: Great Kissers kiss better than any other Sim. They give kisses that are not easily forgotten.

Benefits: Kisses from Great Kissers are more readily accepted by other Sims and have larger positive effects on the relationship.

Shortcomings: None

Unique Features: None

Green Thumb 

Description: Green Thumbs are the best gardeners. They find solace and comfort in their gardens and can revive plants in the worst conditions.

Benefits: Green Thumb Sims learn the Gardening skill faster than other Sims and start off with a Gardening skill book in their personal inventories. They create higher quality harvestables and can revive dead plants.

Shortcomings: None

Unique Features: Green Thumb Sims have the Talk to Plants interaction with their gardens. This interaction can remove the Lonely moodlet.

Grumpy 

Description: Grumpy Sims are rarely in a good mood. They simply don't want to be happy.

Benefits: None

Shortcomings: Grumpy Sims naturally have decreased moods. It takes more work to make them happy.

Unique Features: Grumpy Sims cannot have the Excitable, Hot-Headed, Good Sense of Humor, or Neurotic traits.

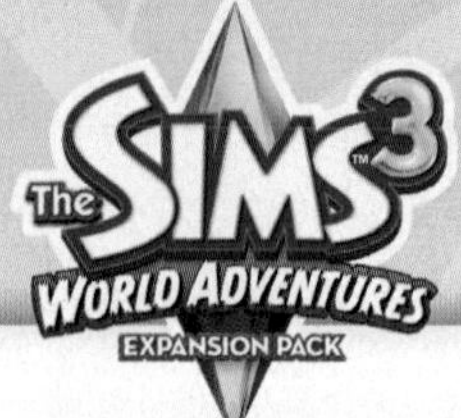

Handy 

Description: Handy Sims are the best tinkerers. They will never fail when repairing or upgrading a household item, which makes electrical objects far less dangerous.

Benefits: Handy Sims learn the Handiness skill faster and start out with a Handiness skill book in their personal inventory. Handy Sims never fail when repairing or upgrading objects.

Shortcomings: None

Unique Features: Objects repaired by Handy Sims have a lower chance of breaking again.

Hates the Outdoors 

Description: Sims who Hate the Outdoors despise being outside and will remain indoors whenever possible.

Benefits: None

Shortcomings: These Sims get the Plagued by Outdoors negative moodlet when they are outside for longer than just a few minutes. (Travel to work is excluded.) These Sims make poor anglers because they don't like being outside.

Unique Features: They cannot have the Loves the Outdoors trait.

Heavy Sleeper 

Description: Heavy Sleepers will sleep through any situation, no matter how loud or alarming. They also tend to snore.

Benefits: Heavy Sleepers are not awakened by loud appliances or music, letting them get a full night's sleep.

Shortcomings: Heavy Sleepers sleep through bad events, too, like burglaries and fires. Not even the alarms for these rouse the Sim.

Unique Features: Heavy Sleepers cannot have the Light Sleeper trait. They also get the Sleep at Work tone for careers.

Hopeless Romantic 

Description: Hopeless Romantics passionately seek their soul mate. They want romance and true love, and surround themselves with cheesy romantic television and novels.

Benefits: Hopeless Romantics are more receptive to romantic socials and get an environment bonus if they are in the same room as a romantic interest in their lives.

Shortcomings: The Stood Up and Heart Broken negative moodlets are more potent with Hopeless Romantic Sims.

Unique Features: Hopeless Romantics have more fun reading romance novels and if they are writers, they create higher quality romance novels.

Hot-Headed 

Description: Hot-Headed Sims are quick to anger. Broken household objects, conversations gone awry, or even the slightest negative moodlet will send them into a boiling rage.

Benefits: None

Shortcomings: Negative moodlets related to anger are more potent. Hot-Headed Sims have increased negative reactions to getting fired and broken objects.

Unique Features: Hot-Headed Sims react poorly to negative socials, such as Mock or Break Up.

Hydrophobic 

Description: Hydrophobic Sims are terrified of swimming. They loathe every second they have to spend in the pool.

Benefits: None

Shortcomings: This Sim hates the water and will experience negative moodlets whenever around it.

Unique Features: Hydrophobic Sims never automatically get in the pool. They will not play with the rubber duckie in the bath, excluding them from Duck Time moodlet.

Inappropriate 

Description: Inappropriate Sims talk about the wrong thing at the wrong time, never think to dress properly, and never think to apologize when they've wronged someone. They enjoy mocking others with harsh words.

Benefits: Inappropriate Sims can rummage through other Sims' trash cans to find cool things (and trash).

Shortcomings: Inappropriate Sims cannot Apologize—they simply do not have this social option. They have the Make Fun Of social that is just cruel to other Sims.

Unique Features: Inappropriate Sims cannot have the Friendly trait.

Insane 

Description: Insane Sims respond to events in life unpredictably. They say what they want, do what they want, and even wear what they want, even if it doesn't make sense to anyone else.

Benefits: Insane Sims are not frightened by ghosts.

Shortcomings: Insane Sims have a random response to a marriage proposal, no matter the level of the relationship.

Unique Features: Insane Sims will sometimes put on inappropriate outfits for occasions, like formal wear for going to bed. Insane Sims can fish in swimming pools. Insane Sims have the Talk to Self social, which removes the Lonely moodlet.

Kleptomaniac 

Description: Kleptomaniacs "accidentally" end up with things owned by others. They often permanently borrow items from work, school, or even their neighbors' homes.

Benefits: None

Shortcomings: Kleptomaniac Sims often come home with stolen objects, which can severely damage relationships.

Unique Features: Stolen objects are tagged with the object's origin. Kleptomaniacs get the Return to Owner interaction with stolen objects that results in Returned Stolen Object moodlet.

Light Sleeper 

Description: Light Sleepers toss and turn throughout the night and are awakened by the slightest sound or bump.

Benefits: Light Sleepers always wake up when a Burglar arrives.

Shortcomings: Light Sleepers have trouble getting Fully Rested and are easily woken by music, children, and noisy objects.

Unique Features: Can use the Research Sleep techniques interaction on computer, but this has no specific benefit. Light Sleepers cannot have the Heavy Sleeper trait.

Loner 

Description: Loners enjoy time spent alone more than time spent with others.

Quite shy, they never approach anyone who isn't a close friend. They prize their solitude and get nervous around large groups.

Benefits: Loner Sims do not mind being by themselves. In fact, they get the Enjoying Solitude moodlet.

Shortcomings: Loners get the Too Many People negative moodlet in social situations.

Unique Features: Loner Sims cannot have the Party Animal trait.

Loser 

Description: Losers encounter woe and misfortune throughouts their lives, beginning with school and continuing into their career. They will fail, and fail often. They won't get mad even when life falls apart. They'll just cry.

Benefits: Loser Sims will get a nice mood bump from the Winner moodlet in the rare event they actually win a game.

Shortcomings: Losers rarely win at games, such as chess or videogames. Losers complain more often in conversations.

Unique Features: Loser Sims cannot have the Charismatic or Brave traits.

Loves the Outdoors 

Description: These Sims love spending time outdoors and find special joy amid nature.

Benefits: Sims get great moodlets for being outside and love careers like Athletic, Science, and Military, and enjoy talking about the outdoors.

Shortcomings: Loves the Outdoors Sims need to be outside more often, which can be disruptive at times.

Unique Features: Sims cannot have the Hates the Outdoors trait at the same time.

Lucky 

Description: Lucky Sims are closely followed through life with comforting sense of luck. They win often and they win big.

Benefits: If a Lucky Sim gets at least four hours of straight sleep, they have a chance at the Feeling Lucky moodlet. This staves off misfortune, like fires, broken objects, and burglaries. Lucky Sims also have a greater chance of getting raises at work.

Shortcomings: None

Unique Features: Lucky Sims have increased chances at winning chess games or videogames.

Mean-Spirited 

Description: Mean-Spirited Sims love to fight, mostly because they never lose in a brawl. They take satisfaction with every new enemy made and dream of new ways to be nasty to others.

Benefits: Mean Sims always win fights. Of course, that means they had to get into a fight in the first place. Every enemy a mean Sim has contributes to the Sim's overall mood. In other words, the more enemies they have, the better mood they'll be in.

Shortcomings: Mean-Spirited Sims regularly make enemies and often veer toward negative socials.

Unique Features: Mean-Spirited Sims cannot have the Friendly trait.

Mooch 

Description: Mooches can mooch food and money from their neighbors, who for the most part, just go along with it.

Benefits: Mooch Sims can actually get free food and Simoleons from other Sims.

Shortcomings: While many Sims just roll with it, not everybody likes a Mooch.

Unique Features: Mooch Sims have the Have Snack interaction on other Sim's lots and the Mooch interactions in conversations.

Natural Cook 

Description: Natural Cooks can improve any dish, making their food the most delicious.

Benefits: Natural Cooks learn the Cooking skill faster than other Sims and start off with a Cooking skill book in their personal inventory. They never start kitchen fires and never burn food.

Shortcomings: None

Unique Features: Natural Cooks can learn recipes just by trying foods on other lots.

Neat 

Description: Neat Sims always find the time to clean, regardless of their mood. They are easily devastated by filthy surroundings, but will never leave a mess behind.

Benefits: Neat Sims will automatically clean up their surroundings and clean objects more thoroughly.

Shortcomings: Neat Sims get negative moodlets around dirty surroundings or unclean Sims.

Unique Features: Neat Sims have the Clean House interaction, which sets them to clean every filthy/dirty surface or object in a house.

Neurotic 

Description: Neurotic Sims will freak out at the most minor of provocations. They become stressed easily and can be difficult to mellow. Luckily, they take solace in sharing their worries with others.

Benefits: Neurotic Sims have a self-interaction to freak out, which gives them a mood boost for a while (at the mood expense of nearby Sims).

Shortcomings: Neurotic Sims take longer to shake stress. Sims can automatically Freak Out after an unfortunate event, such as burning food or breaking an object.

Unique Features: Neurotic Sims can use a new Freak Out interaction that is disruptive to nearby Sims. At the end of the Freak Out, they get the Tranquil moodlet.

Never Nude 

Description: Never Nudes despise nudity and will never completely remove their clothing.

Benefits: None

Shortcomings: None

Unique Features: Never Nude Sims wear swimwear into the bath or shower.

No Sense of Humor 

Description: Sims with No Sense of Humor tell terrible jokes, so they tend not to tell them. They don't enjoy the jokes of others, either. Humor is simply wasted on them.

Benefits: None

Shortcomings: No Sense of Humor Sims have weak reactions to jokes or humorous socials.

Unique Features: No Sense of Humor

Sims cannot have the Good Sense of Humor or Schmoozer traits.

Over-Emotional 

Description: Over-Emotional Sims experience great mood swings when both good and bad things happen. They are constantly shedding tears of joy, whether it's at a wedding or just on the couch watching romantic television.

Benefits: Over-Emotional Sims get an extra bump out of positive moodlets.

Shortcomings: Over-Emotional Sims also get an extra dip out of negative moodlets.

Unique Features: Over-Emotional Sims have extreme reactions to events such as getting a raise/promotion, having a child, or getting married.

Party Animal 

Description: Party Animals love to party, and others love to party with them. When a Party Animal hosts a party, everyone comes and has a great time. Wooo!

Benefits: Any Sim invited to a party from a Party Animal will attend regardless of relationship. These Sims have a greater chance bringing gifts to a Party Animal's party.

Shortcomings: None

Unique Features: Party Animals have the Wooo! social. If the other Sim reacts positively, the Party Animal gets the Awesome Party and Life of the Party moodlets.

Perfectionist 

Description: Perfectionists spend more time cooking, writing, or even painting, but what they eventually finish is noticeably better than average. Perfectionists accept nothing shy of perfection.

Benefits: Perfectionist Sims have the chance to make higher quality painting, novels, recipes, and homework.

Shortcomings: If a Perfectionist Sim is making a high-quality piece of art or food, the action takes longer.

Unique Features: The Perfectionist Sim always makes the bed after waking up from sleep.

Schmoozer 

Description: Schmoozers are really good at befriending neighbors and co-workers, and sucking up to their bosses. They love to flatter and are very good at it.

Benefits: Schmoozer Sims more effectively socialize/suck-up with co-workers and bosses.

Shortcomings: None

Unique Features: Compliments from Schmoozers are always accepted and always improve a relationship. The Chat social is replaced with Schmooze.

Slob 

Description: Slobs constantly leave messes in their wake. To make matters worse, they won't offer to pick up or clean. Luckily, common filth won't offend their senses.

Benefits: Slob Sims are not negatively affected my messes or bad smells. Slob Sims can eat spoiled or burnt food without negative effects.

Shortcomings: Objects used by Slobs get dirtier faster than when used by other Sims.

Unique Features: Slobs can use the Lick Dish Clean interaction.

Snob 

Description: Snobs are very hard to impress, though they love hearing about themselves and will never turn down a compliment. They dream of owning only the finest things and being associated with the highest echelon of neighborhood Sims.

Benefits: Snob Sims love mirrors and expensive objects. They also always accept compliments regardless of relationship.

Shortcomings: Snobs are very hard to impress in conversations.

Unique Features: Snobs often wish to make money, date wealthy Sims, take well-paying jobs, and buy new objects -- particularly mirrors!

Technophobe 

Description: Technophobe Sims hate television. They rarely watch television and always look for alternate entertainment.

Benefits: None

Shortcomings: Technophobes have negative reactions to computers and televisions.

Unique Features: Because Technophobes do not like computers or televisions, they have a difficult time repairing them and have a harder time learning the Writing skill.

Unflirty 

Description: Unflirty Sims do not appreciate romantic advances and are difficult to woo. It's not that they don't want to love, it's just difficult for them.

Benefits: None

Shortcomings: Unflirty Sims have negative reactions to romantic socials, such as kisses or flirtatious jokes.

Unique Features: Unflirty Sims cannot have the Flirty trait. They also have fewer romantic socials.

Unlucky 

Description: Things rarely go right for Unlucky Sims. They lose at everything they touch.

Benefits: The Grim Reaper sometimes takes pity on Unlucky Sims who die of accidents and revives them.

Shortcomings: Unlucky Sims occasionally get the Feeling Unlucky moodlet after four hours of sleep, which affects their chances of burning food, setting fires, and losing games.

Unique Features: Unlucky Sims cannot have the Lucky trait.

Vegetarian 

Description: Vegetarian Sims never choose to eat meat and doing so makes them ill.

Benefits: Vegetarians live longer than other Sims.

Shortcomings: Vegetarian Sims who eat meat earn the Nauseous moodlet.

Unique Features: Vegetarian Sims cannot prepare recipes with meat in them. Vegetarians can also cook vegetarian versions of some recipes, such as veggie burgers and tofu dogs.

Virtuoso 

Description: Virtuosos have a natural gift with musical instruments and make the best musicians.

Benefits: Virtuosos learn the Guitar skill faster than other Sims and start with a Guitar skill book in their personal inventory. They earn more Simoleons from tips.

Shortcomings: None

Unique Features: Virtuoso Sims tend to sing in the shower.

Workaholic 

Description: Workaholics love to work and rarely become stressed from working. Their mood suffers when they miss work, but they can make it up by working from home. Workaholics make the best employees.

Benefits: Workaholics finish homework faster and have fun doing it. Workaholics have a better chance at getting raises at careers. They get the Likes Work moodlet when working.

Shortcomings: Workaholics suffer from the Missing Work moodlet if they accidentally miss a shift.

Unique Features: Workaholics can check in at work via the cellphone. These Sims can also work from home on the computer, which helps with career advancement.

HIDDEN TRAIT

There is a hidden trait that can only be earned through genetics: Pyromaniac. The Pyromaniac trait is sometimes given to children of Firefighters. Pyromaniacs can set objects on fire and get a positive moodlet from doing so. Of course, this ruins the object. Pyromaniacs can also take a fruit and turn it into a Flame Fruit, which Pyromaniacs have fun eating.

Lifetime Wishes

At the very end of the Create a Sim process, you select a Lifetime Wish for your new Sim. This wish is the Sim's main goal in life—it is the dream that ultimately defines them. While you do not necessarily have to play the game strictly to satisfy these wishes, they do give you some structure. Plus, fulfilling a Lifetime Wish rewards your Sim with Lifetime Happiness points—a lot of them. Lifetime Happiness points are a currency that your Sim banks when you help them satisfy smaller wishes or maintain high spirits. While you can amass a lot of Lifetime Happiness points by fulfilling the day-to-day wishes and making sure your Sim is consistently happy, there is no bigger payout than the Lifetime Wish.

NOTE

Look for more information about day-to-day wishes and Lifetime Happiness points in the "A Day in the Life" section of this chapter.

Lifetime Wishes

Become a Creature-Robot Cross Breeder

- Reach Level 9 in the Science Career

The complexity of circuitry and oddity of organics perennially perplex the scientific community. Your Sim must have excellent Handiness expertise and enough experience with gardening and fishing to know what organic beings need to thrive when fused with machines.

Become a Grand Master in Chess

- Chess Legend
- Master the Logic Skill

Logic is cold and calculated, and chess is the battleground for those who adhere to it. A Sim who can master the path of logic and reach the coveted rank of Chess Grand Master will forever be enshrined in memory.

Become a Master Thief

- Reach Level 10 in the Criminal Career (Thief branch)

Lightning quick reflexes (honed at the gym of course) and impeccable teamwork will take your Sim far, but only the most cat-like thieves reach the rank of Master Thief. The path begins with the local crime organization and leads to pilfering the world's jewels!

Become a Superstar Athlete

- Reach Level 9 of the Athletic Career

Earning a championship jersey means developing the utmost athletic perfection and a tight bond with teammates, thus fostering victory even when the game seems lost.

Become an Astronaut

- Become an Astronaut in the Military Career
- Reach Level 10 in the Military Career

Astronauts are incredible pilots who have endured years of rigorous athletic training. An astronaut's thirst for adventure is quenched only by daring space missions.

Celebrated Five-Star Chef

- Reach Level 10 of the Culinary Career

Bustling kitchens filled with fiery stoves and flamin' hot dishes are in store for Sims desiring the Five-Star Chef epithet. Your Sim will need to build relationships with kitchen staff and develop Cooking skills.

CEO of a Mega-Corporation

- Become a CEO in the Business Career

Your Sim can become a purveyor of profits and margins that make board members smile. Your Sim must successfully schmooze co-workers and the ever-present boss to ascend the corporate hierarchy.

Culinary Librarian

- Learn Every Recipe

By mastering the Cooking skill and perusing the bookstore for recipes, your Sim can become a walking library of culinary expertise.

The Emperor of Evil

- Reach Level 10 of the Criminal Career (Evil branch)

Your Sim can become the leader of the world's most diabolical organization. Strong evil office relationships are a must, as is possessing enough Athletic ability.

Forensic Specialist: Dynamic DNA Profiler

- Reach Level 10 in the Law Enforcement Career (Forensic branch)

Special Agents in the field require the best data to apprehend criminals and only the finest analytical minds will suffice. After all, criminals leave only so many useful clues, making the work challenging. Students of Logic with a knack for Painting make the best forensic analysts.

Gold Digger

- See Ghost of Wealthy Spouse

Some paths to acquiring wealth are more devious and selfish than others. Gold Diggers seek to marry the incredibly wealthy and yearn to see the premature demise of their

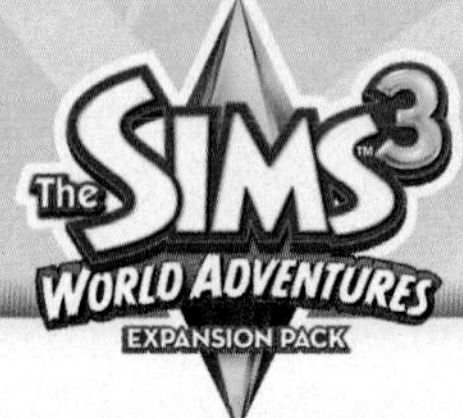

spouse. It's the only way to really enjoy the money—alone and rich.

Golden Tongue, Golden Fingers

- Master the Guitar Skill
- Master the Charisma Skill

Kindly spoken words and softly strummed strings are the fastest way to a Sim's heart and an excellent way to make friends. Charisma is a highly social endeavor, whereas guitar is for those who love learning and performing music. A master of both is an irresistible charmer.

Heartbreaker

- Be the Girlfriend/Boyfriend of 10 Different Sims

Why settle for a long-term romantic relationship or monogamy when there are so many attractive Sims out there? Your Sim can find a lifetime's enjoyment by seeing many different Sims. Just keep your Sim's many former lovers at a reasonably safe distance.

Hit Movie Composer

- Reach Level 10 in the Music Career (Symphonic branch)

The composer must be well-liked by the musicians of the symphony, a master of music, and one who truly understands logic to grasp the science of sound.

Illustrious Author

- Master the Painting Skill
- Master the Writing Skill

The arts delight most Sims. However, for each successful artist there are dozens of has-beens and failures. Your Sim can write and paint toward a lifetime of artistic success, but it won't be easy.

International Super Spy

- Reach Level 10 in the Law Enforcement Career (Special Agent branch)

The forces of justice and order need champions to foil the nefarious plans of those who would do the citizenry harm. Only Sims in peak physical condition who use logic to solve troubled situations and look smashing in evening wear need apply at the Police Department.

Jack of All Trades

- Reach Level 5 of 4 Different Careers

Being tied to a single job isn't for everyone. Your Sim will be a jack of all trades, or at least four, by climbing halfway up the corporate ladder of four careers.

Leader of the Free World

- Reach Level 10 in the Political Career

The Leader of the Free World must be a passionate and charismatic politician who can raise immense campaign funding. It is an unenviable position where a Sim must constantly adjust to unexpected problems. The world needs great leaders—like your Sim.

Living in the Lap of Luxury

- Have Household Net Worth of 100,000 Simoleons

A life of extreme wealth is one of comfort and privilege, but also one of fulfillment. If your Sim owns a fabulously furnished home and has enough money to live in luxury, satisfaction will be had.

Master of the Arts

- Master the Guitar Skill
- Master the Painting Skill

The artisan can paint images that incite the humorless to laugh and the inarticulate to eloquence. The addition of Guitar skills can make your Sim the envy of the community.

Perfect Garden

- Plant and Grow 8 Different Species of Perfect Plant

The most delicious fruits and vegetables are harvested from a perfect plant. Perfect plants grow from only the best seeds, which drop from the branches of generation-spanning plants that have been well tended and loved. Only fanatically patient outdoorsmen can plant such a garden.

Perfect Mind, Perfect Body

- Master the Athletic Skill
- Master the Logic Skill

Seeking personal perfection through rigorous mental and physical training is a noble goal that guarantees a lifetime of challenge. Your Sim may one day stand on the peak of physical Sim achievement, but not without much sweat and mental strain.

Presenting the Perfect Private Aquarium

- Have at Least 13 Different Species of Perfect Fish in Fishbowls

The ultimate fishermen can reel in incredibly majestic fish; so large they're practically bursting out of their scales. Truly dedicated fishermen spend hours casting and re-casting until the fruits of the deep blue are caught. Your Sim can create an amazing private aquarium by catching the most magnificent fish for a private collection.

Renaissance Sim

- Reach Level 10 with 3 Different Skills

True scholars are not satisfied with mastering a single subject. Reach the top level of several skills to become a Renaissance Sim.

Rock Star

- Reach Level 10 in the Music Career (Rock branch)

The path of rock appeals to many a young Sim, but the perilous journey is completed by few. Your Sim must join the music career, survive the early years of rock servitude, and master the guitar to become the greatest rock star the world has ever known.

Star News Anchor

- Reach Level 10 in the Journalism Career

Great Charisma and an epic level of literary eloquence are required to succeed in the fast-paced field of journalism.

Super Popular

- Be Friends with 20 Sims

Popularity is a sign that the community enjoys the friendship of your Sim. Unselfish socialization is a worthwhile pursuit.

Surrounded by Family

- Raise 5 Children from Babies to Teens

For family focused Sims, the pitter patter of little feet makes parenthood worthwhile. A house full of children can mean a tight budget, little personal time, and few luxuries, but there's always somebody to play with or something new to teach.

Swimming in Cash

- Have 50,000 Simoleons in Household Funds

Simoleons fuel the world and for some fiscally minded Sims, personal happiness as well. Scrimping and saving to live in an efficient home, working hard at work, and succeeding at lucrative personal side projects will allow your Sim to swim in the metaphorical pool of money.

Tinkerer

- Master the Logic Skill
- Master the Handiness Skill

Logic and Handiness are natural bedfellows, partners of invention and discovery. Logic leads to great finds like eerie nebulas, whereas Handiness unlocks interesting household improvements.

World Renowned Surgeon

- Reach Level 10 in the Medical Career

Only the greatest surgeons defeat disease. Your Sim must be able to make logically brilliant, split-second decisions at the operating table. The medical profession is only for incredibly dedicated Sims who are mentally above the rest.

NOTE

You can create multiple Sims at the beginning of a game and than define their relationships within a single household, such as spouses, house mates, siblings, and parents. Families and house mates share Simoleons.

Creating a House

Now that you have created a new Sim (or a new household of Sims), it is time to give them a place to hang their hat. A Sim's home is a Sim's castle—in some cases, a clever player can deliver on that adage literally. Much like working with Create a Sim, you have nearly limitless tools for putting up a personal paradise for your Sim. You are limited only by your initial bank account. However, as your Sim earns more Simoleons, you can keep building onto a house and eventually put together a real dream house.

That same budget also prevents you from an initial spending spree in Buy Mode, which is where you shop for the objects that fill a house. But like building on to a house, as your Sim rakes in the Simoleons, you can amass quite a treasure trove of items and goodies.

Now, you do not have to build a house. You can choose from plenty of pre-built houses or buy a furnished joint with all of the objects you need for a basic existence (toilet, shower, fridge, etc.). And, you can even take a pre-built life a step further by assuming a pre-made scenario with one of the many families already living in either Sunset Valley or Riverview.

NOTE

To learn about the different scenarios you can try, just click on the houses when choosing to play as an existing family.

Building Basics

Building a basic house with the tools provided by *The Sims 3* is easy. Using Build Mode and Buy Mode, you access a series of tools and cursors that let you drop new objects and building components on to your lot. The tools are the same in each mode.

Hand Tool [H]: The Hand tool is used to move objects around your house or property. To grab an object, left-click on it. To drop the object, left-click again. To rotate an object, click and hold the left mouse button on the object and move the mouse around. The object will spin to face the cursor as you drag the mouse.

NOTE

One major upgrade to *The Sims 3* is the ability to use freeform placement and rotation. Hold the [Alt] key while using the Hand tool, and objects won't stick to the grid as you move them, and they won't snap to specific rotation angles while you're rotating them. Instead, they will move smoothly during placement and rotate to any angle, allowing for extremely precise and natural-looking floor plans.

Create a Style [R]: This tool enters the Create a Style menu, which allows you to customize objects. Personalize objects with new colors and textures. The Create a Style tool is fully explained later in this chapter.

Eyedropper Tool [E]: The Eyedropper tool copies the color or texture of an object so you can easily place it on another object. You can also use this tool to copy decorations, such as wallpaper. Click on the tool and then click on the object/surface you want to replicate. Then, click on the object/surface you want to copy the texture or color set to.

Sledgehammer Tool [K]: Want to destroy an object, wall, or floor? Click on the Sledgehammer tool. Once the cursor turns into a hammer, click on an object to immediately destroy it. Simoleons are instantly returned to your bank, minus any depreciation.

NOTE

The Sledgehammer tool has also been upgraded from previous *The Sims* games: it now can delete many things at once. To delete multiple objects, click down on an object you want to delete, then hold and drag over an area, and it will delete any objects within the highlighted area. If you want to delete lots of flooring, click and hold on a floor tile, then drag out over an area of floor tiles you'd like to delete. Similarly, if you'd like to delete many walls, click on a wall segment, then drag along an entire wall or drag out over multiple rooms to delete all the walls in the highlighted area.

Build Mode

Build Mode is the tool set for actually constructing a house. There are multiple building elements available in Build Mode, such as a foundation, floor coverings, walls, windows, and doors.

1 Foundation
2 Floor Covering
3 Walls
4 Wall Covering
5 Doors
6 Windows
7 Roof
8 Stairs
9 Arches
10 Columns
11 Fences
12 Gates
13 Pool
14 Fireplaces
15 Trees/Flowers/Shrubs/Rocks
16 Terrain Tools
17 Water Tool
18 Terrain Paints

Note

World Adventures adds a Basement tool to this menu that largely automates the process of creating a cellar. This is actually quite useful for the new Nectar Making skill that Sims learn when vacationing in France.

Buy Mode

Now that you have built your house and laid out the general floor plan, it is time to outfit the place with appliances, furniture, and other objects. You can view the catalog of objects by room or by function. The top icon (1) sorts by room—which lets you click on the Room tabs along the top of the tool. The small chair icon (2) sorts by function.

After selecting an object category, such as a chair or table, you can look at the individual objects. Each object is accompanied by a photo of the object, a description, price, and any related properties, such a comfort rating or how the object addresses a need.

1 Sort by Room
2 Sort by Function
3 Household Inventory
4 Object Buy Field
5 Kitchen
6 Bathroom
7 Bedroom
8 Living Room
9 Dining Room
10 Study
11 Kids Room
12 Outdoor
13 Objects

Build Mode

If you decide to build your own house, then you need to understand the basics of construction. The tools in Build Mode make this process smooth and simple, but let's go through the process of building a single-story house with a small backyard pool.

Before breaking ground, you need to know about an essential pair of tools that makes building easier and helps you see inside not only your house, but also community lots when your Sim is on the premises: Change Wall Mode and Change Floors.

Change Wall Mode [Home] and [End]: Toggle through three different views of your house—walls down, cutaway walls, and walls up.

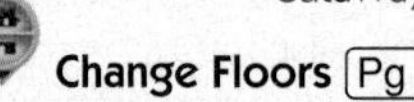

Change Floors [Pg Up] and [Pg Dn]: Scroll up and down the different floors of your house with these two buttons.

Walls down view

Cutaway walls view

Walls up view

Foundation

The first step to building a house is laying down the foundation. The foundation is what supports your house and is especially useful for deciding on a general layout. If you are building your first house after just starting a new game, then you need to think small. Be frugal with the foundation (it's §4 per square) and build a house that encapsulates the essential rooms: bathroom, bedroom, kitchen, and some kind of living area. If you spend all of your Simoleons on a huge foundation, you will run out of money way too soon.

To lay down a foundation, click on the Foundation tool in Build Mode and then stretch the cursor across your purchased lot to create a rectangle. When you release the left mouse button, the foundation is filled. If you want to make a house that is not a rectangle, then attach different pieces of foundation to make your new shape.

There is a second type of foundation: deck. If you want to create a deck for your house, switch to the deck option in the Foundation tool from Build Mode and then follow the same steps with dragging the cursor to lay down the planks.

> **TIP**
>
> Use a foundation to make a nice, flat surface on an uneven lot.

Walls

After laying the foundation, it is time to erect some walls. Left-click on the wall in Build Mode to switch to the wall tool. The cursor changes to an arrow with a small wall symbol over it. You now have three ways to put up walls:

Create Wall: Create walls manually by dragging the cursor along the edges of a foundation or directly across it.

Create Room: Erect four walls to instantly create a room. Drag the cursor across the foundation to expand the pre-made room.

Create Diagonal Room: This option creates a whole room, but does so along the diagonal of the square grid. Use this option to create unique rooms.

There is no limit to the number of walls you can create—that is dictated by your household funds because walls cost §70 per panel. While you definitely need to enclose your house, you do not need to enclose all of the rooms inside the house. You should, of course, enclose the bathroom. The bedroom needs to be enclosed, too, to keep out sound from the rest of the house. Otherwise, noises can wake your Sim and put them in a bad mood.

> **NOTE**
>
> Walls are required to build second (or third) stories on your house. You must have enough walls to bear the load of an additional story. If you meet resistance while setting down the floor for a second story, place additional walls on the floor below it.

> **TIP**
>
> Hold shift to switch between Create Wall and Create Room. When you release Shift, you automatically return to Create Wall.

Wall and Floor Coverings

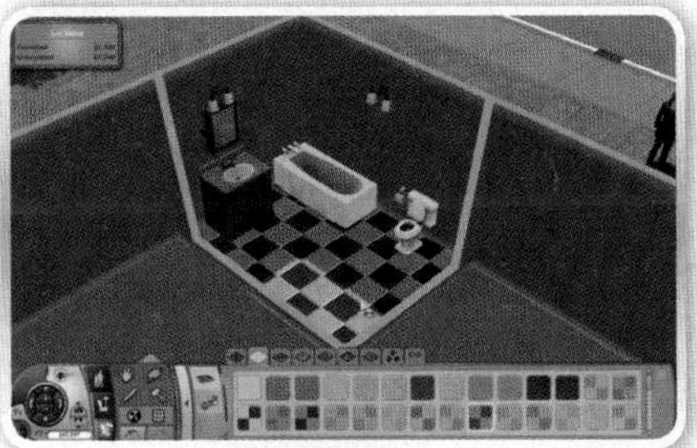

Who wants to live in a house with exposed dry wall or concrete floors? Decorate these flat surfaces with coverings, such as carpet and wallpaper. There are hundreds of wall and floor coverings for a variety of prices, ranging from §4 to §21 per unit of area.

> **CAUTION**
>
> There is actually a negative moodlet called Unfinished Room that overcomes Sims who walk into rooms with exposed surfaces.

Wall coverings are divided into the following categories:

- Paint
- Wallpaper
- Tile
- Paneling
- Masonry
- Rock & Stone
- Siding
- Misc.

There are many floor covering categories, such as carpet, tile, and stone.

- Carpet
- Tile
- Wood
- Stone
- Masonry
- Linoleum
- Metal
- Misc.

Doors and Windows

Naturally, once you create walls for your house and the individual rooms, you need windows and doors. You can also install an arch as an alternative to a door, although that does not block noise like a door does. You always need to install a door on the exterior of your house instead of an arch. An arch just invites Burglars and curious neighbors.

There are many types of doors for your house, from exterior to interior doors. There are also glass doors that serve two purposes.

Not only are they access points for a house, but they also let in sunshine, which many Sims find pleasing.

Windows are important not just as decoration, but also to allow daylight into a house. Sims can read by daylight instead of always needing a lamp or artificial light source. There are many window options in Build Mode across a spectrum of prices. Many windows also accommodate drapes and curtains, which can be purchased through Buy Mode.

Tip

Do you have a Sim who likes nature? Consider placing giant glass panels in the walls so they can soak up the joy of the great outdoors.

Stairs and Railings

The primary function of stairs is to connect two stories of a house either inside the house or provide access to an upper story (or balcony) from outside. Stair prices range from §10 to §120 per segment, which can get quite costly. When creating stairs, select the type of stairs you want from Build Mode and then drag them into the house. The stairs automatically "clamp" to the next story, however, only if you have sufficient room for the stairs. While you may adjust the width of the stairs, you cannot adjust the incline. If the marker around the base of the stairs is red, then the stairs will not fit.

Note

You can choose to automatically have railings placed along with stairs or do it yourself. Or not at all.

Columns

Columns serve dual purposes in Build Mode. Not only are they attractive features when artfully placed around a house, but they also bear the load of upper stories. If you want to create an outdoor balcony for your house, use columns to support it. You can also use columns inside to support an upper floor when you do not want to extend a load-bearing wall across a room. Different columns support different amount of area of an upper floor. The cheapest column, for example, supports a 4x4 grid of floor.

Roof

No house is complete without a roof. When you initially select the Roof tool from Build Mode, you are dropped into the Autoroof function, which stretches a roof across the structure as soon as you select a style. You can turn Autoroof off and opt for topping your dwelling on your own, which is a fun way to design such features as gables. Roofs are free, so feel free to experiment without any hit to your household funds.

Fireplaces

Like columns, fireplaces are both decorative and functional. There are several types of fireplaces to choose from. Some are freestanding and some must be "locked" onto a wall. When you install a fireplace, a chimney is automatically extended up to the roof-even if it has to go through additional floors above it. However, you can share a chimney with multiple fireplaces on multiple floors by installing them directly above and below each other. Fireplaces can also be installed outside.

Fireplaces add fun to a house. Sims can also warm themselves by a fireplace, which results in a mood boost. After lighting a fire, your Sim can poke at it, which they find amusing.

Always extinguish a fire before the last Sim leaves the house, though, to avoid catastrophe. When a house catches fire, the Fire Fighter Service Sims arrive—but only if you have a smoke alarm in the room. Without this alarm, you risk extensive damage to your house.

Gates and Fences

Fences make good neighbors. To add a fence to your lot, choose the Fence tool from Build Mode and then stretch it along the ground just as if you were extending a wall. There is a Create Yard option that lets you stretch a rectangle of fencing across your lot, just like creating a room inside with the Wall tool. You can also add gates to fences to give access to outdoor features, like gardens.

NOTE

While fences can be stretched across uneven terrain, gates must be installed on flat ground.

Swimming Pools

Sims love to swim—unless they have the Hydrophobic trait. Swimming is fun and good exercise. Plus, if a Sim likes the outdoors, swimming in an outdoor pool gives a nice little mood boost. Select the Pool tool from Build Mode to dig a pool on your lot, just like laying down a foundation.

NOTE

Swimming pools are expensive! Each square of pool costs §80.

Terrain Tools

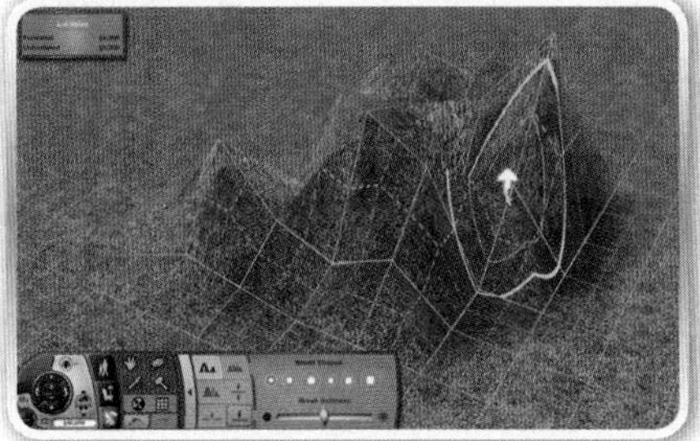

The Terrain tools allow you to perform effortless landscaping on your lot. These tools let you sink the ground, install ponds, build mounds, and smooth rough surface edges. To access the Terrain tools, just select them from Build Mode.

Foliage

Beautify the exterior of your house with trees, flowers, and shrubs. Sims love a landscaped lot complete with trees, artfully placed rocks, and fresh blossoms. Unlike harvestables, which must be tended to grow, the trees and plants you install in Build Mode do not require any upkeep. They are gorgeous year-round.

Buy Mode

Sims love stuff and Buy Mode is how you give it to them. Buy Mode is like an insta-catalog where you purchase objects and items and then immediately install them in a house or on a lot. When you enter Buy Mode, the game is paused so no time passes while you consider the hundreds of shopping options. When you select an object from Buy mode and place it on your lot, the funds are immediately deducted from your household account.

While you are still in Buy Mode, you can return an object for a full refund. Just use the Sledgehammer tool to dismiss the object and the Simoleons reappear in the household funds. However, if you exit Buy Mode and then go back into it to remove an object, you are dinged for object depreciation.

TIP

Want to place an object anywhere, at any angle? Hold Alt while holding down the left mouse button and moving the mouse. Now you can rotate an object in very small increments.

DEPRECIATION AND APPRECIATION

As soon as you buy an object and then exit Buy Mode, the object loses value. The immediate value hit is significant, but not devastating: 15 percent. With each additional day, the object loses more value: 10 percent per day. The value of an object finally bottoms out at 40 percent of its original value. So, if you bought the SimmerChar Dual-State Stove for §400, the object would lose §60 on the first day. The next day, it would lose another §40. If you sold the object back after two weeks of use, you would get §160 back.

However, not everything in this world goes down in value upon purchase. Some art actually increases in value. And if your Sim is an artist, the paintings created on the easel will also grow in value over time. The masterworks of a true artist will skyrocket in value, so it can definitely pay to work on those painting skills.

BILLS

Every Monday and Thursday, the postal worker drops off a stack of bills in your mailbox. You have to pay approximately §6 for every §1,000 of stuff you own. For example, if you spent §14,500 on building and objects, your bills will come out to around §85. So keep this in mind when shopping. To pay your bills, click on the mailbox and choose the Pay Bills interaction or choose the Auto Bill Pay option.

You cannot ignore bills and hope they go away. You can pick up bills from your mailbox and attend to them in a timely manner. Bills change color as you ignore them, indicating the growing need to attend to them. Here's the color chart:

1 day old: Yellow

2 days old: Orange

3 days old: Red

If you do not pay your bills within three days—the normal bill cycle—you can count on a visit from the Repo Man on day four. The Repo Man will enter your house without warning and take objects without mercy until he has reached the number of Simoleons you currently owe. Once you enter day four of bills, you cannot quickly pay them and shoo away the Repo Man. It's too late by that time.

You can have as many rooms in your house as your Simoleons allow, but there are some essential rooms that your Sim cannot function without: bedroom, bathroom, and kitchen. Your Sims would certainly appreciate any other rooms in their new digs, but let's just go over the required areas and the critical objects you must place in those rooms.

Bathroom

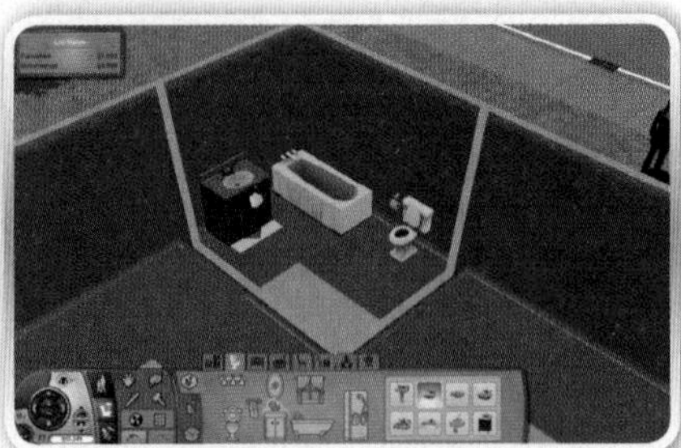

The bathroom is positively critical for your Sims' well-being. Without a place to attend to hygiene and bladder needs, your Sims will not be able to function properly in polite society. You must install a toilet so your Sims can relieve themselves in a timely manner. A bathtub or shower is also essential for keeping clean. If your Sims do not wash on a regular basis, not only with their overall mood suffer, but relationships with friends and work will also take a hit. Install a sink and mirror in the bathroom, too, so your Sim can brush teeth as well as primp and pose. Looking good is often akin to feeling good, you know.

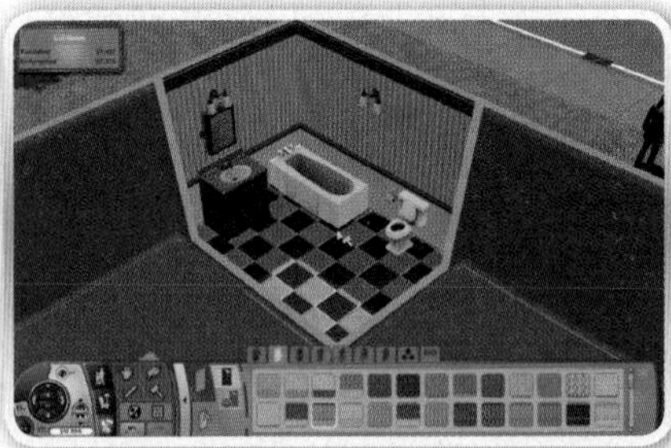

When you create a bathroom, make sure you leave enough room along the side of the bathtub for a Sim to bend over and turn on the faucet. If you put something too close, like a counter, just use the Hand tool to move it over and create the needed space.

Bedroom

Sims need their beauty rest. After a long day of work or play (or, hopefully, a nice combination of both), Sims get sleepy. While a Sim can take a catnap on a couch, to get the kind of rejuvenating rest needed to greet a whole new day and effectively perform at work, Sims need a bed. A modest bed will do the trick at first. You can place other useful objects in the bedroom, such as a dresser, but the bed is your top priority.

Sims do fancy checking themselves out. If you have a little money to spare, put a mirror in the bedroom. A dresser is useful, too, because it lets Sims change their outfits.

Kitchen

Sims need to keep hunger at bay to function, and that means they need to eat food. If Sims get too hungry, not only does their mood greatly suffer, but they can eventually pass out and lose valuable time recovering. Build a small kitchen for starters, with a refrigerator, stove, and sink. A dishwasher is useful to be sure, but dishes can be easily cleaned in the sink at first. A fridge by itself is not exactly helpful after a few days, so make sure you hit up the grocery store for food, especially if you plan on being a cook. You can also dine out, but it is much cheaper to eat at home.

The kitchen does not need to be its own room with a door. It can just be a small nook off the living room to save money and space. However, noise from the kitchen will wake Sims within earshot, especially Sims who are light sleepers.

TIP

If your Sim is going to pursue a career in cooking, a kitchen is absolutely essential. Splurge on this room at the expense of other parts of the house.

Create a Style

So, you just bought a bed for your house, but you want to change the color of the duvet cover? It's easy to accomplish this design feat with the Create a Style tool. The Create a Style tool for changing the appearance of an object works quite similar to making adjustments to a Sim's clothes in Create a Sim. To change the colors or textures, left-click on the Create a Style button (the palette). Now, left-click on the object you want to alter.

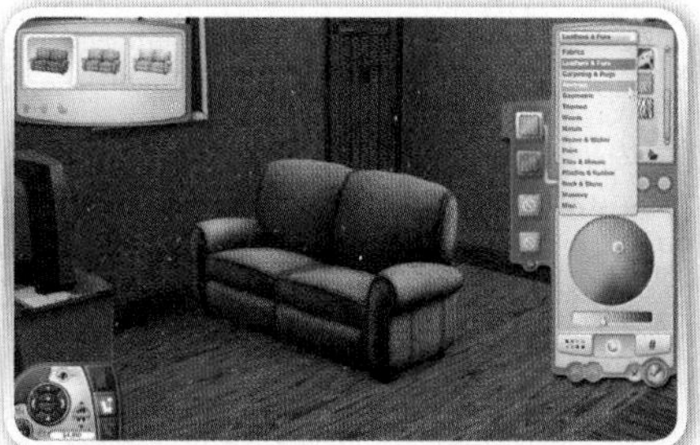

When the Create a Style toolkit appears on the screen's right side, you see the current colors and textures used in the currently selected object. In the case of this bed, the pattern for the duvet cover, the wooden frame textures, and the metal knobs on the bed all appear on the pane to the right. To make changes to any of the textures, left-click on the desired texture. Now, you can either adjust the color with the color wheel or color palette or select a different texture from the texture box in the top-right corner.

The textures are divided into several categories, such as wood, metal, abstract, and geometric.

NOTE

To save a customized object, just click the folder icon in the upper-left corner, right below all of the pre-set versions of the object. Now you can grab a replica of it at any time.

If you want to make objects in a room match, you can easily apply the same textures and patterns from one object to another by grabbing the texture pane and dragging it on to the object you want to match. You can either pull the entire set of textures on to the new object or grab a single texture (such as the wood from the bed frame) and then drag it on top of the piece of furniture you want to match. In this case, pulling the wood texture from the bed onto the dresser changes the pattern so the set now matches.

When you drag a pattern onto another object with multiple textures, you must designate which pattern you want to replace.

A Day in the Life

Once you create a Sim and a place for them to call home, it is finally time to venture into the world and start living it up. The journey will not always be easy, but it will be full of fun and surprises. However, before taking on that first brave day, you need to be familiar with a handful of terms that will not only appear throughout this entire guide, but also be critical to succeeding within the game.

REQUIRED READING

- **Wishes:** Every Sim has desires, both immediate and long-term. When you created a Sim, you gave it a Lifetime Wish. However, Sims also come up with smaller wishes each day that they would love for you to help them fulfill. Fulfilled wishes boost your Sim's mood and award Lifetime Happiness points.
- **Lifetime Happiness Points:** These are the ultimate barometer of your Sim's fulfillment. When you complete a wish, your Sim earns Lifetime Happiness points. You also earn these points when you boost your Sim's mood over a certain threshold. Lifetime Happiness points can be traded in for Lifetime Rewards, which affect your Sim's personality and aptitude.
- **Skills:** Sims can learn a variety of talents, such as writing, fishing, painting, and athletics. These skills are often tied into careers or hobbies. Certain activities increase your skill ranking. You can track your Sims' skills in their Skill Journals.
- **Careers:** In order to maintain their households, Sims must have a constant source of income. Careers provide that. There are a multitude of career tracks in Sunset Valley, from athlete to journalist. Sims can also seek out part-time jobs or turn their skills into moneymaking opportunities, such as penning books from home. Each career has several levels of promotion.
- **Opportunities:** From time to time, Sims encounter opportunities that result in rewards when completed. Opportunities are typically related to careers and skills, but special opportunities pop up just by exploring Sunset Valley and talking to people. Rewards include job promotions, physical objects, Simoleons, or relationship boosts.
- **Moodlets:** *The Sims 3* introduces a new measurement of your Sim's happiness—moodlets. Moodlets are factors that affect your overall mood. They are good, bad, and neutral. Most moodlets have a timer that denotes how long they affect overall mood. Some negative moodlets can be eliminated by correcting behavior or environment. To make your Sims' life better and earn more Lifetime Happiness points, adjust your Sims' life so they experience more positive moodlets.
- **Needs:** As in *The Sims™ 2*, Sims have individual needs like Bladder, Hunger, Hygiene, Social, Fun, and Energy. These needs are affected by environment, activities, and relationships. While mood and moodlet take center stage in making sure your Sim is happy, don't neglect basic needs. When buying objects for your lot, be sure to keep an eye on how certain objects affect specific needs. For example, a nicer bathtub or shower will increase your Sim's Hygiene rating.
- **Socials:** Socials are the interactions that take place between Sims. There are literally hundreds of socials. Not all socials are available right away. Some are unlocked by developing skills. Other socials are activated by the traits you give your Sims. Use socials to direct a conversation and engage other Sims, paying attention to their likes and dislikes so you can build better relationships. Who knows what could happen? Playfully teasing the right Sim could lead to a lifelong love, while joking with a sourpuss could result in a new nemesis.

Mood

There are a handful of ways to measure your Sim's life progress, such as Simoleons or the current career promotion, but mood is how you measure your Sim's immediate condition. Your Sim's happiness and/or misery is displayed right there on the Mood meter—shaped like an upside-down exclamation point—which turns green when the Sim is pleased and bright red when something is seriously amiss. There is a yellow point in the middle of the Mood meter that gives you a warning. Inject something fun or enjoyable into your Sim's day or mood will continue to plummet.

To succeed in life, you must keep your Sim happy. Pushing the Mood meter in to the green indicates happiness. And if you can boost the Sim's mood all the way into the "bubble" at the top of the meter, then you know your Sim is truly happy. As long as the Mood meter is in that bubble, the Sim accumulates Lifetime Happiness points. This lasts until the mood drops out of the bubble, even if the Sim is still shown to be happy by a largely green meter.

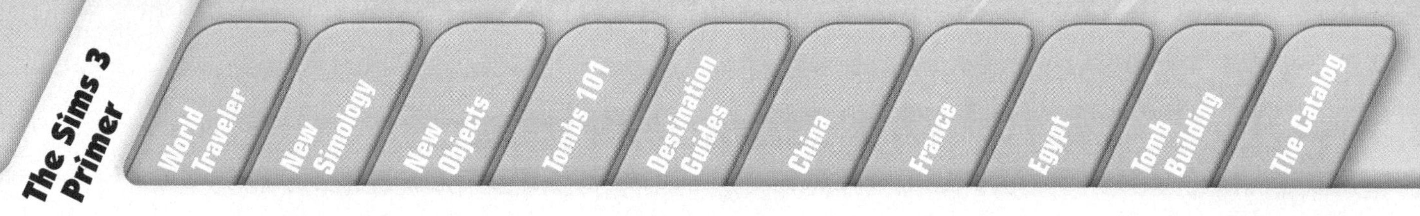

Moodlets

Mood is a bird's-eye view of everything the Sim is feeling at that given moment. Moodlets are slivers of that mood. These smaller emotions, feelings, and cravings are not passive indicators—these are real-time assessments that should never be ignored.

Some moodlets demand immediate attention, such as moodlets that indicate hunger or a lack of hygiene. These negative moodlets contribute to a decreased overall mood, which affects so much of your Sim's life, such as their performance at work. Negative moodlets can typically be dispelled with an action, such as taking a shower to get rid of the Grungy moodlet.

There are three types of moodlets: positive, neutral, and negative. To keep mood up, you need to do more things that inspire positive moodlets. Moodlets have varying degrees of effect on overall mood. Some moodlets are very minor and do not necessarily cause a mood swing. However, these little annoyances can add up to an unhappy Sim if they are ignored. To combat these, rectify any conditions causing a negative moodlet and seek out activities that cause positive moodlets.

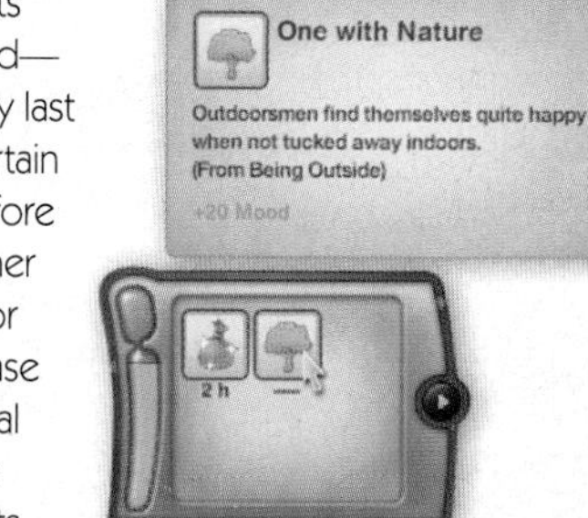

Moodlets are timed—they only last for a certain time before they either vanish, or in the case of several negative moodlets, lead into worse moodlets. While a moodlet is active, it contributes to the overall mood. There is no state of decay. As soon as the timer on a moodlet expires, that moodlet's effect on the overall mood vanishes.

Here is a list of all of the moodlets your Sim can feel, broken down by effect—positive, negative, and neutral. The duration of each moodlet is also included so you know how long the effects of a moodlet will influence overall mood.

POSITIVE MOODLETS

Moodlet	Effect	Duration in Hours	Description
Minty Breath	5	4	Sims love to be around those with Minty Breath. It sure beats the alternative.
Feeling Lucky	5	23	Today is Sim's lucky day. Who knows what good will happen?
Heard Theater Music	10	Variable	The music pulsing from the inside of the theater sounds awesome. Perhaps tickets are still available!
Educated	10	Variable	Exploring the local halls of culture and learning may teach even the most studious individual a thing or two.
Impressed	10	0	Touring public place sometimes reveals unexpected and impressive sights.
Let Off Steam	10	Variable	Having a friendly ear to complain to helps when you need to vent.
Decorated	10	Lasts as long as Sim is in room	Sims enjoy well furnished homes. By the looks of things, this place isn't so bad!
Brightened Day	10	3	Good Sims know exactly what to say to make someone's day better.
Had a Nice Nap	10	5	Having a great, refreshing nap may be just enough to hold back the onset of sleep.
I Am Beautiful	10	4	Recognizing beauty, even one's own, is just a benefit of vanity.
New Car Smell	10	2	Ah, that new car smell is so factory fresh!
Fascinated	10	2	Some Sims take joy in things ordinary Sims might otherwise overlook.
Got a Good Deal	10	8	Saving a few Simoleons is pure satisfaction!
Saw Great Movie	10	16	Sims have a special place in their hearts for movies on the silver screen, and a special place in their stomachs for the buttery popcorn.
Flattered	10	Variable	Compliments are quite flattering!
Intrigued	10	Variable	Juicy gossip satisfies eager ears!
Attractive	10	Variable	When a Sim looks this good, it's difficult for others not to notice. Wowza!
Hilarious Conversation	10	Variable	Some Sims should be stand-up comedians with the humor they're dishing out.
Tranquil	10	8	Nothing can stress or anger Sims who have reached their happy place.
Squeaky Clean	10	7	Experience the clean sensation of practicing personal hygiene!

POSITIVE MOODLETS, CONTINUED

Moodlet	Effect	Duration in Hours	Description
Cheered Up	15	3	Gobs of sobs are stopped by the kind words of others.
Duck Time	15	5	Rubber duckies make hygienic cleansing fun!
Calmed Down	15	3	Sometimes all an Angry Sim needs is an understanding voice to help them get through a bad mood.
Enjoying Solitude	15	Variable	Introverted Sims like it best at times when others completely and utterly stay away.
Buzzed	30	3	Caffeine can really wake a Sim. Use this time wisely, because after the high comes the low...
The Life of the Party	15	3	Not only do party animals love to party, but other Sims love to party with them. Wooo!
Excited	15	3	Excitable Sims tend to get, well, excited.
Great Kiss	15	3	Great kissers give amazing smooches.
Inspired	15	4	A genuine and original work of art can inspire and render viewers speechless upon experiencing.
Oddly Powerful	15	5	The feeling of power is...intense! Science has bestowed Super Sim capabilities!
Fiendishly Delighted	15	6	Sims of the Evil persuasion take pleasure in the misfortune of others.
Fulfilled	15	6	The satisfaction of having a wish come to fruition feels great!
Returned Stolen Property	15	8	Kleptos enjoy returning things even more than...ending up with them. After all, it's more difficult to do the right thing, even when it follows the wrong thing.
Fresh Start	15	24	Moving into a new location provides a clean slate many dream of!
Likes Work	10	Variable	Work isn't quite the daily grind for everyone. Bring on the overtime!
Out After Curfew!	15	Variable	Being out after curfew is totally radical.
Pristine Picture	15	Variable	The pixels are dancing daintily on the television, perfectly in harmony within the highest resolutions money can buy.
Cozy Fire	15	5	Sims enjoy the warm cheery glow of their fireplaces...poke them for extra warmth!
Pumped	15	4	If Sims work out long enough, they get Pumped. Workouts are even more effective while Sims are pumped.
Sweet Venue/Party	15	Variable	The choice in venue for this party is excellent. It sure beats the standard house party.
Adrenaline Rush	15	3	An Adrenaline Rush will keep this Sim pumped and running around everywhere for some time to come!
Feeling Calm	15	Variable	It turns out it was just anxiety getting the best of your Sim. The object wasn't left turned on and impending disaster wasn't looming. But, double checking helps to calm the anxiety.
Comforted	15	3	A quick cry on the shoulder helps the sadness go away.
Sugar Rush	15	Variable	Filling up on sugary goodness makes everything more fun!
New Stuff!	20	2	Sims love getting new things for their homes!
My Love!	20	Variable	Sims in love swoon and flutter about like fools oblivious to the world around them.
Pregnant	20	Lasts until birth	The wonder of creating new life makes pregnancy an exciting time for most Sims.
One With Nature	20	Variable	Outdoorswomen find themselves quite happy when not tucked away indoors.
New Home	20	24	It's a new place to call home!
Read a Masterpiece	20	24	Turning the last page of a masterpiece is like falling in love...it's a beautiful thing.
Saw Great Game	20	16	The fans are rowdy, the food is messy, but when combined with a sports game, it's an experience Sims love!
Cuddle Time	20	5	Teddy bears make excellent sleeping companions.
Exhilarating Shower	20	4	It makes sense that if a Sim uses quality plumbing, they get quality showers.
Awesome Party	20	3	Party plus Party Animal usually equals Awesome Party. It's simple math!

POSITIVE MOODLETS, CONTINUED

Moodlet	Effect	Duration in Hours	Description
Great Adventure	20	3	Sim had such an amazing time! How could this adventure possibly be topped?!
New Friend	20	8	Meeting someone new and hitting it off well enough to call them a friend is spiffy!
Nicely Decorated	25	Lasts as long as Sim in room	Well designed décor stands out in a good way and tends to make everyone happier.
Entertained	25	Variable	Sim is entertained.
Winner!	25	8	Sims never tire of the thrill of victory.
I Am the Greatest!	25	8	It doesn't really matter how you got there. Being at the top means being at the top; you are the best!
Virtually Victorious!	25	8	Success! Sims love the (virtual) taste and smell of (virtual) victory.
Saw Great Concert	25	16	Sims unanimously agree that experiencing a concert is well worth the potential inner-ear damage.
Saw Great Play	25	16	Sims love to watch people on stage doing funny and unexpected things right before their eyes. Sometimes they get the strangest feeling of déjà vu.
Honor Student	25	24	Hard work and a nose to the books pays off with the satisfactory acceptance into the Honor Roll.
Warmed	25	3	There is nothing like the feeling of a warm flame to make a Sim happy.
Saw Great Symphony	30	16	A feast for the ears, Sims devour the mellifluous melodies of symphonies with jubilee.
Threw a Great Party	30	24	Sims love a great party and the host who throws them.
Celebrity	30	Variable	Sims love being recognized by their fans. Celebrity status is so cool!
Superior Equipment	30	Lasts as long as Sim near object	Food made with top-of-the-line equipment just has that superior flavor!
Beautifully Decorated	40	Lasts as long as Sim in room	Rooms adorned with the most expensive sculptures and paintings improve life dramatically.
Having a Blast	40	Variable	Sim is having so much fun it's almost criminal.
First Kiss	40	24	A Sim's first kiss can leave them glowing for a long time.
First Romance	40	48	Love has bloomed for the first time. Could this be the real thing?
Wedding Day	40	24	Sims love to celebrate this incredibly important day with a party...just make sure everything goes to plan!
Celebrated Birthday	40	24	Birthday parties are the best!
Father of the Bride	40	24	Seeing a daughter married makes a father so proud.
Father of the Groom	40	24	Seeing a son married makes a father so proud.
Mother of the Bride	40	24	Seeing a daughter married makes a mother so proud.
Mother of the Groom	40	24	Seeing a son married makes a mother so proud.
Charitable	50	24	It feels great to help out other Sims, especially when they are in need.
Newly Engaged	50	24	With a ring on the finger, vows and true love forever aren't far behind.
Just Married	50	48	Sims always enjoy the joyful period following the marriage. Let's hope the love lasts...
Divine Meal	75	168	Sim has experienced a meal so exquisite, so divine, that it defies description. (i.e., Ate Ambrosia)
It's a Boy	80	24	Bouncing baby boys are delightful additions to any family!
It's a Girl	80	24	Gurgling baby girls are delightful additions to any family!
It's Triplets	80	24	Three babies! Hope your Sims wanted a big family.

POSITIVE MOODLETS, CONTINUED

Moodlet	Effect	Duration in Hours	Description
It's Twins	80	24	Wow, your Sims were lucky enough to have twins. Double trouble!
Good/Great/ AmazingMeal	Variable on cooking skill	Variable	Yummy! Sim enjoyed that meal more than the standard fare.
Comfy	Variable on quality of the chair	Variable	Nothing beats a good seat for comfort except perhaps a better seat.
Well Rested	Variable on quality of the bed	Variable	It's easy to wake up on the right side of the bed when you get plenty of time in the bed.
Beautiful View	Variable on trait	Variable	Would you look at that view!
Beautiful Vista	Variable on trait	Variable	This...house...is...incredible! Somebody really knows how to live.
Enjoying Music	Variable on music preference	Variable	It's hard not to enjoy a beat this solid.
Fit Atmosphere	Lasts as long as Sim is in gym	Variable	Exercising at the gym really improves the quality of the workout.

NEUTRAL MOODLETS

Moodlet	Duration/Effect	Description
Learning Quickly	Indicates sped-up learning	Sim is picking up on this skill really quickly–how satisfying!
Cozy Fire	Lasts as long as Sim is in front of fire	Sims enjoy the warm cheery glow of their fireplaces...poke them for extra warmth!
Has to Pee	Alerts that Sim must use bathroom	Your Sim needs to go. Like, "go."
Hungry	Alerts that Sim must eat	Your Sim's a wee bit peckish. The stomach growling isn't far behind.
Sleepy	Alerts that Sim must go to bed	Get Sim to bed soon, to avoid the wrath of the truly tired.
Stuffed	Sim is completely full	Forcing Sims to eat when they are not hungry may lead to loss of appetite and weight gain.
Garlic Breath	Lasts 3 hours	Whoa! It might be time to scrub away that garlic with a toothbrush.
Fatigued	Variable	Activity of the athletic variety naturally leads to a little muscle fatigue.
Baby is Coming	Indicates birth is soon	Uh oh! The water has broken, contractions have started, and the baby is on its way! Get the mother to a hospital soon or sit tight until the baby arrives!
Power Study	Indicates sped-up homework/learning	That quiet library atmosphere makes reading, studying, and working so much more efficient!

NEGATIVE MOODLETS

Moodlet	Effect	Duration in Hours	Description
On Fire	-200	1	Contrary to popular belief, being on fire is not healthy and can lead to symptoms including panic, burns, and death. Best find some water quickly!
Starving	-80	0	Allowing Sims to starve is quite cruel! Get Sim some food immediately to avoid an unnecessary death.
Heart Wrenching Scene	-60	Lasts until leaving	Witnessing a break up is truly heartwrenching. Hopefully the two Sims can reconcile and find new love elsewhere...
Betrayed	-50	24	Being cheated on is tough to move past. Talking it out with the other Sim would speed the healing process.
Mourning	-50	48	The death of a loved one affects those closest to them. Sims can mourn at a tombstone or move it to a graveyard to feel more at peace.
Heart Broken	-50	48	A broken heart is an affliction only time and tears can heal.

NEGATIVE MOODLETS, CONTINUED

Moodlet	Effect	Duration in Hours	Description
Vile Surroundings	-40	Lasts until leaving or cleaning	This room is so fetid and foul. Sims were not meant to endure such a lax household cleaning philosophy!
Exhausted	-50	0	At this level of sleep deprivation, even the floor looks like a good bed to this Sim.
Failing	-40	18	Having to stare at a failing grade on a report card just stings. Homework completion and a good mood will improve low marks.
Desolate	-50	0	When Sims get really, really lonely, they need to talk to somebody. Anybody.
Singed	-40	0	Fire burns quickly, but it will burn a Singed Sim even faster, so avoid hot situations.
Singed Electricity	-40	0	Sims find it unenjoyable to be electrocuted, especially because it may stop their heart. Until this wears off, Sims should steer clear of further potentially electrifying activities.
Horrified	-35	8	Terrible things have been seen underneath the mausoleum. Explorers beware.
Stressed Out	-40	Variable	Sim is in desperate need of some entertainment. The daily grind has ground the enjoyment of life to a halt!
Really Has To Pee	-30	0	The bladder situation has only gone from bad to worse; find a bathroom soon!
Missed the Wedding	-30	24	It's a bad, bad, bad idea to miss the wedding. It takes two to tango and your Sim missed the dance.
Rejected Proposal	-30	6	It hurts to propose and be rejected. The good news is that Sims can try again as many times as they like. Of course, each rejection will hurt just as much.
Fired	-30	Variable	Ouch! Getting thrown out of the workplace never feels good. Time to find a new job...
Missing Work	-30	0	Workaholics don't get stressed from working, but from not working.
Lost a Friend	-25	Variable	The loss of a friend hurts, but can be easily rectified by giving them a call and rekindling the friendship.
Scared	-25	3	Scaredy-cats are scared of pretty much everything, but they really show it when their life flashes before their eyes.
Virtually Terrified!	-25	3	Yikes! That snaggle toothed monster looked far more realistic than expected. Who knew monster breath would be so...fragrant...in virtual reality.
Too Many People	-15	0	Certain Sims may not feel too comfortable around large groups.
Nauseous	-25	2	Sim isn't feeling so hot. You may want to keep her around a bathroom.
Filthy Surroundings	-30	Lasts until leaving or cleaning	The grime and muck is really starting to pile high. It won't be long before it starts paying rent.
Plagued by Nature	-20	0	It's often best for Sims who Hate the Outdoors to spend as little time out there as possible.
Stir Crazy	-15	Lasts until leaving house	Sims should leave the house frequently for sanity's sake. Shake well with a community marinade for best results.
Tired	-40	0	When Sims get too tired, their mood begins to go south.
Very Hungry	-40	0	Gnawing hunger is not a good feeling for Sims. Feed regularly to avoid.
Hydrophobic	-20	Lasts until away from water	There's just too much water for Sim to enjoy this moment.
Drowning	-40	Lasts until taken out of water	Sims breathe air. Anything else gets a little...suffocating.
Stuff Taken	-15	24	Sims really like their stuff, and when someone grabs it, they take it quite personally.
Rejected By Ex	-20	6	Sims don't like getting rejected, especially by someone who used to like them. Sims will have less luck socializing while they stew over a rejection.
Witnessed Betrayal	-20	6	Witnessing the romantic betrayal of a loved one is quite devastating.
Detention	-20	4	Aww shucks! Nobody likes spending time in detention!
Embarrassed	-20	3	Situations like this should be avoided at all costs...they're hard to live down.

NEGATIVE MOODLETS, CONTINUED

Moodlet	Effect	Duration in Hours	Description
Aching Back	-20	4	An aching back is quite the nagging problem. A massage would surely help.
Buzz Crashed	-10	3	Caffeine buzzes wear off eventually, leaving a sad Sim. Walk it off or have another cup!
Disgusted	-5	Lasts until leaving or cleaning	Revolting sights and smells will have this effect on Sims, so it's best to move them away.
Afraid of the Dark	-15	0	Heading inside or finding a bit of sunlight will take care of this cowardly affliction.
Disappointed	-15	24	Some Sims just hate it when they blow a chance to impress others.
Caught After Curfew	-15	3	It's so unfair! Why don't parents understand?
Offended	-15	3	Offense, when given, will require a healthy dose of time to forgive and forget. Or the dreaded apology.
Humiliated	-15	3	Humiliation tends to rear its ugly head just behind the heap of insulting comments.
Threw a Lame Party	-15	8	Some Sims throw awesome parties. Others throw parties that compare roughly with a stomach virus.
Crying Baby	-15	Lasts until leaving or baby stops crying	If the baby can't be quieted, it's best to get as far away as possible.
Feeling Anxious	-15	Variable	Neurosis overtakes some Sims with a feeling of anxiety that can only be solved by confronting the problem head on.
Anxious to Advance	-15	0	It's been a long time since a promotion has been earned or a skill has been improved... too long!
Overworked	-15	12	All work and no play makes it so that Sim needs to lay off putting in all that extra effort.
Upset	-15	3	It's hard to endure the rough patches with those you care about.
Itchy	-15	4	There's just no way to scratch the cursed itch!
Bad Night's Sleep	-15	6	Sleeping on a cheap bed would make any Sim grumpy.
Dirty Surroundings	-15	Lasts until leaving or cleaning	Garbage, filth, and grime do not improve one's surroundings.
Enemy!	-10	Lasts until Sim leaves	The presence of garbage would be preferred to that of a hated enemy!
Unfinished Room	-10	Lasts until room finished	This room needs proper flooring and wall covering of some sort to be considered complete.
It's Dark	-10	Lasts until room brightens	A little light would certainly improve things. Perhaps some windows to let natural light in, as well?
Strained	-15	Variable	Sim could stand a few hours of fun to iron out the stress.
Sore	-10	6	Sims may occasionally feel a little pain, but the results are usually worth it. Sometimes a massage can help...
Technophobia	-10	3	Some Sims really can't stand watching TV no matter what the channel.
Can't Stand Art	-10	3	One Sim's art is another Sim's garbage. Some Sims just don't appreciate the finer things in life.
Rude Awakening	-10	1	Loud noises and ruckuses will disturb sleeping Sims. Keep those stereos off and the conversations somewhere else, and don't light the bedroom on fire.
Dislikes Children	-10	Last until Sim or child leaves	Some Sims just don't find children to be adorable bundles of joy.
Rude Guest	-10	4	Sims don't like it when other Sims are rude, especially houseguests!
Rejected First Kiss	-10	6	It's sad when a Sim gets rejected for a first kiss. Very sad. A rejected sim needs time to cool off before their social skills will be back on track.
Bad Reception	-10	Variable	Cheap television sets don't always provide the most pristine picture.
Tired From Moving	-10	6	It's been a long day, but it's good to be home and settled in.
Creeped Out	-10	Variable	Ewww! Someone sure is acting creepy!

NEGATIVE MOODLETS, CONTINUED

Moodlet	Effect	Duration in Hours	Description
Cold Shower	-10	3	Freezing jets of water will dull any mood. Perhaps it's time to upgrade the shower...
Tastes Like Fridge	-10	Variable	Every bite shouldn't contain flavors from everything else in the fridge. Quality fridges never have this problem!
Uneven Cooking	-10	Variable	At least the left-most portion was cooked correctly...right? Maybe a nicer stove would burn better.
Lonely	-15	Lasts until Sim finds company	Communication is a must for Sims. A quick chat will fix things right away.
Smelly	-10	Lasts until shower	Sims don't like to stink. More importantly, Sims don't like other Sims that stink.
Grungy	-5	Lasts until shower	Yuck! That layer of grime growing might mean it's time for a bath or shower.
Wasted Food	-5	Variable	Don't throw away good food! There are starving children in Strangetown!
Creepy Graveyard	-5	Variable	Graveyards are terrifying places filled with dead bodies, the ghosts of the bodies, and fear.
Boring Conversation	-5	3	Yawn! Will they ever stop talking?
Feeling Unlucky	-5	23	Today is NOT Sim's lucky day. Nothing good can come of this.

Mood Boosting Tips and Tricks

We have collected a host of suggestions for increasing the appearance of positive moodlets as well as minimizing negative moodlets. Because a good mood has such a far-reaching effect, use these tricks to maintain a smile on your Sim.

Food Boosts

The simple act of eating can have a very positive effect on your Sim. Not only does it negate hunger, but quality food can also put a Sim on cloud nine (or clouds one through eight, depending on how good the meal is). Here are some tricks for maximizing mood through eating:

- Develop the Cooking skill. As your Sim approaches level 10, they make higher and high quality meals. Quality meals result in the Good Meal, Great Meal, and Amazing Meal moodlets depending on the skill of the cook and the number of times the recipe has been prepared.
- Sims get better at a recipe the more they make a dish. Fortunately, they do not get tired of eating the same thing so if your Sim masters a dish like Goopy Carbonara and keeps making it, Sims get moodlet boosts for eating it.
- Place leftovers in the fridge of Excellent or Perfect recipes and eat them whenever the Sim is hungry. Buying a more expensive fridge helps leftovers keep longer so you waste little time making additional servings every day and can enjoy a quick mood boost from eating good food.
- When a Sim finally reaches level 10 of the Culinary career, they get a special fridge that not only keeps leftovers for a long time, but Sims get the Superior Equipment moodlet just for walking past it.
- If your Sim makes a new recipe and does a poor job resulting in a disgusting meal, don't eat it. Just rely on a quick meal to satiate hunger. The Sim is sad over wasting food, but the mood hit for the Nauseous moodlet is worse.
- At level 10 of the Cooking skill, Sims can buy the Baked Angel Food Cake recipe. Eating a serving of this recipe results in the Warm Fuzzies moodlet, which gives an easy mood boost for five hours.
- Eating out at the diner or bistro always results in a food-related mood boost. Sure, it costs Simoleons, but the eight-hour moodlet boost will pump up your Sim's overall mood. Try eating at the bistro or diner before going to work for an extended mood boost.
- Dining at the bistro occasionally (but not too often) results in the Divine Meal moodlet. This moodlet boost lasts for an entire week and offers +75 to your Sim's mood. Talk about a happiness generator.
- Feed Ambrosia to your Sims so they get the coveted Divine Meal moodlet. The recipe is available from the bookstore once Sims reach level 10 of the Cooking skill. However, the recipe does not come cheap. It costs §12,000 and it's worth every single Simoleon.
- No time to cook? Just grab a quick snack. If you let your Sim get too hungry, they get the Very Hungry and Starving moodlets. These negative moodlets last a long time and are terrible to have, especially before going to work.
- In addition to buying a good fridge, splurge on a good stove. This reduces the chances of preparing a meal that results in the negative Uneven Cooking moodlet while working on new recipes.

Environment Boosts

Sims are affected by their surroundings at home. You can boost mood by making sure your Sims have a pleasant pad. Sure, it may cost a little money to get the best stuff and make your Sims happy, but maxing out mood is almost always worth the expenditure.

- Sims love new stuff. In fact, buying a new object for the house results in the appropriately named New Stuff! moodlet, which is a quick mood booster.
- Keep your lot clean. It doesn't take that long to pick up dishes or make sure objects in the bathroom are clean. Mop up puddles right away, too. Dirty houses result in negative moodlets like Filthy Surroundings. Walking through a dirty house on the way to work is a real mood-killer.
- Master the Painting skill so your Sims create Masterpieces. Masterpieces add huge

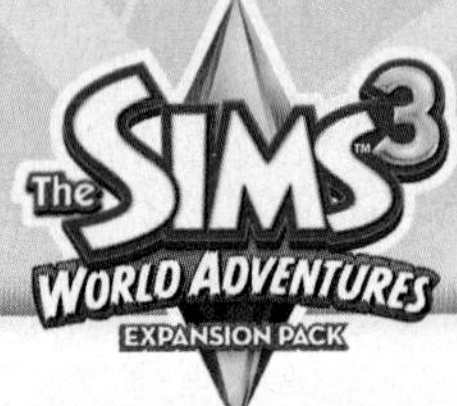

environmental boosts to rooms that help foster the Decorated moodlets.

- Spend some Simoleons on nice objects such as paintings and sculptures so Sims get the Decorated moodlets just for passing through a room.
- Install a fireplace in your Sim's house. When Sims walk past it while a fire crackles, they get the Cozy Fire moodlet. If they linger near the fireplace, they get the Warmed moodlet.
- Speaking of heat, if a gardening Sim grows a Flame Fruit and keeps it in their personal inventory, they always enjoy the Warmed moodlet.
- Place a swimming pool on your lot. Sims get the Lovely Pool moodlet when they are near it.
- Buy the rubber duckie from the supermarket and place it on the tub in your house. Every time Sims take a bath, they get the Duck Time Fun moodlet. That's an easy mood booster.
- All Sims like music. Place a stereo in your house and play music for your Sims so they get the Enjoying the Music moodlet. The potency of this moodlet increases with the quality of the stereo. If a Sim with the Handiness skill upgrades the stereo so it plays music in all rooms, all Sims in the house enjoy the moodlet boost when music is played.
- In addition to digging on music from a stereo, Sims also like the sound of the guitar. A skilled musician can cause the Enjoying the Music moodlet, too.
- Not all chairs are created equal. When browsing the chairs, look at the comfy rating. The higher the rating, the comfier the chair. (And, chances are, the more expensive the chair, too.) However, spend the extra Simoleons for the comfy chairs and sofas. Sitting in one—even for just a few moments—results in the Comfy moodlet.
- Your Sim gets the Pristine Picture moodlet boost from watching a quality TV. If a handy Sim tinkers with it, the chance of getting this moodlet increases. It's another easy way to boost overall mood.

Social Boosts

With the exception of Loner Sims, Sims love to be social. Many positive moods come from being a gadfly or a schmoozer, so consider these tricks while dealing with other Sims. Your next social interaction could put your Sim's mood up into the green!

- Parties put Sims in good moods. If you put together an awesome party that your guests enjoy, you get the Threw a Great Party moodlet, which lasts an entire day.
- Know a Sim who is a Great Kisser? A little smooch from this Sim results in a nice little moodlet, Great Kiss. On the way out the door, that's an easy pick-me-up.
- Meeting a new Sim is always enjoyable, but when your Sim converts that acquaintance into a friendship, they can enjoy the New Friend moodlet. So, get out there and socialize. Just watch out for clumsy conversations so you don't end up with negative moodlets like Embarrassed or Boring Conversation.
- If you have multiple Sims in your household, have them stop and compliment each other for a moment to get the Flattered moodlet.

Need Boosts

Each Sim has six primary needs. Addressing these needs often boosts the overall mood. Because we already dealt with food-related mood boosts, these strategies are related to the remaining needs.

- It's tempting to push your Sims to the limits of sleep in order to squeeze as much into a day as possible. However, getting a full night's sleep gives the Well Rested moodlet for a full 10 hours. That's a great moodlet to have before going to work.
- Got a spare hour? Take a nap. The Had a Nice Nap moodlet is a quick fix that adds a nice mood bump for a few hours.
- Obviously, Sims like to have fun. Giving your Sim something to do they enjoy (often related to traits, such as giving a good book to a Bookworm) will bring on the Entertained moodlet. Keep it up for six hours and that moodlet turns into the Having a Blast moodlet, which is an even bigger mood booster.
- Hygiene is an important need. It's not just that Sims do not like being around stinky Sims, but taking care of Hygiene needs can often result in a positive mood boost.
- The Minty Breath moodlet boost is a quick hit for very little effort. Just brush your Sim's teeth at any sink. Make it a habit.
- Buy a quality shower and enjoy the Exhilarating Shower moodlet boost. Get this right before heading out the door to work (along with a quality meal) to have a great day at the office.
- Whoa—is your Sim afflicted by the Strained moodlet? Get rid of it as soon as possible with a massage or fun activity!

Out and About Boosts

There are many ways to boost your Sim's mood outside the house. Many community lots such as the theater have positive effects on mood, so if your Sim is down in the dumps, try these suggestions for turning that frown upside-down:

- If your Sim has the Loves the Outdoors trait, just going out into nature results in the One with Nature moodlet. It's an easy mood booster achieved by just going outside, so consider making sure your Sim has this trait.
- Visiting a city park gives Sims the Beautiful Park moodlet. It offers a nice mood bump. However, you can kick your mood up another notch by bringing a stereo when heading to the park. Place the stereo on the ground near your Sim and play some music. Now your Sim not only gets the Beautiful Park moodlet, but also the Enjoying the Music moodlet.
- Many facilities such as the theater or science facility offer tours. If your Sim has a trait that is related to the location, take the tour and enjoy the Impressed and/or Fascinated moodlets.
- The day spa is a positive moodlet factory. Buying treatments at the day spa results in a variety of moodlets—all of them positive. The more expensive the spa treatment, the better the effect. The body treatments, for example, result in the Rejuvenated moodlet. If you spring for the top treatment, you can get up to +100 on your mood for 24 hours. You are effectively buying happiness!
- Go to the movies! This is a cheap way to get an extended mood boost called Saw a Great Movie. It lasts for 16 hours, so if you catch a flick the night before work, you'll enjoy the effect of the moodlet for the majority of the next day's shift.
- On your way out of the house, stop by the mailbox and donate some Simoleons to charity. The more Simoleons you donate, the bigger the boost from the Charitable moodlet. The moodlet lasts an entire day, so it's an effective way to pump up a Sim.

Needs

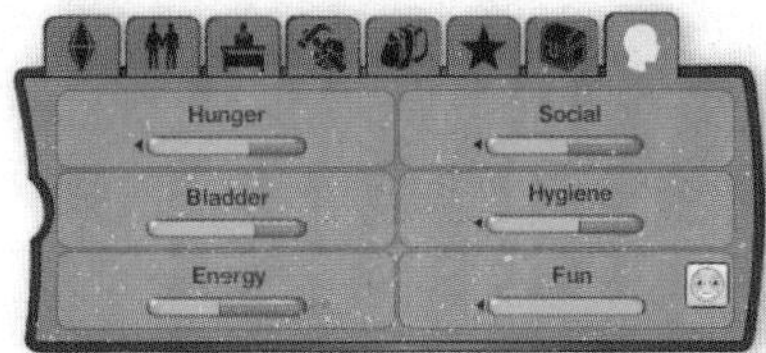

Needs are not as central to *The Sims 3* as they were in previous editions of the series. Needs are still important—after all, Sims gotta use the bathroom and eat when they are hungry—but these needs now manifest themselves through moodlets. For example, when a Sim is terribly hungry, they let you know through the Hungry moodlet that appears right in the moodlet box that is always visible.

There is still a Need panel you can reference to get a closer look at exact need levels. This a helpful way to head off a potential negative moodlet. There are six needs to monitor:

- Bladder
- Hunger
- Energy
- Hygiene
- Fun
- Social

Each need in the Needs panel is accompanied by a meter that shows you the exact level of the need at that moment, such as whether or not the need is being met (the meter appears green) or the need has been ignored for far too long (red). If you check in on the Needs panel and you see that the Hunger meter is yellow, the satisfaction of that need has dropped below 50 percent and is on its way to red territory. When that meter turns red, a negative moodlet associated with that need appears and the Sim's overall mood takes a hit.

CAUTION

While more attention is paid to moodlets, you ignore the Needs panel at your own risk. Just pop into the Needs panel and survey the satisfaction levels, thus heading off a negative moodlet.

Wishes

It is through wishes that Sims feel both fulfilled and productive, but not all wishes are equal. In fact, there are other ways to define a Sim's life besides Lifetime Wishes. The day-to-day desires of Sims are also very important, such as the desire to chat with another Sim or learn a new recipe. These smaller wishes commonly factor into the overarching Lifetime Wish, and also help with skill development and the career advancement.

Fulfilling a promised wish to a Sim results in the acquisition of Lifetime Happiness points. The reward is not nearly as much as a Lifetime Wish, but the points from fulfilling smaller wishes really add up over time.

NOTE

Not every wish is worth the same number of Lifetime Happiness points to every Sim. Depending on a Sim's wants, traits, and needs, a wish is worth a different amount than it would be to another Sim.

Making Wishes Come True

Almost as soon as your Sims move into their new houses, they start expressing wishes and desires via the Wish panel at the bottom of the screen. Sims can have up to four active wishes at any time and express one in the arched bubble above the Wish panel. To promise a new wish to a Sim, left-click on it. That moves it into the Wish panel. If you find an incoming wish more appealing than a promised wish but have no more empty slots, right-click on one of promised wishes to remove it. There is no penalty for getting rid of a promised wish.

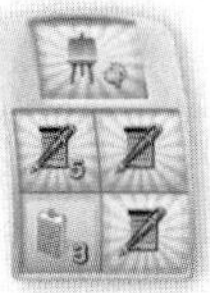

The Wish panel

CAUTION

You cannot undo a denied wish—once it's gone, it's gone. It may come back later, but don't count on it.

Once added to the Wish panel, a wish stays there until it is either fulfilled or denied. The number of Lifetime Happiness points for a promised wish do not deteriorate over time either. If you hold on to the Have a Baby wish for several days before attempting to fulfill it, it is still worth the same number of Lifetime Happiness points as the first moment it appeared.

Wishes are not universal. Every Sim wants different things, although you may see similar wishes appear within Sims in the same household that have similar traits, skills, or careers. Ages also affect the wishes, as a child will want different things than an adult. It is also important to note that some promised wishes disappear when a Sim ages up. Because the Sim is moving into a new age group and possibly gaining a new trait that affects personality, that Sim is likely to have totally different desires.

Lifetime Happiness Points

Whether you accumulate Lifetime Happiness points by boosting mood up into the bubble or by fulfilling wishes, they all go into the same pot. These Lifetime Happiness points can then be traded for Lifetime Rewards, which are a collection of special objects, skill modifiers, or personality tweaks that can make your Sim's life easier or send it spiraling into an entirely new direction.

LIFETIME REWARDS

Lifetime Reward	Cost	Function
Steel Bladder	10,000	Never have to go pee
Change Lifetime Wish	10,000	Pick a new Lifetime Wish to replace current one
Dirt Defiant	15,000	Hygiene concerns be gone!
Hardly Hungry	25,000	Don't have to eat as often
Professional Slacker	5,000	Does not lose career performance for using the Slack Off tone at work
Speedy Cleaner	5,000	Sim can clean objects faster
Fast Metabolism	5,000	Change body shape faster
Multi-Tasker	10,000	Increased career performance / Do homework faster
Extra Creative	30,000	Paintings are always higher-than-average quality
Acclaimed Author	30,000	Increased royalty checks (from Writing)
Super-Green Thumb	20,000	Harvestables are of universally higher quality
Never Dull	15,000	Always interesting (never boring when socializing)
Discount Diner	5,000	Free restaurant meals
Complimentary Entertainment	5,000	Free theater shows
Bookshop Barginer	10,000	Cheaper books
Office Hero	5,000	Popular w/ peers (Increased Relationship Gain during "Hang with Co-Workers")
Vacationer	15,000	Reduce performance decay for missing work
Legendary Host	5,000	Everyone Invited shows up to your parties and they have a higher quality
Haggler	15,000	Permanent shopping discount (at stores)
Long Distance Friend	20,000	No relationship decay when apart from LTRs
Fast Learner	15,000	Develop skills faster
Attractive	10,000	Sims with appropriate preference start in a high relationship to you
Observant	5,000	Instantly learn traits when socializing (tunable number of traits learned)
Opportunistic	10,000	Increase opportunity rewards (earn 2x reward)
Fertility Treatment	10,000	Increases chance of conception and chance of twins or triplets
Mid-life Crisis	20,000	Change traits
Collection Helper	40,000	This adds marks on Map View that help spot collectibles like metals and beetles
Body Sculptor	30,000	Instantly change body shape with this wish
Mood Modifier	60,000	Remove negative moodlets...most of the time
Food Replicator	50,000	Freely duplicate meals without the shopping or cooking time
Teleportation Pad	75,000	Quick way of getting from home to specific destinations

Opportunities

As you live each day, your Sim encounters opportunities related to social situations, careers, and skills. These opportunities often come out of nowhere—just as they do in real life. Opportunities provide short-term goals, but they are not mandatory. There is no penalty for dismissing an opportunity or for not completing an opportunity. However, because each opportunity has a reward, such as Simoleons or a promotion, it pays to pursue them as best as you can.

NOTE

You get many opportunities from being social, so definitely get out there and mingle.

Many opportunities are time-sensitive. If you are presented with an opportunity with a time limit, such as participating in a cook-off, you are given the deadline right up front. Keep these deadlines in mind because many opportunities actually require a little work. You cannot expect to complete an opportunity with just 10 minutes left on the clock.

To track your active opportunities, use the Opportunity panel. There are three opportunity categories: skill, career, and special. You can only have one opportunity in each category at a time. You cannot stack opportunities or bank them for later.

Skills

Sims love to learn—they are just waiting for a little nudge from you. Sims can pick and eventually master a variety of skills, from writing to gardening to learning how to play the guitar. Learning a skill is a good way to shape a Sim's personality, especially if aligned with a specific trait, such as the Gardening skill and the Green Thumb trait. Skills are also a great way for Sims who do not want a traditional career to make money and contribute to the household. Some skills can also be treated as part-time jobs, like growing harvestables or working on a novel.

Development

Any Sim can learn any skill—all it takes is a time commitment and a drive to be the best. Some traits help a Sim master a skill sooner or at least more efficiently. The Bookworm trait lets Sims read faster, which helps speed the process of learning from books.

There are ways to speed skill development though, and some skills actually help out with the development of other skills. Skills such as Fishing and Gardening are intertwined because the fish caught while practicing the Fishing skill can fertilize harvestables that boost your Gardening skill. Quality fish caught with higher Fishing skill also boost the quality of recipes cooked while practicing the Cooking skill.

- Some skills can be first learned by reading a book or taking a class, which gives you a full level boost. Learn the first few levels of a skill by doing. When the levels are getting harder to attain, attend a class or pick up a book. You will reduce the time required to reach that next level.
- Use public equipment whenever possible to save money. The Athletic skill, for example, is improved by using gym equipment. You can buy gym objects, but why not head to the gym and use their stuff for free? While there, you can also meet other Sims and begin socializing.
- Sims learn a little faster when they are in a good mood, so do things that give Sims positive moodlets before and while trying to master a skill. For example, learning the Logic skill by playing chess at the park can give your Sim the Comfy and Beautiful Park moodlets.
- Cheap equipment can slow skill development. At first you may only be able to afford a cheap stove, for example. But when you can afford it, trade up. Your Sim will learn a little faster.

Skill Journal

Sims don't start out with any skills. When a skill is first learned, it is added to the Skill panel, and an entry in the Sim's Skill Journal tracks the development of the skill. The journal charts more than current skill level, though. Skills that produce tangibles, such as Writing or Painting, have each created work logged in the journal. Other journal entries track time spent doing various activities.

The Skill Journal also details Skill Challenges, which are specific titles bestowed on a Sim if they complete a set of requirements. Sims who complete a Skill Challenge are rewarded with a special benefit. The journal takes the guesswork out of each challenge because the requirements are expressly detailed.

Athletic

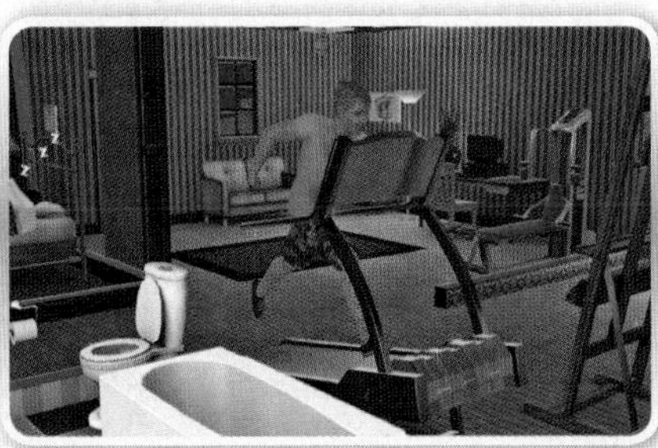

Want to feel the burn? Develop the Athletic skill to positively affect your Sim's health in a variety of ways, from body shape to longevity. There are two types of exercise: strength and cardio. Using the weights improves muscle definition, while cardio drops pounds.

Acquire by: Take Athletic Class, Use Exercise Equipment, Swim, Read Athletic Book, Workout with TV, Workout with Stereo

Development tools: Shut-In Treadmill, Exercise Queen, Pool, TV, Stereo

Development Benefits

Developing the Athletic skill is essential for the Professional Sports career, but it's also useful for the Law Enforcement career. If Sims want to excel at work, they must hone this skill on home equipment, at the gym or pool, or on the machines at the stadium. Sims can also exercise at home with the TV or a stereo, but the workout is not as effective as one with dedicated equipment. The higher the Sim's skill, the longer they can exercise without earning the Fatigued moodlet.

Here are the benefits of developing the Athletic skill:

Level 1: As soon as Sims hit the first level of this skill, they can choose to jog to locations as exercise.

Level 3: Sims can earn the Pumped moodlet from extended workouts once they reach level 3.

Level 5: Once Sims reach level 5 of the development ladder, they also run faster when directed around town on foot via the Go Here interaction.

Level 6: At level 6, athletic Sims learn the Train interaction, which lets them help other Sims improve their Athletic skill. It requires an exercise machine. When another Sim is getting trained by a level 6 athlete, the exercising Sim loses weight and gains Athletic skill faster than if they were exercising alone.

As the Athletic skill is developed, Sims earn new "tones" for workouts. These special tones modify a workout, which can lead to earning or avoiding certain moodlets. The Don't Break a Sweat tone is good for minimizing the amount of Hygiene decay so

the Grungy moodlet doesn't kick in as soon. Use these tones to get the best possible workout for the current situation:

Don't Break a Sweat (Level 1): Bad Hygiene is a real problem with extended workouts. Use this tone to work out without a heavy Hygiene decay.

Good Pacing (Level 3): Good Pacing lets you increase the length of a workout before the Fatigued moodlet takes effect.

Push Self (Level 5): Use Push Self to increase the speed of building muscle, dropping pounds, and gaining skill. However, after Push Self is used, Sims wake up with the Sore moodlet.

Quick Burst (Level 7): Quick Burst allows your Sim to get a lot of body shape change and skill much faster than usual, but the Sim gets fatigued and sore much more quickly as well. Working out with other tones until fatigued will always yield more skill and body shape change than working out until fatigued using Quick Burst, but Quick Burst gives you faster skill gains.

Skill Challenges

- **Body Builder:** Body Builders have dedicated at least 60 hours to strength workouts. This dedication pays off, because they are never fatigued after strength workouts.
- **Marathon Runner:** Marathon Runners must run at least 500 kilometers before they earn this title. However, accomplishing this incredible feat guarantees them a longer, healthier life.
- **Fitness Nut:** Fitness Nuts have spent 75 hours focusing on cardio workouts. All that time experiencing the burn means they are no longer fatigued after cardio workouts.

Charisma

Everybody knows someone who can breeze into a room, seamlessly enter any conversation, and suddenly become the focal point. The key to such feats is Charisma. This skill is essential for Sims who want to effectively socialize. Tuning this skill unlocks new social interactions that simplify befriending other Sims and developing meaningful relationships.

Acquire by: Take Charisma Class, Read Charisma Manual, Practice Speech in a Mirror

Development tools: Books, Socials, Mirror, Parties

Development Benefits

Enhancing the Charisma skill opens exciting new avenues of conversation as well as a special social that guarantees a smooth recovery from any conversational snafus. However, developing the skill requires more than just taking a class and then practicing your charismatic moves with a book or by talking into the mirror. It requires making friends and maintaining relationships during the course of the skill development. Each level of the skill requires a specific number of friends and relationships. Without these connections, you cannot advance up the skill tree, no matter how long you practice that wolfish grin in the mirror.

Here are the number of friends and relationships required to develop the Charisma skill:

CHARISMA – DEVELOPMENT

Level	Required Friends	Required Relationships
1	0	0
2	0	2
3	1	3
4	2	4
5	3	6
6	4	8
7	5	10
8	6	15
9	8	20
10	10	25

TIP

Sims who develop the Charisma skill increase the effectiveness of social interactions at work, such as Meet Co-Workers or Suck Up to Boss.

NOTE

Whenever you use a positive social, the Charisma skill gets a little boost.

Practice your Charisma skill by working on your speech in the mirror at home.

Charismatic Sims get additional greetings that start a conversation right, such as Amusing Introduction and Friendly Introduction. These greets are more potent than regular greets. As the skill develops, more greet modifiers appear that increase the social weight of the greeting and can steer the conversation. Here are the modified greetings with each advancing level:

CHARISMA – GREETINGS

Level	Greet Modifier	Type of Greet
1	Friendly	Friendly
2	Amusing	Funny
3	Interesting	Impressive
4	Flirty	Romantic
5	Affectionate	Romantic
6	Funny	Funny
7	Impressive	Impressive
8	Hilarious	Funny
9	Loving	Romantic
10	Hot	Romantic

Three special socials unlock as you develop the Charisma skill. Once you reach a specific level, you learn these new socials:

Charming Introduction (Level 1): Sometimes, introductions are the toughest part of the conversation. Sims with high Charisma levels become more adept at introductions, as seen by the modified greets. Once charismatic Sims reach level 10, their Charming Introduction rockets them into Friend status right away.

Get to Know (Level 3): This social helps with discovering the traits and interests of other Sims. Once learned, this social becomes more powerful as the Sim approaches level 10 of the skill. Eventually, there is no possibility of rejection when inquiring about traits and interests.

Smooth Recovery (Level 5): Oops. You said the wrong thing. If you have the Smooth Recovery social, you can try to revive the conversation. If may not always work, but as the skill nears level 10, the chance of success increases.

Skill Challenges

Celebrity: Celebrities are Acquaintances with at least 25 local Sims. Celebrities build relationships faster due to a hefty starting relationship bonus.

- **Personable:** Personable Sims have learned at least 50 traits of their friends and neighbors. They learn traits more quickly when conversing with new people.
- **Super Friendly:** Super Friendly Sims can honestly say they have at least 20 Friends. It seems like an impossibly large number of relationships to juggle, but for Super Friendly Sims, friendships never decay.
- **Everybody's Best Friend:** To be Everybody's Best Friend, have at least 10 Best Friends. Your Friends skip Good Friend and jump immediately to Best Friends.
- **Comedian:** Comedians have successfully told 100 jokes, which amounts to quite a few laughs. Jokes told by Comedians rarely fall flat.

Cooking

Save for using the bathroom and sleeping, no activity is more crucial to a Sim than eating. Food is a central part of every Sim's life, so having a Sim around who can actually cook is a boon to everybody's mood. However, very few Sims are awesome in the kitchen right away—even those with the Natural Cook trait. Cooking must be practiced. It's hard work, but it has great rewards. Very few things offer a pick-me-up quite like a good meal.

Acquire by: Class, Prepare Meals, Read Cookbook

Development tools: Books, Meal Preparation Interactions, Foodstuffs, Recipes

Development Benefits

Sims must eat to survive. At first, Sims have access to just a handful of recipes, but can also just grab quick meals out of the fridge. Quick meals have zero prep time, are eaten quickly, and reduce hunger. However, quick meals and snacks do not help develop the Cooking skill, nor can they be served to groups of Sims like a full meal.

TIP

Ditch the cheap stove as soon as possible so you stop getting the Uneven Cooking moodlet. Plus, more expensive stoves help with both the speed of preparing a recipe and the quality of the end result.

The shortcomings of quick meals make developing the Cooking skill so important. Not every member of a household needs to excel at the skill, but a general acquaintance with it is very useful. Prepared meals build the Cooking skill while being made, can serve groups of Sims, and if made well, can improve mood.

Quality of Food

As the Sim develops the skill, the food they make improves. The more recipes learned also improves the variety of dishes served, which has a positive effect on every Sim who eats them. When a Sim first tries to cook a recipe, there is a good chance they will fail and create a disgusting version of the dish. It is still edible, but it hits Sims with a negative moodlet. A recipe's quality is affected by the Sim's level of Cooking skill and the number of times they've cooked the dish. Eventually, a dish the Sim once botched will provide great happiness, inspiring moodlets such as Good Meal and Amazing Meal.

TIP

Recipes that use harvestables grown by a Sim with the Gardening skill also use the quality of the harvest to determine the quality of the meal. The better quality the harvestable, the better the meal.

Recipes Learned

Two types of recipes are opened by developing the Cooking skill: learned recipes and acquired recipes. Learned recipes are purchased in the bookstore, but cannot be opened until the skill reaches a specific level. The acquired recipes are those automatically gifted when the Sim reaches a specific cooking level.

LEARNED RECIPES

Recipe Name	Level Required
Autumn Salad	0
Waffles	0
Mac and Cheese	0
Pancakes	1
Peanut Butter and Jelly	1
Hot Dogs	1
Goopy Carbonara	2
Grilled Cheese	2
Spaghetti	4
Sushi Roll	4
Stu Surprise	5
Hamburger	6
Key Lime Pie	7
Grilled Salmon	8
French Toast	9
Dim Sum	9
Lobster Thermador	10

ACQUIRED RECIPES

Recipe Name	Level Required
Ratatouille	1
Fish and Chips	3
Cookies	3
Fruit Parfait	4
Cheesesteak	5
Cobbler	6
Eggs Machiavellian	7
Tri-Tip Steak	8
Stuffed Turkey	9
Baked Angel Food Cake	10
Ambrosia	10

NOTE

All recipes are tracked in the Cooking Skill Journal, including the number of times each recipe has been made.

TIP

At level 10 of the Cooking skill, you can learn the coveted Ambrosia recipe. This special recipe requires Baked Angel Food Cake and Deathfish. If Ambrosia was made properly, eating it will extend your Sim's life a little during the current age.

Skill Challenges

- **Star Chef:** Star Chefs have prepared at least 50 meals, so they clearly know their way around the kitchen. The dishes they prepare are higher quality and thus more pleasing.
- **World-Class Chef:** World-Class Chefs have prepared at least 75 dishes and are masters of the kitchen. World-Class Chefs prepare meals significantly faster.
- **Menu Maven:** Menu Mavens have learned to prepare all recipes. Recipes are earned by improving the Cooking skill and can be purchased at the bookstore. Menu Mavens prepare higher quality food.

Fishing

The Fishing skill is good for three things: keeping food on the table, earning money, and relaxing. Sims with the Angler trait have a head start on other Sims who pick up a rod and reel, but any Sims can take a class to advance the Fishing skill or just plop a bobber in the water and start learning through experience.

Acquire by: Take Fishing Class, Read Fishing Book, Fishing

Development tools: No tools needed

Development Benefits

The Fishing skill begins one of three ways: reading a book, taking a class, or just going out to a body of water and using the Fish interaction. Once the Fishing skill is underway, the skill increases either by continued reading or continued fishing. Just having a hook under the surface is enough to develop the skill, but this is a slow way to learn. The skill actually gets a bump when you catch a fish. And the bigger the fish, the bigger the skill bump.

TIP

Certain traits in addition to Angler affect the Fishing skill. Loves the Outdoors Sims get great moodlets from just being outside and fishing. Hates Outdoors, Easily Bored, or Clumsy dampen the ability to catch fish.

When a fish is hoisted out of the water, the Sim holds it up and the weight of the fish is automatically logged in the Skill Journal. If it's a new type of fish, that is also noted.

Once the Sim reaches level 3 with the Fishing skill, they can choose the Bait interaction at the water's edge to use a specific type of bait while fishing. Bait is essential if a Sim hopes to catch more than just the basic fish. Gaining levels also unlocks the ability to catch certain fish. However, just unlocking a type of fish does not guarantee actually catching it.

Using any bait slightly increases the chance of catching all fish. It also drastically increases the chance of catching the fish that loves that specific bait type. Higher quality bait tends to catch bigger fish, but only for fish that specifically like that bait. So use Perfect bait to catch the biggest fish. You can also use bait to catch fish that are somewhat higher level than your Sim's Fishing skill. Sims can catch fish up to 3 levels higher than their skill by using the right bait, although it will be harder to catch those fish until the Sim is higher skill.

Each fish has one favorite type of bait, and you should use that bait to catch that fish. Here is a table with the bait that each type of fish prefers:

FISHING

Fish	Skill Level Required	Commonality	Locations Found	Preferred Bait	Minimum weight	Maximum weight	Value at min weight	Value at max weight	Skill Points for Catching
Minnow	0	Common	Lakes, Ocean/Hatchery	Apple	0.1	0.5	5	11	120
Anchovy	0	Common	Ocean/Hatchery	Tomato	0.1	0.5	5	11	120
Goldfish	1	Common	Lakes	Lettuce	0.1	2	6	16	132
Alley Catfish	1	Uncommon	Lakes, Ocean/Hatchery	Cheese	0.1	5	6	20	132
Jellyfish	2	Common	Ocean/Hatchery	Grapes	0.1	10	8	19	140
Rainbow Trout	2	Common	Lakes	Egg	1	10	9	18	140
Red Herring	3	Common	Lakes, Ocean/Hatchery	Hot Dogs	1	10	5	5	160
Tuna	3	Common	Ocean/Hatchery	Onion	2	40	11	25	160
Piranha	4	Uncommon	Lakes	Watermelon	5	15	14	30	185
Tragic Clownfish	4	Uncommon	Lakes, Ocean/Hatchery	Bell Pepper	5	40	13	32	185
Siamese Catfish	5	Common	Lakes, Ocean/Hatchery	Minnow	3	25	14	41	220
Blowfish	5	Uncommon	Ocean/Hatchery	Potato	5	40	13	47	220
Salmon	6	Common	Ocean/Hatchery	Lime	10	50	14	45	255
Black Goldfish	6	Common	Lakes	Goldfish	5	25	16	49	255
Shark	7	Uncommon	Lakes, Ocean/Hatchery	Red Herring	1	150	7	70	295
Swordfish	7	Common	Ocean/Hatchery	Anchovy	20	60	17	60	295
Angelfish	8	Uncommon	Lakes, Ocean/Hatchery	AlleyCatfish	2	60	21	85	340
Vampire Fish	8	Rare	Graveyard	Garlic	25	80	55	225	1,000
Robot Fish	9	Rare	Science Facility	Piranha	250	1,000	50	275	1,000
Lobster	9	Common	Lakes, Ocean/Hatchery	Tuna	5	50	25	120	400
Deathfish	10	Rare	Graveyard	Angelfish	20	80	200	1,000	1,500

Skill Challenges

- **Amateur Ichthyologist:** Amateur Ichthyologists have caught at least one of every fish type. Their deep understanding of marine life helps them catch the bigger fish.
- **Commercial Fisherman:** Commercial Fisherman have caught at least 350 fish. They catch more fish in less time than normal Sims.

Gardening

Gardening is a great skill for Green Thumb Sims, Sims who want to cook, and Sims who like the outdoors. This skill tree lets you turn a backyard into a harvestable-growing paradise. But gardening is a lot of work and takes time to master.

Acquire by: Take Gardening Class, Read Gardening Book, Plant Seed

Development tools: Gardening Books, Seeds

Development Benefits

Learn the Gardening skill by taking a class or reading a Gardening book. You can also plant a seed and cultivate it to start developing the skill. Once the skill has been acquired, Sims can choose the Plant interaction from seeds and other harvestables in their personal inventories. Once a seed has been planted, Sims can water it. As they continue leveling, they unlock two more critical interactions: Weed and Fertilize.

Here are the unlockable interactions or specials for the development of the Gardening skill:

Weed (Level 2): Once the Weed interaction is unlocked, Sims can pull up choking weeds before they damage a harvestable. The higher the skill level, the less time it takes to clear weeds around a plant.

Fertilize (Level 3): Fertilizing is key to growing the best harvestables. No one fertilizer is better for a particular plant. The quality of the fertilizer is what affects the potential growth of the harvestable.

Uncommon Seeds (Level 5): Once the Sim reaches this level, they can plant uncommon seeds.

Revive Plant (Level 6): If a Sim has the Green Thumb trait, this interaction is unlocked at level 6. A dying plant can be rescued with a pretty high success rate by using this interaction on it.

Rare Seeds (Level 7): Once the Sim reaches this level, they can plant rare seeds.

Special Plants (Levels 8, 9, and 10): At level 8, you get the first of three special gardening opportunities from the chef at the bistro. There is one opportunity per level: 8, 9, and 10. Once all three have been completed, the Sim receives Omni Plant seeds and the ability to plant them.

NOTE

What's an Omni Plant? Imagine a plant that grows into whatever fertilizer you give it. Give the Omni Plant a book and the Omni Plant will soon blossom great texts.

TIP

Grow garlic and watermelon for simple cash crops. Just keep planting the highest quality of these harvestables and churn that garden until it becomes a money machine.

The better care you give a plant and the higher your Gardening skill level, the better quality fruit a plant produces. Plants range from Horrifying to Perfect, just like prepared recipes from the Cooking skill. Better quality harvestables are worth more when sold.

To raise the best harvestables, you must show no mercy with your plants. Keep growing as many as you can and dispose of the lowest quality ones, so you keep breeding higher quality harvestables. Combine this tactic with raising your skill level to keep growing better harvestables. Using quality harvestables in your cooking improves the quality of recipes, which in turn gives out better meal-related moodlets.

Seeds

Sims need seeds to grow harvestables. Not all seeds are easy to grow into successful plants, though. Sims must level up the Gardening skill to plant all types of seeds: common, uncommon, and rare.

Many seeds can just be bought from the EverFresh Supermarket, such as grape or tomato. Just buy the fruit and then plant it. However, Sims can also find seeds by exploring. Every morning, there are new seeds in new locations, so look around daily to see what's on the ground. The farther away from houses and commerce buildings Sims look, the more likely they are to find uncommon and rare seeds. Seeds are unknown when found. To discover what the seed will grow, it must be planted and nurtured. Once you grow a harvestable from a found seed, you recognize that seed in the wild.

Fertilizer

There are many different types of fertilizer to use on your plants to help them grow into high-quality harvestables. Here's a full list of the best fertilizers:

FERTILIZERS

Ingredient	Effectiveness	Fish	Effectiveness
Cheese	1	Anchovy	1
Burger Patty	1	Goldfish	1
Egg	1	Alley Catfish	1
Lettuce	1	Rainbow Trout	2
Tomato	1	Minnow	3
Onion	1	Jellyfish	3
Potato	1	Tuna	3
Apple	1	Salmon	4
Lime	1	Black Goldfish	4
Grapes	1	Swordfish	4
Watermelon	2	Red Herring	5
Steak	3	Tragic Clownfish	5
Bell Pepper	3	Siamese Catfish	5
Garlic	3	Piranha	5
Flame Fruit	3	Blowfish	5
Life Fruit	4	Shark	6
		Lobster	6
		Angelfish	7
		Vampire Fish	7

Skill Challenges

- **Master Planter:** A Master Planter must plant every type of plant available. Once you have mastered the varieties, you can reduce weed growth significantly on future plants.
- **Botanical Boss:** Botanical Bosses must harvest at least 75 Perfect fruits and vegetables. The plants of Botanical Bosses almost never die from neglect.
- **Master Farmer:** Master Farmers have harvested at least 650 fruits and vegetables. The plants of Master Farmers remain watered and fertilized longer, meaning their gardens are more efficient.

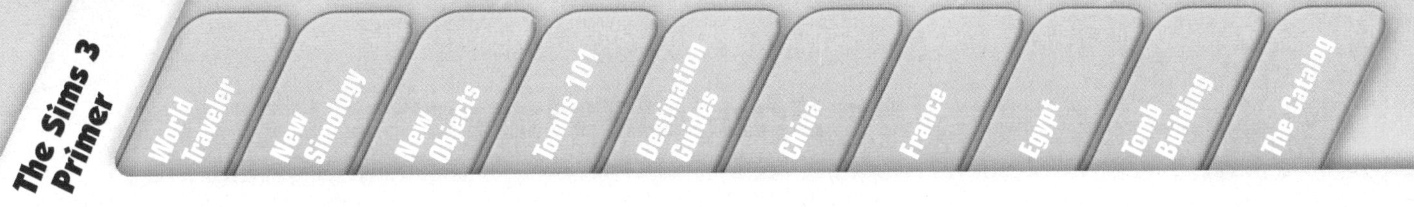

Guitar

Who doesn't love the gift of music? A smooth jam lilting on a summer's breeze brings joy to all who hear it. So why not become the source of such aural pleasures by picking up the guitar and developing this skill. The Guitar skill can be enjoyed by any Sim, not just those who have embarked on the Music career.

Acquire by: Take Guitar Class, Play Guitar

Development tools: Guitar

Development Benefits

To get started on the Guitar skill, take a Guitar class or just pick up a guitar for the Sim's household. The guitar can slide into the Sim's personal inventory, so they can take it to the park or the beach.

Once Sims know how to play, they only have a few available compositions. Only by leveling up the skill does the Sim learn more music and eventually reach a point where they can buy sheet music from the bookstore and really play some impressive tunes. As the skill improves, the Sim gets better at playing music and makes fewer mistakes. Here's the level progression of the Guitar skill:

Level 1–4: Sim learns at least two basic practice-level songs per level.

Level 5: Sim earns three new songs—real songs that other Sims enjoy listening to.

Level 6–10: Sim learns at least one new song per level and performs it without fail.

Level 5 is particularly important to this skill. At this level, the Sim stops just noodling around with the Play interaction and moves up to the Perform interaction. Other Sims get the Enjoying Music moodlet if around a performing Sim. Level 5 Sims can also Serenade other Sims, which is a romantic social that can aid a romantic conversation following the song's conclusion.

Guitar-playing Sims can also Play for Tips in public locations. This is not the most lucrative activity, but it does add some extra change to the household bank account. The higher your skill, the more you make in tips. To really make money with this skill, practice hard and be sure to socialize. Soon, you will receive opportunities to play at parties or venues. That's where the real money is.

Sheet Music

You can buy sheet music from the bookstore or earn it from opportunities and give it to your Sim to practice. To learn from sheet music, left-click on the music from the Sim's personal inventory and select the Learn interaction. The Sim starts playing the song and when the meter is full, the Sim knows the song by heart and can perform it.

> **CAUTION**
>
> Sheet music cannot be shared among Sims. Once sheet music is learned, it disappears.

Skill Challenges

- **Master Guitarist:** Master Guitarists learn to play every song awarded to them and available for purchase at the bookstore. After learning so many songs, they receive a special master track!
- **Guitar Star:** Guitar Stars must play at 10 parties and venues in the town to earn their title. Afterward, they earn more money for tips and performances.
- **Money Maker:** Earn §5,000 playing the guitar to earn a new master track to perform. Money can be earned through tips or by completing opportunities.

Handiness

Stuff breaks. But when it does, it's usually inconvenient. Sims with the Handiness skill are suddenly valuable folks to have around.

The Handiness skill is good for repairing broken objects, and can even ensure against future calamity.

Acquire by: Take Handiness Class, Read Handiness Book, Try to Repair an Object

Development tools: Handiness Skill Books, Tinkering with Objects, Repairing an Object, Upgrading an Object

Development Benefits

Once the Handiness skill has been acquired via a course or a book, Sims can further develop it at home by either Tinkering with objects or attempting to Repair a broken object, such as a stove, stereo, dishwasher, or toilet. Any mechanical or electric object has the potential to break after every use. When an electrical object breaks, it typically smokes or sparks. A broken toilet is clogged and refuses to flush. When this happens, the Repair interaction becomes available.

When the Repair option is selected, a handy Sim will start working on the object. Depending on the level of the Handiness skill, the Sim risks getting electrocuted by the object. This causes the Singed moodlet, which drops the overall mood. (Remove this moodlet with a bath or shower.) The higher the Handiness skill, the less chance the Sim will be shocked while repairing the object.

This is the risk of trying to fix an electrical object when the Handiness skill has not been adequately developed.

A repaired object is not back to 100 percent. Once an object breaks, it has started its steady downhill slide. The chance of a repaired object breaking again goes up. The more it breaks and is repaired, the higher the chance of repeat breaks until the object finally goes absolutely kaput and must be replaced.

> **TIP**
>
> If you're lucky, insurance will kick in a few Simoleons to cover the costs of replacing an object destroyed by fire.

Upgrading

Once the Handiness skill reaches level 3, the Sim learns the Upgrade interaction. Upgrading lets a Sim add a new effect or function to an existing object. This is not a universal interaction once learned. Subsequent levels after earning the Upgrade interaction unlock extra upgrades that the handy Sim can install. Upgrades can provide many benefits, from making an object unbreakable or self cleaning or fireproof to strictly improving it, for instance the stereo's speakers can be improved to produce a bigger Enjoying Music moodlet.

Here is the list of objects that can be upgraded, the function of the upgrade, and the level required to perform the upgrade:

UPGRADING

Level	Object	Upgrade	Failure Effect
3	Inexpensive Shower	Prevents ever getting Cold Shower moodlet	Causes puddle that must be mopped
3	Dishwasher	Silences noisy dishwashers that disturb other Sims	Dishwasher just makes louder noises while running
3	Doorbell	Change doorbell to a pleasing sound	Doorbell makes awful noise
3	Stereo	Increase area of effect	Electrocution
3	Window	Improves insulation which lowers bills	None
4	Stove	Make stove fireproof so it never catches fire	Stove catches fire and burns up
4	Coffeemaker	Add timer function so coffee is ready in morning	Electrocution
6	Trash Compactor	Improve capacity	Electrocution
6	Shower	Improve water pressure to cause the Exhilarated moodlet	Causes puddle that must be mopped
7	Gas Fireplace	Fireplace starts when Sim enters room	Fire breaks out in fireplace
7	Stove	Improves food quality	None
8	Stereo	Increase mood gain of Enjoying Music	Electrocution
8	Stereo	Wire House with Speakers so music plays in all rooms	Electrocution
8	Computer	Improves graphics to make games more fun for Sims	Electrocution
9	Grandfather Clock	Increase value of clock	Decrease resale value of clock
6 through 10	Television	Unlock extra channels. Higher the skill, the more channels unlocked.	Electrocution

> 
>
> **TIP**
>
> Each object can only have one upgrade at a time, so choose wisely.

At level 3, a Sim can add a self-cleaning upgrade to objects that get dirty, such as the stove or refrigerator. At level 6 of the skill, Sims can upgrade any mechanical/electrical object so that it is unbreakable with the Prevent Breakage interaction. This upgrade takes time, but doing so helps develop the skill. Success with these upgrades is not guaranteed. If the upgrade fails (there's a small chance of this happening) then the object is either broken beyond repair or gets dirty and must be cleaned. Finally, at level 10, the Sim gets a membership card to a guild. Build Mode objects are then 25 percent off.

Skill Challenges

- **Electrician:** Electricians have repaired at least 10 electrical objects. The experience gained means they will never be electrocuted by an electrical object again.
- **Plumber:** Plumbers have repaired at least 10 plumbing objects. They are so good at repairs that plumbing objects repaired by them never break again.
- **Tinkerer:** Tinkerers have finished at least 10 unique upgrades on household items. Installing the "Unbreakable" upgrade on multiple objects only counts as one unique upgrade, so it helps to experiment with different upgrade options! Tinkerers never fail when upgrading objects.

Logic

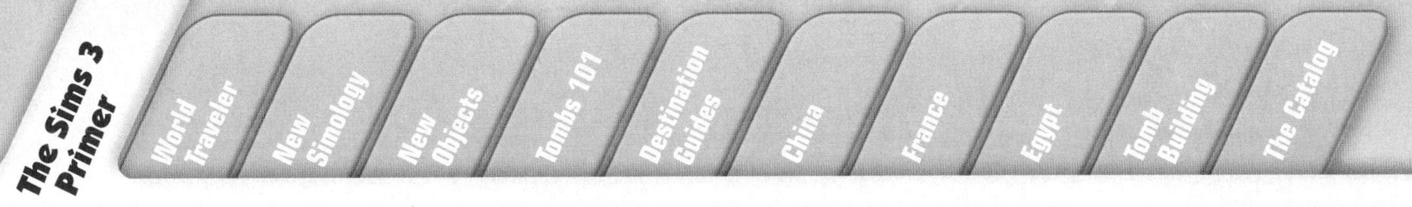

Intelligence is always a treasured asset, so pursue the Logic skill to improve your Sim's brainpower. The Logic skill involves the use of the telescope and chess set objects, but also gives Sims additional computer interactions.

Acquire by: Take Logic Class, Read Logic Book, Play Chess, Use Telescope

Development tools: Chess Set, Telescope, Logic Books, Computer

Development Benefits

The development of the Logic skill starts with attending the Logic class at the science facility, reading a Logic book, or playing chess at a chess board (at home or in a public location). This skill has many benefits beyond the ability to win chess matches. For example, this skill unlocks the Solve the Unsolvable interaction with the computer, which gives the logic-minded Sim a chance to earn some Simoleons at home. (This interaction is not a guaranteed success.)

As this skill is developed, it shortens the time it takes to develop other skills, with the exception of Athletic and Charisma. This skill also increases the chance of winning all varieties of games. Winning games gives Sims a mood boost.

At level 3 of the Logic skill, Sims have a new interaction with the telescope. They can now do more than just Stargaze, they can Search Galaxy. This is another money-making opportunity for Sims, as every new celestial body found earns them a little extra cash from the science facility. New finds are logged in the Skill Journal, too. When a Sim finds a new object in the heavens, they can name it.

At level 5, Sims unlock the ability to Tutor other young Sims: children and teens. Tutoring not only develops the Logic skill, but it helps the student and can provide a mood bump. Tutored Sims always do better in school, so if a child suffers from lagging grades, interacting with a logical Sim is a great remedy. If the mentored student has the Logic skill, too, they develop the skill while being tutored, but at a slower pace.

> **TIP**
>
> There is a "hidden" skill: Chess. Like other skills, the more you play chess, the better you get at it. You will soon start winning more and more games.

At level 5 Logic skill, Sims can start talking about the things they find while using the telescope. Talking about a celestial object is a friendly social that improves the building relationship between two Sims. However, for a real social bump, tell a Sim that you named a celestial object after them. This instant relationship builder helps with making new friends or developing a romantic relationship.

At level 10 Logic skill, the Sim can tutor any other Sim from teen to elder in any of the skills with the exception of Athletic and Charisma. The catch is that the logical Sim must also have the skill they are teaching and they cannot teach past their current level. For example, if Catherine has level 5 Writing skill, she cannot tutor Chris past level 5. This development process is much faster than reading a skill-related book but not as fast as actually practicing the skill.

Skill Challenges

- **Grand Master:** Chess Grand Masters have reached the coveted fifth level of the competitive chess circuit. Those who engage Grand Masters in chess improve their abilities in Logic and Chess twice as quickly.
- **Celestial Explorer:** Celestial Explorers have discovered 20 celestial bodies through their telescope. Their extensive knowledge of the heavens allows them to discuss the stars with their friends and neighbors.
- **Teacher Extraordinaire:** Teachers Extraordinaire have spent at least 20 hours tutoring young Sims. Because of this, they are twice as effective when tutoring.
- **Skill Professor:** Skill Professors have spent at least 30 hours tutoring other Sims in different skills. Because of this, they are twice as effective when teaching skills to others.

Painting

One of the hardest skills to develop, Painting is also one of the most rewarding. Watch in wonder as Sims create works of art before your very eyes, working from inspiration they gathered from themselves or your own input. Like Writing, this is a personalized skill that requires a lot of direction from you. But once this skill is mastered, it's not only satisfying, but very lucrative. Great paintings can sell for a pretty penny.

Acquire by: Take Painting Class, Practice at Easel

Development tools: Easel

Development Benefits

The Painting skill is actually fairly easy to acquire, but it is not exactly cheap. You must either pay for a Painting class at the community school or spring for an easel. With an easel, use the Practice interaction on the easel to pick up a brush and just mess around. After a considerable amount of time, the skill is acquired. Once level 1 of the Painting skill has been acquired, though, the development path is pretty clear: practice, practice, practice.

The Dabble interaction is replaced by Practice and you can choose the size of the canvas you want the Sim to practice on. The smaller the canvas, the faster the painting is completed. The size of the canvas also factors into the price a painting fetches, but more on that in a moment. The Practice interaction disappears when there is a canvas on the easel—then you can only continue practicing unless you chose to Scrap the Painting and start all over with a new one.

Once a Painting is completed, a Sim can either Sell it and earn a few Simoleons, put it in personal inventory, or drag it right onto the wall. You can also give the painting a name.

At level 5 of the skill, Paint replaces Practice as the interaction with the easel. Now the Sim can start earning money with this skill. As soon as the Sim unlocks skill level 6, they can paint a Brilliant painting, which is worth a decent number of Simoleons and can add environmental bonuses to rooms and inspire the Decorated moodlet. At level 9, the Sim has the chance to create a Masterpiece painting, which is even more valuable than a Brilliant painting.

The value of a painting is determined by several factors. The canvas size partially determines the value, as does the number of paintings a Sim has produced. Brilliant or Masterpiece paintings get massive value boosts, too. There is a degree of randomness in a painting's value. One somewhat morbid factor greatly enhances a painting's value: death. If the painter is deceased, the painting's appreciation accelerates.

TIP

At skill level 5, a Sim's paintings increase in value over time. Keep checking the painting to see its current appreciation.

BROWNIE BITES

This is a little sinister, but it's a great trick. If you have an elder Sim in the house, make them a painter. Concentrate on that skill. Make them painting factories. Get them to produce as many quality works as possible before they die. Then, once they do pass, all of their paintings are worth more!

Skill Challenges

- **Brushmaster:** Brushmasters have painted at least 35 paintings, and as a result paint much faster than normal painters.
- **Proficient Painter:** Proficient Painters have proven their worth by painting at least six Brilliant paintings. They then paint far more Brilliant paintings and Masterpieces than less proficient painters.
- **Master Painter:** Master Painters have painted at least five Masterpieces. Every painting they sell is worth much more than normal paintings.

Writing

Writing is another personalized skill that is deeply involving but also rewarding. Sims who learn the Writing skill unlock a world of possibilities when they sit down to the computer. Naturally, the Bookworm Sim has a jump on this skill thanks to the relevant trait. But any Sim with time and dedication can become a bestselling author.

Acquire by: Attend Writing Class, Read Writing Book, Practice Writing at Computer

Development tools: Computer, Books

Development Benefits

Once the Writing skill has been acquired, Sims have several new interactions at the computer. The Refine Writing Skill is a good way to continue developing the skill. No novels come out of this activity—just skill development. Once a writer reaches level 2 of the skill, they can start writing novels.

When the Sim pushes back from the computer, the development is added to the Skill meter. Continue Writing Novel and Scrap Current Novel are two more interactions that affect a novel-in-progress. A scrapped novel tosses out an incomplete work but the skill development remains.

Various novel genres are unlocked as the skill is further developed. The higher the genre in the skill tree, the more it is worth when published. Here are the genres, the levels required to unlock them, and the reactions they can cause it their readers:

NOVEL GENRES UNLOCKED BY WRITING

Genre	# of Books Required
Fantasy	Write 3 sci-fi novels
Satire	Write 3 humor novels
Autobiography	Write 3 biographies
Vaudeville	Write 3 of each: drama, sci-fi, humor, mystery, romance

NOVEL GENRES UNLOCKED BY SKILL LEVEL

Genre	Level
Fiction	0
Non-Fiction	0
Science Fiction	1
Trashy Novel	2
Drama	3
Children's Book	3
Humor	5
Historical	6
Mystery	8
Romance	10
Masterpiece	10

CAUTION

You can only work on one novel at a time. If you want to start a new novel in a newly unlocked genre, you must scrap the current novel.

Royalties

A Sim who's writing a novel regularly submits chapters to an agent and gets a small stipend. It's enough to live on, but nothing extravagant. Once a novel has been completed, though, the royalties start rolling in. When the novel is finished, the Sim is immediately told if the book is good or not and if it is a success. The royalty amount is listed, as well as how the amount will be paid out. (Typically, royalties

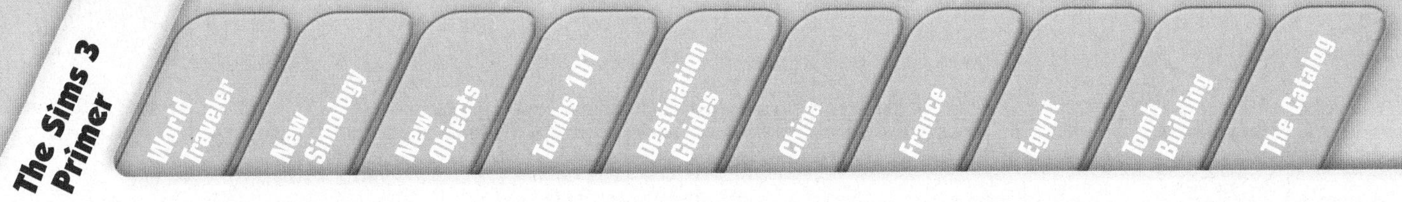

are paid over the course of several weeks with lump sums dropped into the household account at a specific time on a specific day.)

The royalty amount is decided by: level of Writing skill, desirability of the genre (check the Skill Journal, which also tracks the number of books written and the amount pulled in so far), and a certain degree of randomness. The author's traits can also affect the amount of royalties paid. Here are the traits that boost the profitability of specific genres:

TRAITS – GENRES

Genre	Trait
Trashy Novel	Flirty
Drama	Commitment Issues
Sci-Fi	Computer Whiz, Genius
Humor	Good Sense of Humor, Inappropriate, Mean-Spirited
Satire	Grumpy, Hot-Headed, Over-Emotional
Mystery	Genius
Romance	Hopeless Romantic
Historical	Perfectionist
Children's Book	Artistic, Childish, Family Oriented
Vaudeville	Bookworm
Autobiography	Charismatic, Unlucky, Daredevil, Insane, Kleptomaniac

Skill Challenges

- **Speed Writer:** Speed Writers are so prolific that they've earned §15,000 in royalties. Speed Writers write much faster than normal writers.
- **Prolific Writer:** Prolific Writers have written at least 20 books in their career. They are so well known that they tend to write far more Hits and Best-sellers than their counterparts.
- **Specialist Writer:** Writers must pen at least five novels in a specific genre to be known as a Specialist Writer. Such Specialist Writers write far more Hits and Best-sellers in their particular genre than most.

Careers

While everybody would prefer a life of leisure, you must find a source of income if you want to succeed. There are multiple ways to rake in the Simoleons, including the advancement of certain skills as detailed earlier in this chapter. However, there are more traditional ways of finding an income: careers.

To sign up for a career, you simply report to the building that headquarters the job, such as the military base or police station. Applying is as easy as left-clicking on the location and then choosing the offered career. When your Sim reports to the job location, the career is immediately offered and the starting position/salary flashed on-screen. If you accept, you are given a schedule and expected to show up at the designated times.

There are multiple ways to advance a career. Promotions are the most common benchmark of success and always come with a one-time Simoleon bonus, but there are social aspects to each career that involve getting to know co-workers, which has the potential to widen your circle of friends. While at work, you can set the "tone" for your performance, which affects how you interact with co-workers or approach the job itself. As you advance, your schedule changes and your salary rises. Typically, there are perks or benefits for hitting certain promotions.

TIP

Going to work in a good mood boosts your chances of promotion. Go see a movie the night before work to get the powerful Enjoyed a Great Movie moodlet that lasts almost the entire next day.

Tones

Although you do not actually see what your Sim is up to when they are on the job, you can dictate their general behavior for that work day through tones. Tones include behaviors such as working hard, getting to know co-workers, and sucking up to the boss. Some careers have unique tones, such as the Do a Side Job tone of the Criminal career. Many of these tones play into earning promotions at work, so look at the provided promotion metrics for each career to see what tones are best for the next step in that career.

NOTE

Not all tones are available from the first day. In some careers, additional tones are earned when you reach specific promotions.

RETIRING

Later in life, Sims can retire from a career and make a pension. This pension is smaller than the wages normally made at that promotion level, but it is a great way to pull in daily income for necessary food and objects while pursuing skills.

Business

The Business career unfolds exactly as you might expect. Sims dutifully report to work in the morning to attend meetings and climb the corporate ladder. As you approach the top of the career ranking, the requirements to reach each new promotion become harder to juggle. But that should be expected for a career with such incredible financial rewards. You cannot coast. You must work hard, appealing to both the boss and co-workers so that one day that corner office is yours.

Work Location: Doo Peas Corporate Towers

BUSINESS CAREER

Level	Position	Work Days	Start Time	Length of Day	Average Daily Pay	Weekly Average Pay	Pension Pay	Metrics for Promotion
1	Coffee Courier	M, T, W, TH, F	8 AM	6	160	800	40	Mood, Relationship w/ Boss
2	Filing Clerk	M, T, W, TH, F	8 AM	6	208	1,040	50	Mood, Relationship w/ Boss
3	Report Processor	M, T, W, TH, F	8 AM	6	271	1,355	70	Mood, Relationship w/ Boss, Relationship w/ Co-Workers
4	Corporate Drone	M, T, W, TH, F	8 AM	6	353	1,765	90	Mood, Relationship w/ Boss, Relationship w/ Co-Workers
5	Department Head	M, T, W, TH, F	8 AM	7	530	2,650	130	Mood, Relationship w/ Boss, Relationship w/ Co-Workers
6	Division Manager	M, T, W, TH, F	8 AM	7	689	3,445	170	Mood, Relationship w/ Boss, Relationship w/ Co-Workers, Meetings Held
7	Vice President	M, T, W, TH, F	8 AM	7	896	4,480	220	Mood, Relationship w/ Boss, Relationship w/ Co-Workers, Meetings Held
8	CEO	M, T, TH, F	8 AM	6	1,434	5,736	280	Mood, Relationship w/ Boss, Relationship w/ Co-Workers, Meetings Held
9	Venture Capitalist	M, T, TH, F	8 AM	6	1,721	6,884	330	Mood, Relationship w/ Co-Workers, Meetings Held
10	Power Broker	M, T, TH	8 AM	3	947	2,841	400	Mood, Relationship w/ Co-Workers, Meetings Held

BUSINESS TONES

Tones	Description
Hold Meetings	Available to schedule meetings, slows performance growth
Meet Co-Workers	Build relationship with co-workers
Chat at Water Cooler	Build relationship with co-workers
Suck Up to Boss	Build relationship with boss
Power Work	Work hard to increase performance, but adds stress

Benefits and Rewards

To work your way up this career, you must have a good relationship with the boss. This can be achieved by the Suck Up to Boss tone, but this risks alienating co-workers. This turns into a problem later in the career when your relationship with co-workers becomes a metric by which your promotion is judged. Being charismatic can help with this career because after meeting co-workers on the job, you can then improve those relationships outside working hours.

The Business career is the easiest to master because it requires the fewest skills.

Once you reach the Division Manager promotion, you can start holding meetings and meeting opportunities come regularly. Making these meetings becomes a critical metric for making additional promotions. Here, the career starts to consume a lot of time and attention.

One of the key benefits of this career comes at the top promotion to Power Broker. Now, you have complete control over working hours by choosing to hold meetings at your whim. You are paid for these meetings, too, so you have control over how much money is made during that specific day. A day full of meetings is very lucrative. This flexibility allows the Power Broker to pursue different skills or attend to a household without worrying about a heavy work schedule.

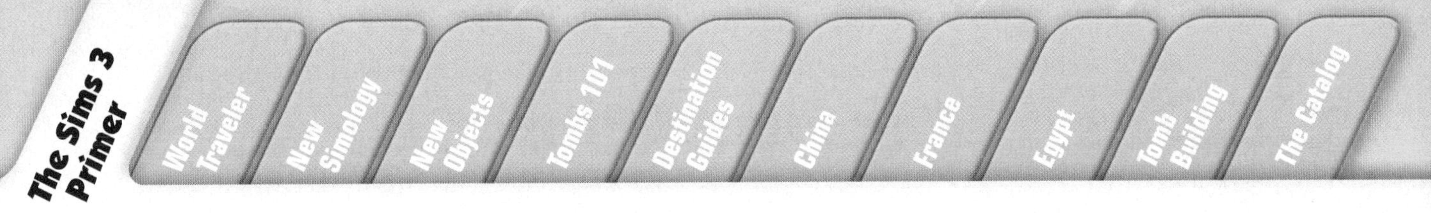

Criminal

Who hasn't harbored thoughts of engaging in criminal activity? The Criminal career allows you to try out being a bad guy. The Criminal career actually branches into two different tracks: Thief and Evil. Each of these branches has a different reward for reaching the top.

Work Location: Outstanding Citizen Warehouse Corp.

CRIMINAL CAREER

Level	Position	Work Days	Start Time	Length of Day	Average Daily Pay	Weekly Average Pay	Pension Pay	Metrics for Promotion
1	Decoy	SU, M, T, F, S	10 AM	6	100	500	30	Mood, Athletic Skill
2	Cutpurse	SU, M, T, F, S	10 AM	6	140	700	40	Mood, Athletic Skill
3	Thug	SU, M, T, F, S	9 PM	6	190	950	50	Mood, Athletic Skill
4	Getaway Driver	SU, M, T, F, S	9 PM	6	240	1,200	60	Mood, Athletic Skill, Relationship w/ Accomplices
5	Bagman	SU, M, T, F, S	9 PM	6	310	1,550	80	Mood, Athletic Skill, Relationship w/ Accomplices
6	ConArtist	SU, M, T, F, S	9 PM	6	375	1,875	90	Mood, Athletic Skill, Relationship w/ Accomplices

CRIMINAL CAREER – THIEF

Level	Position	Work Days	Start Time	Length of Day	Average Daily Pay	Weekly Average Pay	Pension Pay	Metrics for Promotion
7	Safe Cracker	SU, M, T, F, S	9 PM	5	480	2,400	120	Mood, Athletic Skill, Relationship w/ Accomplices
8	Bank Robber	SU, T, F, S	9 PM	5	610	2,440	120	Mood, Athletic Skill, Relationship w/ Accomplices
9	Cat Burglar	SU, T, F, S	9 PM	4	900	3,600	180	Mood, Athletic Skill, Relationship w/ Accomplices
10	Master Thief	SU, T, F, S	9 PM	4	2,100	8,400	400	Mood, Athletic Skill, Relationship w/ Accomplices

CRIMINAL CAREER – EVIL

Level	Position	Work Days	Start Time	Length of Day	Average Daily Pay	Weekly Average Pay	Pension Pay	Metrics for Promotion
7	Henchman	M, T, W, TH, F	9 PM	6	650	3,250	160	Mood, Athletic Skill, Relationship w/ Leader
8	Evil Sidekick	M, T, TH, F	9 PM	6	850	3,400	170	Mood, Athletic Skill, Logic Skill, Relationship w/ Leader
9	Super Villain	M, T, TH, F	9 PM	5	1,200	4,800	230	Mood, Athletic Skill, Logic Skill, Relationship w/ Leader
10	Emperor of Evil	M, T, F	9 PM	5	2,100	6,300	300	Mood, Athletic Skill, Logic Skill

CRIMINAL TONES

Tones	Description
Work Hard	Work hard to increase performance, but adds stress
Take It Easy	Relax at work. Slower performance, but less stress.
Practice Illicit Activities	Increases athletic skill at work
Meet Accomplices	Build relationship with co-workers
Conspire with Accomplices	Build relationship with co-workers
Do a Side Job	Perform this tone to earn side cash
Grovel to Leader	Build relationship with boss

Benefits and Rewards

The Criminal career sounds shady, but it has definite benefits. For example, no one will rob the home of a Sim who's on the Criminal career track. Criminal career Sims also occasionally come home with an object in their personal inventory, snatched while out on a job. The criminal Sim can also use the Do a Side Job tone to earn extra cash while at work, but this takes time away from getting to better know accomplices (the equivalent of co-workers in the Criminal career), which is an important metric for earning promotions.

TIP

If you also have the Athletic skill, you can improve it by selecting the Practice Illicit Activities tone.

Thief Branch

The Thief branch of the Criminal career starts you toward becoming the Master Thief. Right away, you earn the Sneak interaction for going to a location. When you Sneak onto a lot, other Sims do not detect you. Sleeping Sims will not wake up either, so you can actually rob while performing this interaction.

As soon as you reach the Bank Robber promotion, you receive a valuable piece of art as a bonus. At the top of the career track, the Master Thief, the Sim receives an extremely valuable statue called The Fox. This statue can be placed on the Sim's lot, which offers a huge environmental bonus. Whenever the Sim chooses to View the statue, they get the I Am the Best moodlet, which is a positive boost to overall mood.

Evil Branch

The Evil branch of the Criminal career has different rewards and a different means of reaching the top job: Emperor of Evil. You must use the Grovel to Boss tone a lot to advance along the Evil track because the relationship with the boss is a metric used to dole out promotions.

At level 9—Super Villain—the Sim gets a black limo. But when you finally get that top promotion, you earn the Aura of Evil. This has a powerful effect on other Sims. Criminal Sims or Sims with the Evil trait get a relationship boost from the Aura of Evil. However, the Aura of Evil has a negative effect on Sims with the following traits: Cowardly, Loser, and Neurotic. These Sims are afraid of the Aura of Evil and will flee. Sims with the Good trait or in the Law Enforcement career will actually boo at the Aura of Evil Sim. Building a good relationship with these Sims is extremely difficult.

Culinary

Sims who want to pursue a Culinary career should head to either the bistro or the diner. This is not one of the higher paying careers, but it does come with a lot of perks, such as the consistent development of the Cooking skill while at work and discounts at the restaurant of employment.

Work Locations: Little Corsican Bistro or Hogan's Deep-Fried Diner

CULINARY CAREER

Level	Position	Work Days	Start Time	Length of Day	Average Daily Pay	Weekly Average Pay	Pension Pay	Metrics for Promotion
1	Kitchen Scullion	SU, M, T, F, S	3 PM	6	148	740	40	Mood, Cooking Skill
2	Spice Runner	SU, M, T, F, S	3 PM	6	190	950	50	Mood, Cooking Skill
3	Vegetable Slicer	SU, M, T, F, S	3 PM	6	230	1,150	60	Mood, Cooking Skill, Relationship w/ Boss
4	Ingredient Taster	SU, M, T, F, S	3 PM	6	280	1,400	70	Mood, Cooking Skill, Relationship w/ Boss, Relationship w/ Co-Workers
5	Line Cook	SU, M, T, F, S	3 PM	5.5	460	2,300	110	Mood, Cooking Skill, Relationship w/ Boss, Relationship w/ Co-Workers
6	Pastry Chef	SU, M, T, F, S	3 PM	5.5	590	2,950	150	Mood, Cooking Skill, Relationship w/ Boss, Relationship w/ Co-Workers
7	Sous Chef	SU, T, F, S	3 PM	5.5	680	2,720	130	Mood, Cooking Skill, Relationship w/ Boss, Relationship w/ Co-Workers
8	Executive Chef	SU, T, F, S	3 PM	5	750	3,000	150	Mood, Cooking Skill, Relationship w/ Boss, Relationship w/ Co-Workers
9	Chef de Cuisine	SU, F, S	3 PM	5	1,005	3,015	150	Mood, Cooking Skill, Relationship w/ Boss, Relationship w/ Co-Workers
10	Five-Star Chef	SU, F, S	3 PM	4	1,400	4,200	200	Mood, Cooking Skill, Relationship w/ Boss, Relationship w/ Co-Workers

CULINARY TONES

Tones	Description
Work Hard	Work hard to increase performance, but adds stress
Take It Easy	Relax at work. Slower performance, but less stress.
Practice Cooking	Increases cooking skill at work
Meet Co-Workers	Build relationship with co-workers
Hang with Co-Workers	Build relationship with co-workers
Suck Up to Boss	Build relationship with boss

Benefits and Rewards

Because cooking is such an important part of every Sim's life, the Culinary career has benefits that extend far beyond a daily paycheck. The Culinary career offers the Practice Cooking tone, which lets you advance the Cooking skill while earning a paycheck. Using this tone may come at the expense of not hastening an improved relationship with the boss or with co-workers (essential to promotion), but being a good cook is a mood booster for your Sim and potentially all other Sims in a household.

Improving your Cooking skill is an important part of the promotion game in the Culinary career. Make sure you practice at home and don't rely on too many quick meals or snacks.

Good food is a mood booster for all Sims, so the benefit of occasionally getting free meals from work to take back to the lot is a real happiness generator. This benefit does not happen until the Sim reaches Ingredient Taster. But once it happens, expect to see free meals on a regular basis. And if you have multiple Sims in a household, that free meal will have enough servings to satisfy all.

Dining out is another mood booster that benefits from the Culinary career. At the Sous-Chef level, Sims get a discount at the restaurant where they work. This saves money, especially on dates, which can get pretty expensive after a while. Once the Sim reaches Executive Chef, the discount extends to both restaurants.

Sims in the Culinary career get two very cool equipment bonuses. At the Pastry Chef position, the Sim earns the food processor, which speeds up the cooking process at home. The real prize, though, comes at the final promotion: Five-Star Chef. The Sim is awarded the Master Chef Fridge. This fridge gives the Superior Equipment moodlet to any Sim who walks near it. Also any recipe that uses food out of the fridge will come out high quality.

Journalism

As a journalist, Sims must chase down the facts not only during work hours, but on their own time, too. Such dedication is as reward in it itself, for the pursuit of truth is the noblest profession of all.

Work Location: Doo Peas Corporate Towers

JOURNALISM CAREER

Level	Position	Work Days	Start Time	Length of Day	Average Daily Pay	Weekly Average Pay	Pension Pay	Metrics for Promotion
1	Paper Boy	M, T, W, TH, F	8 AM	6	225	1,125	60	Mood, Writing Skill
2	Automated Spell-Checker Checker	M, T, W, TH, F	8 AM	6	259	1,295	70	Mood, Writing Skill
3	Freelance Writer	M, T, W, TH, F	8 AM	6	298	1,490	80	Mood, Writing Skill, Stories Written
4	Professional Blogger	M, T, W, TH, F	8 AM	4	301	1,505	80	Mood, Writing Skill, Stories Written
5	Anonymous Source Handler	M, T, W, TH, F	8 AM	5	482	2,410	120	Mood, Writing Skill, Charisma Skill, Stories Written
6	Investigative Reporter	M, W, TH, F	8 AM	5	627	2,508	120	Mood, Writing Skill, Charisma Skill, Stories Written
7	Weather Man	M, W, TH, F	8 AM	5	753	3,012	150	Mood, Writing Skill, Charisma Skill
8	Lead Reporter	M, W, TH, F	8 AM	5	942	3,768	180	Mood, Writing Skill, Charisma Skill, Stories Written
9	Editor-In-Chief	M, W, TH, F	8 AM	5	1,178	4,712	230	Mood, Writing Skill, Charisma Skill, Stories Written
10	Star News Anchor	M, W, TH, F	8 AM	4	1,532	6,128	300	Mood, Writing Skill, Charisma Skill, Stories Written

JOURNALISM TONES

Tones	Description
Work Hard	Work hard to increase performance, but adds stress
Take It Easy	Relax at work. Slower performance, but less stress.
Practice Writing	Increases Writing skill at work
Discuss Latest News	Build relationship with co-workers
Hang with Co-Workers	Build relationship with co-workers
Suck Up to Boss	Build relationship with boss

Benefits and Rewards

Like other careers where a certain skill is in play, pursuing the Journalism career lets a Sim advance their Writing skill while at the office. Sure, this is to the exclusion of seeking better relationships with the boss or co-workers, but it also opens up more genre possibilities for writing lucrative novels at home in the Sim's spare time.

Joining the Journalism career also allows the Sim to develop a new genre for writing at home: stories and reviews. Stories and reviews are selected from the computer interaction list, just like choosing to write a novel. It does not take nearly as long to write a story or review as a novel, and no royalties are awarded for completing a story or review. However, writing stories and reviews are essential for promotions. If you want to reach the very top of the career track, you must spend considerable time outside the workday creating articles at home. These stories and reviews go into the Sim's personal inventory and are recognized at work.

To get the material for writing stories and reviews, you must interview Sims around town. You should also visit the stadium to see sporting events and stop into the restaurants. These three things give you plenty to write about—but they take time to attend, and that's on top of the time it takes your Sim to write the story or review. At least visiting the stadium and going out to eat is a good mood boost, so there is a nice side benefit for taking the time to do your research.

Not every promotion takes stories and reviews into consideration, though. You really need to work on Charisma skill to keep getting ahead. The Charisma skill ranking is an important metric for promotion. This just adds to the career workload, as you must now juggle improving the Writing skill, improving the Charisma skill, and writing articles outside of work hours. Fortunately, the work hours in this career are slightly lower than others, giving you extra free time for these career-related pursuits.

When you finally reach the top of the career track—Star News Anchor—you unlock a new social: Tell Intriguing News Story. This social is perfect for situations where you want to boost a relationship with another Sim.

Law Enforcement

Not everybody in Sunset Valley or even idyllic Riverview is on the up-and-up. With a criminal element afoot, the city needs its fair share of Law Enforcement officers. This career branches, and the two tracks lead to different rewards. The Law Enforcement career also uses a number of skills as metrics for promotion, so having a well-rounded Sim is a plus.

Work Location: Police Station

LAW ENFORCEMENT CAREER

Level	Position	Work Days	Start Time	Length of Day	Average Daily Pay	Weekly Average Pay	Pension Pay	Metrics for Promotion
1	Snitch	M, T, W, TH, F	9 AM	6	235	1,175	60	Mood, Logic Skill
2	Desk Jockey	M, T, W, TH, F	9 AM	6	278	1,390	70	Mood, Logic Skill
3	Traffic Cop	M, T, W, TH, F	9 AM	6	329	1,645	80	Mood, Logic Skill, Relationship w/ Partner
4	Patrol Officer	M, T, W, TH, F	9 AM	6	389	1,945	100	Mood, Logic Skill, Relationship w/ Partner, Reports Written
5	Lieutenant	M, T, W, TH, F	9 AM	6	460	2,300	110	Mood, Logic Skill, Relationship w/ Partner, Reports Written

LAW TONES

Tones	Description
Work Hard	Work hard to increase performance, but adds stress
Take It Easy	Relax at work. Slower performance, but less stress.
Chat with Partner	Build relationship with co-workers
Build Independent Case	Side work that can result in extra cash
Use Workout Facility	Build Athletic skill at work to expense of performance
Suck Up to Boss	Build relationship with boss

Benefits and Rewards

The Law Enforcement career takes a few interesting turns but comes with some exciting rewards and side benefits. One of the tones for work is to Build Independent Case, which detracts from dealing with co-workers or the daily workload, but is quite useful if successful. If the case ends up being a success, the Sim has a chance at an immediate promotion. However, if the case fails, the Sim risks losing the respect of co-workers.

TIP

The current Logic skill level is what determines the chance of success, so build up that skill before trying out this tone.

At level 3, the Sim can apprehend Burglars, which goes a long way toward getting a promotion. At level 5, the Sim gets a police car, which improves travel time. At level 5, the Sim chooses a branch of the career to pursue. Each branch has an different end reward.

WRITING REPORTS

One of the metrics for doling out promotions is the number of reports written. Sims in the Law Enforcement track create reports on other Sims by conducting interviews with the Question social. (This social is not negative.) During the questioning, the interviewer discovers the other Sim's traits, which is actually quite useful for social situations outside the workday.

After rifling through somebody's trash, take a shower. Your Sim is likely going to stink.

Reports can also come from rifling through garbage cans. Use this interaction to look through another Sim's trash until you receive the notice that you have enough information on the person whose trash you were inspecting to write a report.

If during these interactions, the Sim discovers that the subject is part of the Criminal career track, the chance of promotion greatly increases.

CAUTION

Rummaging through the trash leads to the Disgusted moodlet. Be ready to shower after extensive garbage-sifting sessions.

Branching Career Rewards

Advance the Logic skill to succeed in all branches of the Law Enforcement career. Get started with a Logic book or chess set (home or park) to get a jump on the first promotions. When the career branches after the fifth promotion, two more skills come into play. The Painting skill must be developed for the Forensics branch, and the Athletic skill must be advanced for the Special Agent branch. After the split, the Logic skill is still critical to getting promotions.

The Forensics branch has a reward as soon as you earn its first promotion: laptop. The laptop computer is placed in the personal inventory and can be used at home. The top reward for the career is a new computer interaction: Run Analysis. This is a lengthy interaction, but it results in a payday. This is a good way to make additional money when not at work.

The Special Agent branch of the career has two special rewards that are given out at level 10: Tell Impressive Story and Raid Warehouse. Tell Impressive Story is a special social. It immediately impresses the Sim it is directed at. The Raid Warehouse interaction directs the Sim to enter the warehouse at night and disappear for a few hours. If the raid is a success (based on mood, Athletic skill, and Logic skill), the Sim has the potential to earn two different rewards. A mild success at the warehouse results in a small monetary bonus. A big success results in a huge payday.

Medical

The Medical career is not for a Sim who likes to keep a strict schedule. As this career develops, the schedule turns chaotic and occasionally disruptive thanks to the unpredictable needs of patients at the local hospital. If you don't mind the idea of being pulled into work in the middle of the night, then the Medical career's rewards may be worth the potential inconvenience. Especially the final reward for becoming a World Renowned Surgeon...

Work Location: Sacred Spleen General Hospital (Sunset Valley), County Care General Hospital (Riverview)

MEDICAL CAREER

Level	Position	Work Days	Start Time	Length of Day	Average Daily Pay	Weekly Average Pay	Pension Pay	Metrics for Promotion
1	Organ Donor	M, T, W, TH, F	9 AM	6	128	640	40	Mood, Logic Skill
2	Bed Pan Cleaner	M, T, W, TH, F	9 AM	6	150	750	40	Mood, Logic Skill
3	Paramedic	M, T, W, TH, F	9 AM	7	190	950	50	Mood, Logic Skill
4	Medical Intern	M, T, W, TH, F	9 AM	10	330	1,650	80	Mood, Logic Skill, Medical Journals Read
5	Resident	M, T, W, TH, F	9 AM	9	700	3,500	170	Mood, Logic Skill, Medical Journals Read
6	Trauma Surgeon	M, T, W, TH, F	7 PM	8	810	4,050	200	Mood, Logic Skill, Medical Journals Read
7	Gene Therapist	M, T, TH, F	9 AM	5	960	3,840	190	Mood, Logic Skill, Medical Journals Read
8	Infectious Disease Researcher	M, T, TH, F	9 AM	5	1,050	4,200	200	Mood, Logic Skill, Medical Journals Read
9	Neurosurgeon	M, T, TH, F	9 AM	8	1,800	7,200	350	Mood, Logic Skill, Medical Journals Read
10	Deadly Disease Specialist	M, T, TH, F	9 AM	5	2,400	9,600	460	Mood, Logic Skill, Medical Journals Read

MEDICAL TONES

Tones	Description
Work Hard	Work hard to increase performance, but adds stress
Watch TV in Ready Room	Relax at work. Slower performance, but less stress.
Chat with Medical Personnel	Build relationship with co-workers
Do Boss's Paperwork	Build relationship with boss
Sleep in Ready Room	Napping at work helps with energy
Suck Up to Boss	Build relationship with boss

Benefits and Rewards

The Medical career is one of the most stressful careers, so to advance, you need activities in the Sim's life that will counteract the Stressed Out moodlet. Mood is a major factor in promotions, so be sure to sleep when possible (the Sleep in Ready Room tone helps out with this) and have an activity that lowers tension, such as reading, exercise, or socializing.

As soon as you reach the Medical Intern promotion, get ready for a hectic schedule. The Sim gets a beeper and has to come into work at odd hours. Shifts start growing, too, so be ready to spend lots of time at the hospital as you work farther up the promotion ladder. Medical Interns earn the Give Medical Advice social, which helps out pregnant Sims. Pregnant Sims who regularly seek medical advice (or receive it) assist the development of the pregnancy, which can lead to the baby getting highly desirable traits.

When you reach the Medical Intern position, you start receiving medical journals, too. These are critical for future advancement because the number of journals read is a metric for deciding promotions alongside mood and Logic skill. In your off time, be sure to read these medical journals because the game keeps track of this statistic.

TIP

The Medical career does not factor relationship with co-workers or the boss into promotions. The quality of work is what really counts.

At the Resident level, Sims get two new socials: Give Good Medical Advice and Brag About Being a Doctor. The Give Good Medical Advice has a greater benefit to expectant mothers—in fact, the medical Sim can even deduce the sex of the baby. The Brag social impresses other Sims in conversation. If the other Sim is already romantically interested in the medical Sim, that romance is further enhanced.

NOTE

The Neurosurgeon promotion turns Give Good Medical Advice into Give Amazing Medical Advice, which is even more beneficial to expectant mothers.

Military

Fortunately, peace has broken out in the world and Sims in the Military career need not worry about shipping out to war. They do have a goal that takes them outside of town, though. Way outside of town. As in, into space.

Work Location: Fort Gnome Military Base (Sunset Valley), Fort Salas Military Base (Riverview)

MILITARY CAREER

Level	Position	Work Days	Start Time	Length of Day	Average Daily Pay	Weekly Average Pay	Pension Pay	Metrics for Promotion
1	Latrine Cleaner	M, T, W, F	7 AM	7	280	1,120	80	Mood, Athletic Skill
2	Grease Monkey	M, T, W, F	7 AM	8	350	1,400	100	Mood, Athletic Skill
3	Grunt	M, T, W, F	7 AM	8	385	1,540	110	Mood, Athletic Skill, Handiness Skill
4	Squad Leader	M, W, F	7 AM	7	655	1,965	150	Mood, Athletic Skill, Handiness Skill, Relationship w/ Superior
5	Flight Officer	M, W, F	7 AM	7	754	2,262	170	Mood, Athletic Skill, Handiness Skill, Relationship w/ Superior
6	Wing Man	M, W, F	7 AM	6	868	2,604	190	Mood, Athletic Skill, Handiness Skill, Relationship w/ Superior
7	Fighter Pilot	M, W, F	7 AM	6	999	2,997	220	Mood, Athletic Skill, Handiness Skill, Relationship w/ Superior
8	Squadron Leader	M, W, F	7 AM	6	1,149	3,447	250	Mood, Athletic Skill, Handiness Skill, Relationship w/ Superior
9	Top Gun	M, W, F	7 AM	5	1,322	3,966	290	Mood, Athletic Skill, Handiness Skill, Relationship w/ Superior
10	Astronaut	M	7 AM	18	6,000	6,000	430	Mood, Athletic Skill, Handiness Skill, Relationship w/ Superior

MILITARY TONES

Tones	Description
Work Hard	Work hard to increase performance, but adds stress
Goof Off	Relax at work. Slower performance, but less stress.
Hang Out with Fellow Soldiers	Build relationship with co-workers
Suck Up to Superior	Build relationship with boss

Benefits and Rewards

To advance in the Military career and earn benefits, Sims must develop two different skills: Athletic and Handiness. (Fortunately, the Handiness skill can be learned right on base through a class.) Other metrics contribute to the chance of promotion, too, including the relationships with fellow soldiers and base superiors. Naturally, mood is also a factor. Working hard and keeping these skills in active advancement leads to some fun rewards.

For example, as soon as the career begins, you start saluting other soldiers of superior rank. But at level 4, Squad Leader, inferiors start saluting you. When you reach the Top Gun rank, random Sims in town are also inspired to salute you. Citizen salutes are positive and will start any social encounter with an impressed context.

At level 10, the Sim becomes an Astronaut. Becoming an Astronaut changes the Show Sim the Jet interaction to Show Sim the Spaceship. Show Sim the Spaceship is a huge romance booster.

Music

Let a little music fill your life with this exciting career track. This career is not about the money—it's about the music. Or, at least it's about the music at first with the extra benefit of truckloads of Simoleons later on when you're filling stadiums with fans who cannot wait to hear your next overblown anthem. The Music career has two branches, the Rock and the Symphonic tracks.

Work Location: Wilsonoff Community Theater

MUSIC CAREER

Level	Position	Work Days	Start Time	Length of Day	Average Daily Pay	Weekly Average Pay	Pension Pay	Metrics for Promotion
1	Fan	M, T, TH, F, S	15	6	125	625	30	Mood, Guitar Skill
2	Roadie	M, T, TH, F, S	15	6	148	740	40	Mood, Guitar Skill
3	Stagehand	M, T, TH, F, S	16	6	175	875	50	Mood, Guitar Skill, Relationship w/ Band
4	Band Manager	M, T, TH, F, S	16	5.5	263	1,315	70	Mood, Guitar Skill, Relationship w/ Band
5	Music Talent Scout	M, T, F, S	17	5.5	311	1,244	60	Mood, Guitar Skill, Relationship w/ Band

ROCK CAREER

Level	Position	Work Days	Start Time	Length of Day	Average Daily Pay	Weekly Average Pay	Pension Pay	Metrics for Promotion
6	Lyricist	M, T, F, S	6 PM	5	483	1,932	100	Mood, Guitar Skill, Relationship w/ Band Members, Concerts Performed
7	Backup Vocalist	M, T, F, S	7 PM	5	628	2,512	120	Mood, Guitar Skill, Relationship w/ Band Members, Concerts Performed
8	Lead Guitarist	T, F, S	8 PM	4.5	817	2,451	160	Mood, Guitar Skill, Relationship w/ Band Members, Concerts Performed
9	Pop Icon	T, F, S	9 PM	4	1,144	3,432	200	Mood, Guitar Skill, Relationship w/ Band Members, Concerts Performed
10	Rock Star	N/A	N/A	N/A	N/A	N/A	350	Concerts Performed

SYMPHONIC CAREER

Level	Position	Work Days	Start Time	Length of Day	Average Daily Pay	Weekly Average Pay	Pension Pay	Metrics for Promotion
6	Quartet Member	M, T, F, S	3 PM	5.5	467	1,868	90	Mood, Guitar Skill, Relationship w/ Musicians
7	Orchestra Seat	M, T, F, S	3 PM	5.5	608	2,432	120	Mood, Guitar Skill, Relationship w/ Musicians
8	Orchestra Lead	M, T, F, S	3 PM	5.5	791	3,164	160	Mood, Guitar Skill, Logic Skill, Relationship w/ Musicians
9	Conductor	M, T, F, S	3 PM	5	1,029	4,116	200	Mood, Guitar Skill, Logic Skill, Relationship w/ Musicians
10	Hit Movie Composer	M, T, F, S	1 PM	5	1,801	7,204	350	Mood, Guitar Skill, Logic Skill, Relationship w/ Musicians

MUSIC TONES

Tones	Description
Work Hard	Work hard to increase performance, but adds stress
Slack Off	Take it easy at work to reduce stress
Chill with Band/Musicians	Build relationship with co-workers
Meet Band/Orchestra Members	Meet co-workers
Study Music Theory	Build Guitar and Logic skills
Practice Performance	Prepare before a concert so it goes better

Benefits and Rewards

Naturally, the key to advancing in this career is the development of the Guitar skill. A class at the theater is a good way to get a head start on the career. At first, you do not even need the Guitar skill because you are just a Fan and Roadie. But keeping on top of the skill before it becomes critical to advancement has nothing but advantages. The Guitar skill is a constant metric for promotions no matter which branch you choose when you reach the sixth promotion.

To continue moving up the career ladder, you must maintain a good mood and have a good relationship with co-workers, who are called band or orchestra members depending on the career path taken. Use the Study Music Theory tone because it helps build the Guitar skill—and the Logic skill, which is a critical measure for the Symphonic branch. In the Rock branch, you need to practice for gigs because performing concerts is a key to advancement.

Rock Branch

The next promotion following the Music Talent Scout in the Rock branch is Lyricist. When you reach this promotion, you can start holding concerts. Use this interaction on the theater and stadium to stage two- or four-hour concerts that are measured as part of the promotion process. (This interaction is only available between noon and midnight.)

Once inside the Rock branch, the relationship to other band members is no longer important. When the Sim becomes the Backup Vocalist, they unlock the Wave interaction to use wherever music is playing. It's a fun action that boosts mood.

Keep performing concerts and keep up the Guitar skill to reach the pinnacle of the branch: Rock Star. At this level, your carpool is replaced by a pastel limo that will take you anywhere. At this level, the Sim can also select venues and choose to Hold Autograph Session, just like the Athlete career. The goal is to sign as many autographs as possible with the other Sims on the lot. The more signed, the more money is awarded for the session.

Once the Sim achieves Rock Star, they no longer have a work schedule. Money is earned exclusively by holding concerts. The concert at the stadium takes twice as long than one at the theater, but the salary is double.

Symphonic Branch

The Symphonic branch of the Music career unfolds a bit differently than the Rock branch. In this track, relationships with other musicians are very important, so be sure to use that tone to get ahead. Keep advancing the Guitar skill whenever possible, too.

Once you close in on the Orchestra Lead promotion, develop the Logic skill. (Practice Music Theory is a good way to boost the Logic skill while at work.) Once you reach level 8 of this career—Orchestra Lead—you earn free admission to activities at the theater. This is great for boosting moods.

The highest level of the career—Hit Movie Composer—comes with an object reward: 85g Audio Explosion. This high-end stereo boosts the fun of Sims in its listening radius and can be used to develop the Athletic ability.

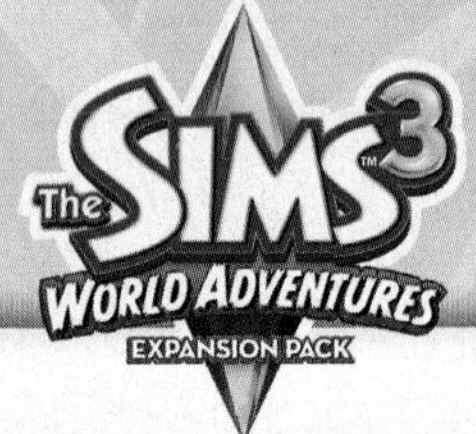

Politics

Politics is no career for the timid Sim. This highly social career track requires a great deal of socializing. Because this is such a social career, the Charisma skill is required. Also required: no fear of asking other Sims for money. Campaigns don't pay for themselves, you know.

Work Location: City Hall

POLITICAL CAREER

Level	Position	Work Days	Start Time	Length of Day	Average Daily Pay	Weekly Average Pay	Pension Pay	Metrics for Promotion
1	Podium Polisher	M, T, W, TH, F	9 AM	6	140	700	40	Mood, Charisma
2	Ballot Counter	M, T, W, TH, F	9 AM	6	185	925	50	Mood, Charisma
3	Campaign Intern	M, T, W, TH, F	9 AM	7	230	1,150	60	Mood, Charisma
4	Yes-Man	M, T, W, TH, F	9 AM	6	270	1,350	70	Mood, Charisma, Relationship w/ Boss
5	City Council Member	M, T, W, TH, F	9 AM	5.5	375	1,875	90	Mood, Charisma, Relationship w/ Boss, Campaign Money Raised
6	Local Representative	M, W, TH, F	9 AM	5.5	500	2,000	100	Mood, Charisma, Relationship w/ Boss, Campaign Money Raised
7	Mayor	M, W, TH, F	9 AM	5	650	2,600	130	Mood, Charisma, Relationship w/ Boss, Campaign Money Raised
8	Governor	M, W, TH, F	9 AM	5	800	3,200	160	Mood, Charisma, Relationship w/ Boss, Campaign Money Raised
9	Vice President	M, W, F	9 AM	4.5	1,200	3,600	180	Mood, Charisma, Relationship w/ Boss, Campaign Money Raised
10	Leader of the Free World	M, W, F	9 AM	4.5	1,900	5,700	280	Mood, Charisma, Campaign Money Raised

POLITICAL TONES

Tones	Description
Work Hard	Work hard to increase performance, but adds stress
Chat with Co-Workers	Build relationship with co-workers
Meet Co-Workers	Meet co-workers
Run Errands for Superior	Build relationship with boss
Suggest New Course of Action	Research new ideas that can possibly increase performance or relationships

Benefits and Rewards

At first, mood is the only metric used to measure performance and award promotions. But to get ahead, be sure to start practicing Charisma early on through various means, such as taking a class at City Hall or practicing in the mirror at home. Having a good Charisma level will make it much easier to advance early in this career.

The Yes-Man promotion is given out to a Sim who has a good relationship with the boss, so use the Run Errands for Supervisor tone early on, too. Getting in good with the boss is preferable to being popular with co-workers. To move up to the City Council position, though, you need to start raising campaign contributions, which is another metric for promotion. The social Ask for Campaign Donation usually results in a small Simoleon transfer, although hitting up a wealthy Sim elicits a larger donation. Fortunately, this social is positive.

CAUTION

You cannot use the Ask for Campaign Contribution social on household members.

NOTE

Here's a nasty bit of business with campaign contributions: every so often, you will be asked if you want to transfer money out of the campaign kitty and into the household account. This is risky. If caught, the Sim is expelled from the career.

TIP

Political Sims can throw Campaign Fundraisers, which are just like parties. (See the Relationships chapter for details on how to throw a party.) If the party is successful, the host receives campaign contributions at its conclusion.

Once you reach the Local Representative position, you have a new social: Give Inspirational Speech. You can use this positive social on a single Sim or in a group setting. It gives everybody a positive impression of you and sets up healthy relationships. Yes we can, indeed.

At higher levels you get two nice benefits. At the Governor level, a black limo drives you everywhere. As Leader of the Free World, your Sim gains the Aura of Leadership, and other Sims wave at you wherever you go. This boosts the relationship with other Sims and can also result in the Celebrity moodlet.

Professional Sports

The Professional Sports career charts a course from zero to hero. The Sims slowly become deeply involved with the local sports team. At first, they are a fan with a dream. Then, they join the team and start working up the ranks. Soon, shifts are replaced by sporting events where winning and losing directly affect mood.

Work Location: Llama Memorial Stadium

PROFESSIONAL SPORTS CAREER

Level	Position	Work Days	Start Time	Length of Day	Average Daily Pay	Weekly Average Pay	Pension Pay	Metrics for Promotion
1	Rabid Fan	M, T, W, TH, S	3 PM	6	75	375	30	Mood
2	Snack Hawker	M, T, W, TH, S	3 PM	6	150	750	60	Mood
3	Toddler Sports Coach	M, T, W, TH, S	3 PM	6	195	975	70	Mood, Athletic Skill
4	Minor Leaguer	M, T, F, S	3 PM	6	254	1,016	80	Mood, Athletic Skill, Relationship w/ Team
5	Rookie	M, T, F, S	3 PM	5	381	1,524	110	Mood, Athletic Skill, Relationship w/ Team, Win-Loss Record
6	Starter	M, T, F, S	3 PM	5	667	2,668	200	Mood, Athletic Skill, Relationship w/ Team, Win-Loss Record
7	AllStar	M, T, F, S	3 PM	4	801	3,204	230	Mood, Athletic Skill, Relationship w/ Team, Win-Loss Record
8	MVP	M, T, F, S	3 PM	4	962	3,838	280	Mood, Athletic Skill, Relationship w/ Team, Win-Loss Record
9	Superstar	M, T, F, S	3 PM	3	1,155	4,620	330	Mood, Athletic Skill, Relationship w/ Team, Win-Loss Record
10	Sports Legend	M, T, F, S	3 PM	3	1,386	5,544	400	Mood, Athletic Skill, Relationship w/ Team, Win-Loss Record

PROFESSIONAL SPORTS TONES

Tones	Description
Prepare for Game	Get ready for next game. Increases chances of winning next game.
Meet Teammates	Build relationship with co-workers
Hang with Teammates	Build relationship with co-workers
Slack Off in Locker Room	Take it easy at work to reduce stress
Work Out in Gym	Develop Athletic skill

Benefits and Rewards

Naturally, this is a great career for a Sim with the Athletic trait and developing the Athletic skill. Once you reach the Toddler Sports Coach position, you can start using the Work Out at Gym work tone, which lets you continue developing the Athletic skill at work, albeit at a slower pace than at home or on personal time. (Up until this promotion, reporting to work does not increase the Athletic skill.)

Once the Minor Leaguer position is reached, the Sim can begin interacting with other team members, which casts a wider net of Sims to socialize with and make friends. The Rookie promotion starts the game part of the career. Now work is often replaced by practice and the career keeps a running tally of the team's win-loss record. The higher the Sim's Athletic skill, the greater the chance of winning the game, which in turn improves the Sim's mood with the Winner moodlet. The chance of winning a game is also improved by the Prepare for Game tone.

TIP

Members of a Sim's household can see a sporting event for free.

Once the Sim reaches the top promotion—Sports Legend—two things happen. One, the Sim can now perform the Sponsorship Deal interaction at businesses for Simoleons at least once a week. Two, the Sim can also Hold Autograph Sessions at venues where they are handsomely rewarded for signing autographs for as many Sims on the lot as possible.

Science

A mind is a terrible thing to taste—er, waste. This career celebrates that organ between the ears, the cortex that pulses with thoughts and desires. The Science career requires a keen sense of Handiness and a real green thumb, as well as a desire to both observe and collect.

Work Location: Landgraab Industries Science Facility (Sunset Valley), Soil and Water Research Facility (Riverview)

SCIENCE CAREER

Level	Position	Work Days	Start Time	Length of Day	Average Daily Pay	Weekly Average Pay	Pension Pay	Metrics for Promotion
1	Test Subject	M, T, W, TH, F	9 AM	5.5	240	1,200	60	Mood, Gardening Skill
2	Lab Tech	M, T, W, TH, F	9 AM	5.5	288	1,440	70	Mood, Gardening Skill
3	Useless Contraption Manipulator	M, T, W, TH, F	9 AM	5.5	346	1,730	90	Mood, Gardening Skill, Handiness Skill
4	Fertilizer Analyst	M, T, TH, F	9 AM	5	485	1,940	100	Mood, Gardening Skill, Handiness Skill
5	Carnivorous Plant Tender	M, T, TH, F	9 AM	5	582	2,328	120	Mood, Gardening Skill, Handiness Skill
6	Aquatic Ecosystem Tweaker	M, T, TH, F	9 AM	5	699	2,796	140	Mood, Gardening Skill, Handiness Skill, Fishing Skill
7	Genetic Resequencer	M, T, TH, F	9 AM	4.5	839	3,356	160	Mood, Gardening Skill, Handiness Skill, Fishing Skill
8	Top Secret Researcher	M, T, TH, F	9 AM	4.5	1,007	4,028	200	Mood, Gardening Skill, Handiness Skill, Fishing Skill
9	Creature-Robot Cross Breeder	M, T, F	9 AM	4.5	1,209	3,627	180	Mood, Gardening Skill, Handiness Skill, Fishing Skill
10	Mad Scientist	M, T, F	9 AM	4.5	1,814	5,442	260	Mood, Gardening Skill, Handiness Skill, Fishing Skill

SCIENCE TONES

Tones	Description
Work Hard	Work hard to increase performance, but adds stress
Relax in Specimen Closet	Relax at work. Slower performance, but less stress.
Meet Fellow Scientists	Meet co-workers
Hang Out with Fellow Soldiers	Build relationship with co-workers
Assist Boss with Research	Build relationship with boss
Do Independent Experiment	Doing this tone builds toward promotion or at least performance boost

Benefits and Rewards

The benefits of the Science career are plentiful, but you must be attentive to skills to receive the promotions that award them. The immediate skill required for the career is Gardening, which can be learned at the science facility or through a book. Get a jump on Gardening as soon as you join the career. Later in the career, two additional skills come into play: Handiness and Fishing. At no point are relationships a metric for advancement because, warranted or not, scientists aren't exactly known for their social graces.

Do not wait until you close in on a promotion that requires Fishing or Gardening to start learning those skills. Develop those skills early.

One of the most useful tones in this career is Do Independent Experiment. While performing this tone, you do side experiments that have a chance of resulting in great things. These experiments take time and you will not complete one in just a day. If the project is a success, though, you might get an immediate promotion.

From time to time, scientists come home with extras in their personal inventories, such as a fish or seed. They will be either common or uncommon fish or seeds. Upon reaching the Top Secret Researcher and Creature-Robot Cross Breeder promotions, though, the Sim receives a seed for a special plant. These seeds are rare and will grow into one of the following: Flame Fruit, Life Fruit, Money Tree, or Omni Plant.

Do Science to It!

Upon reaching the height of the career, the Sim receives a new interaction to perform on household objects: Do Science to It. This interaction works on seats, beds, electronics, and appliances. It acts like an upgrade. Once the interaction is complete, the Sim stands back to look at what was accomplished. If the upgrade goes well, the following may happen:

- Object gets environmental boost.
- Object broadcasts music, giving all Sims in the area the Enjoying Music moodlet.
- Object earns random upgrade from Handiness upgrade list.
- Object starts broadcasting random moodlets that affect Sims in the room: Attractive, Beautiful Vista, Cheered Up, Comforted, Feeling Lucky, New Car Smell, New Stuff, Oddly Powerful, Tranquil, or Warmed.

Conversely, this interaction can have negative effects, too. These things can go wrong:

- Object catches fire and is burned until useless.
- Object randomly electrocutes Sims who try to use it later.
- Object disappears—forever.
- Object breaks and must be repaired.
- Object starts broadcasting random negative moodlets that affect Sims in the room: Upset, Tastes Like Fridge, Stir Crazy, Offended, Buzz Crash, Horrified, or Disgusted.

PART-TIME WORK

In addition to these full-time careers, Sims can pick up part-time jobs at the supermarket, cemetery, bookstore, or day spa. These jobs are for just four hours a day, four days a week. These jobs are designed not to interfere with life too much. For example, a teen might take a job at the supermarket that starts after school at 4 PM and lasts until 8 PM. Or an adult could grab a late-night 6 PM to 10 PM gig helping bury bodies at the cemetery.

Part-time jobs include tones, just like the full-time jobs. However, because relationships and skills don't determine job performance, the tones are limited to: Business As Usual (average amount of work), Work Hard (put in extra effort), and Take It Easy (minimal effort). Each part-time job has only three career levels with minimal raises between each promotion. To get ahead at a part-time job, just show up in a good mood and put in a decent day's labor.

Part-time jobs can be quit via the cell phone. You can go back to work at the same place, but if you wait too long between quitting and going back, you lose any promotions and must start over.

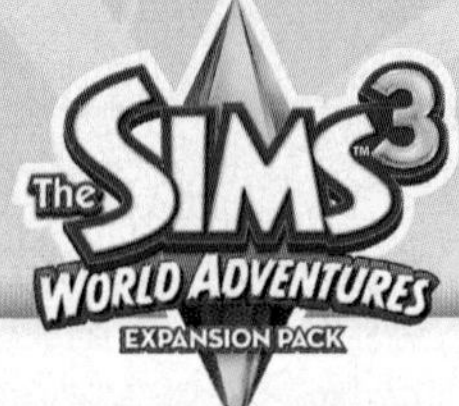

Relationships and Socializing

Relationships in *The Sims 3* actually unfold not that differently from those in the real world. How you treat other Sims is the biggest metric in your overall relationship with them. If you insult another Sim, expect them to get upset in the immediate conversation and for that to have a lasting effect on your relationship. Conversely, a constant stream of support or praise will boost the immediate interaction and lead to a longer-lasting positive relationship. Developing a successful romance means spotting if the other party is receptive to your advances and knowing when to cool your jets.

The social structure of *The Sims 3* is not navigated with obvious metrics. There is a touch of mystery in conversations that makes socializing more organic. You need to consider the current attitude of the Sim in the conversation, often referred to as the Target. (Your current Sim is known as the Actor.) That attitude affects the long-term status of your relationships with different Sims.

Let's detail some basic concepts that will assist with understanding how relationships work: long-term relationship (LTR), short-term context (STC), and commodities. Understanding these three factors is the key to brushing back some of the mystery of social interaction.

Long-Term Relationship (LTR)

The long-term relationship represents the state of the relationship between two Sims, which extends beyond the time during which a conversation is taking place. LTR essentially describes the way two Sims view each other at a given moment. Every Sim outside the family starts out as a Stranger. Once initial contact is made, the LTR moves up to Acquaintance and can never fall back into Stranger. However, Acquaintance is the proverbial fork in the road. From here, the LTR can blossom into friendship or deteriorate into rivalry.

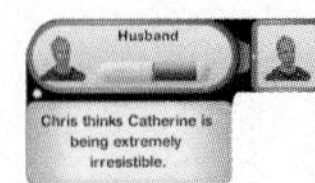

The LTR is visually measured by the bar below the portrait of the Sim you are conversing with. If the relationship develops in a positive manner, the right half of the bar fills. Positive relationship status is noted with green. If the relationship is souring, that meter empties back out and can even dip into the left side, which is red. The red bar denotes a negative LTR.

NOTE

The natural tendency of the LTR is to decay toward zero from either end of the relationship spectrum. Zero puts you back into Acquaintance territory. Decay occurs naturally with each passing day that you do not contact a Sim you have a relationship with.

How to achieve the different LTRs is explained in the Friendships (and Enemies) section of this chapter, but here is a list of all of the LTRs:

- Stranger
- Acquaintance
- Disliked
- Distant Friend
- Friend
- Good Friend
- Best Friend
- Best Friends Forever (teens only)
- Romantic Interest
- Ex-Spouse
- Ex
- Enemy
- Old Enemies
- Partner
- Fiancee
- Spouse

Short-Term Context (STC)

Short-term contexts are what a Sim thinks about the other Sim in the course of the current conversation, not as an LTR. The STC is displayed in the conversation box in the screen's upper-left as the conversation unfolds. For example, the box may say that "Jenny thinks Sasha is being amusing." STC is affected by the kind of socials used in a conversation. Each social has a commodity attached to it that directs the course of a conversation. These are all of the STCs:

- Dull
- Drab
- Insufferably Tedious
- Odd
- Creepy
- Frightening
- Very Scary
- Impolite
- Insulting
- Unforgivably Rude
- OK
- Friendly
- Very Friendly
- Amusing
- Funny
- Hilarious
- Flirty
- Seductive
- Hot
- Awkward
- Very Awkward
- Steamed

Not all STCs are symmetrical. One Sim can have a totally different impression of a conversation than the other. The only symmetrical STCs are those associated with the following commodities: friendly, funny, amorous, and steamed. It is very possible that Jenny could think Sasha is being Dull while Sasha does not.

STC also modulates the way socials are accepted. Instead of just hot and cold, STCs and their respective commodities temper reactions. Depending on your LTR and STC, you can see different degrees of reaction to a social. Trying to kiss a Sim on the cheek in the context of the Flirty STC will be a lot more successful than the Friendly STC.

NOTE

The STC of a conversation contributes to the kind of decay an LTR undergoes each day.

Commodity

So, each STC is associated with a commodity? What's a commodity? Think of these as the general categories a social or

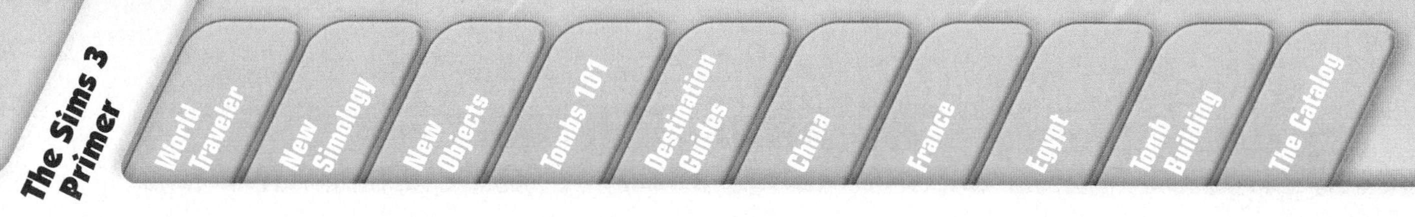

STC falls under. They are based on specific emotions we all feel, such as awkwardness or love. Use the commodity of a social to inspire an STC, which in turn affects the overall LTR. Here are the seven commodities:

- Boring
- Funny
- Creepy
- Amorous
- Insulting
- Awkward
- Friendly
- Steamed

As you look at the different STCs and socials in this chapter, check the associated commodities so you can push a conversation in the desired direction.

Decay and Normalizing

Relationships do not operate under inertia. They decay over time if not tended to, even if that time period is as short as 24 hours. This is why regular socializing is so important. Decay is not necessarily a negative slide. While positive relationship can indeed decay into mere Acquaintance, a negative relationship can normalize into the far more desirable Acquaintance. (Apparently Sims don't keep grudges quite like we do.)

TIP

Decay can be slowed by something as simple as a phone call.

As mentioned, the STC of a conversation contributes to LTR decay. These commodities dictate the decay. The amount of decay is also determined by the LTR itself. An LTR above zero, which starts heading toward positive territory, will have a different amount of decay from a specific STC/commodity than a negative LTR, which is below zero. No hard math on-screen shows the numerical value of an LTR, but you can sort of eyeball it.

Here's an example of how this decay works: Jenny and Sasha are Good Friends. If their last encounter was Impolite, then after a few days, the LTR will decay to just Friends. Conversely, if Jenny and Sasha have the Disliked LTR, the relationship will normalize into Acquaintance if the last STC was Friendly.

NOTE

Decay and normalization are not confined only to friends and pre-marriage Sims. This also applies to familial relationships, such as father or wife. However, the bonds of blood are far deeper than those of friends, so it takes a lot more to adversely affect a familial relationship. Not that it cannot be done. You can absolutely sour a familial relationship with insulting socials.

Friendships (and Enemies)

Now that we've explained the four basics of socialization—LTR, STC, commodity, and decay—let's look at how relationships bloom and wither...and what you can do to affect the course of these relationships. Naturally, Sims want friends. Social is a need, after all. Socializing and having friends have various effects on the course of your Sims' lives.

Friendships are a universally positive thing. Having friends, particularly in an expanded social circle, opens you up to a wealth of opportunities for receiving good moodlets. Positive moodlets are the key to earning those coveted Lifetime Rewards. Friendships can result in such pleasing moodlets as Flattered or Nicely Decorated, such as if you are invited over to a friend's house that has some great environmental bonuses.

Achieving the different LTRs is done through conversations—and conversations are made up of socials. But there is much more to a conversation/STC than just employing a handful of socials. A Sim's personality is hugely important in determining which socials can be used—and should be used. And it's not only the traits of the Actor that matter. Learning the traits of the Target is also quite important.

The Art of the Conversation

So, you've approached another Sim, you left-clicked on them, and now you are staring at a menu of different social options. How do you navigate the social structure of a conversation? Well, your options are partially defined by your LTR, current mood, age, and your traits. Categories of socials include things like Friendly, Funny, Mean, Romantic, and Special. Special leads to socials that are encouraged by the Actor having a specific trait, such as Bookworm. Inside the Bookworm menu, there will be options to talk about books or the bookstore.

The menu of available social categories appears around your Sim's head. Left-click on an option to see what socials are available.

Now, select a social from the category to add it to the action queue.

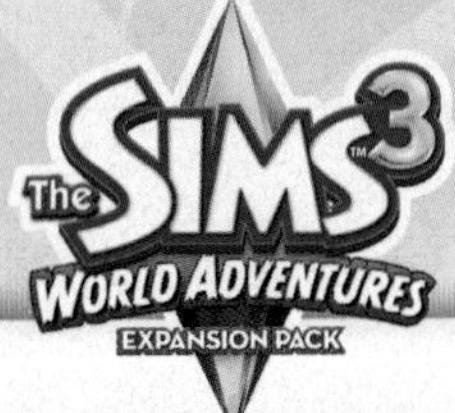

NOTE

Social menus have a maximum of 12 options. If there are more than 12 available to a Sim, the friendly socials are the first to get cut from the menu of options.

When you select a social, it is added to your list of activities in the upper-right corner, just as if you were stacking interactions with objects. When a current social ends, the next one automatically begins. But stacking socials is not a wise strategy because you do not want to just babble away about a topic that the other Sim is just not interested in listening to. Use socials and then watch for reactions. A positive social with a positive effect is noted with a chime and a blue symbol of two Sims next to each other. A negative reaction is noted by two red Sims and a minus symbol.

Being Boring

Talking about the same things over and over gets boring to most Sims. The positive effect of a positive social is weakened the more you use it. Repeating a social can also affect the STC. Continuous droning about the same subjects will nudge the STC into Dull, Drab, or Insufferably Tedious territory. If the conversation ends on one of those STCs, the LTR suffers.

When a relationship is suffering due to a boring conversation, red symbols appear over the Sims' heads.

The default number of times you can repeat a social without getting boring is two. And if you break apart a conversation, you can use a social more than twice without any STC worries. Some socials can be used more than twice without dullness setting in, such as Chat. Chat has four uses before it is boring in a single conversation. However, it can be "recharged" so that the social can be used six times before it is boring. To recharge a social, you just need to break it up in the conversation. For example, let's say you use Chat four times in a row. The other Sim is not bored, but is about to be if you use it one more time. So, you change course and Talk About Books. After that social runs its course, you have recharged Chat once. Now you can use Chat again without it being boring. However, if you tried to use it again without another recharge, the social would be considered boring.

Family and Aging

Few bonds in this world are more powerful than family—and family is a strong force inside *The Sims 3*, too. The family is a close unit that is always on the lookout for each other's best interests, both socially and with the tending of moods and needs.

Time is a constant that cannot be avoided in *The Sims 3*. It is a steady drumbeat in the back of every day, sometimes barely audible above the din of career, socialization, and the little joys of life. Over time, Sims age. They transition between the stages of life, from toddler to child, from adult to elderly. And at the end of the strange, fascinating trip that is life, Sims will die.

There are seven stages of life in *The Sims 3*: baby, toddler, child, teen, young adult, adult, and elder. Each stage has a different number of days that completes an age. At the end of the age, the Sim transitions into the next age. Here are the number of days in each age:

Baby: 2 days

Toddler: 7 days

Child: 7 days

Teen: 14 Days

Young Adult: 21 days

Adult: 21 days

Elderly: 16 days (minimum)

AGE TRANSITIONS

When a Sim closes in on the transition date, you are given a two-day warning. If the Sim about to age up is younger than a young adult, this transition period is extremely important. When a toddler transitions to a child and a child transitions to a teen, the Sim picks up an additional trait. If the Sim is doing well in life by specific metrics at the point of transition, you get to pick that new trait. If the Sim is struggling, then the trait is either randomly chosen or is chosen from a list of negative traits.

Baby

The most helpless of all Sims, the baby requires a lot of care. Fortunately, this age lasts only a couple days and parents are given the time off from their careers to tend to the baby. Babies are typically carried around by their parents (or adult/elder Sims). While carrying a baby, Sims must limit their interactions to sitting (not in front of a table), using the phone, and any socialization that does not require touching. Babies have fewer needs than other Sims, but the needs they do have are critical. Here is what you need to monitor on a baby:

- **Energy:** Babies tend to get tired much faster than other ages. When a baby gets tired, it can fall asleep, as long as it is not in the middle of an activity. Babies typically sleep in a crib, though, so make sure you buy one if your household has a baby in it.
- **Hygiene:** Babies need to relieve themselves like every other Sim, but they do so in their diapers. This makes the baby Smelly, which can cause a negative moodlet on other Sims if the Change Diaper interaction is not selected after the baby alerts you of its stinky predicament.

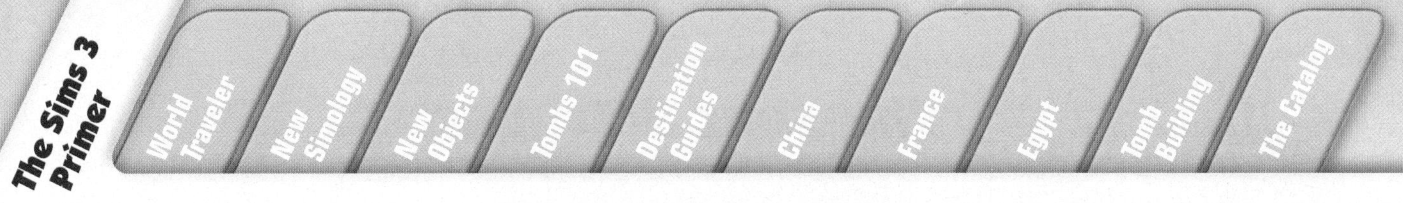

- **Hunger:** Babies need a lot of feeding, but not the kind of food you prepare in the kitchen. Babies need bottles. To feed a baby when it needs it, select the Feed Baby interaction on the baby.
- **Social:** Babies need interaction and entertainment, so be sure to regularly play with your new baby.

CAUTION

You must attend to the baby or the baby will get the Lonely moodlet. You must also feed the baby regularly so the Hunger need never drops into the red. If you neglect a baby (or any Sim younger than young adult), you risk a visit from a Social Worker. The Social Worker will take away a child who is being neglected.

Toddler

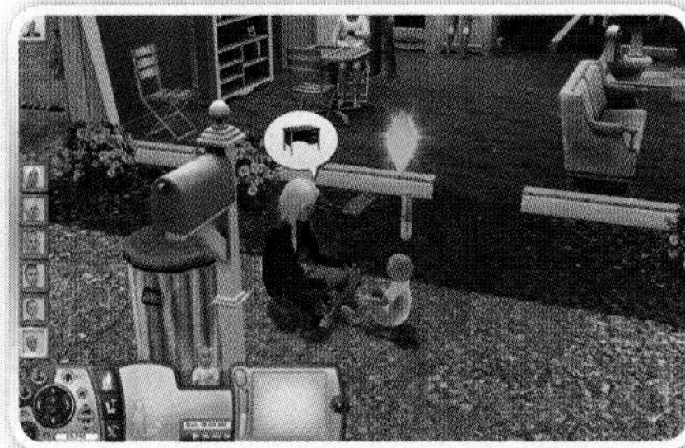

Babies age up into toddlers. Toddlers cannot take much better care of themselves than babies, but at least they are somewhat mobile, thanks to the ability to crawl, and they can amuse themselves via toys. Toddlers can be taught how to walk via a special interaction with an teen or older Sim. In fact, teaching a toddler to walk is one of three critical lessons you need to teach a toddler before it ages up into a child. The other necessary lessons are Teach to Talk and Potty Train. Toddlers need attention like babies, so if a toddler starts to fuss, you should definitely pick it up and socialize with it.

Toddlers love toys. You can keep them busy for hours by giving them a few toys to play with, like the baby xylophone.

Toddlers have four needs that must be attended to:

- **Energy:** Toddlers need to sleep a little less than babies, but they still get sleepy on a much more regular basis than older Sims.
- **Fun:** To keep toddlers in a good mood, you need to either play with them or direct their attention to some toys. You can purchase several toys in Buy Mode from the Kids Room catalog.
- **Hunger:** Toddlers need to eat. You can either go the bottle route or feed a toddler in a high chair, which can also be purchased from the Kids Room catalog. To feed a toddler actual food, you need the food processor to puree the meal.
- **Hygiene:** Toddlers use diapers. If not potty trained, a toddler will fill its diapers and demand immediate changing. If a toddler has been taught to use the potty, it can use the training potty.

You need to teach the toddler for it to properly age up. If you have not taught the toddler all three skills before it ages, you cannot choose the third trait it receives during the transition.

Teach to Walk and Teach to Talk are selectable when you left-click on the toddler. The older Sim sits down next to the toddler and starts the lesson. Lesson progress is viewable just like learning a skill in adulthood. A blue bar appears over the toddler's head and fills over the course of the lesson. When the bar fills to the max, the skill has been taught. To handle potty training, you need to buy the small training toilet from Buy Mode. As soon as the toddler has learned any of these skills, that skill vanishes from the interaction menu.

TIP

Elder Sims are great teachers for toddlers.

Child

Child Sims have survived being a toddler and are ready to take on a little responsibility of their own: school. Child Sims can socialize and make friends with other children, feed themselves with quick snacks from the fridge, and even learn a few of the skills that will give them a leg up on teen and adult life. Children still like to play, so let them have a little fun with toys and games when not working on homework for school and socializing with the family.

A child who gets regular good grades and has an A at the time of the age transition gets to choose the next trait. Anything less and the trait is either random or purposefully negative. However, in addition to going to school, children can learn a few skills, such as Cooking.

Teen

Teen Sims graduate to high school and are impressed with a whole new level of responsibility. Teen Sims can get part-time jobs to help contribute to the household worth, although doing so leaves them less time to get homework done or be social, both of which are important activities for the teen. Teen Sims must pay attention in school and get homework done so when they graduate to adulthood, they can select the fifth and final trait.

TIP

When Sims reach teen, they get to choose a Lifetime Wish.

Teen Sims share a lot with adult Sims. They can perform most socials at this point, save for marriage and WooHoo. Romance is a big part of the teen experience, as teens want to have relationships and go steady with another teen. (Teens cannot be romantic outside of their age level.)

Teens have a special LTR: Best Friends Forever. This is the teen version of Best Friends. To designate this special friend, use the BFF social on a fellow teen with a high relationship. BFFs long to hang out together. Teens can only have one BFF at a time. If a teen chooses a new BFF, the relationship with the previous BFF takes a significant hit and has an insulting STC.

TIP

Teen Sims can learn all skills, just like adult Sims. This is a good time to figure out what kind of skills you want to nurture and get an early start on them.

Young Adult/Adult

Adult Sims have great responsibilities to take care of their charges and maintain a positive household, all while juggling career, skills, and socializations. It's not an easy task. There are thousands of choices to make, from sitting down to write a book to going into the military to looking for butterflies up at SimHenge. But it's the stage and all of its freedoms that makes *The Sims 3* such a wonderful experience.

Elder

Elder Sims are not that different from adult Sims. They learn skills, have careers, like to socialize, and still have Lifetime Wishes. However, they are nearing the end of the great arc of life. But they still deserve to live this final age with grace and poise. Keep elder Sims active even if they retire from work (and enjoy a nice pension) by continuing to develop skills and relationships. That way, when death finally does knock on your front door, there are zero regrets and the family that the elder Sim leaves behind has a wealth of memories, lessons, and Simoleons.

World Traveler

Others define us by the company we keep, but we define ourselves by the experiences we've had and the ones we are planning. One of the greatest experiences we can have is to travel. The awe of new sights. The thrill of unfamiliar sounds. The intoxication of new smells. Travel is an expansion of personal borders by crossing physical ones.

Until now, the farthest away from home that Sims could explore was the city limits of Sunset Valley or Riverview. But with *World Adventures*, Sims can finally leave their city lives behind and take flight to exotic new places. Sims can now see things like a nectary in France, a zen garden in China, and the depths of a creepy tomb in Egypt. They can learn new cultures from the Sims in these exciting locations, and taste new foods. And when the Sim finally returns home to a career or the rest of a household, they bring these new experiences with them, enriching not only their own lives, but the lives of those around them.

What's New?

This guide is designed to help you get the absolute most out of your vacation plans. Sims cannot jet off to new countries for an indefinite amount of time. Their visas only allow them short stays overseas, at first. By completing special adventures on their trips, Sims earn points for their visas. The more points you bank, the longer you can stay the next time you visit. When a Sim finally maxes out a visa for a particular location, they may purchase special vacation homes there for use the next time they visit.

These adventures are typically trips to tombs and catacombs beneath the surface. In these dark places, Sims must seek out hidden chambers and learn how to survive dangerous traps. The rewards of raiding these tombs includes more than just points on a visa. Sims will discover valuable treasures and relics. These relics can be sold for Simoleons or taken back home and put on display.

While on holiday, Sims are encouraged to open their minds and hearts, to take in new cultures, learn new skills, and establish new friendships. The methods of learning the new skills—Martial Arts, Nectar Making, and Photography—and socializing with other Sims is very similar to how it's done in *The Sims 3*, which was detailed in the previous chapter. While Sims do not necessarily need to embark on personal journeys to develop new skills or make new friends, you only get a portion of the *World Adventures* experience by slipping into the tombs. During each trip, balance both exploration and personal growth so that when your Sims finally bid adieu to the vacation destination, they go home with wonderful memories as well as souvenirs.

The Basics of Travel

Once you have *World Adventures* all set up, your Sims can leave on their first vacation. It only takes one phone call or a click on the computer to get the Sim in a cab, whisked off to the airport, and on their way to your choice of the three possible locations—Egypt, China, or France. However, before boarding, you need to know some essentials about travel. Not only do you need to understand what's involved with travel on the departure end of the trip, but also the basics of an adventure at the destination.

Before You Go...

As mentioned, all you need to do to travel to a new location is dial it up on the phone in your Sim's inventory or choose the Travel interaction from a computer. It is as easy as ordering a pizza or arranging babysitting. However, travel is not cheap. Each trip costs Simoleons and the price of travel goes up with each consecutive trip that lasts longer than the previous. These costs only cover getting there and getting back. Once you are at your destination, you need additional Simoleons to purchase goods at merchants such as foodstuffs and other essentials. (You have to take care of Hunger, Sleep, and Hygiene on your travels, you know.) Here are the opening prices of each three-day trip:

- **China:** §1,300
- **Egypt:** §1,600
- **France:** §1,900

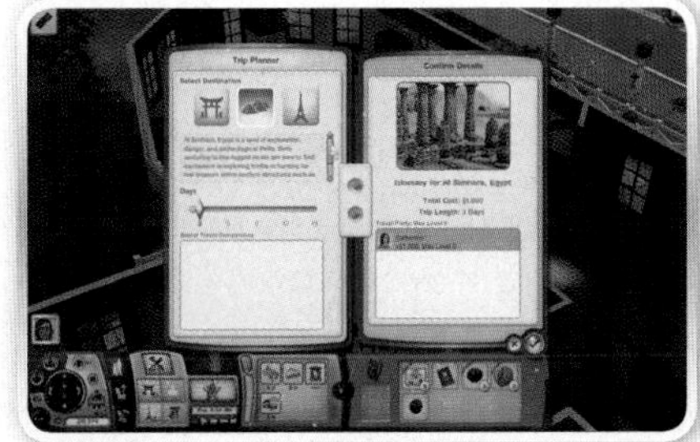

The Trip Planner pops up after the Sim has arranged to travel. Use the Trip Planner to select your destination, the length of the stay (within the boundaries of your current visa level), and which members of a multi-Sim household are going on the vacation.

Caution

Visibly pregnant Sims cannot travel. Neither can babies or toddlers. Child Sims require an adult in order to travel.

The Visa

Why is your Sim limited to only three days? Well, that's because your Sim's visa is only good for three days of travel when you take your first trip. Your Sim has one visa for each location. Each visa has four levels to it if you count the zero level when you first receive the visa. To stay longer at a destination, you need to raise the level of the visa. To raise your visa level, you must undertake adventures at each destination. When you complete an adventure, the Sim who offered it to you adds points to your visa. The more points you accumulate, the higher your visa level.

Points on a visa are not transferable. They are unique to the location where they are earned. Just because your Sim completed an adventure in China and earned a new visa level allowing them to stay five days does not mean they can now start staying five days in Egypt. The visa level for Egypt must also be bumped up to enjoy a similar benefit.

Here are the visa levels and the required number of points for each level:

VISA LEVELS

Visa Level	Points Required	Max. Length of Stay
1	50	5
2	150	7
3	300	9

The Special Merchant will not sell you some goods unless you have a certain visa level. It's one of the many reasons to increase your visa level as soon as possible.

Higher visa levels do more for your Sim than just allow for an extended stay. Certain objects and perks cannot be bought unless your Sim has a specific visa level. Some adventures at each location are not offered to Sims until they reach a suitable visa level.

Base camp's great, but why not vacation in luxury?

When your Sim reaches the highest visa level at a location, they can buy a vacation home. (Or vacation homes, if your Sim is loaded.) Now, the Sim does not have to use the general facilities at base camp any more. They can stay at their vacation home instead. Plus, the vacation home is a great place to store all of the cool relics and treasures found on travels.

Note

A special Adventure Reward called the Certificate of Partnership extends your stay even longer. Buy it from the Special Merchant who tours near the market in each location.

At the end of your vacation, your Sim is automatically returned home. Now, even if you want to head right back out on another adventure, the travel option on your Sim's phone is grayed out. You must wait two full days before going on another trip. Don't be bummed. Use that time to practice some useful skills, go to work, and catch up with your household.

Tip

Sims with the Adventurous trait only need to wait one day before traveling again.

Frozen Time

When you saw that you could stay on a vacation for several days, you thought about how that would affect aging, right? After all, your Sim only has a certain number of days before they age up. If you spend all of your days on vacation, how will you fit in all of the career-building and skill-developing back at home to satisfy a Lifetime Wish?

Well, you're in luck—aging and the earliest stage of pregnancy freezes on vacation. You do not have to worry about blowing important aging days while cavorting around the dunes of Egypt or the tombs of China. Time picks right back up when you return to your home town, though.

You can use this to your advantage, especially when you can stay for a long time at a location. Most locations have skill-building objects, such as the gym equipment at the martial arts facility in China. Work on those skills while on vacation so you don't consume precious time. When you return home, you enjoy the benefits of an increased skill level (such as earning a promotion at work) without losing any days doing it.

Base Camp

When you first arrive at a destination, you are dropped off at base camp. Base camp provides temporary housing for your Sims while they are on vacation. As such, it contains all the necessary amenities, such as showers, a bed, and a place to prepare food. Each destination's base camp looks different, but they all have the same amenities. For example, the guest quarters at base camp in China are quite luxurious compared to the tents in Egypt. But, you can get a decent night's sleep in each place, and that's what matters.

Egypt's base camp

China's base camp

France's base camp

While the bed and running water at base camp are important, perhaps the most interesting amenity at each location is the Adventure Board. When you first arrive, be sure to check the Adventure Board for new adventures. If one is open and you accept it, the Sim you need to see for the adventure is then marked in map view.

However, you are not required to immediately check the Adventure Board. You can just laze about at base camp and take it easy. Use it as a home away from home for trips when you just want to work on one of the new skills or do a little souvenir-shopping.

TIP

You aren't the only vacationer. Base camp is sometimes filled with other travelers. This is a great place to make new friends. Chat up your fellow adventurers while making breakfast.

Ancient Coins

While most merchants take Simoleons, there is a special currency often used while on vacation: Ancient Coins. Ancient Coins are found while exploring tombs and are sometimes awarded when completing an adventure. Look for Ancient Coins in piles on the floor in tomb chambers or inside treasure chests. Pocket as many as you can find, because while you can trade Simoleons for cool relics, the Special Merchant only accepts Ancient Coins.

The number of Ancient Coins found in tombs changes with each visit. Just because one Sim found 25 in a treasure chest in a particular room doesn't mean another Sim will find the same amount in the same spot.

NOTE

In addition to Ancient Coins, your Sim can collect relics while traveling. For a complete explanation of relics as well as a breakdown of how they fit into different collections and what they are worth, please see the "Relics" section of this chapter.

Markets & Merchants

As any traveler knows, shopping abroad is tremendous fun. You find items and objects completely foreign from the stores back home. These trinkets make for wonderful gifts as well as reminders of previous travels. In *World Adventures*, there are plenty of merchants at each destination ready to relieve you of Simoleons in exchange for goods and gear. Merchants have all sorts of things for sale, from new recipes and books to relics.

When visiting the markets on consecutive trips, you will discover that inventories change. A merchant may not have the same relic selection on your next trip, so if you spy something you like, you may want to splurge for it right away. It may be a while until you see it at a merchant again.

NOTE

The steady inventory for each shopkeeper, such as the bookseller, is located in the individual destination chapters.

The market at each location is plainly marked on the map so you can make a beeline to it upon your first visit.

Markets are not just for buying stuff, though. Markets often double as social centers at destinations, too, just like the Central Park in Sunset Valley or the plaza in Riverview. Socialize at the market with different Sims as well as shopkeepers and merchants. These are great places to make new friends. And who knows? You might even find a special someone while shopping for trinkets and go home with the best souvenir of all—love.

Survival Gear

Merchants at all three locations offer a few of the same objects, such as tents and dried food. These objects fall under the "general necessity" category: items you need if you plan on doing some tomb exploration and are not always near base camp or a vacation home.

Although these objects are called out in the new object catalog later in this guide, these necessities are important to know about right up-front. Before going on an adventure that takes you into the underworld, consider stocking up on some of these objects.

Dried food: Time may effectively stop on a vacation, but that rumble in your Sim's tummy does not. Food is easily available at base camp or the market, but when you are in a tomb, you need to have something portable to nosh on. If you did not bring fruit or something with you, then buy dried food. There are three kinds of dried food to pick from, each of varying quality. The higher quality the dried food, the more expensive it is. However, quality equals satisfaction. Eating higher quality dried food results in a better Meal moodlet, which in turn can help keep your Sim's spirits high.

Tent: Exploring is exhausting. Sims will get tired while out on an adventure. Sometimes it takes too long to get back to base camp before your Sim gets so tired it affects their mood. Other times, you just don't want to sacrifice time traveling to base camp—that's time that could be spent looking for secret doors! Buy a tent so your Sim can sleep away from base camp or a house. There are multiple tents. The more expensive the tent, the more comfortable it is for your Sim.

TIP

Occasionally, Sims wish to sleep in a tomb. Having a tent lets you indulge this wish and pick up some Lifetime Happiness points.

You can even take the tent home with you and use it back there. If you really want to go nomad, sell the house and use a tent instead for a portable bed. Just be sure to hit up the gym for showers...

Shower in a Can: Let's face it—the underworld is a bit dingy. Your Sim's Hygiene will drop as they root around tombs for treasure. If they get stinky, they offend not only other Sims but also themselves. Mood takes a hit. Avoid this with Shower in a Can, a portable bath. This canned shower only has one use, but it is just as good as taking a normal shower.

TIP

Shower in a Can has an alternate, life-saving secondary use. If your Sim is caught in a fire trap in a tomb, the Shower in a Can will put out the flames.

Camera: The camera is not technically an essential object like food or a portable shower, but it is still an important travel item, and all general stores at each destination stock it. The camera is required for building up the new Photography skill. Plus, photos are another good way to make some extra Simoleons on the side, which can fund future trips.

Special Merchants & Adventure Rewards

Each location has a Special Merchant. This merchant is not anchored to a physical store, but moseys around the marketplace at each destination from 9 AM to 6 PM. Special Merchants sell Adventure Rewards, which are similar to Lifetime Rewards in that these rewards cannot be purchased with Simoleons. Adventure Rewards are bought with Ancient Coins. Some Adventure Rewards cannot be bought until your visa is at a specific level, too.

Adventure Rewards are not like relics or other objects bought at the market. These particular items affect your travels. So save up those Ancient Coins! You will undoubtedly want many of these rewards to use during your travels, such as the Mummy Snacks. These snacks will keep a rampaging mummy off your tail. (What? A rampaging mummy will chase you? Oh, more on that in the Tombs 101 chapter.) Use this shopping list when browsing the Special Merchant's goods:

ADVENTURE REWARDS

Adventure Reward	Cost (in Ancient Coins)	Visa Level Required	Destination
Pemmican	10	1	All
Potion of Liquid Courage	40	1	All
Sands of Understanding	100	1	China
Avornalino Grapes	20	1	France
Mummy Snacks	100	1	Egypt
Skeleton Keystone	400	2	All
Escape Dust	75	2	All
Master Thief's Coin	750	2	China
Meloire Grapes	25	2	France
Tear of Horus	1,600	2	Egypt
The Sultan's Tabernacle	2,500	3	All
Certificate of Partnership with China	1,350	3	China
Certificate of Partnership with France	1,000	3	France
Certificate of Partnership with Egypt	1,200	3	Egypt
Gralladina Fran Grapes	40	3	France
Carnerlet Nuala Grapes	50	3	France

New Skills

You can learn three new skills while traveling the world: Martial Arts, Nectar Making, and Photography. All three of these skills may be learned while on trips, but the benefits of the skills extend far beyond the limits of your visa. These skills can be brought back home and used there, too. A Sim who returns to Riverview with a bottle a sweet nectar not available at the EverFresh Supermarket will be a popular Sim indeed. And woe to the Burglar who tries to rob a Sim with an advanced Martial Arts skill.

Martial Arts

Martial Arts is the skill learned in China. It's separate from the Athletic skill. It is originally learned by either reading a book about the skill or by checking into the dojo in Shang Simla. There, Sims will find the necessary equipment to train up the skill, such as Board Breakers.

Sims who learn Martial Arts become excellent fighters. They don't go around picking fights, though. This is a defensive skill, but one that pretty much guarantees that a Sim forced into a brawl will walk away the victor.

Nectar Making

Sims who visit France can begin mastering the fine art of making nectar. Visit the Nectary to check out a public Nectar Maker and start squashing fruit to make batches of the delicious beverage. Adding quality fruits to the Nectar Maker will result in better nectar, which means better moodlets for drinking the stuff, as well as better prices when selling it.

Buy a Nectar Maker and install it back home so you can keep developing the skill when not in France.

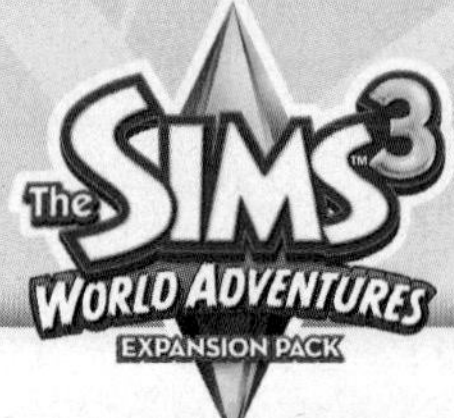

Nectar ages well in a cellar. That means you better make a basement for your house if you pursue this skill. There is a brand-new tool in Build Mode for easily constructing basements. Be sure to check out how to do it in the Nectar Making section of the New Simology chapter.

Photography

Photography is not tethered to any one destination. It can be developed in any of the three travel spots by either reading the beginner's book or by just buying a camera from a shop and snapping some pictures. Photos are added to different collections. When you complete a collection, you boost the skill. It costs Simoleons to take photos, but the benefits of completing collections and eventually mastering the skill make it as valuable as the Painting skill.

TIP

There are three cameras, but the medium- and high-quality cameras can be purchased only in Egypt.

NOTE

The full progression of each skill and tips for how to speedily develop it are detailed in the New Simology chapter.

Relics

Ancient Coins are not the only things to seek while on vacation. Relics are special treasures to buy or find and then bring home as interesting souvenirs to show off. Find relics in rubble piles, inside treasure chests, and even just lying around inside tombs. For the less adventurous, relics can also be purchased at merchants.

NOTE

Relics are generally categorized by culture: Chinese, French, and Egyptian. As you collect relics from each culture, it is logged in your Adventure Journal.

Relics can also be sold for profit, just like the collectibles back in your home town. In fact, this is a great way to make Simoleons while on vacation. Some relics are worth as little as 100 Simoleons. Some are worth as many as 4,000 Simoleons. You can see how a vacation might pay for itself (and then some) with a lucky find.

NOTE

Not every relic found is valuable. Sometimes you discover wrecked relics that are worth very little.

But perhaps you would rather keep these relics for yourself? After all, relics are extremely attractive and go a long way toward sprucing up a lot back home in Sunset Valley or Riverview. Placing relics in your house adds to the environmental rating of the room, which can result in a moodlet boost just for walking though it, such as Nicely Decorated.

Each relic belongs to a collection, too. There are nine collections:

- Canopic Jars
- Gold Figurines
- Zodiac Animals
- Chinese Vases
- Dangerous Creatures
- Dropa Stones
- Egyptian Tomb
- Chinese Tomb
- French Tomb

When you complete a collection, just being around it gives you a nice moodlet boost called Wondrous Collection. Depending on the collection, you get a different moodlet boost. Here are the moodlets associated with each collection:

RELIC MOODLETS

Wondrous Collection	Moodlet Value
Canopic Jars	10
Chinese Vases	10
Dropa Stones	15
Gold Figurines	20
Zodiac Animals	20
Dangerous Creatures	25
Chinese Tomb	30
Egyptian Tomb	30
French Tomb	30

NOTE

These and all new moodlets are discussed in the New Simology chapter.

Much like Ancient Coins, you will not find the same relics in the same places with each tomb visit. (The maps for each tomb in the individual location sections show what kinds of relics to expect in certain locations.) But, here is a chart that shows the value for each relic, the destination in which the relic is found, and which collection it belongs to.

RELICS—EGYPTIAN TOMB

Relic	Location	Which Tomb?	Minimum Value	Maximum Value
Sigil of the Tomb of Discovery	Egypt	Tomb of Discovery	§100	§100
Sigil of the Tomb of the Burning Sands	Egypt	Tomb of the Burning Sands	§100	§100
Sigil of the Tomb of the Rock	Egypt	Tomb of the Rock	§100	§100
Sigil of the Tomb of the Desert Ocean	Egypt	Tomb of the Desert Ocean	§100	§100
Sigil of the Criminal Headquarters	Egypt	Criminal HQ	§100	§100
Sigil of the Ancient Library	Egypt	Ancient Library	§100	§100
Sigil of James Vaughan's Command Center	Egypt	Command Center	§100	§100
Sigil of the Great Sphinx	Egypt	Soulpeace Chambers	§100	§100
Sigil of Queen Hatshepsut's Quarters	Egypt	Hatshepsut's Quarters	§100	§100
Sigil of the Bazaar Basement	Egypt	Bazaar Tomb	§100	§100
Sigil of the Passage to the Underworld	Egypt	Temple of Death	§100	§100
Sigil of the Copper Quarry	Egypt	Copper Quarry	§100	§100
Sigil of the Sanctuary of Horus	Egypt	Sanctuary of Horus	§100	§100

RELICS—CHINESE TOMB

Relic	Location	Which Tomb?	Minimum Value	Maximum Value
Symbol of Pangu's Haven	China	Temple of the Axe	§100	§100
Symbol of the Annex of the Resolute Fist	China	Resolute Fist Retreat	§100	§100
Symbol of the Tomb of the First Emperor	China	Tomb of the Dragon Emperor	§100	§100
Symbol of the Temple of the Dragon	China	Temple of the Dragon	§100	§100
Symbol of the Halls of the Lost Army	China	Rice Paddy Hidden Temple	§100	§100
Symbol of the Hot Springs Cave	China	Hot Springs Hidden Temple	§100	§100
Symbol of Dong Huo's Treasure Trove	China	Dong Huo Treasure Trove	§100	§100
Symbol of the Market Caverns	China	Market Caves	§100	§100
Symbol of the Resolute Fist Retreat	China	Ancient Monk Retreat	§100	§100

RELICS—FRENCH TOMB

Relic	Location	Which Tomb?	Minimum Value	Maximum Value
Signet of the Nectary Cellars	France	Nectar Catacombs	§100	§100
Signet of the Tomb of Isael	France	Tomb of Isael	§100	§100
Signet of the Tomb of Jean Necteaux	France	Tomb of Necteaux	§100	§100
Signet of the Museum Catacombs	France	Museum Catacombs	§100	§100
Signet of Tuatha's Garden	France	Faerie Tomb	§100	§100
Signet of King's Burial Ground	France	Forgotten Burial Mound	§100	§100
Signet of the Maze of the High Ruler	France	Forgotten Burial Mound	§100	§100
Signet of Smuggler's Cavern	France	Forgotten Burial Mound	§100	§100
Signet of Le Chateau du Landgraab	France	Chateau du Landgraab	§100	§100

RELICS—CANOPIC JARS

Relic	Location	Minimum Value	Maximum Value
Little Pharaoh Canopic Jar	Egypt	§400	§900
Weeping Canopic Jar	Egypt	§400	§900
Mummified Canopic Jar	Egypt	§400	§900
Canopic Jar of the Cat	Egypt	§400	§900
Canopic Jar of the Eagle	Egypt	§400	§900

RELICS—GOLD FIGURINES

Relic	Location	Minimum Value	Maximum Value
Cobra	Egypt	§1,500	§2,500
Horus	Egypt	§1,500	§2,500
Sphynx	Egypt	§1,500	§2,500
Seth	Egypt	§1,500	§2,500

RELICS—ZODIAC ANIMALS

Relic	Location	Minimum Value	Maximum Value
Dragon	China	§1,600	§3,000
Snake	China	§1,600	§3,000
Tiger	China	§1,600	§3,000

RELICS—CHINESE VASES

Relic	Location	Minimum Value	Maximum Value
Vase of Maroof	China	§350	§800
Vase of Barooka	China	§350	§800
Vase of Amin	China	§350	§800
Vase of Life	China	§350	§800
Vase of Nosylla	China	§350	§800
Vase of the Empress	China	§350	§800
Vase of Nebu	China	§350	§800
Vase of the Dragon	China	§350	§800

RELICS—DANGEROUS CREATURES

Relic	Location	Minimum Value	Maximum Value
Ammit the Destroyer	Egypt	§2,500	§4,000
Anubis	Egypt	§2,500	§4,000
Fu Dog	China	§2,500	§4,000
Gargoyle	France	§2,500	§4,000

RELICS—DROPA STONES

Relic	Location	Minimum Value	Maximum Value
Dropa Stone of the Vortex	China	§700	§1,200
Dropa Stone of the Sky	China	§700	§1,200
Dropa Stone of the Endless Sands	Egypt	§700	§1,200
Dropa Stone of the Enlightened	Egypt	§700	§1,200
Dropa Stone of the Stars	France	§700	§1,200
Dropa Stone of the Fleur	France	§700	§1,200

Adventures

When Sims arrive at their destinations, they have so many different options. Shop? Learn a skill? Socialize? The most thrilling activity at each destination, though, is the adventure. Adventures are similar to opportunities in *The Sims 3*, but are typically tied to a specific task, such as diving into a tomb or looking for a special relic.

Adventures are usually given out by Sims who live at the destination. They present you with an opportunity that you can accept or decline. If you accept, the adventure goes into your Adventure Tracker (more on that in a moment) and you're off to fulfill the task at hand. If you complete an adventure, you are typically awarded points for your visa and some Ancient Coins.

Some adventures have multiple steps and might require additional trips to a destination to complete. However, the harder the adventure, the greater the reward.

NOTE

All of the adventures for each destination are cataloged and detailed in the China, Egypt, and France chapters. Use the maps in each of those chapters to complete the adventures.

WHY ADVENTURE?

There are many reasons to take on an adventure. The most obvious is to increase your visa level so you can spend longer at a destination. But the adventure itself is often the reward. Adventures send you on cool missions to explore dark tombs and seek out unseen treasures. If you combine going on adventures with all of the stuff to do above ground, you can have wonderful, well-rounded vacations that leave your Sim fulfilled on all levels. And your Sim usually brings home a suitcase full of neat stuff, like relics.

Adventure Journal

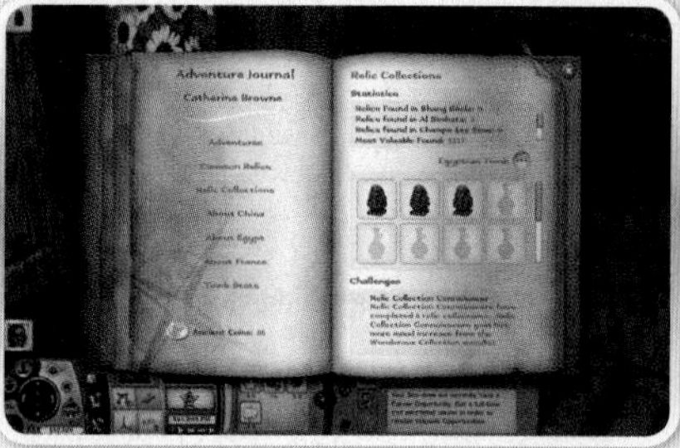

As soon as you take your very first trip, you receive an Adventure Journal. This is similar to a Skill Journal, which you use to track the progress of skills such as Writing and Guitar. The Adventure Journal keeps track of all relevant statistics regarding your travels, so keep an eye on it.

The journal also monitors your progress toward fulfilling a handful of Adventure Challenges. These are the adventure equivalent of Skill Challenges. When you meet certain criteria, your Sim gains a challenge title. This title comes with benefits, such as increased ease of performing a certain action or the improved value of having certain relics.

- **Adventures**: This page tracks all current adventures, organized by the three destinations. The details of the current adventure are displayed here for easy access. If you have no active adventure, then this page reminds you to visit the Adventure Board or answer the phone to embark on a new adventure.
- **Common Relics**: This page charts the number of relics found by locations and all information relevant to your personal history.
- **Relic Collections**: As mentioned, there are nine relic collections. This page in the journal tracks your progress toward completing each collection.
- **About China**: This page displays the current visa level and stats (such as how long you've spent there) for China.
- **About Egypt**: This journal page shows your current visa level and stats for Egypt.
- **About France**: This page reveals your current visa level and stats for France.
- **Tomb Stats**: This journal page tracks dozens of tomb statistics such as how many traps you have disarmed, the number of treasure chests found, and the number of rubble piles cleared.

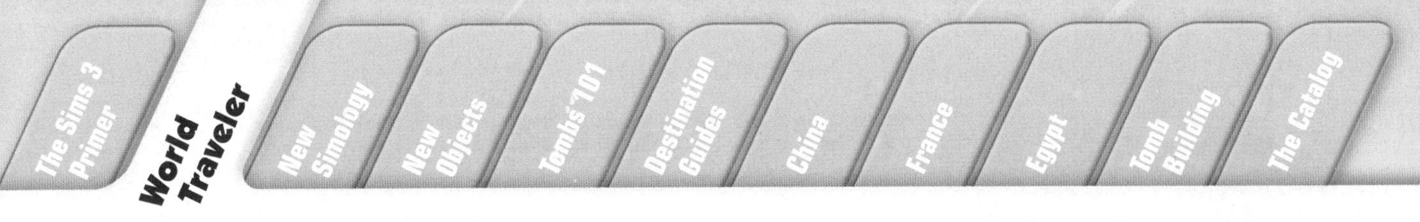

Common Relics

The Common Relics page of the journal offers a top view of your efforts to collect relics throughout your adventures. Every time you collect a relic, it is recorded in this section of the journal. Now, the journal does not record the exact moment or place the relic was found. But it does record important information such as how many relics have been found in each destination, the number of relics analyzed by your Sim, the oldest relic found, and the most valuable relic discovered.

There is a single Common Relics challenge:

- **Historical Hoarder**: A Historical Hoarder has collected 20 relics from each culture. Relics discovered by Historical Hoarders are 50 percent more valuable.

Relic Collections

The general categorization of relics is by culture. But relics are also divided into nine different collections. These collections are tracked in this page of the Adventure Journal. Every time a relic from a new collection is discovered, that collection is logged in the journal so you can track which of the nine collections you have thus far uncovered, and how many relics within that collection you've found. This is a great resource for Sims who seek to complete entire collections for reasons of art, mood, or just that natural drive to finish off a collection.

There is a single Relic Collections challenge:

- **Relic Collection Connoisseur**: Relic Collection Connoisseurs have completed six relic collections. The Wondrous Collection moodlet is 50 percent more powerful on Relic Collection Connoisseurs.

Tomb Stats

This page of the Adventure Journal tracks your activities in the tombs. This is where you can monitor how many keys you have used, how many traps you've disarmed, how many rubble piles you've cleared away, and more. Most of these stats are just for fun. Why not track how many switches you've stood on? (And how fast can you push that stat into triple digits?)

Three challenges will make you want to revisit this page often and check specific tomb states. These challenges are related to exploration, and every time you complete one of them, you get a benefit that helps with scouring the tombs. Here are the three challenges related to tomb stats:

- **Rubble Excavator**: After excavating 10 rubble piles, you'll excavate them 35 percent faster.
- **Well Spelunker**: After diving into 10 dive wells, you'll clear them 80 percent faster.
- **Hazmat Sim**: After disarming 10 traps, you'll have an 80 percent higher chance of successfully disarming them.

Adventure Board

When you first arrive at a destination, you are dropped off at base camp. Each base camp has an Adventure Board. Check out this board to read about new adventures and opportunities being offered by Sims at the location. Later on, Sims may offer missions and adventures over the phone, but the Adventure Board is definitely the best place for new travelers to start.

Adventure Tracker

The Adventure Tracker is a useful tool that appears above the Moodlet window. It appears after you've accepted an adventure, and it tells you the current objective. In some cases, left-clicking on the Adventure Tracker will send your Sim to the stated goal. For example, if you have grabbed the relic from a tomb sought by another Sim, clicking on the Adventure Tracker will direct your Sim to return to the relic-requester.

TIP

Click on the little arrow in the lower-right corner of the Adventure Tracker to toggle it on and off.

Tombs

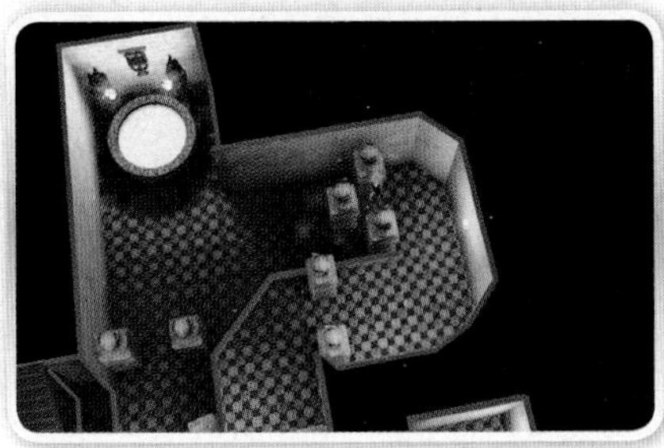

Tombs are a major part of your travels. You will likely spend as much time under the surface as you do mingling with Sims or working on skills in the sunlight. There are dozens of tombs across the three destinations to explore, each filled with tricks, traps, and most importantly treasures. The more adventures you accept, the more complex the tombs become. At first, they seem like a straightforward collection of rooms. Soon, though, you start stumbling upon hidden chambers and devious traps. The harder it is to reach the bottom of a tomb, the likelier it is you will find greater relics.

Tombs are spooky places, full of mystery. Do you really want to put your hand in that hole?

Tombs are dangerous places, though. There are many ways to get in trouble while poking around the underworld, such as ancient traps. There are many ways to get around traps or even disable them, but as you know from just having a fireplace, any time you start dealing with things like fire, you are flirting with danger. And then there are the mummies...

Note

For everything you need to know about surviving tombs, check the Tombs 101 chapter.

Catherine's First Trip

We've gone over the basics of travel, but let's see how it all works before getting too deep into tomb technology, the development of the three new skills, and mapping out each destination. And what better guide for this first trip abroad than Catherine Browne? Well, the Sim Catherine Browne. Back home, Catherine has already boosted many skills such as Writing and Painting and is earning decent money from selling collectibles, such as gems and metals. She's saved up for this trip and is now ready to pick up the phone and make those first travel arrangements.

For her first trip, Catherine goes to China. Because this is her very first trip, it's limited to just three days. But you can pack a lot into just three days: shopping, socializing, and tomb exploration. Here is Catherine's trait breakdown so you can see how those choices might potentially play into an adventure:

- **Trait 1:** Adventurous
- **Trait 2:** Loves the Outdoors
- **Trait 3:** Bookworm
- **Trait 4:** Natural Cook
- **Trait 5:** Photographer's Eye
- **Lifetime Wish:** Seasoned Traveler

Brownie Bites

Now, I had created a Catherine Browne Sim for playing *The Sims 3* so I could build skills, socialize, and do all the things needed in order to write *The Sims 3* Primer. However, when it came time to go on an adventure, I wanted to create a brand-new Catherine Browne that used some of the new traits offered in *World Adventures*. I also wanted to strive for one of the new Lifetime Wishes. I chose Seasoned Traveler, which is the dream of getting level 3 visas in all three destinations. These new traits and new wishes are all detailed in the New Simology chapter, along with the new skills and new ways to socialize with other Sims.

(And it didn't hurt that *World Adventures* offers a whole bunch of new clothes, too. How do you like my scarf?)

Before leaving, make sure that you have unfinished business taken care of because some wishes do not survive travel and vanish. If you are close to fulfilling a smaller wish, such as chatting with a Sim, try to wrap it up. When you reach your destination, new wishes flood into your Sim's head and you will be tempted to zero in on those. Rather than dismiss a bunch of promised wishes, go ahead and finish up the easiest ones.

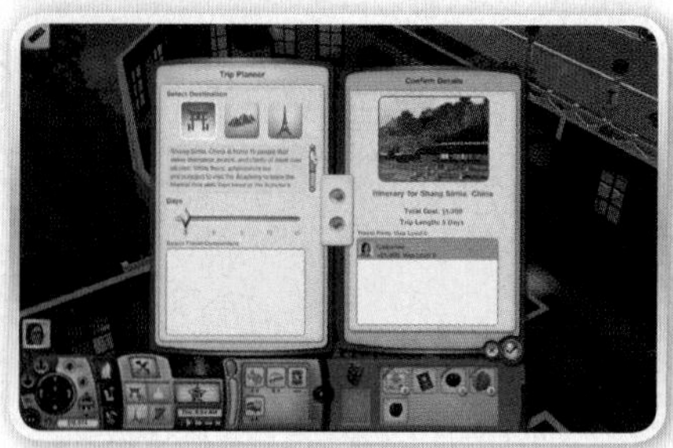

As soon as everything is in order and Catherine has enough in her household funds for the trip, I access the phone and choose the Travel interaction. This opens the Trip Planner. I've already decided on China, so I select it from the planner. The money for the trip is subtracted from the household funds and a taxi immediately pulls up to the house. Catherine hops in the cab and it drives out of the city, presumably to take her to the airport where she will fly off into the horizon.

Day One

This is Catherine's first trip to China, so her visa is at zero. Not only does this limit Catherine's trip to just three days, but it means that when Catherine touches down in China, she is dropped off at base camp. In China, base camp is actually quite lovely and accommodating. The giant facility has everything she needs inside, such as beds, a kitchen, and bathrooms.

First things first: check the Adventure Board.

The Adventure Board is Catherine's first stop because I want to make sure she can spend more time in China on her next visit. To do this, I need to earn points for her visa. The best way to do this is to undertake adventures offered by the locals. When you first visit a destination, there is always an adventure waiting for you on the Adventure Board.

The first adventure in China is called Seeking Adventure? It is the first step in a multi-part adventure that will take Catherine into a tomb. The message on the board asks for a traveler (Catherine in this case) to contact

Xi Yuan. When you accept this adventure, it gets added to the Adventure Tracker above the moodlet panel. Left-clicking on it sends Catherine directly to Xi Yuan, although if you zoom out to map view, you can also see Xi Yuan highlighted with a small token bearing her face.

NOTE

The same Sims will not always offer the same adventures. Whereas Xi Yuan offered this adventure to Catherine, Seeking Adventure? might be offered by Ai Pei in your session.

When Catherine visits Xi Yuan to follow up on the next step of the adventure, she is awarded a handful of visa points. See we're already on our way to increasing the visa level to 1. Xi Yuan tells Catherine about the next step of the adventure: Treasure Hunter.

Treasure Hunter is a mission to seek out a relic at the bottom of a nearby tomb. This tomb is actually beneath the Hall of the Lost Army, which is the giant temple in the center of the Forbidden City. (The Forbidden City is the massive city center at the heart of China.) If Catherine can recover the ancient relic rumored to be at the bottom of the tomb for Xi Yuan, she will reward her with visa points, Simoleons, and Ancient Coins. "Yes, please" to all three of those things! Before leaving, Catherine receives a keystone, which is a critical object for opening a door in the tomb.

Before going into the tomb to seek out the treasure, though, Catherine needs some survival gear. Because I want to get the most out of the three days (trust me, three days can fly by when you are first exploring a destination and undertaking an adventure), I do not want to spend too much time traveling back to base camp at night to use the facilities. So, we head for the market inside the Forbidden City.

The shops in the market are all neatly aligned, making it easy to pop in and out of the bookstore, food place, relic shop, and the general store.

Catherine can shop at the other stores later, and she will because I definitely want to pick up the entry-level Martial Arts skill book and at least one recipe from the bookstore. But because time is of the essence, we go straight for the general store and buy a tent, two Showers in a Can, and several portions of dried food. I spring for the medium quality so Catherine gets a pleasant moodlet bump when she eats them.

With the goods in Catherine's inventory, it's off to the Hall of the Lost Army. Standing on the floor switch opens up the stairs leading down into the tomb.

Using the keystone on the panel next to the door at the bottom of the steps opens the tomb.

Catherine explores the first part of the tomb, using floor switches to open doors.

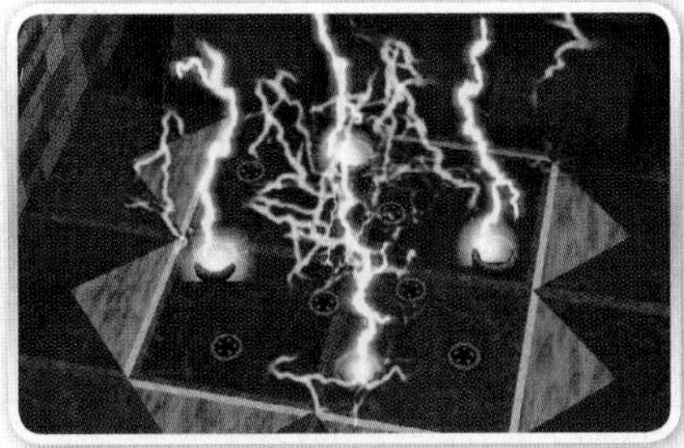

There's an electric trap in one of the tomb chambers. Catherine can turn the trap off by pushing one of the statues on top of it.

Some of the switches must be uncovered by clearing away rubble piles. Clearing away the rubble piles increases Catherine's Athletic skill.

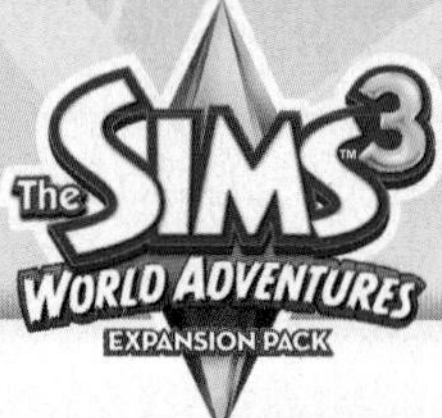

Because Catherine got something of a late start on the day and spent a little time in town, it's already starting to get late. Catherine's mood is starting to go south because she is sleepy. Because I want to get right back into that tomb first thing in the morning, I send Catherine back up to the surface to pitch a tent right next to the Hall of the Lost Army. We'll sleep out here for the night.

Note

Don't forget that all of the information you need to excel at tomb exploration (as well as survive it) is contained in the Tombs 101 chapter.

Day Two

Morning dawns on Catherine's second day. She really needs to complete the tomb today so we can get some social stuff, shopping, and skill-building done on the third day of the trip. As soon as Catherine is awake and out of the tent, she uses a Shower in a Can to ward off any negative Hygiene moodlets. A quick bite of dried food and then it is back to the tomb.

Catherine continues exploring the tomb, pushing deeper into its depths by unlocking doors. A chamber contains several treasure chests and these chests contain relics. I direct Catherine to move some of the statues around the room so she can open the chests and take whatever is inside.

Tip

Like clearing rubble piles, moving the heavy statues in a tomb increases the Athletic skill.

One of the chests holds Ancient Coins. Those will be great for buying Adventure Rewards as soon as Catherine's visa level goes up to at least 1.

Deeper exploration of the tomb reveals a dive well. Catherine uses the dive well to swim to a secret room. A treasure chest in the secret room holds the keystone for a nearby locked door. With the keystone, Catherine can enter the chamber that Xi Yuan was talking about—the one with the ancient relic.

Once Catherine has the ancient relic described by Xi Yuan, she can return to the surface to finish the adventure.

Brownie Bites

By the way, I am not trying to be all clever and obtuse by calling the goal of this adventure an "ancient relic." *World Adventures* is full of randomness, so you can replay the adventures multiple times with different Sims and not always see the same thing. The merchant at the bookstore may sell the same books, but the merchant's appearance is never the exact same. The identity of the Sim who sends you off on a new adventure is always different. The loot in the treasure chest changes because getting the exact same number of Ancient Coins or the exact same vase out of a chest with each visit to the same tomb would be boring.

Now that Catherine has the relic, it's time to return to Xi Yuan to hand it over and receive her rightfully earned rewards.

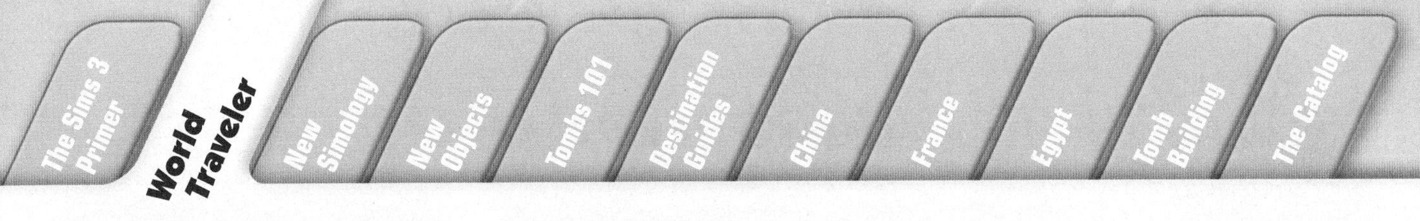

Sure enough, Xi Yuan happily takes the relic and rewards Catherine. Her visa level goes up to 1. Now she can stay in China for five days on her next visit.

It is starting to get late, so Catherine heads back to base camp. There, she can get a good night's sleep in a real bed and make breakfast in the kitchen in the morning. Tomorrow, she will finish her first excursion with some skill-building, play time, and socializing.

Day Three

After taking care of morning rituals such as eating, showering, and using the restroom, Catherine heads back to the city to do a little shopping. She goes to the bookstore and buys Martial Arts Vol. 1: Wax On Philosophic. This book will teach her the Martial Arts skill and get her started on a journey of physical and mental enlightenment.

I find a nice bench or sofa somewhere and plop Catherine down to do some reading. As soon as she finishes that book, she is a level 1 martial artist.

At the completion of the book, Catherine gets on her bicycle and rides to the Phoenix Martial Arts Academy. There is martial arts equipment here—a Training Dummy and a Board Breaker for her to work with so she can raise that skill level up to 2 before the day is out. Because level 1 cannot use the Board Breaker, Catherine works on the Training Dummy first.

Once she reaches level 2, Catherine gives the Board Breaker a few good whacks before it gets too late.

TIP

Working on the Martial Arts skill decreases Hygiene. It doesn't take long before Catherine is Smelly. Fortunately, she can use the shower at the Martial Arts Academy before heading back into the Forbidden City.

Back at the Forbidden City, Catherine returns to the general store to buy the Training Dummy. I want her to keep working on this skill. The purchased dummy is immediately transferred to the household inventory where it can be placed on the lot in Buy Mode once she returns home. I also buy some Golden Dragon Fireworks. You'll see why in a moment.

Because Catherine has a wish to meet a local, I mingle with the folks walking around the Forbidden City. A family swims in one of the pools. Catherine approaches the little boy on the edge of the pool and engages in friendly conversation, which satisfies the wish. There are some easy Lifetime Happiness points right there.

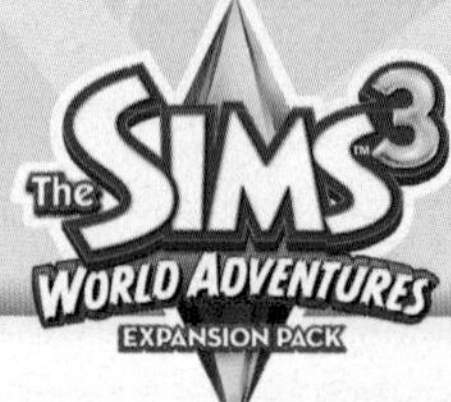

Once Catherine is on friendly terms with the little boy, a new interaction appears in the social menu: Learn Song. When I choose this, the little boy starts teaching Catherine a song.

Catherine follows along with the boy, singing parts of it back to him until she has the song down. Now Catherine can share this song with other Sims. And not only that, but singing with the little boy was a lot of fun for Catherine. She's in a great mood. The trip is almost over, so let's end it with a bang and see if we cannot get Catherine all the way to the Having a Blast moodlet.

Catherine places the fireworks on the lawn in the Forbidden City. I choose the Launch interaction on the fireworks and Catherine automatically stands back. I stand back, too, in a sense, by pulling the camera all the way out to map view. This gives me a great view of the fireworks.

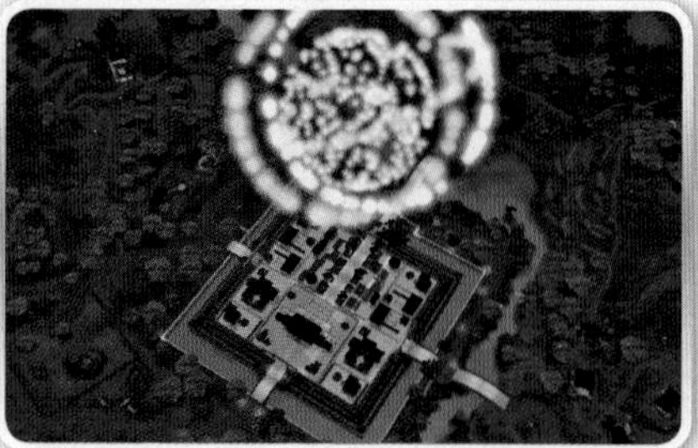

What a great way to end a first vacation.

Back at Home

Catherine arrives home, fulfilled. She cannot go on another trip for at least 24 hours, but that's okay. There is plenty to do at home, such as finish a novel and continue practicing the Painting skill. Plus, she did buy a recipe to bring home: Egg Rolls. After reading the recipe for a few minutes, she's got it down and can add the exotic dish to her library of recipes. In fact, because she's feeling a wee bit peckish, why not fry up a trio of egg rolls now and remember the trip?

Within just three days, Catherine has had fun exploring a tomb, making new friends, developing an all-new skill, and lighting fireworks, and she's even brought home some treasures. In fact, she can hardly wait to go back to China and see what else lies just beneath the surface. But France is so tempting this time of year...

...and wouldn't it be fun to play snake charmer in the markets of Egypt? Come on, 24 hours, hurry it up!

New Simology

World Adventures adds more than just new real estate for you to explore; it offers all-new traits, wishes, skills, and more that only deepen the possibilities for your Sims' drives and dreams. Now, Sims have new avenues to express their artistry—photography. New Sims just moving in can have adventure and discipline as pieces of their personalities. There are also new wishes—both large and small—that extend far beyond the borders of a Sim's hometown.

This chapter charts the new building blocks for a Sim's lifetime adventure. But choosing to incorporate many of these new traits or wishes into your Sim's life does not only affect their travels. The skills they develop or the goals they aspire to fulfill also influence behavior, attitude, and living back on their own lots in their home cities.

Personality

A Sim's personality is made up of many factors, from the traits you select when in the final stages of the Create a Sim tool to the dreams and wishes you promise them as they enjoy their days. *World Adventures* introduces many meaningful ways to further define them. *The Sims 3* Primer that opened this book explained all of the traits, moodlets, skills, and wishes that come with the base game. Use that primer in conjunction with New Simology to understand how to develop the personalities of Sims who come into being with *World Adventures* as part of the equation.

New Traits

As you know, when you create a Sim (or when a Sim not yet an adult ages up) you give them a series of up to five traits. These traits are the foundation for their personality. Traits affect so much, so choose carefully. These new traits are designed to affect a Sim who will be going on an adventure from time to time, but these traits affect more than just behaviors and activities while a Sim is on a vacation. After all, giving a Sim a trait to help them in their travels means one less trait that could prove beneficial for their careers or the original skill sets.

Adventurous 

Description: Adventurous Sims enjoy traveling and exploration more than other Sims, can go on new trips sooner, and improve their visa levels more quickly.

Benefits: Adventurous Sims get a positive Adventuring moodlet while on vacation.

Shortcomings: Sim tends to get the Stir Crazy moodlet faster, which prevents them from lazing indoors for extended periods of time.

Unique Features: The Recently Traveled moodlet does not last as long for an Adventurous Sim, meaning they can skip off on another trip sooner than other Sims.

Disciplined 

Description: Disciplined Sims do not fool around. They have the dedication and perseverance to become the best martial artists in town.

Benefits: Sim learns the Martial Arts skill noticeably faster and has an increased chance of successfully sparring. Disciplined Sims developing the Martial Arts skill also fail less at using the Board Breaker or the Training Dummy.

Shortcomings: None

Unique Features: Any martial arts–related activities provide fun for a Disciplined Sim.

Photographer's Eye 

Description: Sims with the Photographer's Eye naturally learn Photography more quickly than other Sims and tend to earn more Simoleons for the photos they take.

Benefits: Sims with this trait develop the Photography skill faster and their photographs are worth more.

Shortcomings: None

Unique Features: Sims with the Photographer's Eye trait have a series of new socials such as "Talk About Cameras," "Discuss SLR Cameras," and "Rant about Dark Rooms." These help establish relationships with other Sims who are interested in Photography or have the Photographer's Eye trait.

Hidden Traits

The above three traits are selectable when you are finishing up Create a Sim or adding a new trait to a Sim who is aging up. However, there are two hidden traits that you cannot select: French Culture and East Asian Culture. These traits are inherent in the non-player

Sims who live in their respective destinations. These traits are also slowly picked up by a Sim the longer they remain in France or China.

These traits affect behavior when in the related destination. For example, when in China, a Sim with the East Asian Culture trait will always eat with chopsticks. The French Culture trait causes a Sim with the hidden trait to greet other Sims in France with the double-cheek kiss.

These traits are passed down genetically. If a Sim marries a non-player Sim from France or China and has a baby, there is a 70 percent chance the baby will acquire the hidden culture trait.

Existing Traits

So, when creating a new Sim or aging up a Sim who will go on travels, should you automatically load them up with these new traits? Not necessarily. You need to find a balance, because Sims still spend a great deal of time back in Sunset Valley or Riverview. That's where they need to work or concentrate on developing the original skills, such as Charisma. (Not that the original skills cannot be developed abroad. It's just that you are likely to be a little keener on exploring a tomb than painting or playing the guitar.)

Some of the existing traits are quite useful when traveling, too. The Athletic trait, for example, isn't going to hurt you when you develop the Martial Arts skill or try to move giant statues inside the tombs. The Loves the Outdoors trait will consistently help boost your Sim's mood while they are on a trip because so much time will indeed be spent outside of a house or building. The Angler trait will help your Sim with fishing—and there are lots of new places to fish while on a trip.

So, find the right balance for you. If you know you want to dig into the new Photography skill and take photos both home and abroad, then by all means, give your new Sim the Photographer's Eye skill. If you want to travel all the time, then the Adventurous trait is also extremely beneficial. But guess what? If you fill three of the five available trait slots for an adult Sim with the new traits, you are going to miss out on all the benefits of the existing traits that help with careers and skills. That may make life back home a little tougher than necessary.

New Wishes

Back home in Sunset Valley and Riverview, Sims have litany of wishes that flash through their heads. Raise Painting skill level. Kiss a Sim. Land a promotion. Grow a great plant. Well, just because a Sim flies to a new destination doesn't mean their wishful desires take a vacation, too. While Sims are exploring new destinations, they regularly dream up new wishes. These wishes help define their trips, as your Sims often crave to meet locals, learn songs, possess exotic relics, and try something fun (and sometimes dangerous) in the underworld tombs.

Of course, there are two types of wishes—Lifetime Wishes and the day-to-day wishes. *World Adventures* introduces all-new wishes in both categories. When wishes of either category are fulfilled, the Sim earns Lifetime Happiness points. These are traded in for all sorts of perks and new objects called Lifetime Rewards. *World Adventures* adds new Lifetime Rewards, which are listed following the lists of new wishes.

Lifetime Wishes

Lifetime Wishes are determined by the traits you select for your Sim. *World Adventures* introduces eight new Lifetime Wishes. As you might expect, choosing the Disciplined trait is likely to cause one of the martial arts–related Lifetime Wishes to appear. The Photographer's Eye will inspire the appearance of the Visionary or World-Class Gallery Lifetime Wishes.

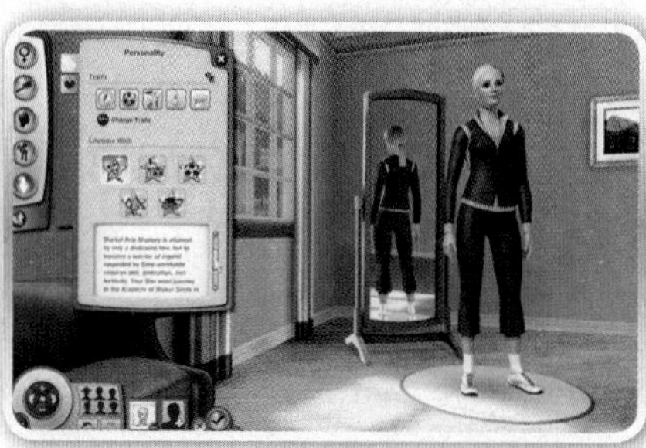

Picking a Lifetime Wish in Create a Sim

One thing you must be aware of when selecting a Lifetime Wish new to *World Adventures* is that if you are the kind of player who zeroes in on satisfying the Lifetime Wish, doing so completely alters the trajectory of your Sim's life. The Seasoned Traveler Lifetime Wish, for example, is all about traveling to new destinations. To satisfy this wish, you won't be spending a lot of time at home. So you need to be vigilant about household funds to make sure your Sim can keep jetting off into the horizon.

Seasoned Traveler 

- Max Out Visa Level for All Three Destinations

Sophisticated Sims who travel extensively and spend time in foreign locales become worldly and wise, but only those who work hard at earning the respect and trust of the locals can get a coveted max level visa in France, China, and Egypt. Through opportunities and adventures abroad your Sim will befriend others and become welcome wherever they go.

> **TIP**
>
> The speediest way to fulfill this wish is to concentrate on exploring tombs and going on adventures for Sims. Collecting and photography? That can wait!

Physical Perfection 

- Master the Martial Arts Skill
- Master the Athletic Skill

On the path to Martial Arts mastery, Sims must hone their bodies and minds through challenges and rigorous training. Your Sim must seek out the Academy in Shang Simla to start practicing the basic moves. Only through hard work and dedication will your Sim sculpt the perfect body and attain the skills necessary to rise in the ranks of Martial Arts mastery.

> **TIP**
>
> Training with equipment and battling other martial artists will quickly develop the Martial Arts skill. But what about the Athletic skill? The Athletic skill raises along with the Martial Arts skill, so you learn both at once by doing Martial Arts.

Visionary 

- Master the Photography Skill
- Master the Painting Skill

Whether slowly crafted through the precise stroke of the brush on canvas, or captured in a moment by the eye of the camera's lens, artistic works can evoke in Sims feelings of beauty, anger, excitement, and joy. Mastering the artistic skills of Painting and Photography is a sure path of happiness for Sims who value the creative arts above all else.

TIP

If this is your selected wish, grab a camera as soon as possible and start taking photos. Use the Photography section of this chapter to develop that skill. The Painting skill (which is detailed in *The Sims 3 Primer*) can be worked on abroad as well as at home. Look for easels at base camps or other community lots while at exotic destinations.

World-Class Gallery 

- Have a Current Collection of Photographs Worth at Least §25,000
- Have at Least 10 Photographs from Each Collection

Sims with keen aesthetic judgment value photographs of all sizes and subjects. Whether it's a beautiful foreign landscape or a candid portrait snapped on city streets, collectors have an eye for beauty and value. A World-Class Gallery is built by Sims who want a collection rivaled by none.

TIP

The Photography skill section of this chapter includes a table showing you all of the different photo collections. Use that table as a checklist for taking the necessary photos for this Lifetime Wish.

Private Museum 

- Have a Current Relic Collection Worth §20,000

Collectors and purveyors of the ancient arts have a keen eye for beauty, detail, and value. Relics of all kinds interest them, and they actively seek out new acquisitions in tombs, markets, and dig sites to expand their collections. Only the most persistent and dedicated Sims possess a Private Museum.

TIP

This Lifetime Wish is best satisfied by both exploring the tombs in search of treasure and constantly checking the inventory of relic merchants at the markets. Their inventories change with every visit!

Martial Arts Master 

- Master Martial Arts Skill
- Achieve Grand Master Rank

Martial Arts Mastery is attained by only a dedicated few, but to become a warrior of legend respected by Sims worldwide requires skill, dedication, and fortitude. Your Sim must journey to the Academy of Shang Simla to compete in the Tournament Sparring Matches in order to earn the rank of Grand Master.

TIP

Use the Martial Arts skill section of this chapter to see how to best develop this talent as well as what is necessary to work your way up to the rank of Grand Master. It's not as hard as you may think!

Bottomless Nectar Cellar 

- Have a Current Collection of Nectar Bottles Worth at Least §10,000
- Have at Least 50 Bottles of Nectar in Your Nectar Cellar

High-quality nectar comes with a heavy price tag, but Sims of discerning taste know that it is worth the cost. Nectar obsessed Sims seek to stock a cellar full of nectar racks with the finest, tastiest juices infused with the sweetest fruits, and be known by friends as a true connoisseur of fine nectar.

TIP

To achieve this dream, you must work on the Nectar Making skill, which is detailed later in this chapter. But in addition to creating fine nectars, you must also create a cellar beneath your house to store all of the goods.

Great Explorer 

- Fully Explore 6 Tombs in Each Location

With a thirst for knowledge and experience, explorers are always in search of their next big adventure! Though they face hardships untold and dangers unnumbered, nothing will stop explorers from traversing the deepest, darkest tombs found around the world.

TIP

The best way to fulfill this Lifetime Wish is to spread your travel around each destination and always seek new adventures. Check the Adventure Board and answer the phone when it rings. And when you do dive into tombs, be on the lookout for secret doors and whatnot. Until a Sim discovers the final room in a tomb, it is not considered cleared.

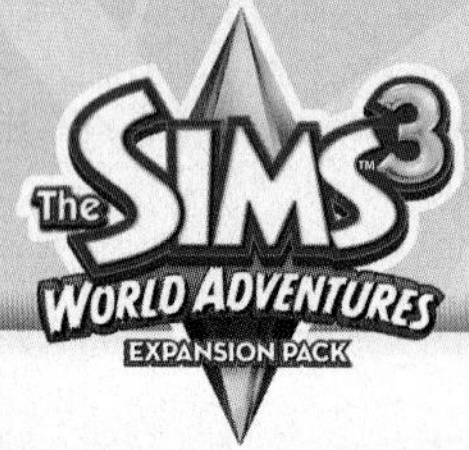

Wishes

As Sims visit destinations and explore, they come up a new stream of wishes related to travel. These new wishes mingle with the wishes you promise (or dismiss) back in Sunset Valley or Riverview. The decision to jettison promised wishes from back home to accommodate incoming travel wishes is entirely yours. Pursuing wishes related to setting foot in Egypt, France, or China can send your travels off in new, exciting directions. But you have to make room if you do promise these wishes, which means dismissing little dreams that might not have been too difficult to achieve back home.

What follows is a complete list of all of the new wishes your Sims potentially consider while on one of their adventures:

WISHES

Wish
MARTIAL ARTS
Beat someone in a ranked sparring match.
Break *X* boards.
Break a space rock board.
Lose a sparring match against someone.
Meditate.
Meditate for *X* hours.
Spar with someone.
Train with Board Breaker.
Train with Training Dummy.
Visit a dojo.
Win *X* ranked sparring matches in a row.
Win martial arts tournament.
NECTAR MAKING
Build a nectar cellar.
Buy some nectar.
Drink a perfect bottle of nectar.
Drink nectar older than *X* years old.
Drink nectar worth more than *X* Simoleons.
Drink some nectar.
Grow some nectar grapes.
Learn to make nectar.
Make *X* bottles of nectar.
Make nectar with [fruit].
Make nectar worth at least *X* Simoleons.
Make some nectar.
Visit a Nectary.

WISHES, CONTINUED

Wish
PHOTOGRAPHY
Take *X* photos.
Take a photo of [subject].
Take photo of someone.
Take photo worth at least *X* Simoleons.
TOMB EXPLORATION
Defeat the mummy.
Disarm a trap.
Enter a room with a disarmable trap.
Enter a room with a hidden door.
Enter a tomb room.
Escape from the mummy.
Escape from tomb I'm in.
Explore a dive well.
Fear level above *X*.
Find *X* Simoleons more worth of relics.
Find a hidden door.
Find a relic.
Find relic worth at least *X* Simoleons.
Find some ancient coins.
Find some phat lewtz.
Fully explore a tomb.
Go exploring in a tomb.
Open a treasure chest.
See a dive well.
See a mummy.
Sleep in tomb.
TRAVEL
Buy first vacation home in China.
Buy first vacation home in Egypt.
Buy first vacation home in France.
Call someone at home.
Eat a good luck fortune cookie.
Get Chinese visa to level *X*.
Get Egyptian visa to level *X*.
Get French visa to level *X*.
Go inside a pyramid.
Go on a trip.
In China.
In Egypt.

WISHES, CONTINUED

Wish
TRAVEL, CONTINUED
In France.
Invite Sim to stay with you (from another place).
Meet a foreign Sim.
Return home from trip.
See the Terracotta Army.
Travel for at least *X* consecutive days.
Travel with someone.
Visit a French café.
Visit a market.
Visit a museum in France.
Visit a pyramid.
Visit a Scholar's Garden.
Visit China.
Visit Egypt.
Visit France.
Visit the Forbidden City.
Visit the Sphinx.
Visit the Temple of Heaven.
Visit the Temple of Queen Hatshepsut.
WooHoo in tent with someone.
MISC.
Eat Mummy Snack.
I'm a mummy.
Call someone.
Have Adventurous Trait.
Have Disciplined Trait.
Have Photographer's Eye Trait.
Practice Skill.

New Moodlets

By now, you understand how the mood system works—your overall mood is determined by a series of smaller, fleeting emotions called moodlets. There are three types of moodlets: positive, negative, and neutral. Strive to do things that give your Sims positive moodlets so they can keep banking Lifetime Happiness points.

MOODLETS

Moodlet	Effect	Duration	Description
			POSITIVE
Adventuring	10	240	Moodlet earned by Adventurous Sims only for 4 hours the first time they visit a new destination, or for an unlimited amount of time while exploring tombs (until leaving the tomb).
Blessing of the Sphinx	25	2,880	Seek this blessing from the Sphinx to cure your mummy problems. Dispels Mummy's Curse.
Boosted Courage	25	180	Drink the Potion of Liquid Courage to dispel fear and feel safe and secure.
Carbed Up!	35	180	Eating Pemmican (an Adventure Reward) satisfies more than hunger.
Eye Candy	10	30	Sim is near another Sim with the Eye Candy LTR.
Full of Life	50	480	Sims who drink fine nectar made by a level 10 Nectar Maker get not only a mood boost, but extended life.
Good Memories	10	180	Sims who reminisce upon photos earn this happy moodlet.
Good Nectar	Varied	480	Imbibing fine nectar makes a Sim feel good. The better the bottle, the bigger the boost.
Love Is in the Air	10	Varied	Incense from the French incense holder inspires feeling of amour.
Meditative Focus	None	15	Earned by meditating, this moodlet helps Sims develop skills faster, win chess matches, do better at school or work, and even thwart tomb traps.
Neuronic Synergy	10	Varied	Incense from the Chinese incense holder boosts mental capacity.
Promising Fortune	10	180	A positive fortune cookie from the Fortune Cookie Maker leaves Sims feeling hopeful.
Saw Great Fireworks Show	10	960	Watching awesome fireworks makes Sims squeal with delight.
Slept Like a King/Queen	Varied	Varied	Sleeping in the Sultan's Tabernacle inspired wonderful rest. The longer the sleep, the longer and stronger the moodlet.
Snake Kiss	25	120	Sim has developed Snake Charming enough that the snake will allow the Sim to kiss the top of the snake's head.
Totally Mellow	10	Varied	Burning Egyptian incense has a soothing effect on Sims. Dispels stress.
Went to [Destination]	15	2,880	When coming home from one of the three destinations, Sims enjoy this cozy moodlet.
Wonderous Collection	Varied	15	As Sims complete relic collections, the potency of this moodlet grows.
Zen	20	Varied	Enter the Chinese garden to earn this moodlet. It helps Sims learn Martial Arts faster as long as it lasts. It also helps students do homework faster.
			NEGATIVE
Bad Nectar	Varied	120	Poor quality nectar leaves a sour taste in a Sim's mouth.
Fear	None	Varies	Getting spooked by bugs or a mummy has a negative impact on a Sim.
Forebording Fortune	-10	120	If a Sim gets an unfortunate fortune cookie, they feel down. A good fortune cheers them up, though.
Foul Food	-25	45	Snob Sims do not like dried food. Not one bit.
Hurt Hand	-25	180	Failing at the Board Breaker while performing martial arts hurts!
Knocked Out	-25	30	A Sim can be rendered unconscious by a trap or a mummy attack.
Mummy's Curse	-25	20160	If a mummy attack ends in a curse, this deadly moodlet starts counting down. Quick, to the Sphinx!
Snake Bite!	-25	45	A bite from a snake in the snake charmer basket really stings.
Soaked	-5	120	Getting drenched in a dive well may help a Sim with fire traps, but it still leaves them feeling all wet.

NOTE

Many of these moodlets have positive effects on your Sims beyond making them happy. The incense-related moodlets can boost romance and concentration. The Zen moodlet helps with developing the Martial Arts skill or working on homework.

Brownie Bites

You can buy three objects to inspire special moodlets: incense holders. Each destination has its own specific incense holder that, when ignited in a Sim's presence, conjures up a specific positive moodlet. China's Honorary Incense Holder of Jun Pao brings about the Neuronic Synergy moodlet, which helps with learning and development. France's Little Boy Soldier's Incense Holder causes the Love is in the Air moodlet, which improves the romance possibility of social interactions. Egypt's Mazzamesses II Incense Holder brings about the Totally Mellow moodlet, which negates stress.

To get the moodlet, place the incense holder in the same room as the Sim and ignite it. After a few minutes within close proximity of the incense holder, the Sim experiences the specific moodlet related to the incense. Keep in mind, lighting incense costs per use. The Egyptian incense is §35. Chinese incense is §85. French incense is §120.

Traveling Moodlets

When you whisk your Sims off on a vacation, they leave a lot of moodlets back home. Only a fraction of moodlets remain in effect when you touch down in your new destination. Here are the moodlets that survive travel:

- Betrayed
- Blessing of the Sphinx
- Charitable
- Completely at Ease
- Divine Meal
- First Kiss
- First Romance
- Heartbroken
- Honor Student
- Mummy's Curse
- It's a Boy
- It's a Girl
- It's Twins
- It's Triplets
- Just Married
- Mourning
- Newly Engaged
- Nice Nails
- Relaxed
- Smooth Skin
- Rejuvenated
- Threw a Great Party

Tip

The moodlets associated with treatments from the Day Spa travel with you to your destination. Because being in a good mood helps with everything from skill development to socializing, why not stop into the spa before departing on a trip? Splurging for one of the big packages can result in a positive moodlet that lasts for the entire trip.

Lifetime Rewards

When your Sims' spirits are high or they satisfy wishes large and small, they earn Lifetime Happiness points. These points measure fulfillment. The more you have, the happier your Sim. But these points are not just for show. Lifetime Happiness points can be traded in for Lifetime Rewards, which are special perks and cool objects that will undoubtedly help your Sim.

Use this list of Lifetime Rewards to see what's possible for Sims who are truly blessed with a player like you. The more wishes you fulfill and the happier you keep your Sim, the more of these rewards they can possess.

LTR List

Lifetime Reward	Benefit	Cost
Carefree	Sim gains Fun 25% faster than normal.	20,000
Eye Candy	Sim has an aura that gives everyone near them the "Eye Candy" moodlet (unless there is a better environment moodlet already). Sim glows frequently with sparkles.	5,000
Prepared Traveler	When this Sim is in a group going to a destination, the maximum possible duration of the trip is increased.	10,000
Learned Relic Hunter	Increases the chance of finding higher value collectibles and relics.	15,000
Change of Taste	Allows the player to reselect a Sim's favorites, like food or music.	5,000
Meditative Trance Sleep	Sim has learned how to get more out of sleeping and now requires less sleep per day.	30,000
No Bills Ever	Any household that has a Sim with this reward no longer receives bills.	15,000
Jetsetter	Any trips to destinations that include this Sim cost less.	5,000
No Jealousy	Other Sims never get jealous when this Sim does anything that would cause envy.	10,000
Inappropriate but In a Good Way	This Sim isn't affected by inappropriateness (i.e. can eat out of host's fridge, sleep in their beds, etc).	5,000
Stone-Hearted	This Sim isn't super close to anyone, and deep inside isn't as affected by those around them. Sim does not receive these moodlets: Rejected by Ex, Rejected First Kiss, Rejected Proposal, Betrayed, Heartbroken, Lost a Friend, Mourning, Witnessed Betrayal, Humiliated, Embarrassed, Enemy!, Offended.	10,000

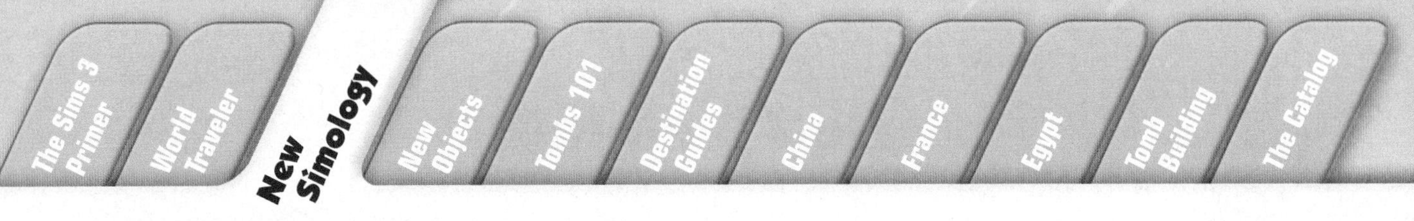

NOTE

Not all of these Lifetime Rewards are specific to new activities in *World Adventures*. For example, the No Bills Ever reward is universal—it simply removes the cash drain of bills. However, that will certainly help you save Simoleons for additional trips.

Skills

You cannot define a Sim's lifetime only by fulfilled wishes and the company they keep. Sims desire to grow in other ways, too. Careers are one way in which a Sim's life is given structure and meaning, but there are no new careers in *World Adventures*. (And why would there be? These are vacations!) Another way Sims are defined is by the skills they develop and hopefully master.

World Adventures introduces three new skills: Martial Arts, Nectar Making, and Photography. The only way to start developing these skills is through travel. You cannot start the Martial Arts skill without leaving home. Sure, you could buy a book about Martial Arts and then read it on the comfort of your sofa back in Riverview—but you still had to at least visit China to buy the book from the merchant.

Development

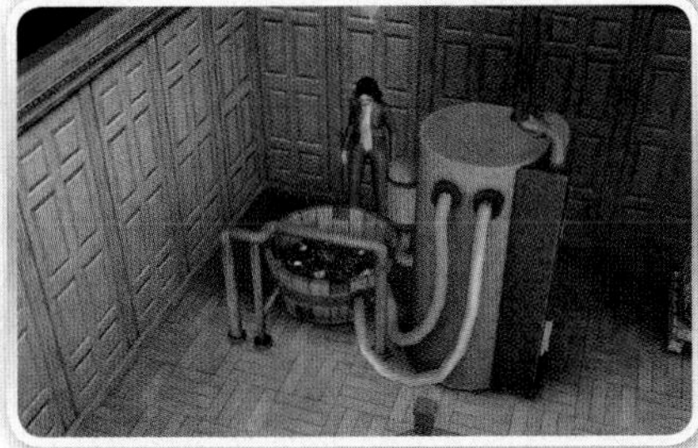

There is no limit on who can learn any of these skills. Certain traits make it easier to develop some of these skills. For example, the Photographer's Eye accelerates the development of the Photography skill. But specific traits are not required to start learning a skill. All it requires is drive and time.

There are a handful of ways to develop a skill. Some are learned and further refined by reading books related to the skill. Some skills are developed by simply doing. Working with a Training Dummy builds the Martial Arts skill. Wielding a camera around the neighborhood develops the Photography skill. Squashing grapes in your cellar with your very own Nectar Maker improves the Nectar Making skill.

Use these tips to speed skill development:

- Sims in a good mood develop a skill slightly faster.
- Expensive equipment does help develop a skill. The cheap camera suffices for first developing the Photography skill. But as you get into the top half of the skill, you really should splurge on a better camera.
- Use community equipment when just starting out to save a little cash. You can use Training Dummies and Board Breakers at the dojo in China for free while visiting. The same goes for the public Nectar Maker at France's Nectary.
- Unless you feel pressed for time to start developing a new skill, save books on the subject for skill levels higher than 2. Reading a book reduces the amount of time needed to attain the next level. However, this is within reason. Reading the beginner's level skill book for Martial Arts is not going to do you a tremendous amount of good when working toward level 9.

Check the bookstores in each destination for volumes that will help with skill development.

Martial Arts

Sims desiring strong minds as well as bodies should consider traveling to China to learn the new Martial Arts skill. This skill requires serious training, not just on specific martial arts equipment, but also in sparring matches with other Sims. While much of this skill is developed in China due to the prevalence of other Sims who share it, it can be practiced at home if you buy equipment.

Acquire by: Reading Martial Arts book, practicing on Training Dummy

Development tools: Books, Training Dummy, Board Breaker, Sparring, Tournaments

Available ages: Teen, Young Adult, Adult, Elder

Development Benefits

There are two ways to begin learning the Martial Arts skill—and both exist only in China. The first way is to purchase a Martial Arts skill book from the bookstore in the Forbidden City.

The other way to start learning the Martial Arts skill is to practice on a Training Dummy. Direct your Sim to the Training Dummy and choose the Practice interaction. Your Sim will start attacking the Training Dummy, but badly at first. Stick with it, though, because over time, your Sim will get better. Soon, they are smacking that Training Dummy around like nobody's fool.

TIP

One of the big benefits of developing the Martial Arts skill is that your Sim will almost always win in a fight (against a Burglar, etc.). When your Sim is at the top of the skill, they never lose a fight.

Once your Sim reaches level 2 of the skill, they can begin training on the Board Breaker. This set-up allows them to practice a concentrated chop on a board placed between two blocks. You can place various materials on the Board Breaker. The easiest to break is the foam board, so even though you can try any of the boards, it's best to start here. As you advance, try out the other boards, such as balsa wood, oak, thin stone, and space rock.

NOTE

Once you are breaking oak boards, you'll notice other Sims crowding around to watch your feats of strength.

CAUTION

Failing a board break actually hurts your Sim—they get the negative Hurt Hand moodlet. To get rid of the moodlet, you need to wait three hours until your hand feels better. So, don't get too cocky with the Board Breaker!

When your Sim reaches level 5 of the skill, they unlock the new Meditate action. Meditation has multiple benefits. The first is that meditating improves mood. The Sim earns the new Meditative Focus moodlet, which is positive. The longer you meditate, the longer that moodlet lasts.

TIP

Loner Sims achieve the benefits of meditation faster than any other Sim.

Meditating also removes many negative moodlets: Anxious to Advance, Bored, Creeped Out, Disappointed, Disgusted, Embarrassed, Horrified, Humiliated, Mourning, Offended, Rejected, Rude Awakening, Stir Crazy, Stood Up, and Upset. All can be banished by meditating. You just need to do it long enough to remove those moodlets, so make sure you have a little time before attempting to meditate a bad moodlet away.

CAUTION

Absent-Minded, Excitable, and Neurotic Sims require additional time to achieve the benefits of meditation.

TIP

Visit the garden in China to get the Zen moodlet. While you are totally Zen, you develop the Martial Arts skill faster.

After meditating for a very long time, the Sim starts to actually float! They have hit the maximum Meditative Focus. This opens up a new interaction: Zeneport. Click on an open spot on the map and the Sim will be zapped to the new location. However, teleporting uses up all of the focus. It removes the Meditative Focus moodlet.

One of the greatest benefits of Meditating is that the effects of the Meditative Focus moodlet are universally awesome. Having this moodlet active means your Sim will develop a skill faster, do better at work or school, and even improve your performance on an adventure. There is no downside to meditating except for the consumption of time.

Belts

As you improve the Martial Arts skill, your Sim earns new belts. These belts physically appear on your Sim when they don the martial arts outfit, the gi, which is now an available outfit just like swimwear or formal wear. The belts do not have specific enhancements, but denote which skill level your Sim has.

BELTS

Skill Level	Belt
1	White
2	Yellow
3	Orange
4	Green
5	n/a
6	Blue
7	n/a
8	Brown
9	Black
10	Black & Gold

Sparring and Tournaments

When you reach level 1 of the Martial Arts skill, you get a new social interaction with other Sims who also possess the skill: Spar. When you challenge another Sim to spar, you both start a friendly match. This is not a knock-down, drag-out fight. This is sparring for the benefit of improving the skill. In fact, sparring with another Sim actually improves the skill faster than using a Training Dummy as long as you are a lower skill level than the other Sim in the sparring match.

Once you reach level 4 in the skill, you can enter tournaments. Tournaments only happen in China. To enter a tournament, pick up the phone and use the Challenge Spar Tournament Contender interaction. The opponent quickly arrives at your location. Now, left-click on the rival and choose the Challenge to a Ranked Sparring Match interaction. This begins the match.

If you are victorious enough, you get to advance a rank in the tournament. Fortunately, you cannot drop down a rank, no matter how many times you may fail a sparring match.

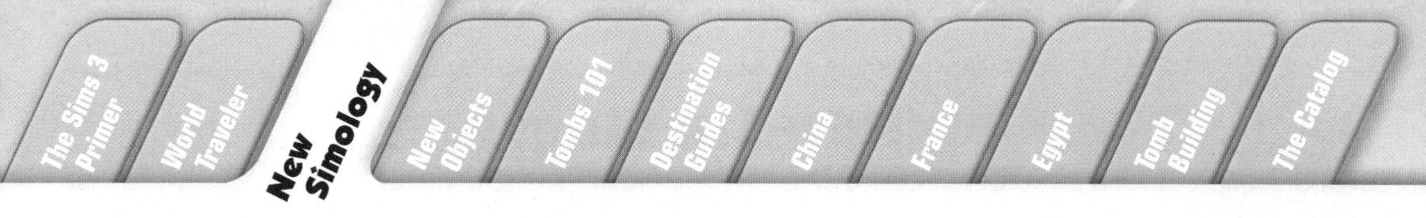

The top rank in the Martial Arts tournament is Grand Master, which helps fulfill one of the Lifetime Wishes.

Skill Challenges

- **Grand Master:** Reach tournament level 5 to attain the title "Grand Master."
- **Master of Meditation:** Meditate 150 hours to be known across the land as the "Master of Meditation"... or "MOM" for short.
- **Sim Fu King:** Participate in 75 sparring matches.
- **Timber Terminator:** Break at least 150 oak or greater toughness boards.

Nectar Making

When visiting France, be sure to check out the Nectary at the base of the rolling hills and sample a fine bottle. But don't just stop there. Head downstairs at the Nectary and check out the Nectar Maker. This piece of equipment allows you to make your very own nectar, which is not only a valuable beverage, but the effects of sharing the nectar with other Sims will definitely improve your social standing.

Acquire by: Using Nectar Maker, Reading Nectar Making book

Development tools: Nectar Maker, Books

Available ages: Teen, Young Adult, Adult, Elder

How to Make Nectar

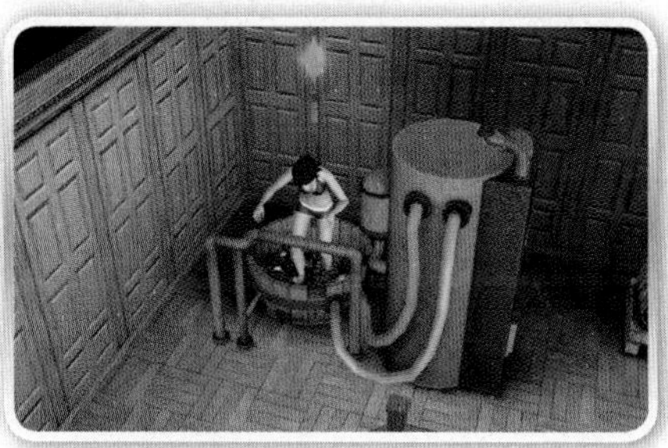

Whether using the Nectar Maker at the Nectary or one purchased at the general store in France and installed at home, the process of making nectar remains the same. First, place fruits in the Nectar Maker. You can use grapes or other fruits to create a satisfactory blend. Once the barrel of the Nectar Maker is full, squish the fruit into a pulp.

As soon as the fruit has been squished, it is time to use the Make Nectar interaction on the Nectar Maker. The machine starts to rattle and hum, turning the pulpy fruit into a liquid beverage. The machine then places the nectar into easily portable or storable bottles and you get to name the batch. As the process happens, the Sim develops the Nectar Making skill, as seen by the blue meter overhead.

NOTE

Make sure the Nectar Maker is clean before using it! If the Nectar Maker is dirty, it still works, but the nectar bottles produced are lower quality and not worth as much.

Any fruit grown via gardening or bought from a shop can be used to make nectar. However, there are now several varieties of grapes that can be grown. These grapes originate in France. The grapes are of differing color, growth speed, and rarity.

GRAPES

Grape	Rarity	Growth Speed
Cherimola Blan Grape	Common	Slow
Renoit Grape	Common	Slow
Avornalino Grape	Uncommon	Medium
Meloire Grape	Uncommon	Medium
Cranerlet Nuala Grape	Rare	Fast
Gralladina Fran Grape	Rare	Fast

NOTE

Some of the best grapes can be bought from the Special Merchant in France.

Though there are new grapes introduced in *World Adventures* specifically for nectar making, there are no specific recipes for making nectar; Sims just add grapes and other fruit to the Nectar Maker. Different combinations of grapes and fruits yield different results, but these impromptu recipes do not affect quality or bottle value. Instead, the quality of the nectar is determined by the quality of the ingredients and the skill level of the Sim making it. There are additional quality modifiers, such as upgrades a Handy Sim performs on the Nectar Maker, additional interactions earned by improving the Nectar Making skill, as well as benefit from skill challenges.

NOTE

Each destination has a new plant. Grapes are the new fruits for France. In Egypt, Sims will find pomegranates and cherries. China has plums and pomelos. Use these new fruits when making nectar and come up with some fun, flavorful batches.

TIP

Making nectar is a fun activity that almost always inspires a positive moodlet.

Development Benefits

As you develop the Nectar Making skill, you get better at making higher value batches of bottled nectar. Reaching specific skill levels also unlocks new interactions with the Nectar Maker. These interactions let you further customize your batches of nectar, such as making concentrated nectar for extra-fine batches or going for mass-produced nectar.

Make Concentrated Nectar (Level 4): This new interaction makes fewer bottles of nectar per session. However, the concentrated nectar is higher quality.

Mass Produce (Level 7): Making nectar with this interaction increases the number of bottles produced, but quality suffers.

Extended Nectaration (Level 9): Making nectar with this interaction takes significantly longer, but the resulting bottles are very high quality.

Nectar Maker Upgrades

The Handiness skill allows Sims to upgrade objects. The Nectar Maker can undergo three upgrades, depending on the Handiness skill level of the Sim performing the action.

Improved Pressing (Level 5): This upgrade increases the number of bottles made in a batch of nectar. If the upgrade fails, the Nectar Maker begins producing fewer bottles. To reverse this error, attempt to upgrade the Nectar Maker again.

Make Unbreakable (Level 6): When successful, this upgrade prevents the Nectar Maker from ever breaking again. If the upgrade fails, the Nectar Maker breaks and must be repaired.

Flavor Enhancement (Level 10): This upgrade improves the value of all nectar bottles produced by the Nectar Maker. If the upgrade fails, it decreases the value of produced bottles until the upgrade is attempted again and is successful.

TIP

Bottles of nectar made by level 10 Nectar Makers using Life Fruit can actually extend life by adding a few days to the aging process.

Skill Challenges

- **Nectar Master:** Make 200 bottles of nectar.
- **Flavorful Feet:** Squish 40 batches of fruit.
- **Vine Vizard:** Harvest 400 bunches of grapes and convert into nectar 400 bunches of grapes of any variety.
- **Mix Master:** Make 15 Nectar combinations.

NECTAR CELLAR

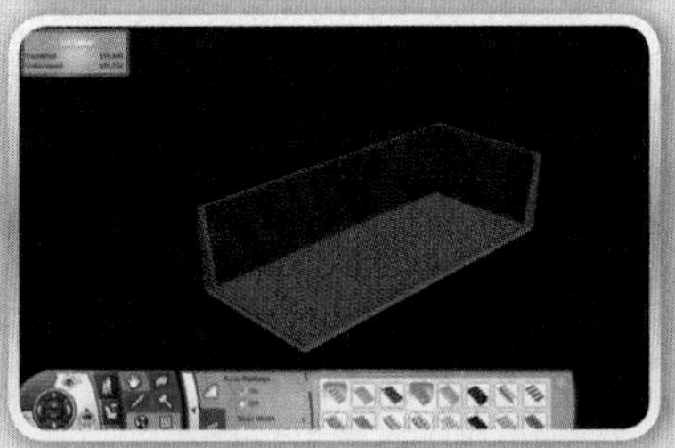

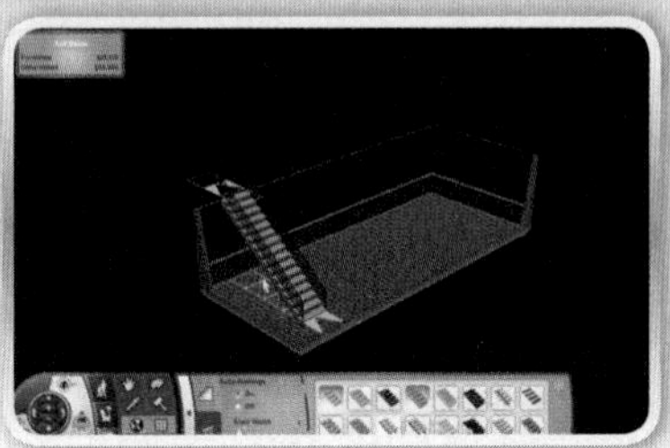

Nectar needs to be aged properly and the best place to do that is in a cellar. To help with building a basement or cellar on your lot, *World Adventures* adds a brand-new Basement tool to Build Mode that makes digging out an underground floor beneath your house as easy as laying a foundation.

To dig out a cellar, go into Build Mode and select the new tool. Now, holding the left mouse button, you can stretch a rectangle across your lot to designate the basement. The basement appears in blue. Once you release the mouse button, the basement is automatically dug. It has a perfectly flat floor and four nice walls.

What is does not have, though, is a means for getting down to the cellar where you will presumably store your nectar bottles or even your Nectar Maker. (You can also hide out in the cellar to avoid unwanted company—a nice side benefit.) Use the stairs tool from Build Mode to create a flight of stairs leading from the surface down to your new cellar. Make sure there is empty space on the floor above for the stairs to come up through.

NOTE

Once you have finished your cellar, feel free to decorate it just like a room in a house. Add some sort of floor and wall covering. Place some lights in there, too. The only thing you cannot add? Windows.

Photography

Much like Writing or Painting, Photography is a highly personalized skill that allows your Sims to express themselves through art. Sims can take photos while exploring a destination as well as back home in their city. The fact that Sims can make Simoleons off those photos is just icing on the cake—the neatly photographed cake, that is.

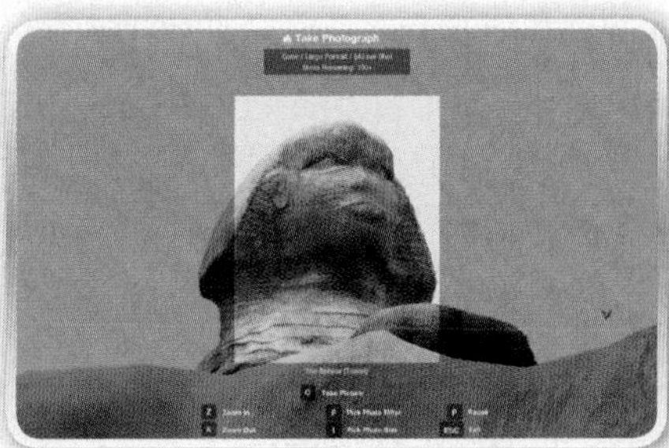

Acquire by: Reading Photography Book, Taking Photos

Development tools: Books, Camera

Available ages: Child, Teen, Young Adult, Adult, Elder

Development Benefits

To start taking photos, you need a camera. You can buy the basic SnapTastic Flimsy-Cam (§250) at all three destinations, but only the general store in Egypt sells the other two cameras. The medium-grade camera is the ChannonTec Outlaw SE (§850). The top-tier camera is the Hikon QX40di Gladiator (§3,250). The more expensive the camera, the more it costs to take a photo with it. Each camera has different properties that are important to budding photographers:

- **SnapTastic Flimsy-Cam:** This camera can only take small photos, which means it only takes low-value photos.

- **ChannonTec Outlaw SE:** The medium-level camera's photos are more valuable than the SnapTastic's. The camera can accommodate medium-sized photos and has minor zoom functionality.

- **Hikon QX40di Gladiator:** This camera allows large photos and has good zoom functionality. It takes the highest-value photos of all of the cameras. This is also the only camera that can take panoramic photos.

NOTE

Photography skill books are only available in Egypt.

CAUTION

You cannot develop the Photography skill past level 3 with books. Once you reach level 3, the skill can only be developed by taking photos.

To start developing this skill, you can either use a camera to take a photo or dive into a Photography skill book. Every time you take a photo, you develop the skill a little bit. At first, you get a moderate amount of skill for taking your photos. The first time you take a photo of a subject, you also earn a decent amount of skill-development. However, the higher the level of the skill, the more photos you need to take to move up to the next tier. And the more often you take a photo of the same subject, the less skill it is worth. If you try to take the same photo of a subject more than twice in a day, you receive zero skill boost for the third and every subsequent shot.

TIP

The more expensive the camera, the more skill you get for taking a shot, too. If you really want to rocket up the skill ladder, splurge on a spendier camera.

To take a photo, click on the camera in your personal inventory, select the Take Photo interaction when left-clicking on your Sim, or just press [⇧Shift] + [C]. The camera interaction is then added to the queue of actions, if there are any. The camera interaction screen then pops up. Use the mouse to frame the subject of your shot. The small, portrait frame is the default framing. Depending on your camera, you can select additional sizes with the on-screen commands. If your camera has zoom functionality, use either the on-screen commands or your mouse wheel. As you gain more skill levels, you also earn more filters for your photos, which you can choose before taking the shot. Click the mouse button to finally take the photo. The photo is then added to your collection.

Photos can be named and hung on the wall at home. Use the Reminisce interaction on a photo to get the Good Memories moodlet.

CAUTION

The lower your skill level, the greater the chance you may screw up the shot. Maybe a finger will slip into the frame. Perhaps the photo will be blurry. There is even a rare chance that a magic gnome will pop up and mess up the shot. When you reach level 5 of the skill, you no longer take bad photos.

As you increase your skill level, you get extra filters and aspect ratios for your shots. These extra filters affect the value of the photo, as does the selected size of the photo. Here are the levels in which you gain photo filters as well as the different value modifiers for filters and sizes:

FILTERS

Skill Level	Filter
2	Black & White
4	Sepia
9	Vignette
10	Panorama

PHOTO VALUES

Size	Multiplier
Medium	50%
Large	70%
Panorama	250%

New Simology

Photo Collections

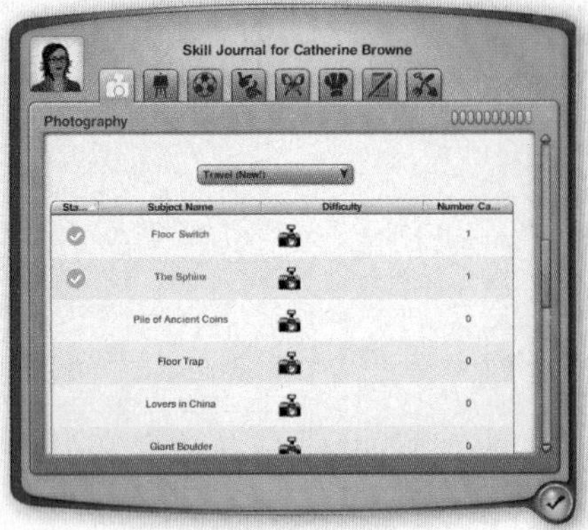

Almost every single photo that you take can be categorized into one of the photo collections. When you first start taking photos, no collections are noted in your Skill Journal. However, when you do take a photo that belongs to one, that collection is "unlocked" and appears in your Skill Journal. Each photo in a collection has a base value, which can be multiplied by the modifiers listed above (filter, size).

PHOTO COLLECTIONS

Subject	How to Capture	Value (in Simoleons)
ARCHITECTURE		
French Market	Photograph a market in France.	75
Market	Photograph a market at any destination.	160
Dojo	Photograph the Phoenix Martial Arts Academy in China.	210
Chinese Garden	Photograph the Scholar's Garden in China.	240
Bookstore	Photograph the bookstore in your home town.	290
Nectuary	Photography the Nectary in France.	230
City Hall	Photograph the City Hall in your home town.	140
Theatre	Photograph the theater in your home town.	150
Hospital	Photograph the hospital in your home town.	160
Stadium	Photograph the stadium in your home town.	140
Mausoleum	Photograph the mausoleum in the cemetery of your home town.	230
AROUND TOWN		
Car	Photograph a car.	1
Bicycle	Photograph a bicycle.	2
Picnic Basket	Photograph a picnic basket.	3
School	Photograph this building in your town.	80
Gym	Photograph this building in your town.	80
Diner	Photograph this building in your town.	80
Park	Photograph this site in your town.	80
Beach	Photograph this site in your town.	80
Bistro	Photograph this building in your town.	80

PHOTO COLLECTIONS, CONTINUED

Subject	How to Capture	Value (in Simoleons)
AROUND TOWN, CONTINUED		
Spa	Photograph this building in your town.	80
Grocery	Photograph this building in your town.	80
Places in Town	Photograph a career building in your town.	80
Police Car	Photograph a police car.	80
BEST OF CLASS		
Nectar Rack	Photograph a nectar rack.	180
Expensive Stereo	Photograph the top of the line stereo for a house.	190
Most Expensive Tent	Photograph the Sultan's Tabernacle tent.	200
Rich and Famous Metal	Photograph valuable metals.	25
Rich and Famous Car	Photograph an expensive car.	25
Money Tree	Photograph a Money Tree.	240
Omniplant	Photograph an Omniplant.	300
Lifesaver	Photograph a Sim at the top of the Medical career.	240
Master Criminal	Photograph a Sim at the top of the Criminal career.	300
Super Cop	Photograph a Sim at the top of the Law Enforcement career.	290
Iron Chef	Photograph a Sim at the top of the Culinary career.	280
Super Star	Photograph a Sim at the top of the Music career.	270
Champion of the Nation	Photograph a Sim at the top of the Military career.	290
Diplomat Extrordinaire	Photograph a Sim at the top of the Political career.	286
Limo	Photograph a limo.	293
CALAMITY		
Thievery	Photograph a Burglar stealing objects.	100
Social Worker	Photograph a Social Worker taking a child from a home.	100
Singed	Photograph a singed Sim.	100
Fight	Photograph 2 Sims fighting.	100
Repo Man	Photograph the Repo Man taking back objects.	100
Slapping	Photograph one Sims slapping another Sim.	100
Being Arrested	Photograph a Sim being arrested.	20
Sick Sim	Photograph a sick Sim.	20
Snake Fail	Photograph a snake biting a snake charmer.	75

PHOTO COLLECTIONS, CONTINUED

Subject	How to Capture	Value (in Simoleons)
CALAMITY, CONTINUED		
Soaked	Photograph a soaked Sim who just came out of a dive well.	10
COLLECTABLES		
Magic Gnome	Photograph any Magic Gnome in any position.	250
White Diamond	Photograph gem with any cut.	75
Topaz	Photograph gem with any cut.	75
Rainbow Gem	Photograph gem with any cut.	75
Luminorious Gem	Photograph gem with any cut.	75
Pink Diamond	Photograph gem with any cut.	75
Tiberium	Photograph gem with any cut.	130
Opal	Photograph gem with any cut.	65
Quartz	Photograph gem with any cut.	25
Geode	Photograph gem with any cut.	50
Space Rock	Photograph any meteorite.	50
Copper	Photograph smelted metal.	50
Iron	Photograph smelted metal.	50
Silver	Photograph smelted metal.	50
Gold	Photograph smelted metal.	50
Mummitomium	Photograph smelted metal.	80
Mercury	Photograph smelted metal.	50
Canopic Jar Collection	Photograph the complete collection of relics.	400
Dropa Stone Collection	Photograph the complete collection of relics.	350
Egypt Statue Set	Photograph the complete collection of relics.	425
China Statue Set	Photograph the complete collection of relics.	245
Dangerous Creatures Statue Set	Photograph the complete collection of relics.	300
EVERYDAY MOMENTS		
Maid	Photograph a maid.	5
Maid at Work	Photograph a maid working.	5
Four Sims Eating	Photograph four Sims eating a meal.	5
Three's a Crowd	Photograph three Sims in a frame.	5
Two's Company	Photograph two Sims in a frame.	5
Five Sims	Photograph five Sims in a frame.	5
Repair Sim	Photograph a repair service Sim.	5
Lovers at Night	Photograph 2 Sims being romantic during evening hours.	5
Cook Cooking	Photograph a Sim preparing a meal.	20

PHOTO COLLECTIONS, CONTINUED

Subject	How to Capture	Value (in Simoleons)
EVERYDAY MOMENTS, CONTINUED		
Politics Demonstration	Photograph a political rally.	35
Playing with Sprinkler	Photograph a Sim playing in a sprinkler.	50
Repair Man Reparing	Photograph a Repair Service Sim fixing an object.	5
Computing	Photograph a Sim using a computer.	6
Chessmatch	Photograph 2 Sim engaged in a chess match.	5
Fishing	Photograph a Sim fishing.	5
Photo of Photographer	Photograph a Sim photographing your Sim.	5
Gardening	Photograph a Sim gardening.	5
Sim Painting	Photograph a Sim painting.	5
Child Being Carried	Photograph a Sim carrying a child Sim.	5
Pizza Delivery	Photograph a Pizza Delivery Sim at a door.	5
Mail Carrier	Photograph a Mail Carrier Sim making the rounds.	100
Area Man/Area Woman	Photograph just 1 normal Sim.	20
Child Playing with Toybox	Photograph a child or toddler Sim playing with the toy box.	75
Child Playing with Easy Bake	Photograph a child or toddler Sim playing with the toy oven.	75
Police Officer	Photograph a Police Officer.	100
Firefighter	Photographer a Firefighter.	100
Babysitter	Photograph a Babysitter.	190
FAMILY		
Family Member	Photograph a family member.	5
Child	Photograph a child related to photographer.	2
Grandchild	Photograph a grandchild of the photographer.	2
Friend	Photograph a friend Sim of the photographer.	2
Dead Relatives	Photograph a ghost of a family member of the photographer.	65
Spouse	Photograph the spouse of the photographer.	2
Two of My Friends	Photograph 2 friends of the photographer.	2
Three of My Friends	Photograph 3 friends of the photographer.	4
Housemate	Photograph a housemate of the photographer.	5

PHOTO COLLECTIONS, CONTINUED

Subject	How to Capture	Value (in Simoleons)
FAMILY, CONTINUED		
Significant Other	Photograph a Sim that is romantic with photographer.	2
HOME SWEET HOME		
Gadgets Galore	Photograph at least 2 electronic objects.	5
Outdoor Stuff	Photograph at least 2 outdoor objects.	5
Bathroom Stuff	Photograph at least 2 bathroom objects.	5
Kitchen Kitsch	Photograph at least 2 kitchen objects.	5
Party Stuff	Photograph at least 2 party-related objects, such as balloons.	5
Decorations	Photograph at least 2 decorative objects.	5
Nice Garden	Photograph at least 2 garden objects.	5
Furniture	Photograph at least 2 furniture objects.	5
Something Yummy	Photograph a prepared recipe.	5
Toys and Hobbies	Photograph at least one toy or hobby-related object.	5
Baby Stuff	Photograph at least 2 baby-related objects, like a potty chair.	5
Toilet	Photograph a toilet.	1
Stuffed Bear	Photograph a stuffed bear toy.	0
PARANORMAL		
Doubly Dead	Photograph a ghost and mummy in the same frame.	300
Ghost	Photograph 1 ghost.	100
Ghost Problem	Photograph 2 ghosts.	200
Serious Ghost Problem	Photograph 3 ghosts.	300
Too Many Ghosts	Photograph 5 ghosts.	500
My Dead Spouse	Photograph the ghost of a dead spouse.	150
Haunted Objects	Photograph a haunted object.	200
My Dead Enemy	Photograph the ghost of an enemy Sim.	300
Mummy	Photograph a mummy.	30
Mummy Having a Snack	Photograph a mummy eat a Mummy Snack.	50
Wandering Ghost	Photograph a ghost just out and about.	30
Death of an NPC	Photograph a Service Sim or non-player Sim being taken by the Grim Reaper.	200
Death on Vacation	Photograph a Sim at a destination being taken by the Grim Reaper.	250
PLANTS		
White Rose	Photograph plant.	35
Red Rose	Photograph plant.	35

PHOTO COLLECTIONS, CONTINUED

Subject	How to Capture	Value (in Simoleons)
PLANTS, CONTINUED		
Sunflower	Photograph plant.	35
Hydrangea	Photograph plant.	35
Tomato Plant	Photograph plant.	35
Apple Tree	Photograph tree.	35
Grape Vine	Photograph any grape vine.	35
Lettuce Plant	Photograph plant.	35
Onion Plant	Photograph plant.	35
Potato Plant	Photograph plant.	35
Watermelon Vine	Photograph plant.	35
Lime Tree	Photograph tree.	35
Bell Pepper Plant	Photograph plant.	35
Garlic Plant	Photograph plant.	35
Death Flower Bush	Photograph plant.	35
Life Plant	Photograph plant.	35
Flame Fruit Plant	Photograph plant.	35
Cherimola Blan Grape Vine	Photograph a Cherimola Blan Grape Vine	35
Renoit Grape Vine	Photograph a Renoit Grape Vine	35
Avornalino Grape Vine	Photograph a Avornalino Grape Vine	35
Meloire Grape Vine	Photograph a Meloire Grape Vine	35
Gralladina Fran Grape Vine	Photograph a Gralladina Fran Grape Vine	35
Cranerlet Nuala Grape Vine	Photograph a Cranerlet Nuala Grape Vine	35
Pomegranate Tree	Photograph tree.	35
Plum Tree	Photograph tree.	35
SIMS IN MOTION		
Sims Dancing	Photograph at least 2 Sims dancing.	75
Sim Solo Dancing	Photograph a Sim dancing alone.	75
Sims Sparring	Photograph 2 Sims sparring.	150
Sim Breaking Boards	Photograph a Sim training with the Board Breaker.	75
Sim Running	Photograph a Sim running somewhere.	75
Sims Playing Catch	Photograph 2 Sims playing catch with a ball.	75
Pushing Statue	Photograph a Sim pushing a statue in a tomb.	75
Pleading to Sphinx	Photograph a Sim pleading to the Sphinx in Egypt.	75

PHOTO COLLECTIONS, CONTINUED

Subject	How to Capture	Value (in Simoleons)
SIMS IN MOTION, CONTINUED		
Martial Arts Training	Photograph a Sim training the Martial Arts skill with the Board Breaker or Training Dummy.	75
Playing Instrument	Photograph a Sim playing an instrument, like the guitar.	75
Sim Making Bed	Photograph a Sim making a bed—any bed.	75
Sim Swimming	Photograph a Sim swimming in any body of water.	75
Rummaging In a Trashcan	Photograph a Sim rummaging through a trashcan, such as a journalist.	75
Sim Putting Out Fire	Photograph a Sim extinguishing a fire that is out of control.	75
Working Out	Photograph a Sim working out on a treadmill or weight bench.	75
Making Nectar	Photograph a Sim using the Nectar Maker.	75
Clearing Pile	Photograph a Sim clearing a rubble pile.	75
Swing Set	Photograph a Sim using a swing set.	75
Air Guitar	Photograph a Sim strumming an air guitar.	75
Voyeur Couch Make Out	Photograph two Sims kissing on the couch.	120
STILL LIFE		
Generic	Generic photograph of an object.	1
Couch	Photograph a couch.	0
Flowers	Photograph some flowers.	3
Garden Decorations	Photograph some garden decorations.	1
Candles	Photograph some candles.	2
Tombstone	Photograph a tombstone or grave marker.	5
Nectar Bottle And Food	Photograph a nectar bottle and a prepared recipe.	5
Tissue Box	Photograph a tissue box.	0
Television	Photograph a television.	0
Video Game	Photograph a video game console.	0
TRAVEL		
Lovers in China	Photograph 2 Sims being romantic in China.	75
Lovers in France	Photograph 2 Sims being romantic in France.	75
Lovers in Egypt	Photograph 2 Sims being romantic in Egypt.	75
Trap	Photograph a trap in a tomb.	100
Pushable Statue	Photograph a pushable statue in a tomb.	120

PHOTO COLLECTIONS, CONTINUED

Subject	How to Capture	Value (in Simoleons)
TRAVEL, CONTINUED		
Giant Boulder	Photograph a giant bolder in a tomb.	120
Pile of Ancient Coins	Photograph an ancient coin pile in a tomb.	160
Floor Switch	Photograph a floor switch in a tomb.	190
Rubble Pile	Photograph a rubble pile in a tomb.	75
Treasure Chest	Photograph a treasure chest in a tomb.	150
Sphinx	Photograph the Giant Sphinx in Egypt.	180
Temple of the Dragon	Photograph the Temple of the Dragon in China.	350
Pyramid	Photograph a pyramid in Egypt.	300
Abu Simbel	Photograph the Tomb of Abu Simel in Egypt.	250
Snake Charmer	Photograph a snake charmer in Egypt.	200
Soulpeace Statue	Photograph the Soulpeace Statue in Egypt.	200
Anubis Torch	Photograph an Anubis Torch in Egypt.	200
Relic	Photograph any relic at any location.	75
Sarcophagus	Photograph a sarcophagus.	120
Shower in a Can Voyeur	Photograph a Sim using a Shower in a Can.	50

NOTE

Any photo that does not fit in any designated collection goes into the Miscellaneous photo collection.

Skill Challenges

- **Photography:** Capture 75 different subjects.
- **Architectural Eye:** Capture 10 unique landmarks.
- **Human Form Expert:** Capture 50 unique Sims.
- **Paparazzi:** Capture 60 different strangers.
- **Shutternut:** Complete 5 different photo collections.

Existing Skills

World Adventures does have some effects on the Fishing and Gardening skills, too. Each destination introduces new plants and fish that you can catch and then bring home. Use the following tables to track how you can further develop these two skills while traveling and what new plants and fish you will encounter abroad.

Fishing

Every new destination has bodies of water that invite a rod and reel. There are several new species of fish in *World Adventures*, and they are as exotic as the destinations you find them in, like Egypt's Mummy Fish. Not every fish can be caught right away. Some require higher levels of fishing skill to land. But as you fish while on vacation, you can continue to develop that useful skill and one day be able to reel in every type of fish.

FISHING

Fish	Location	Preferred Bait	Fishing Level to Catch	Rarity	Fertilizer Quality
Mummy Fish	Egypt	Pomegranate	8	Rare	Great
Crocodile	Egypt	Siamese Catfish	4	Uncommon	Good
Crawfish	France	Frogs	5	Uncommon	Good
Frogs	France	Cherimola Blan Grape	0	Common	Good
Snails	France	Renoit Grape	3	Uncommon	Good
Dragon Fish	China	Tancho Koi	9	Rare	Great
Doitsu Koi	China	Pomelo	0	Common	Good
Kawarimono Koi	China	Plum	3	Common	Good
Ochiba Koi	China	Pomelo	5	Uncommon	Good
Tancho Koi	China	Plum	7	Uncommon	Good

TIP

Each destination chapter contains a map that shows you exactly where to find the new fish.

Gardening

The fruits from the plants—especially the grapes—will help you keep producing sweet nectar at home with your very own Nectar Maker. Each destination has its own unique plants that bear fruit, which can then be transported home and planted on your own lot. If you visit Egypt and pocket a few pomegranates, for example, you could have your very own pomegranate orchard at home up and growing within days.

GARDENING

Plant	Destination	Rarity
Cherimola Blan Grape Vine	France	Common
Renoit Grape Vine	France	Common
Avornalino Grape Vine	France	Uncommon
Meloire Grape Vine	France	Uncommon
Cranerlet Nuala Grape Vine	France	Rare
Gralladina Fran Grape Vine	France	Rare
Pomegranate Tree	Egypt	Uncommon
Plum Tree	China	Uncommon
Pomelo Tree	China	Rare
Cherry Tree	Egypt	Rare

NOTE

Be sure to check out the fish table to see which species makes the best fertilizer.

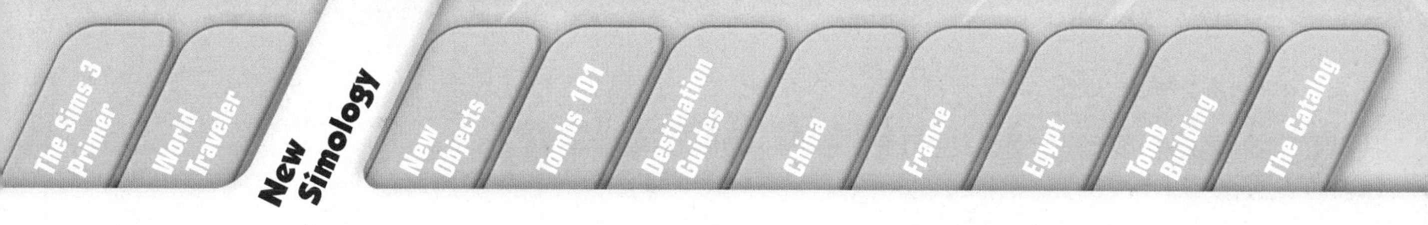

Socials

Just as there are new wishes, skills, and moodlets for Sims in *World Adventures*, there are new social interactions. Socials are the actions between two Sims in a conversation. All of the original socials from *The Sims 3* are still available, but a new set of socials is added to the mix to further stimulate conversation. Some socials are related to traits. Others are inspired by the development of skills.

Use this chart of socials added to *World Adventures* to help guide conversations, especially when abroad and talking with locals. Here is how the chart breaks down:

- **Social:** Name of social as seen in the conversation menu
- **Commodity:** Commodity associated with the social
- **Actor/Target Age:** Ages in which the social is applicable
  - C=Child
  - T=Teen
  - Y= Young Adult
  - A=Adult
  - E=Elder
- **Social Available When?:** What prompts the use of the social
- **Required Trait:** Social is only available when Actor has this trait
- **Social Encouraged by Trait?:** Social is potentially more "powerful" due to Actor's trait
- **Social Prevented by Trait?:** Actor's trait prevents them from using this social
- **# of Uses Before Boring:** Number of uses in a conversation before the social is dull. Default is 2. Exceptions are specified.
- **# of Uses if Recharged:** Number of times the social can be used if another social interrupts the re-use of the social

SOCIALS

Social	Commodity	Actor Age	Target Age	Social Available When?	Required Trait	Social Encouraged By Trait?	Social Prevented By Trait?	# of Uses Before Boring	# of Uses if Recharged
Ask Foreign Visitor to Leave	Neutral	T, Y, A, E	C, T, Y, A, E	While foreign visitor is on lot.					
Ask Every Foreign Visitor to Leave	Neutral	C, T, Y, A, E	C, T, Y, A, E	While foreign visitor is on lot.					
Ask to Pose	Friendly	C, T, Y, A, E	C, T, Y, A, E	Actor wants to take photo.		Photographer's Eye			
Buy Items from Register	Neutral	T, Y, A, E	T, Y, A, E	Actor is inside shop or with merchant.					
Challenge to a Ranked Sparring Match	Neutral	T, Y, A, E	T, Y, A, E	Actor and Target are martial artists.		Disciplined			
Chat Locals	Friendly	C, T, Y, A, E	C, T, Y, A, E	While at destination talking to local Target.				2	1
Discuss SLR Cameras	Friendly	C, T, Y, A, E	C, T, Y, A, E	Actor is into photography.	Photographer's Eye	Photographer's Eye		2	1
Gossip with Locals	Friendly	C, T, Y, A, E	C, T, Y, A, E	While at destination talking to local Target.					
Insult Locals	Insulting	Y, A, E	T, Y, A, E	While at destination talking to local Target.					
Rant about Dark Rooms	Friendly	C, T, Y, A, E	C, T, Y, A, E	Actor is into photography.		Photographer's Eye			
Reminisce About Film	Friendly	C, T, Y, A, E	C, T, Y, A, E	Actor has recently seen movie.				2	1
Sing Song	Friendly	C, T, Y, A, E	C, T, Y, A, E	Actor has learned local song from a destination.			Can't Stand Art		
Sing Song Romantic	Amorous	T, Y, A, E	T, Y, A, E	Actor has learned romantic song from a destination.			Can't Stand Art		
Spar	Neutral	T, Y, A, E	T, Y, A, E	Actor and Target are martial artists.		Disciplined			

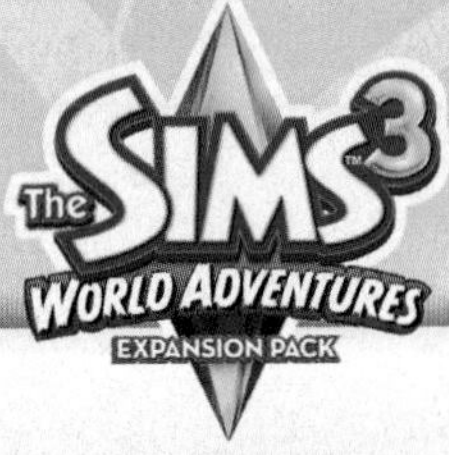

SOCIALS, CONTINUED

Social	Commodity	Actor Age	Target Age	Social Available When?	Required Trait	Social Encouraged By Trait?	Social Prevented By Trait?	# of Uses Before Boring	# of Uses if Recharged
Talk About Cameras	Friendly	C, T, Y, A, E	C, T, Y, A, E	Actor is into photography.		Photographer's Eye		2	1
Talk About Egyptian Pantheon	Friendly	T, Y, A, E	C, T, Y, A, E	Actor is a mummy.				2	1
Talk About Embalming	Friendly	T, Y, A, E	C, T, Y, A, E	Actor is a mummy.				2	1
Talk About Eyeliner Secrets	Friendly	T, Y, A, E	C, T, Y, A, E	Actor is a mummy.				2	1
Talk About Sand	Friendly	T, Y, A, E	C, T, Y, A, E	Actor is a mummy.				2	1
Talk About Trip	Friendly	C, T, Y, A, E	C, T, Y, A, E	Actor has been to at least one destination.				2	
Teach Song	Friendly	C, T, Y, A, E	C, T, Y, A, E	Actor has learned local song. Target does not know song.			Can't Stand Art	3	1
Teach Song Romantic	Friendly	T, Y, A, E	T, Y, A, E	Actor has learned romantic song. Target does not know song.			Can't Stand Art	3	1
Tell Joke Locals	Funny	C, T, Y, A, E	C, T, Y, A, E	While at destination talking to local Target.		Good Sense of Humor			

Note

You'll find a complete list of all social interactions from *The Sims 3* in The Catalog chapter.

Brownie Bites

There is one very special new social in *World Adventures* that I want to call out: Learn Song. This is one of my favorite additions to the game via *World Adventures.* While traveling to destinations and chatting up locals, you can learn songs and take them back home with you. This a wonderful way for the culture of a destination to escape its borders.

Each destination has two unique songs: local and romantic. All locals know the local song. Locals older than children know the romantic song, too. Start a conversation with a local and then choose Learn Song. Pick from the offered songs. Your Sim and the local will then go back and forth with your Sim repeating phrases of the song after the local until the song has been learned.

Once you have learned the song, you can sing it on your own. (There is even a chance your Sim may start singing one of the songs in the shower.) You can also teach the song to another Sim back home.

Not every Sim will react to your songs the same. Sims with the following traits react positively to you singing a song within earshot: Artistic, Easily Impressed, Family-Oriented, Friendly, Excitable, Good, Hopeless Romantic, Party Animal, and Virtuoso. No Sense of Humor, Mean, Hot-Headed, Grumpy, Evil, Can't Stand Art, and Dislikes Children Sims will actually boo.

The romantic song has an alternate use. Now, unlike my singing voice—which causes birds to run into windows on purpose—if your Sim sings the romantic song to a receptive Sim, it will put them in the mood for love.

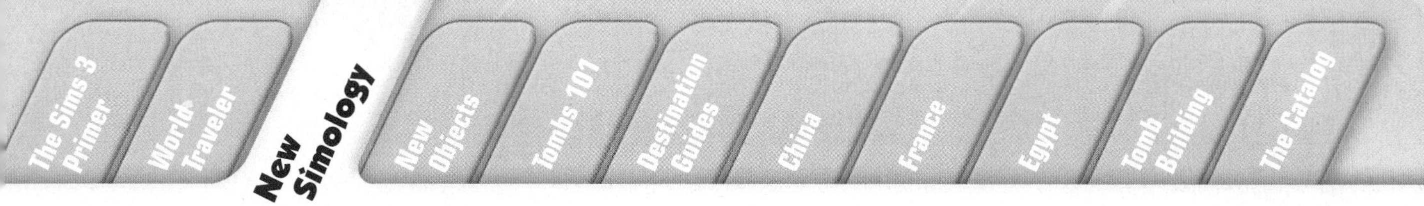

Opportunities

While traveling, Sims are likely to concentrate on going on adventures for locals, exploring tombs, and collecting new goodies. But don't ignore opportunities. Opportunities are occasional events related to your skills and/or career. In *World Adventures*, opportunities arise while you are at a destination and also back home. Sometimes opportunities spur you to travel, such as when the Political career opportunity "As a Leader Should" suggests you go to France or China to talk to locals about their politics. The rewards for completing opportunities include Simoleons, promotions, skill gains, and more.

Here is a full list of the opportunities offered in *World Adventures*, sorted by skills and careers:

ATHLETIC SKILL

Opportunity	Hint
Secret Techniques	Travel to China and Learn Secret Techniques from a leader of the local community then report back to *X* to improve your Athletic skill and receive a travel stipend.
Desert Air… Good?	*X* has done plenty of overseas training courses and has challenged you to run in the desert air of Al Simhara to build endurance and improve your Athletic skill.
Train Local	Travel to France and train a local for 4 hours, then report back to the stadium to collect your cash payment and increase your Athletic skill.

CHARISMA SKILL

Opportunity	Hint
Friendly World	Go to France and Promote the Exchange Program to *X* locals, then report back to the school to increase your Charisma skill and earn Simoleons.
Business Negotiation	Travel to Egypt and use your Charisma to Negotiate a Deal with the seller, then report back to the business office to increase your Charisma skill and earn some money.

COOKING SKILL

Opportunity	Hint
Prepare Crepes	Bring a serving of Excellent Crepes to the restaurant to receive a payment.
We Love Falafel	Bring 2 servings of Falafel to the restaurant to fulfill the order and get paid.
Prepare Stir-Fry	Bring a group serving of Stir-Fry to the diner to receive a payment. You need to learn the recipe first.

FISHING SKILL

Opportunity	Hint
Crocodile Hunting	Bring a Crocodile to the science facility for a cash reward.
To Hunt a Dragon	Bring 3 Dragonfish to the military base to receive payment.
No Warts Please!	Bring 3 Frogs to the restaurant to receive a cash payment.

GARDENING SKILL

Opportunity	Hint
Stomping Grapes	Bring *X* Excellent quality Renoit Grapes to the theater to receive a payment.
Great Plums	Bring *X* Excellent quality Plums to the supermarket to receive your payment.
Pure Pomegranate	Bring *X* Pomegranates of Excellent quality to the supermarket to receive a payment.

GUITAR SKILL

Opportunity	Hint
Play for China	Play your guitar in China to earn some tips.
Play for Egypt	Play your guitar in Egypt to earn some tips.
Play for France	Play your guitar in France to earn some tips.

HANDINESS SKILL

Opportunity	Hint
Try the Traps	Travel to Egypt, enter a tomb, and disable a trap. Then report back to your contact for your payment.
Buyer's Remorse	Go to China and get the broken television from *X*. Find it in your family inventory, repair it, and deliver it to *X* to receive your payment.

HANDINESS SKILL, CONTINUED

Opportunity	Hint
Fix Under Warranty	Travel to France and get the broken stereo, repair it, and return it to receive your payment.

LOGIC SKILL

Opportunity	Hint
A French Puzzler	*X* has asked you, an esteemed puzzle-solver, to go to France and personally solve the puzzle. Travel to France and ask for the answer, then tell it to *X* to get paid.
Riddle War in China	Travel to China and talk to 3 locals to solve all the riddles, then report back to the group at the theater to get your reward.
Senet Strategy	Travel to Egypt and learn Senet from a local, then report back to the military base to earn some cash.

PAINTING SKILL

Opportunity	Hint
Deliver a Painting to China	Travel to Shang Simla and deliver a painting worth more than §750 to earn a cash reward.
Deliver a Painting to Egypt	Travel to Egypt and deliver a painting worth more than §750 for payment.
Deliver a Painting to France	Travel to France and deliver a painting worth more than §750 for payment.

WRITING SKILL

Opportunity	Hint
Deliver a Book to China	Travel to China and deliver one of your books to earn a cash reward.
Deliver a Book to Egypt	Travel to Egypt and deliver one of your books for payment.
Deliver a Book to France	Travel to France and deliver one of your books for payment.

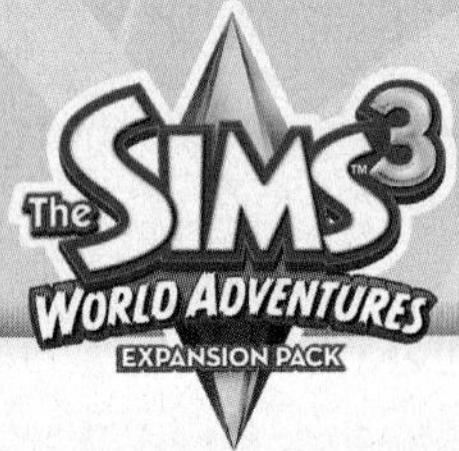

MARTIAL ARTS SKILL

Opportunity	Hint
The Ultimate Challenge	Break the Space Rock on the Board Breaker, then report to the stadium to receive the prize.
Keep It Up	Increase your Martial Arts skill by one level, then report your progress to *X* to earn a cash reward.
Power Measure	Train on the Board Breaker for 2 hours with the power meter in your inventory, then report back to the science facility to increase your Martial Arts skill and collect your compensation.
Meditation Benefits	Meditate until you get the Meditative Focus moodlet then Enlighten *X* to increase your relationship and earn a cash reward.
Help My Friend	Spar with *X* and report back to *X* when you're done to increase your relationship and Martial Arts skill.
Sparring Practice	Spar with *X* to earn a cash reward and increase your relationship.
The Spa Restoration	Go to the day spa and Conduct Relaxation Session to earn a cash reward.
Focus is Key	Go to the business office and Conduct Meditation Workshop to earn a cash reward.
Try the Tourney	Win a Martial Arts tournament match in Shang Simla, then report back to the stadium to receive a cash reward.
Advanced Training	Train *X* for 4 hours to increase your relationship and earn a cash reward.
Training Demo	Go to the stadium and give a Martial Arts demo to earn a cash reward.
Agent Training	Go to the police station and Train Agents to earn a cash reward.
Need Training	Train *X* for 3 hours to increase your relationship and earn a cash reward.
Training for Dummies	Use a Training Dummy for 2 hours, then talk to *X* about your experience to receive a cash reward.
Complete Victory	Travel to China to win the Martial Arts tournament, then report back to the stadium to earn a cash reward.

PHOTOGRAPHY SKILL

Opportunity	Hint
Al Simhara	Take a photograph of the Temple of Abu Simbel in Al Simhara and bring it to the day spa to get paid.
Photo Contest	Bring a high value photograph to the theater for a chance to win!
The Temple of the Dragon	Travel to China and take a photograph of the Temple of the Dragon, then give it to *X* to receive a cash reward.
Egyptian Fashion	Bring one photograph of Egyptian locals to the business office to get receive a cash reward.
French Photos	Take 5 pictures of France and then turn them in to the bistro to receive a cash payment.
Better Photographs!	Advance one skill level in the Photography skill, then report to *X* to earn a cash reward.
Grapestand	Take a photograph of grapes and bring it to the grocery store to get paid.
High Quality Photos	Bring a photograph worth more than *X* to city hall to receive three times its worth.
Photographic Evidence	Go down to the police station and examine the photographs before *X* time to earn a cash reward.
Paparazzi!	Bring a photograph of *X* to *X* to earn a cash payment.
Visa Photograph	Take a photograph of *X* and then deliver it to them to earn a cash reward.
The Pyramids	Deliver a high value photograph of a pyramid to the business office to earn some money.
Intro to Photography	Go to the school before *X* time and teach a Photography class to earn a cash reward.
The Sphinx	Bring a photograph of the Sphinx to the business office to earn a cash reward.

ATHLETIC CAREER

Opportunity	Hint
French Appreciation	Go to France and make some nectar, then report back to work to earn a raise and increase your job performance.

ATHLETIC CAREER, CONTINUED

Opportunity	Hint
The Grand Tour	Travel to Egypt, China, and France then report back to work for a raise.
The Focused Athlete	Learn the Martial Arts skill then report back to work.
The Whole Athlete	Go to China and stay at the Scholar's Garden, then report back to work to increase your job performance.
Tomb Raiding Hero	Go to Egypt and enter the Tomb of the Rock, then report back to work to earn a raise.

BUSINESS CAREER

Opportunity	Hint
Oh, and Bring Gifts	Bring *X* relics to work to earn a raise.
The French Connection	Travel to France to discuss business ventures with the local merchant to earn a raise.
A Priceless Bet	Bring a relic worth at least 750 Simoleons to work with you.

CRIMINAL CAREER

Opportunity	Hint
Chinese Delivery	Go to China and deliver the heavy item in your inventory to a local contact to increase your job performance and earn a raise.
Egyptian Delivery	Go to Egypt and deliver the package in your inventory to a local contact to increase your job performance and earn a raise.
French Delivery	Go to France and deliver the thin package in your inventory to a local contact to earn a raise.
A Better Criminal	Get to skill level 5 in Martial Arts and return to work to earn a raise.

CULINARY CAREER

Opportunity	Hint
Chinese Stir-Fry	Learn the recipe for Stir-Fry, prepare a serving, then bring it to work to earn a raise.
Falafel Portfolio	Learn the recipe for Falafel, then cook a serving and bring it to work to earn a raise.

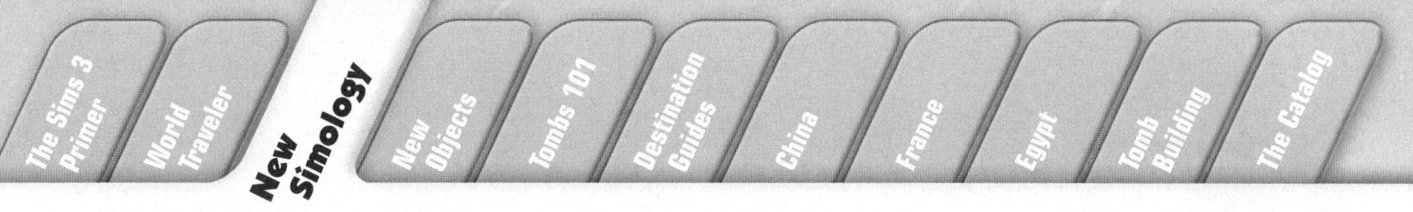

CULINARY CAREER, CONTINUED

Opportunity	Hint
Create-a-Crepe	Learn the recipe for Crepes, cook a serving, then bring it to work to earn a raise.
Culinary Tips	Go to France and interview 4 locals, then report back to work to increase your Cooking skill and job performance.
New High Quality Ingredients	Bring in *X* Outstanding *X fruit* to work to receive a raise, a performance boost, and some extra cash.

JOURNALISM CAREER

Opportunity	Hint
Eye on Egypt	Bring one photo of an Egyptian pyramid to work to earn a raise and increase your job performance.
Historical Interview	Go to China and interview an elder Sim, then report back to work to increase your job performance and receive a bonus.
Exotic Living	Go to France and interview 5 locals, then report back to work to receive a travel stipend and increase your job performance.
Photojournalism	Advance to at least level 1 of the Photography skill, then report to work to earn a raise and increase your job performance.
Museum Photos	Bring 5 photographs of relics to work to earn a raise and increase your relationship with your boss.

LAW ENFORCEMENT CAREER

Opportunity	Hint
Nectar Emergency	Bring *X* bottles of nectar in to work to receive a cash reward and increase your job performance.
Smuggle Check	Bring *X* unique relics to work to earn a raise.
Hard Core Training	Learn the Martial Arts skill and then report back to work for a raise.

LAW ENFORCEMENT CAREER, CONTINUED

Opportunity	Hint
Photo Evidence	Learn the Photography skill and then report back to work with pictures you've taken to increase your job performance and earn a raise.
Improving Disguises	Go to China and meet *X* locals, then report back to the police station to earn a raise.

MEDICAL CAREER

Opportunity	Hint
Preservation Techniques	Bring some Pemmican to the hospital to improve your job performance.
French Seminar	Go to France and attend the seminar then report back to work to receive a travel stipend and increase your job performance.
Scarab Ecology	Bring *X* Scarab Beetles to the hospital to earn a cash reward.
Field Tests	Get bitten by a snake, then return to the hospital for tests.
Research	Go to China and Learn about Herbal Medicine from *X* locals to earn a raise and increase your job performance.

MILITARY CAREER

Opportunity	Hint
Mummitomium?	Collect *X* chunks of Mummitomium and bring them to work to receive your overtime pay and increase your job performance.
The Commander's Cabinet	Bring *X* bottles of excellent quality nectar to work to earn a raise and increase your job performance.
Learn Martial Arts	Learn the Martial Arts skill, then report back to work to earn a raise.
Space Awareness	Travel to France and speak to *X* locals about the space program, then report back to work to earn a raise.
Martial Arts Mastery	Compete in the Martial Arts Tourney, then report to work to claim your prize.

MUSIC CAREER

Opportunity	Hint
Collaborate in Egypt	Go to Egypt and Discuss Musical Influences with 3 locals then report back to work to earn a raise.
New Musical Theory	Go to China, Learn Musical Theory from the Special Merchant, and return to work to earn a raise.
Playing for Others	Go to Egypt and play your guitar to earn §1,000 in tips, then report back to work to increase your job performance and earn a raise.
Spread the Music	Travel to France and Discuss Music with 3 locals, then report back to work to increase your job performance and earn a raise.

POLITICS CAREER

Opportunity	Hint
As a Leader Should	Travel to *X* and Chat Up 4 locals, then return to work to earn a raise.
Foreign Affairs	Bring *X* common relics in to work to increase your job performance and receive some campaign donations.

SCIENCE CAREER

Opportunity	Hint
Assassin Bug Study	Collect *X* Assassin Bugs and bring them to the science facility to increase your job performance and earn a raise.
Relic Research	Bring *X* relics to work to increase your job performance and receive a cash reward.
What Is This... Tiberium?	Bring *X* samples of Tiberium to work to earn a cash reward.
Site Investigators!	Enter a tomb with the PKE Meter in your inventory, then return to work to earn a raise.

New Objects

A Sim's home is a Sim's castle. And once you buy or build your home, you want to fill it with stuff. After all, the appearance of a Sim's house is another method of self-expression. If you are just starting out with a new Sim, the household budget may prevent you from going large right away. But as you start pulling in the Simoleons via careers, skill development benefits, or from successful adventures, you can stock that house with objects that are not only functional, but also fun.

Naturally, the urge to buy objects for your house must be balanced with the desire to go on trips. You only have so many Simoleons...

Object Catalog

World Adventures adds many new objects you can purchase in Buy Mode and place on your home town lot or any vacation homes you are lucky enough to own in the different destinations. These new objects mingle with the original series of objects from *The Sims 3*.

CAUTION

Remember the rules of depreciation when buying these objects in Buy Mode. As long as you sledgehammer the object before leaving Buy Mode, you get the full value of the object back. As soon as you click out of Buy Mode, the object starts depreciating. Each day, the object depreciates 10 percent. The bottomed out value is 40 percent of the original price. The value of an object can never drop below 40 percent unless the object is broken or ruined.

NOTE

Only objects purchased in Buy Mode appear in the catalog. Objects you buy in shops while on trips, such as the Nectar Maker, are detailed either with the associated skills or in that destination's chapter.

Misc. Storage

Since *World Adventures* introduces Nectar Making as a new skill, you need someplace to store your bottles. This category of objects includes two Nectar racks as well as storage unit that can be used to hold small objects.

Displays

Collecting relics is great fun in *World Adventures*. But you cannot just show them off on a plain table. You need a cool display to go with your relic. Use these new displays to proudly show off your collections, or anything else.

The objects in this catalog are listed with prices, important depreciation values, and any effect the object may have on your Sim as well as the environmental rating of a room.

Object	Price (in Simoleons)	Daily Depreciation	Fully Deprec. Value	Environment	Hygiene	Hunger	Bladder	Energy	Fun	Logic	Charisma	Cooking	Athletic	Painting	Guitar	Handiness	Gardening	Writing	Fishing	Stress Relief	Group Activity	Comfort
SMALL APPLIANCES																						
The Juspresso XTi-French Beverage Maker	1,400	140	560					4														
TOILETS																						
Sultan's Throne by Scarab Corp.	1,175	117.5	470	1			10															
MIRROR & DRAPES																						
Admire Moi Mirror	190	19	76	2					3		x											
The Shade-a-Plenty Awning	50	5	20	1																		
The Shade-a-Plenty Awning XL	100	10	40	1																		
Antique Drape	300	30	120	2																		

Object	Price (in Simoleons)	Daily Depreciation	Fully Deprec. Value	Environment	Hygiene	Hunger	Bladder	Energy	Fun	Logic	Charisma	Cooking	Athletic	Painting	Guitar	Handiness	Gardening	Writing	Fishing	Stress Relief	Group Activity	Comfort
END TABLE																						
End of the Line End Table	95	9.5	38																			
Le Petit Table	270	27	108	1																		
Anxious End Table	300	30	120	2																		
BEDS																						
Fit for a King(size)	990	99	396	2				5												3		2
Great Wall Bed from Dynasty Industries	2,400	240	960	4				8												3		3
Delicious Slumber Bed XV	4,200	420	1,680	7				10												3		3
WALL DECORATIONS																						
Papyrus Aplenty	65	6.5	26	2																		
Feathery Fans	95	9.5	38	2																		
Playful Pandas	105	10.5	42	2																		
Pyramids at Sunrise	130	13	52	3																		
The Lofty Wafter	130	13	52	3																		
The Royal Wedding Tapestry	205	20.5	82	3																		
Couple of Khopesh	280	28	112	3																		
Wall Mounted Home Deterrent System	305	30.5	122	4																		
Eternal Life	350	35	140	4																		
Rue de Rodiek	640	64	256	5																		
DRESSERS																						
Dragon Dresser	555	55.5	222	3																		
Great Dresser of Neezer	635	63.5	254	4																		

New Objects

Object	Price (in Simoleons)	Daily Depreciation	Fully Deprec. Value	Environment	Hygiene	Hunger	Bladder	Energy	Fun	Logic	Charisma	Cooking	Athletic	Painting	Guitar	Handiness	Gardening	Writing	Fishing	Stress Relief	Group Activity	Comfort
LIVING CHAIRS																						
The Regal Rester	190	19	76																			2
Practically Yours	260	26	104	1																		2
Simply Elegant Seating	530	53	212	2																		2
SOFAS																						
The Sultan's Sofa	310	31	124																			1
The Proper Loveseat	390	39	156	1																		1
The Cradle of Civilization	1,060	106	424	4																		2
COFFEE TABLES																						
Nosylla's Half-Caf Coffee Table	215	21.5	86	1																		
The Coffee Sarcophagus Coffee Table	270	27	108	1																		
Quaint Coffee Support Structure	280	28	112	1																		
MISC. DECOR & PLANTS																						
Porcelain Dinner Set	30	3	12	2																		
Clay Pots	45	4.5	18	2																		
Rice Basket Carrier from Landgraab Inc.	75	7.5	30																			
Trader Ashai's Baskets	165	16.5	66	3																		
Bonsai! Table Plant	470	47	188	5																		
Fabu Foo	655	65.5	262	6																		
Rodent Repellent	655	65.5	262	6																		
Fragmented Vase	25	2.5	10	1																		
Tomb Block - Half	35	3.5	14																			
Unfinished Cat	35	3.5	14	2																		

Object	Price (in Simoleons)	Daily Depreciation	Fully Deprec. Value	Environment	Hygiene	Hunger	Bladder	Energy	Fun	Logic	Charisma	Cooking	Athletic	Painting	Guitar	Handiness	Gardening	Writing	Fishing	Stress Relief	Group Activity	Comfort
Clothes Hanging on a Line	48	4.8	19.2	2																		
Tomb Block - Full	90	9	36																			
Tomb Wall - Broken	115	11.5	46																			
Really Ruined Column	165	16.5	66																			
Fish Swimming in Stone	180	18	72	3																		
Ruined Ruin Column	300	30	120																			
Used Nectar Barrels	430	43	172	5																		
The Urn of Franco	440	44	176	5																		
Ruin Column	600	60	240																			
A Show of Force	660	66	264	6																		
Gally de Orleans	820	82	328	6																		
The Gazing Pharaoh	1,350	135	540	7																		
Phillippe of Aznac	1,410	141	564	7																		
Gloria	1,475	147.5	590	7																		
Alexia Full of Hair	1,500	150	600	7																		
Mirror to the Undersea World	1,800	180	720	7																		
Sphinx of Simoglyphia	2,200	220	880	8																		
Papyrus Plant	55	5.5	22	2																		
Antique-But-Not Lotus Pot	60	6	24	2																		
Fountain of Flowers	80	8	32	2																		
Desert Lotus	110	11	44	3																		

New Objects

Object	Price (in Simoleons)	Daily Depreciation	Fully Deprec. Value	Environment	Hygiene	Hunger	Bladder	Energy	Fun	Logic	Charisma	Cooking	Athletic	Painting	Guitar	Handiness	Gardening	Writing	Fishing	Stress Relief	Group Activity	Comfort
Box Tree	115	11.5	46	3																		
Ivy Hill Planter Box	130	13	52	3																		
ePedestal	145	14.5	58	3																		
My First Bamboo Garden	290	29	116	3																		
Perma-Palm by Indoor Oasis Inc.	320	32	128	4																		
DINING CHAIRS																						
Perfect Shui Dining Chair from Feng Shui Designs	95	9.5	38																			1
The Chair of Amon	110	11	44																			1
Stone Seat from Tomb Dining Inc.	140	14	56																			2
Dinner Party Perfect Chair	670	67	268	1																		3
DINING TABLES																						
Dynamic Dynasty Dining Table	210	21	84																			
Pharaoh's Feasting Feaster	560	56	224	3																		
Dining Table du Jour	720	72	288	4																		
LIGHTS																						
Simply Radiant Pendant Lamp by Practically Fancy	75	7.5	30	1																		
The Light of Brahman	105	10.5	42	1																		
Far East Fire Hazard by the Paper Light Company	135	13.5	54	1																		
The Sandy Ceiling Light	190	19	76	2																		
The Petite Four Chandelier	300	30	120	2																		
Petite Pagoda	340	34	136	2																		
Francois' Table Lamp	140	14	56	1																		

Object	Price (in Simoleons)	Daily Depreciation	Fully Deprec. Value	Environment	Hygiene	Hunger	Bladder	Energy	Fun	Logic	Charisma	Cooking	Athletic	Painting	Guitar	Handiness	Gardening	Writing	Fishing	Stress Relief	Group Activity	Comfort
Classic Torch	70	7	28																			
Lantern Illuminator	110	11	44	1																		
Classique Torch	125	12.5	50																			
Belsim Torch from Scarab Corp.	590	59	236	2																		
Magic Sun Stick	1,600	160	640	6																		
BOOKSHELVES																						
Posture-Perfect Bookshelf	390	39	156	2					3	x		x				x						
Class-E Bookcase	630	63	252	3					4	x		x				x						
LAWN ORNAMENTS																						
The Politicians' Rock	420	42	168	5																		
The Scholar's Rock	440	44	176	5																		
The Warrior's Rock	455	45.5	182	5																		
VIP Fountain	1,700	170	680	7																		
The Water Breathing Dragon	2,300	230	920	8																		
Hedge Your Bets Fountain	3,800	380	1,520	8																		
OUTDOOR SEATING																						
Umbrella Sculpture	40	4	16																			
Le Grand Amour Park Bench	500	50	200																			1
OUTDOOR LIGHTING																						
Dependable Little Light	90	9	36																			
Laissez-Faire Light Post Extended Version	260	26	104																			
Water Lily Lanterns	340	34	136																			
Laissez-Faire Light Post	400	40	160																			

New Objects

Object	Price (in Simoleons)	Daily Depreciation	Fully Deprec. Value	Environment	Hygiene	Hunger	Bladder	Energy	Fun	Logic	Charisma	Cooking	Athletic	Painting	Guitar	Handiness	Gardening	Writing	Fishing	Stress Relief	Group Activity	Comfort
ROOF DECORATIONS																						
The Roof's End by Roof Akcents	10	1	4																			
Roof Apex by Roof Akcents	15	1.5	6																			
Custom Roof Bar by Roof Akcents	45	4.5	18																			
Dragon's Head Roof Sculpture	45	4.5	18																			
Weather Rooster by Roof Akcents	55	5.5	22																			
The Dragon's Corner by Roof Akcents	190	19	76																			
TREES																						
Tree Shrub	90	9	36	2																		
Small Ash Tree	95	9.5	38	2																		
Small Chinese Elm Tree	110	11	44	2																		
Small Olive Tree	115	11.5	46	2																		
Bougainvillea Tree	130	13	52	2																		
Small Oak Chestnut Tree	135	13.5	54	2																		
Ash Tree	140	14	56	2																		
Banana Tree	145	14.5	58	2																		
Small Chinese Bamboo Tree	145	14.5	58	2																		
Small Cinnamon Tree	150	15	60	2																		
Oak Chestnut Tree	160	16	64	2																		
Olive Tree	190	19	76	3																		
Chinese Elm Tree	195	19.5	78	3																		
Chinese Bamboo Tree	200	20	80	3																		

Object	Price (in Simoleons)	Daily Depreciation	Fully Deprec. Value	Environment	Hygiene	Hunger	Bladder	Energy	Fun	Logic	Charisma	Cooking	Athletic	Painting	Guitar	Handiness	Gardening	Writing	Fishing	Stress Relief	Group Activity	Comfort
Small Chinese Maple Tree	205	20.5	82	3																		
Small Sago Palm Tree	210	21	84	3																		
Cinnamon Tree	240	24	96	3																		
Small Pistache Tree	260	26	104	3																		
Chinese Maple Tree	280	28	112	2																		
Small Al Simharan Palm Tree	280	28	112	3																		
Chinese Cypress Tree	310	31	124	4																		
Sago Palm Tree	320	32	128	4																		
Pistache Tree	330	33	132	4																		
Al Simharan Palm Tree	390	39	156	4																		
SHRUBS																						
Chinese Water Lily	8	0.8	3																			
Bullrushes	11	1.1	4																			
Large Chinese Water Lily	15	1.5	6																			
FLOWERS																						
Lavender	45	4.5	18																			
Peony	50	5	20																			
Chinese Lantern Plant	65	6.5	26																			
Yellow Lilac	75	7.5	30																			
Pink Hydrangea	80	8	32																			
ROCKS																						
Large Horizontal	65	6	26																			

New Objects

Object	Price (in Simoleons)	Daily Depreciation	Fully Deprec. Value	Environment	Hygiene	Hunger	Bladder	Energy	Fun	Logic	Charisma	Cooking	Athletic	Painting	Guitar	Handiness	Gardening	Writing	Fishing	Stress Relief	Group Activity	Comfort
Large Vertical	65	6	26																			
Large Square	68	7	27																			
Large Oval	70	7	28																			
Large Round	73	7	29																			
FIREPLACES																						
A Very Civilized Fire	1,700	170	680	3	6																	
MISC. STORAGE																						
Stone Alcove	535	53.5	214																			
Flavor Savor Nectar Rack	550	55	220																			
The Necteaux	1,200	120	480																			
DISPLAYS																						
Rory's Display Pedestal	250	25	100																			
Di§play Case by BlingBling! - Small	290	29	116																			
Carter's Display Case	310	31	124																			
Rory's Display Pedestal - China	310	31	124																			
Di§play Case by BlingBling! - Medium	320	32	128																			
Rory's Display Pedestal - Egypt	400	40	160																			
Di§play Case by BlingBling! - Large	480	48	192																			
Di§play Case by BlingBling! - Short	550	55	220																			
Di§play Case by BlingBling! - Extra Large	710	71	284																			
Rory's Display Pedestal - France	850	85	340																			
Carter's Display Case - XL Edition	1,250	125	500																			

Tombs 101

Understanding the Underworld

Your Sim slips down the newly revealed steps into the inky unknown. The crackling torch on the wall, newly breathed to life, casts light on an ancient chamber that has not seen illumination for centuries. Shadows are thrown against the wall, making it look as if the Sim is not the only thing moving in this forgotten tomb. But she is. Or at least, she thinks she is.

A lone sarcophagus leans against the far wall. Near it are three treasure chests. Does one of them contain the treasure she was sent to seek? One by one, she opens the chests, feeling around the dust and debris for relics of long ago. She keeps an eye on the sarcophagus as she inches closer to it. Surely the rumors of mummies that walk the tomb in search of living flesh are just stories to keep children from poking around, right?

Finally, she reaches the third treasure chest—the one closest to the sarcophagus. She hoists the lid up and reaches inside. Her fingers feel the unnatural edges of carved stone. This is it. This is the relic. She just has to take it and return to the surface. But the lid of the treasure chest slams shut with a sharp thud, loud enough to wake the dead.

And that's exactly what happens next. A mummy explodes from the sarcophagus, arms outstretched to grab the intruder. The Sim tumbles backward, barely avoiding the mummy's bandaged hands. Centuries of decay have curled the mummy's fingers into claws. She regains her footing and starts to run. There's a fire trap ahead, but if she can make it to the pool of water first and drench her clothes, she can get through the belching pillars of flame unharmed. The mummy will be unable to follow her. The trap that almost killed her on the way down will now be the very thing that saves her life. She starts to run. And she will not stop running until the ground beneath her feet is warmed by daylight.

Tomb Features

Before descending the stairs into a potentially dangerous tomb, you need to know exactly what to expect. These tombs are not happy treasure chambers. They are dangerous places, filled with hidden doors, traps, and even a few unhappy residents. There's a reason the locals ask you to go on these adventures instead of just completing them themselves! This chapter details exactly what you need to know about tomb exploration. All tomb features are explained, from floor switches to dive wells. And we'll even help you survive an encounter with a deadly mummy.

Keystones

Keystones are carved pieces of rock that are used to open doors in tombs. Keystones come in a handful of shapes, such as stars, crescents, and hearts. Once a keystone is discovered (usually found in a treasure chest) and taken, it goes into the Sim's inventory. In some tombs, your Sim will discover special keystones with actual names. These keystones are essential for completing a tomb, because they unlock doors that regular keystones cannot.

Once you have a keystone, you can open a locked door that has a keystone panel next to it. The keystone panels have shaped holes that accommodate only same-shaped keystones. Direct your Sim to insert a keystone into a panel to unlock a door. (If you have the right shaped keystone in your inventory, your Sim automatically fishes out the correct one.) The Sim hoists the heavy keystone into place. After a brief flash of light, the nearby door is magically unlocked and your Sim can pass through it.

TIP

The Skeleton Key Adventure Reward allows Sims to open any door that does not use a special keystone, one that is unique to that tomb or building. With the Skeleton Key, you no longer have to worry about coming to a door and being stopped cold!

Treasure Chests

Most tombs and mysterious structures contain treasure chests. Treasure chests are often filled with relics and other valuables, such as gems or metals. Whenever you spy a treasure chest, be sure to open it and inspect it for goodies. The relics you find in chests can be saved as part of relic collections or sold to fund future explorations.

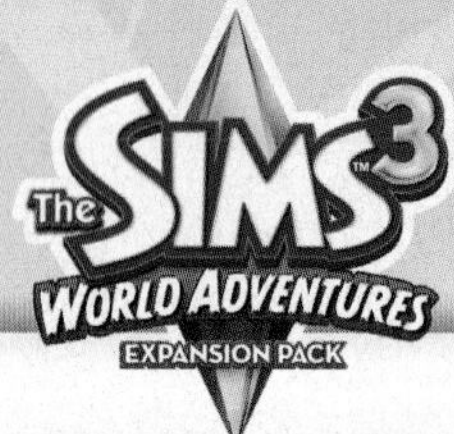

Each destination has its own treasure chest style. Whereas the Egyptian chests are ancient stone, the Chinese treasure chests are made from ornate woods.

Floor Switches and Statues

The main mechanism for opening locked doors in tombs is a floor switch. These panels are usually plain to see on the ground (although some are invisible until you trigger their appearance, such as activating a switch in a wall hole). Floor switches are triggered by the weight of a Sim. Just direct your Sim to the floor switch and they will place their feet firmly on the footprints on the panel.

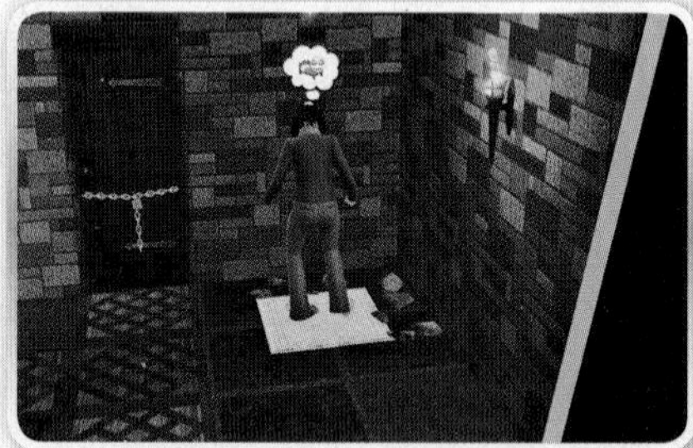

Standing on a floor switch with footprints typically unlocks a door or perhaps disables a trap.

Some floor switches require constant weight and will re-lock a door as soon as a Sim steps off of it. To hold these triggers down, you need to drag something heavy on top of it. Fortunately, many of these tombs are crowded with large statues. These statues are movable.

To move a statue, move the mouse cursor over it. Small yellow arrows appear on each side of the statue as you mouse over them. These arrows show you which directions the Sim can push or pull the statue. When you see the arrow you want to use, click on the statue and choose one of the following interactions: Push, Pull, Push Far, or Pull Far.

Push or Pull just moves the statue a single square on the floor. Pull Far or Push Far tells your Sim to keep moving it until it either hits a wall or you right-click on the interaction in the action queue. This is a good way to move a statue across a room without having to make repeat clicks.

NOTE

Pushing or pulling statues increases your Sim's Athletic skill. You can get quite a workout in some of the larger tombs!

Hole in the Wall

Look for openings in walls. These small holes can contain treasures, but many are switches that open new doors or expose puzzle pieces, such as new floor switches. Sometimes these holes appear only after a Sim steps on a floor switch or clears away a rubble pile.

There is always a good chance that when your Sim reaches into one of these dark holes, they get a nasty surprise: bugs. If the hole is filled with creepy-crawlies, the Sim yanks her hand out and shakes off the bugs. The Sim can then reach back in the hole to see if it contains anything good.

Agh!! Bugs!! Even after shaking them off, the Sim suffers from the Fear moodlet for several minutes.

TIP

Brave Sims do not get the Fear moodlet from bugs in a wall hole.

Rubble Piles

These old tombs have been crumbling for centuries. Rocks, dirt, and debris naturally collect in rubble piles. Sims can dig through rubble piles to search for hidden relics, disguised holes in the wall, or buried floor switches. While Sims dig through a rubble pile, they develop the Athletic skill.

TIP

Sims who discover Pangu's Axe in China can smash through rubble piles in one blow.

SANDS OF UNDERSTANDING

The Sands of Understanding reward is very useful for exploring tombs efficiently and effectively. With this reward, Sims can see hidden objects both good and bad nearby. This reward also speeds up clearing rubble piles and increases the number of Ancient Coins found in treasure chests. Just remember, the reward disappears once it has been used.

Dive Wells

Dive wells are circular pools of water that appear in tombs. These wells are perfect places to get soaked, which is actually quite useful for dealing with traps. (More on traps later in this chapter.) Traps that would burn your Sim can be passed through if your Sim pops out of a dive well sopping wet.

But dive wells are often not just for decoration and trap-thwarting. Sims can jump into dive wells and explore them. Dive wells occasionally act as switches that open up new areas in a tomb or reveal another piece of the mechanism that leads out of a room. Sometimes Sims find treasures and relics among the muck at the bottom of a dive well. Some dive wells also open up into underground tunnels. These tunnels lead to other dive wells inside a tomb. A Sim can use these dive wells as portals to discover new chambers in tombs, find new treasures, and get closer to their goals.

NOTE

When returning to a destination, explore dive wells again to see if new treasures and relics have surfaced at the bottom.

These two dive wells are connected, allowing exploration of the new chamber.

TIP

When Sims swim through dive wells they gain Athletic skill.

Boulders

Some passages in tombs are blocked by giant boulders. These are immovable objects. It doesn't matter if your Sim is it level 10 of the Athletic or Martial Arts skill. That boulder is not moving. However, if you locate Pangu's Axe—a very special relic in China—then you can shatter these boulders with a single click. So, be sure to come back after finding that axe. The treasures tucked behind these boulders are typically of very high value.

NOTE

Please check out the China chapter of this guide for maps of all of the tombs at that destination, including places you might find this valuable relic.

Hidden Doors

Many of the tombs have hidden doors. These doors look like normal walls. But when a Sim triggers a switch that activates the door, the outline of it appears on the wall. Now the Sim can go over to the secret door panel and attempt to open it. It takes a little effort.

Tombs 101

Note

Some secret doors are revealed by inspecting a wall. If a wall panel looks suspicious to you, roll the cursor over the panel. If the cursor changes, click on the panel and choose the Inspect interaction. Perhaps your Sim will discover a chamber of wonders?

Sarcophagus

Many tombs feature a particularly creepy decoration: a sarcophagus. These can be forced open and inspected, just like a treasure chest. Many of them contain relics and other treasures. Some of them reveal secrets in a chamber. But others contain a dangerous cargo: mummies. Mummies are vicious monsters that mean harm to Sims. They should be avoided at all costs because they only seek to hurt your explorers—sometimes with physical violence, sometimes with a horrible curse.

Caution

Some mummies pop out as soon as your Sim gets close to a sarcophagus, startling them. If you see a sarcophagus surrounded by treasure chests, for example, you may want to exercise great caution. Chances are good that it's a trap.

Whew! This sarcophagus only contains treasure.

Look who woke up on the wrong side of the millennium.

Eyes of Horus

The Eyes of Horus are special treasures discovered in the bottom of the Temple of Abu Simbel. These treasures are incredibly useful for exploring tombs. You can place one anywhere in a destination—even deep inside a tomb—and then use the other to teleport to the first Eye's location. Use these as portable teleporters to quickly move around a destination.

Brownie Bites

I've mentioned this before, but it bears repeating—do not go into these tombs without the proper gear. For longer tomb explorations, bring food, at least one Shower in a Can, and a tent. Not only are these the best ways to maximize your time in a tomb—no need to rush back to base camp—but they will keep your Sim's mood bright. Better mood, better time in the tomb.

I always carry at least three Showers in a Can. Not just for cleanliness, either. As you'll see in the next section about traps, the Shower in a Can can be a lifesaver when your Sim accidentally stumbles upon a fire trap. The water will extinguish the flames before any permanent damage is done. And by permanent damage, I really mean the Scorched moodlet.

Food is also important. Dried food is good and the more expensive it is, the better Meal moodlet your Sim gets from eating. But don't be afraid to spend some Ancient Coins on the Pemmican. This special dried food will keep your Sim satisfied for longer and you get the positive Carbed Up! moodlet that will hopefully push your Sim's mood into that green bubble so you earn Lifetime Happiness points while in the underworld.

Traps

Four types of traps await in the tombs or other mysterious buildings: fire, electricity, steam jets, and poison darts. All four of these traps can cause real harm to Sims who carelessly move through a tomb. Some traps are hidden. Others are quite visible, appearing as a series of holes on the floor or even repeatedly going off as ample warning. For example, a fire trap will often belch flames on a regular basis to let your Sim know that the other side of a room will be difficult to reach, but probably contains something valuable. After all, traps are rarely laid for sport. They are for protection.

A Sim who spots the trap in advance will normally refuse to cross it, even if you click on the opposite side and try to order the Sim to "go here." However, if the trap has failed or been disarmed, the Sim will have no problems crossing it.

You can actually spot a hidden trap in advance by having your Sim inspect a suspicious-looking area. If the Sim successfully discovers the trap, the trap appears on the floor in regular view—but it is armed. Now what?

Sims can attempt to disarm traps, but this is a risky proposition. Just click on the trap and choose the Disarm command. While the Sim is working on disarming the trap, a green status gauge appears above their heads, just as if they were reading a book. When the gauge reaches the top, one of three things happens. There is a random chance that the trap will go off while the Sim is attempting to disarm it, thus frightening the Sim (and earning the Fear moodlet). Should the Sim successfully disarm the trap, the trap is now ineffective and can be walked over without worry. If the trap cannot be disarmed, a short message tells you that you need to find another way around.

TIP

Handiness skill gives Sims greater success when disarming a trap.

If a trap cannot be disarmed or you don't want to risk trying to disarm it, you can use the Attempt to Cross interaction. If the trap is just visible on the floor, the Sim will attempt to slink between the holes. If the attempt fails, the trap goes off and the Sim suffers the consequences of that particular trap. Should you Attempt to Cross an active trap, one that is going off in regular intervals, you have a greater chance of making it, but these traps can still be tricky. However, certain conditions thwart the effects of a trap. For example, if you attempt to cross a fire trap, soaking your Sim in water at a nearby dive well will make them impervious to the flames.

NOTE

If you ever get in too much trouble in a tomb with traps or mummies, use the Adventure Reward Escape Dust to be magically teleported back to base camp or an owned vacation home.

CAUTION

Most traps cause the Fear moodlet.

Another way to disarm a trap is to push one of the giant statues that you use to trigger floor switches on top of a trap. The weight of the statue disarms the trap (but only the trap the statue is on—not an entire series of traps) and allows the Sim to safely pass over it.

TIP

Always look for statues that you can push on top of traps. This is the foolproof way to disable a trap.

Fire

Fire traps are one of the most common. This trap emits huge pillars of flames from holes. Sims caught in fire traps catch on fire. Similar to the effect of a kitchen fire, the Sim goes into panic mode. If your Sim is on fire, look for any nearby water to put out the flame. A dive well is perfect. Steam jets traps will also put out the flames. Once the fire is extinguished, the Sim gets the Torched moodlet.

NOTE

Daredevil Sims actually get a big positive reaction from the Torched moodlet. Once the fire is out, the Daredevil also gets the Adrenaline Rush moodlet for three hours.

TIP

On fire? Use a Shower in a Can to put out the flames. Don't expect any Hygiene bump from the Shower in a Can, though.

Sims can get through a fire trap by soaking themselves in a dive well first. As soon as the Soaked moodlet is present, they are drenched and can slip through the trap without harm. If the fire is raging while they move through it, the Soaked moodlet disappears. If the fire trap is off when the Sim tries to cross it, they keep the Soaked moodlet and the puddle of water from their feet disables the trap.

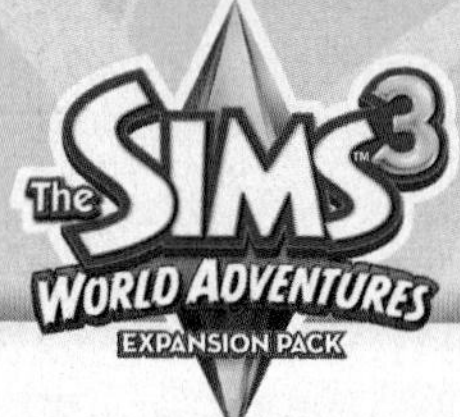

Electricity

The electricity trap looks very similar to the fire trap except that it crackles with blue sparks when it goes off. If the Sim is in a normal state, the shock will just singe them (they receive the Singed moodlet). These electrical bolts will shock a singed Sim into unconsciousness, giving them the Knocked Out moodlet. While knocked out, the Sim is vulnerable to other things, but if they are exploring with another Sim, hopefully that Sim can protect them.

This trap can be disabled by soaking a Sim and then getting water on the trap—while it is not arcing electricity. If you Attempt to Cross and get a water puddle on the trap, it is disabled.

Steam Jets

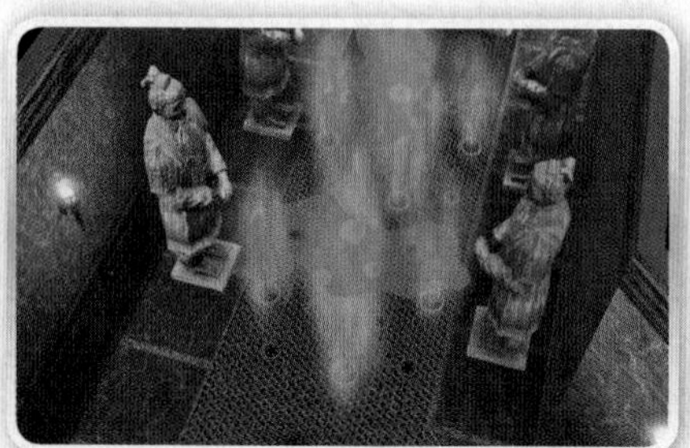

This trap shoots hot blasts of steam through its holes. Soaking your Sim doesn't do much to disable this trap because it is water-based itself. If your Sim is caught in the steam jets, they get Soaked. (But at least the trap can put out flames or remove the Singed moodlet.) This is the weakest of the traps and easiest to cross. Sims won't even get the Fear moodlet from the steam jet trap.

> **NOTE**
>
> Steam jet traps have a Jump In interaction that lets you purposefully leap into active jets to extinguish flames or just get the Soaked moodlet.

Poison Darts

This trap is pretty darn devious. Sims who get caught in it by surprise or who attempt to cross the trap and fail are poisoned by the little spears. The Sim then stumbles backward and passes out. While Knocked Out, the Sim lies on the floor, helpless. Definitely attempt to disarm this trap however you can—using a statue to block the vents is always the best solution.

Mummies!

When you spot a sarcophagus in a tomb, just relax. Not all of them house the reanimated bandaged remains of ancient kings who had their brains pulled out through the nose and stored in a jar buried next to them. (The heart is usually in the next jar over. This would make you pretty upset, too.) But some of them do release dangerous mummies into tombs that threaten your Sim with physical harm and even a curse that eventually causes death.

> **NOTE**
>
> Mummies will not attack child Sims.

When a mummy spots a Sim, it attacks. The mummy jumps on a Sim and goes berserk. (Look, you woke it up—now you have to deal with the consequences.) If your Sim has a high Martial Arts or Athletic skill rating, there is a good chance that you can beat the mummy. But if you lose, one of two things can happen. If you are lucky, the mummy only knocks your Sim unconscious—you have the Knocked Out moodlet and must wait for it to pass before you can get up. If you are not so lucky, the mummy pulls your Sim close and breathes an icky gas. This gives your Sim the Mummy's Curse moodlet, which is a curse.

Ugh, mummy breath!

If your Sim is hit with the Mummy's Curse moodlet, you have a limited amount of time to get rid of the curse before the Sim dies. (It's an awful death, too. There's screaming and burning. And your ghost is dark.) There are a few ways to get rid of the curse. Get to the Sphinx and use the Plead with the Sphinx interaction. Now your Sim can enter and look for the Soulpeace statue. This statue cleanses the curse from your Sim. You can also ditch the curse via the Snake Kiss moodlet, which is achieved by kissing a cobra from the Snake Charmer Basket. (More on this basket—and the hidden Snake Charmer skill—in the Egypt chapter.)

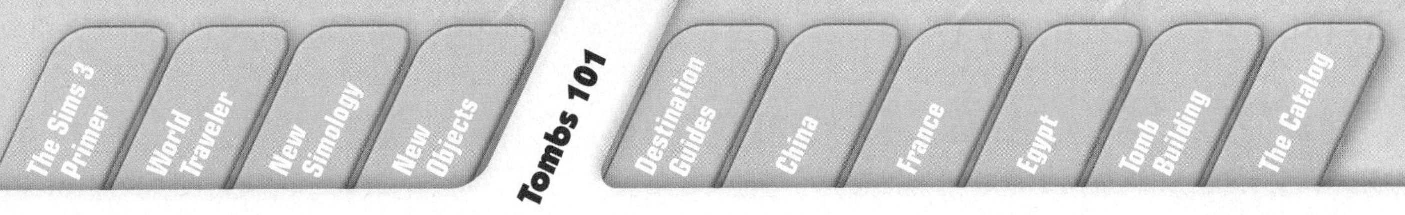

TIP

You can also sleep in the Blessed Sarcophagus to remove the Mummy's Curse moodlet.

There is a way to get an aggressive mummy off your back: Mummy Snacks. This Adventure Reward (purchased from the Special Merchant with Ancient Coins) can be thrown to the ground as your Sim flees. Mummies cannot resist this treat. A mummy will stop pursuit and start noshing on a Mummy Snack. While the mummy is busy eating, Sims can either continue their escape or use this distraction to inspect the mummy's sarcophagus. Surely there is enough room in that thing for a relic as well as a mummy, right?

TIP

If you lead a mummy into a fire trap, it burns up.

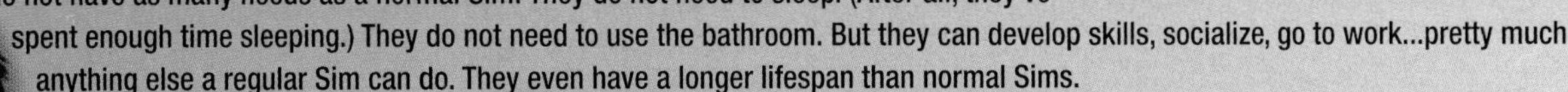

Brownie Bites

Maybe you don't find mummies scary at all? Perhaps you want one to take home and call your very own? Well, if you find all of the pieces of the Sarcophagus of the Kings in the tombs of Egypt, you can assemble the artifact and bring it home. From this artifact, you can summon a playable mummy into your household. Here's what else you need: 5 Canopic Jar relics. Place these objects inside the Sarcophagus of the Kings. If the offering is accepted, the sarcophagus lid swings open and the mummy stumbles out. It's now all yours!

You need to know a few things about playing a mummy. Mummies cannot Try for Baby. Mummies cannot run. Mummies also scare Coward or Neurotic Sims. But mummies also do not have as many needs as a normal Sim. They do not need to sleep. (After all, they've spent enough time sleeping.) They do not need to use the bathroom. But they can develop skills, socialize, go to work...pretty much anything else a regular Sim can do. They even have a longer lifespan than normal Sims.

One last word of warning about mummies: keep them away from fire. If a mummy catches on fire, it burns. That's it. There is no saving it.

Destination Guide

How to Use Destination Chapters

You know about all of the Lifetime Wishes. You have seen the new objects you can buy for your house. You understand how to survive a fire trap. You know exactly which new skill you want to tackle first. You are just itching to get out there and explore. And we're happy to help you get the most out of your travels.

The following three chapters detail everything there is to do at each of the destinations—France, China, and Egypt. Each chapter is broken down into specific sections: touring the sites, shopping, adventure list, and tomb maps. Before heading out the front door, make sure you know how to use each destination chapter so you don't miss a thing.

Touring

Each destination chapter includes a general tour of the site before going into all of the adventures you can undertake as well as the tombs you can explore. These tours include photos of the vacation homes you can buy once you max out your visa for that destination, the location of the markets and store inventories, and maps for all of the different collectibles and fishing spots.

Shopping & Skills

With the exception of relic merchants, the shops at each destination have the same inventory every day. The same camera. The same foods. The same books. Only the relic merchants change their inventories daily, so be sure to check in regularly to see what's new on the shelf. Each destination also has a special merchant, typically strolling around the marketplace—although they have been known to wander to other locations. The special merchants share a common collection of goods, but they also have destination-specific items you definitely should browse.

Check out the skill sections for each destination, too. Each location has a skill that is somehow tethered to it, although skills themselves do not have borders. The Martial Arts skill can be practiced in France by using the Training Dummy at the museum, for example. And Egypt even has its own hidden skill: Snake Charming. Don't miss out on that cool hidden skill. (It may even save your life one day...)

Adventure Lists

Each destination offers dozens of adventures. Learn about them by checking the Adventure Board near base camp, meeting locals, and answering your phone. Some adventures are single outings. You go find something, help someone, and then report back to earn the reward. However, there are many adventure chains—linked adventures to start as one ends. As you complete each adventure in the chain, you may or may not earn a reward when reporting the success of your current step.

Each destination includes a full list of adventures. The adventures are sorted into their chains (if relevant) and include the adventure title, the objective, the reward, and—if applicable—the tomb. The tomb listing lets you know which tomb map to reference to satisfy the adventure objective.

When an adventure requires that you collect a certain number of something, that collectible is usually marked on map view.

Many adventures require talking to locals, perhaps to spread information or learn something. You'll see a new social, always noted in a gold bubble. Often, you need to be acquainted with the local for the new social to be successful. Trying it too early doesn't carry a penalty, but you will get a message saying you need to know the Sim better. So, chat them up, be friendly, learn a song from them—you have to butter 'em up to get what you want.

TIP

The Charisma skill is actually quite useful to develop because many adventure chains involve social situations.

BROWNIE BITES

Adventures are a great way to see a destination—but be sure to take some time during your travels to explore at your own pace. Not every location at a destination is part of an adventure. Some sites are just cool to look at, such as the shipwreck in Egypt that you are never directed toward. So, relax. Take a look around. After all, not all who wander are lost...

Tomb Maps

Many adventures require that you slip into a dangerous underground tomb or a daunting structure, such as a pyramid or chateau. Each destination chapter includes maps of every tomb with traps pointed out so you never get shocked, burned, or soaked without warning. We also call out hidden doors, dive well tunnels, keystone panels—you will not get lost. You will find the treasure. And you will emerge from the tomb victorious!

Many tomb maps also have photos that show you how to solve a tricky puzzle.

Because no two adventurers will have the same experience in a tomb, it is impossible to show you exactly what you will find in every treasure chest or on every pedestal. The relics, gems, and precious metal ingots you find in a tomb are, to a large degree, random; however, we point out specific spots where you are likely to find a valuable treasure. We also point out the locations of the keystones. After all, without a keystone, you aren't going very far in most tombs.

Here are the treasures you can expect to find in a tombs, from bags of Simoleons to metal ingots to relics. When using our tomb maps, use these legends to determine the contents of a treasure drop.

RELICS

Relic	Min. Value (in Simoleons)	Max. Value (in Simoleons)
Small	10	75
Medium	100	200
Large	300	600
Epic	750	1,250
Fragments	n/a	n/a
Collection	n/a	n/a

MONEY BAGS

Money Bags	Min. Value (in Simoleons)	Max. Value (in Simoleons)
§	10	51
§ §	75	140
§ § §	150	300
§ § § §	400	750
§ § § § §	1,000	1,500
§ § § § § §	1,750	3,000

GEMS

Gem	Possible Treasure
Gem Cheap	Aqua, Smoky, Ruby
Gem Aqua	Aqua
Gem Medium	Yellow, Tanzanite, Diamond
Gem Expensive	Rainbow, Crazy, Pink
Gem Egypt	Alabaster, Turquoise
Gem China	Jade, Lapis Lazuli
Gem France	Amethyst, Opal
Gem Soulpeace	Soulpeace
Gem Tiberium	Tiberium
Gem New	Geode, Septarian, Quartz
Gem Emerald	Emerald

METALS

Metals	Possible Treasure
Random Metals	Iron, Silver, Gold, Palladium, Plutonium
Metals China	Mercury, Platinum
Metals France	Titanium, Iridium
Metals Egypt	Copper, Mummitomium

OTHER

Keystone
Adventure Goal
Dried Food
Nectar Bottle
Seed
Magic Gnome

NOTE

The number of Ancient Coins in piles are also random, although some piles are absolute jackpots. If it's tough to get at, chances are good the payout is big.

Collectibles

All three destinations in *World Adventures* have collectibles, just like Sunset Valley and Riverview. However, in addition to the original collectibles, there are all-new ones to pocket. Each destination has maps for the collectibles that pinpoint where you can find the goodies, such as butterflies and gems.

Collectibles are a great way to earn extra Simoleons on the side and decorate your home. There are many adventures, too, that task you with finding collectibles—fortunately, though, the local offering the adventure is kind enough to mark the required collectibles on map view.

Butterflies

Butterflies flit about each new destination, just as they do back home. There are new butterflies for each destination. As before, butterflies can be kept in your house in a terrarium or sold to the science facility in your hometown for extra Simoleons.

Destination Guides

Butterfly	Location	Rarity	Base Value (in Simoleons)
Bamboo	China	Common	20
Dart	China	Rare	430
Crypt	Egypt	Uncommon	65
Cleopatra	Egypt	Extraordinarily Rare	1,200
Pasha	France	Uncommon	110
Glowy	France	Extraordinarily Rare	1,500

Beetles

Beetles skitter about the ground at each new destination—and there are a handful of new beetles in *World Adventures*, too. Keep beetles in terrariums back home or sell them for Simoleons.

Beetle	Location	Rarity	Base Value (in Simoleons)
Scarab	Egypt	Uncommon	180
Assassin	China	Rare	800
Cerambyx	France	Common	70

Gems

That might not be a rock you just stepped over. Look closer. Is there a little color poking out of the dull stone? Then that's a gem. There are several new gems in *World Adventures* located at each new destination.

Name	Location	Minimum Weight	Maximum Weight	Value of Min. Weight (in Simoleons)	Value of Max. Weight (in Simoleons)
Aqua	All	1	105	9	21
Smoky	All	1	105	15	25
Emerald	All	1	105	20	30
Ruby	All	1	105	25	35
Yellow	All	1	105	35	60
Tanzanite	All	1	105	65	95
Diamond	All	1	105	100	200
Rainbow	All	1	105	450	700
Crazy	All	1	105	150	350
Pink	All	1	105	1,200	1,650
Alabaster	Egypt	1	105	9	55
Turquoise	Egypt	1	105	60	70
Lapis Lazuli	China	1	105	12	30
Jade	China	1	105	120	240
Amethyst	France	1	105	18	24
Citrine	France	1	105	35	53
Opal	France	1	55	350	520
Soulpeace	Collection Display interaction	1	11	1,450	2,100
Geode	All	10	25	15	120
Septarian	All	10	25	50	350
Quartz	All	60	105	10	18
Tiberium	All	60	105	75	125

NOTE

To get the Soulpeace Gem, you either need to discover it in a tomb or acquire it through displaying other gems. Here's how you can actually "make" a Soulpeace Gem in your own house: buy a large display in Buy Mode. Then, place one gem of every color on the display. Mix and match the cuts. This will not work if they are all the same or all different. Once you have the collection laid out, click on the display and choose "Activate." Voila! You have a Soulpeace Gem.

When you find a gem on the ground, it is in rough form. You can increase its value by having it cut. Gem cuts cost Simoleons. You unlock additional cuts as you send more and more gems off. There are brand-new cuts in *World Adventures* that look quite nice. Here is a chart of the cuts, including the cost of each cut and how much the cut multiplies the value of the gem:

Gem Cut	Available After # Cuts	Value Multiplier	Cost of Cut (in Simoleons)
***THE SIMS 3* GEM CUTS**			
Emerald	0	1.25	10
Oval	4	1.5	20
Pear	8	1.75	35
Plumbbob	16	2	50
Marquis	30	2.3	75
Crystalball	45	2.6	100
Brilliant	60	3.5	250
Heart	Collect 10 different types of gems	5	1,000

NEW *WORLD ADVENTURES* GEM CUTS

Gem Cut	Value Multiplier	Cost of Cut (in Simoleons)
Split	2.4	45
Tiberium	69	6,500
Skull	10	0

- The Split cut is only available on Geodes and Septarian Nodules.
- The Tiberium cut is only available on Tiberium gems.
- To get the Skull cut, you need to follow a similar system to creating a Soulpeace Gem. First, buy a large display. Then, place the exact same type of gem in all open slots on the display. All of these gems must have different cuts. Once you have the collection assembled, click on the display and choose "Activate." This turns the gems into one large Skull cut gem.

Metals

When you travel the world, you find new things. The new destinations have unique ores that cannot be mined anywhere else.

Metal	Locations	Minimum Weight	Maximum Weight	Value of a Min. Weight (in Simoleons)	Value of a Max. Weight (in Simoleons)
Iron	All	1	52	7	20
Silver	All	1	52	25	35
Gold	All	1	52	40	120
Palladium	All	80	300	300	500
Plutonium	All	0.1	5	1,000	1,800
Mercury	China	1	52	100	400
Platinum	China	1	52	250	336
Copper	Egypt	1	52	15	31
Mummitomium	Egypt	150	450	750	1,200
Titanium	France	75	105	450	700
Iridium	France	1	11	75	155
Supernovium	Collection Display interaction	35,000	55,000	3,500	5,500
Compendium	Collection Display interaction	1,100	5,500	Variable	Variable

NOTE

To get Supernovium and Compendium, you need to follow a similar system to creating a Soulpeace Gem or a Skull cut. Buy a large display. To get Supernovium, place different types of metal in most of the slots of the display (but fill all slots). Then, click the display and choose "Activate" to create Supernovium. To create Compendium, follow the same step but instead of different types of metal, place mostly the same type of metal on the display. (Still, throw one or two different metals in there.) Then, use the "Activate" interaction to make the Compendium.

NOTE

In the wild, you typically find metals in ore form. You can increase their value by smelting them into ingots. Send the ore away to be smelted, which costs §40. When you get the ingot back, its value has increased by 75 percent.

Meteorites

Space rocks crash to the ground all over the world—not just in Sunset Valley or Riverview. Meteorites comes in three sizes. The larger the rock, the more valuable it is. However, size isn't the only factor. Analyze meteorites to find out exactly what they are.

Now, there are some risk to this. The raw value of a meteorite may actually be more than its analyzed value. Once analyzed, you cannot undo the process either. So, are you a betting person? Is that huge meteorite a Kamasite, thus improving the value? Or is it really an Ordinary Chondrite, thus halving the value?

Space Rock	Min. Weight	Max. Weight	Value of Min. Weight (in Simoleons)	Value of Max. Weight (in Simoleons)
Small	1	65	10	30
Large	100	1,050	50	200
Huge	50,000	1,001,000	2,000	4,500

METEORITES VALUES

Meteorite	Value Multiplier
Acapulcoite	0.7
Angrite	1
Ataxite	1.5
Aubrite	1.4
Brachinite	1.2
Carbonaceous Chondrite	5
Chassignite	1.2
Diogenite	0.9
Enstatite Chondrite	6
Eucrite	0.8
Hexahedrite	1.6
Howardite	0.7
Kamasite	1.75
Lodranite	0.8
Lunar	1.3
Mesosiderite	10
Nakhlite	1.1

METEORITES VALUES, CONT.

Meteorite	Value Multiplier
Octahedrite	1.8
Ordinary Chondrite	0.5
Pallasite	4
Rumurutite	3
Shergottite	1
Unusual Bellacite	1.6
Unusual Custerous Gossticite	1.9
Unusual Dukeadite	2.2
Unusual Holmberic	1.8
Unusual Llamatite	2
Unusual Mazzadrayte	2.1
Unusual Pearsonite	2.1
Unusual Rodiekceous	2
Unusual Sporecite	1.7
Ureilite	0.9
Winonaite	1.3

Dig Sites

While off on your adventures, you explore dangerous tombs full of loot and treasure. But you can find relics half-buried on the surface, too. Each destination has many dig sites. When you locate a dig site (you see what looks like some debris poking out of the ground), click on it and choose Excavate. Your Sim will bend down and pull the relic out of the ground after a few moments.

Each destination chapter has dig site maps that show where you are likely to find low-quality relics worth very little, mid-range relics that are worth your while, and high-value relics. You may even find a relic that fits into one of the Relic Collections. There are also sites with relic shards. Relic shards can be assembled into full relics if you collect enough of them.

NOTE

There is a degree of randomness to what you find at each dig site.

Welcome to China

According to your Adventure Journal, Shang Simla is an isolated community in the mountainous region of China. The craggy peaks surrounding the area preserve the idyll, making it a pleasant place to visit. China has a different atmosphere from the other destinations—it is much more peaceful. Locals are more relaxed and less stressed, thanks in no small part to the mental clarity afforded by the destination's beautiful temples and gardens, as well as the local skill: Martial Arts.

However tranquil Shang Simla looks from above, though, its underworld is a much different story. Below the temples and monuments are several dangerous tombs, just waiting for a careless Sim to traipse through and never be heard from again.

Shopping & Skills

The marketplace is in the center of town, within the walls of the Forbidden City. The market fills with locals, giving you ample opportunity to chat up native Sims, learn songs, and make new friends. You can swim in fountains for exercise or stress-reducing pleasure. But even though there are all of these great things to do around the marketplace, you know what you are there for: spending Simoleons.

Emperor's Plaza

There are four merchants in the marketplace: relics, food, books, and general store. The inventories of the relic and food merchants change daily, so check back often to see what new treasures are for sale. The inventories of the book and general stores remain static, though. Here are the useful items and goodies you can buy at the marketplace, plus the wares of the Special Merchant, who is likely not too far from the marketplace during waking hours.

GENERAL STORE

Item	Price (in Simoleons)
Low Quality Dried Food	5
Medium Quality Dried Food	20
High Quality Dried Food	40
Shower in a Can	120
Sim Scouts' Classic Camper	220
Colesim 2br Edition Tent	2,700
SnapTastic Flimsy-Cam	250
Golden Dragon Fireworks	75
Honorary Incense Holder of Jun Pao	1,000
NostalgiCycle	250
Bi-Trike for Kids	250
Fortune Factory Fortune Cookie Maker	1,900

GENERAL STORE, CONTINUED

Item	Price (in Simoleons)
Sheng Hai Training Dummy	325
Board Breaker	550
Jiangzhou's Chest	475

BOOKSTORE

Book	Genre/Skill Level Required	Price (in Simoleons)
GENERAL		
Jimmy Sprocket and the Cave of the Dragon	Children's	486
Toddlers and Chopsticks	Children's	628
Planet Beeboz	Sci-Fi	810
The Year of the Llama	Non-Fiction	933
The Dragon's Age	Fantasy	966
The Life and Time of Mr. Chan	Historical	1,210
Li Bing and the King's Daughter	Fiction	1,311
Imperial Military Tactics	Non-Fiction	1,323
Terracotta Bodyguard II	Fiction	1,355
Raymundo the Dragon	Fantasy	1,385
The Rice Tourist's Companion	Non-Fiction	1,439
How Rain Built the World	Historical	1,906
A Wall Between Us	Romance	2,009
How to Handle Fireworks	Non-Fiction	2,135
Sim Fu: Jumping Kicks	Non-Fiction	2,224
The Memoirs of Chin Han	Historical	2,297
Fishing for the Moon	Non-Fiction	2,394
The International Reader of Fried Rice	Non-Fiction	2,469
Noodles! And Sauerkraut!	Non-Fiction	2,471
The Dragon Ripple	Fantasy	2,475
SKILLS		
Martial Arts Vol. 1: Wax On Philosophic	0	50

BOOKSTORE, CONTINUED

Book	Genre/Skill Level Required	Price (in Simoleons)
FISHING		
Delicate Decorations: Katching Kawarimono Koi (and Doitsu)	0	75
The Art of Koi Ponds: Ochiba and Tancho	3	400
Mythical Fish Vol. 1: Discovering Dragons	7	1,500
RECIPES		
Stir-Fry	6	200
Egg Rolls	2	325

NOTE

The items offered at the food store will change from one trip to the next.

SPECIAL MERCHANT

Item	Description	Cost (in Ancient Coins)	Required Visa Level
Pemmican	Special snack that sates hunger for longer and gives Carbed Up! moodlet.	10	1
Potion of Liquid Courage	Drink this to banish Fear and get an extra boost of courage.	40	1
Sands of Understanding	Use this magical sand to reveal secrets inside a tomb, illuminating the location of relics, traps, and treasures.	100	1
Skeleton Keystone	This special keystone fits any keystone panel except a tomb's unique keystone panel.	400	2
Escape Dust	Tired? Hungry? Just in a bad spot? Use this reward to instantly teleport back to base camp or an owned vacation home.	75	2
Master Thief's Coin	Holding this reward increases the number of Ancient Coins found in tombs or earned by completing an adventure.	750	2
The Sultan's Tabernacle	This portable palace gives your Sim the Slept Like a King/Queen moodlet.	2,500	3
Certificate of Partnership with China	Allows bearer (and any traveling with) to stay at destination longer than possible with current visa.	1,350	3

Buy fireworks from the general store and launch them into the air to put on a great show and have fun.

Fortune Cookies

What's the Fortune Cookie Maker at the general store? This fun machine produces fortunes inside delicious little cookies. There is a Fortune Cookie Maker inside the food shop at the marketplace, so give that a try before you plunk down the Simoleons for your own to take home. When activated, the Fortune Cookie Maker shakes and whirs, eventually spitting out a little cookie with a slip of paper inside. While your Sim munches on the cookie, they read their fortune. If it's a good fortune, they get the Promising Fortune moodlet. If the treat that pops out of the machine is actually a misfortune cookie, then the Sims gets the negative Foreboding Fortune moodlet.

TIP

Did you get a downer of a cookie? Then fire up the machine again and see if you can get a good fortune to reverse the effect of the negative moodlet.

NOTE

You can also leave your own notes inside the fortune cookies created by the machine.

Lucky Sims tend to get good fortunes more often.

Well, did you like the Fortune Cookie Maker? Then buy it from the merchant. The machine is added to your family inventory. When you return home from China, you can place it anywhere in your house and enjoy a fresh fortune cookie at your leisure. If luck is on your side, your whole household can benefit from the good vibes that come from great fortune cookies.

Martial Arts Skill

As you know, each destination in *World Adventures* has a skill that is somehow tethered to it. China's skill is Martial Arts. You can learn this skill by reading a book or just heading up to the Phoenix Martial Arts Academy just outside the Forbidden City and starting in with one of the provided Training Dummies. The academy also has Board Breakers you can use when you develop the skill up to level 2. Expect to find a lot of other Sims around the academy—talk with them, get to know them, and then spar with them. Sparring is a wonderful way to develop the Martial Arts skill while you are in China.

NOTE

The Phoenix Martial Arts Academy has a bathroom with showers so you can wash off the post-training funk.

Phoenix Martial Arts Academy

There are other locations in China where you can practice your Martial Arts skill: Resolute Fist Retreat and the Crane Master Martial Arts Park. The Resolute Fist Retreat has beds and showers in addition to a Training Dummy, Board Breaker, and ample space for sparring. The Crane Master Martial Arts Park is perched high above the Temple of Heaven. It is a small location, but offers the necessary equipment for getting a good Martial Arts training session in.

TIP

Expect a Beautiful Vista moodlet when ascending to the top of the peak with the Crane Master Martial Arts Park.

Resolute Fist Retreat

Crane Master Martial Arts Park

NOTE

The floor switch at the bottom of the Resolute Fist Retreat unlocks the stairs leading down to the Ancient Monk Retreat tomb.

Sight-Seeing

Ready to go on some adventures in China and increase your visa? Then expect to do some sight-seeing around Shang Simla. There are a number of community lots you will visit in addition to the marketplace and skill-related sites detailed earlier. There are tomb entrances to investigate, graveyards to explore, and vacation houses to covet.

Marker	Lot	Marker	Lot
A	Base Camp	J	Land of the Ancestors
B	Emperor's Plaza	K	Temple of Heaven
C	Phoenix Martial Arts Academy	L	Terracotta Army
D	Scholar's Garden	M	Hot Springs
E	Resolute Fist Retreat	N	Dragon Springs
F	Crane Master Martial Arts Park	O	Han's Orchard
G	Abandoned Barn	P	Camp Chrysanthemum
H	Dragon's Maw	Q	Camp Lotus
I	Halls of the Lost Army	R	Camp Orchid
		S	Camp Peony

Community Locations

Abandoned Barn

The Abandoned Barn looks quite ordinary, but it is the entry to a small hidden temple below the earth.

Base Camp

When you first arrive in China, your initial stop is the base camp. The Adventure Board in front of the base camp gets you started on your very first adventure—stop there right away and see what's being offered to curious Sims. Base camp also offers all of the amenities your Sim needs for basic needs, such as beds, showers, and a kitchen. Use base camp at any time—but be polite and clean up after yourself before you leave!

Dragon's Maw

Carved in stone above the Forbidden City, the eyes of an ancient dragon watch over the people of Shang Simla. The Dragon's Maw is the entrance to a tomb of the same name, which your Sim must explore as part of the adventures offered in China. It is not a place

for the weak-hearted. Many traps await those who dare slip through the dragon's teeth and explore its dark belly.

Halls of the Lost Army

The Halls of the Lost Army is a temple in the middle of the Forbidden City. Just below the hall is a tomb where visitors to China can get their feet wet, exploring their very first tomb at the destination. It's not the toughest tomb your Sim will encounter, but woe unto those who take trips to the underworld lightly.

Land of the Ancestors

Nestled in the mountains above the Forbidden City is the Land of the Ancestors, the ancient burial ground of Shang Simla. This graveyard is a quiet place to visit...during the day. Is your Sim brave enough to pay their respects to the ancestors after the sun has set?

Explore the catacombs below the burial ground, just like the cemetery back in your home town.

Scholar's Garden

The peaceful Scholar's Garden is a relaxing respite in a destination that is already stunningly peaceful. Sims walk among the manicured plants and breathe deep the outdoor air. Sims with a developed Logic skill may use the telescope to search the heavens or practice their mental fortitude at the outdoor chess table. Inside the small structure on the garden grounds, Sims may relax in posh chairs and read a selection from the bookshelves.

NOTE

The Scholar's Garden also has a Training Dummy and Board Breaker if you want to break a physical sweat as well as a mental one.

Name heavenly bodies over China by searching the galaxy through the telescope.

Temple of Heaven

The Temple of Heaven jabs its finger into the sky, pointing to the gods above that have shown such great fortune to Shang Simla. Rumor has it that somewhere below the Temple of Heaven, though, is a magical artifact with the power to shatter that which the gods created: stone. If your Sim wants to break through the giant boulders that block many paths in tombs, they must prove themselves worthy to enough locals to earn the right to attempt the Pangu's Axe adventure.

Pangu's Axe is located in the Temple of Heaven—it is the only place you will find this treasure and only as part of the "Pangu's Axe" adventure.

Pangu's Axe lets you smash through giant boulders in other tombs. Go back to previously explored tombs with that magical axe and open new areas with great treasures.

Terracotta Army

It is said that the emperors of old would need a great army to escort them into the underworld. And so vast platoons of terracotta soldiers were fashioned from ancient clay and erected on the site where the emperor's physical body was buried. The Terracotta Army is a breathtaking sight to behold, but below the clay hooves of the horses that shall fight for the emperor in the afterlife is the Tomb of the Dragon Emperor. Does your Sim dare set foot on such hallowed ground?

Camp Sites

We've all been there. You're halfway done with an adventure but the Sleepy moodlet is about to turn red. You don't want to spend a bunch of time hoofing it back to base camp. Traveling Sims are always welcome to take a snooze or use the bathroom facilities at any of China's camps.

TIP

Warm yourself by the fire pit before tucking into that tent.

Camp Chrysanthemum

Camp Lotus

Camp Orchid

Camp Peony

Vacation Homes

Once Sims have achieved level 3 of their visa, they can buy vacation homes in China to enjoy during their extended stays. Here are the available homes in China:

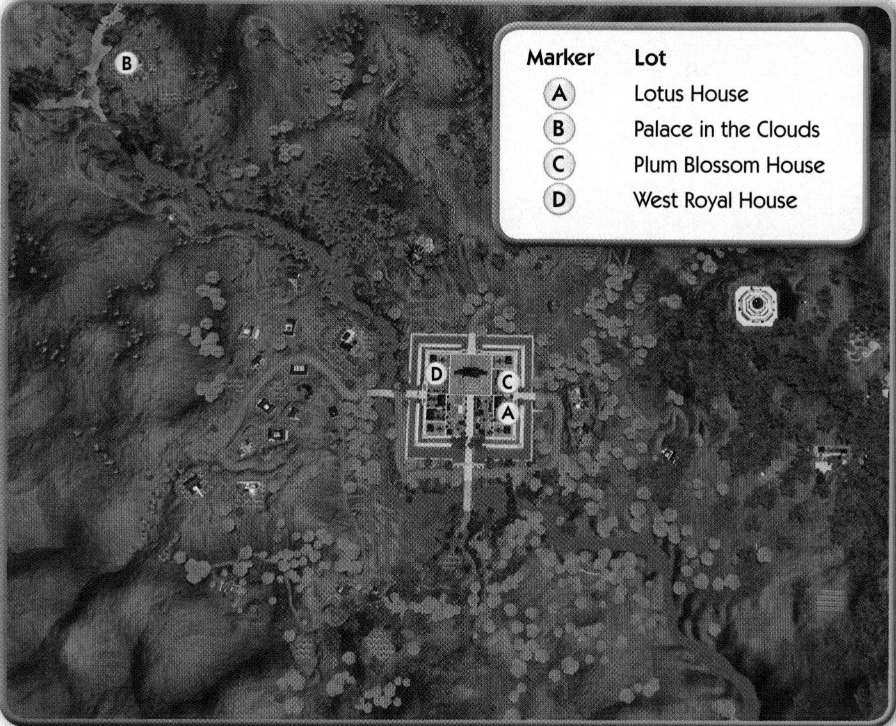

Marker	Lot
A	Lotus House
B	Palace in the Clouds
C	Plum Blossom House
D	West Royal House

Lotus House

Palace in the Clouds

Plum Blossom House

West Royal House

NOTE

Sims can also buy empty lots and build their own vacation homes on them.

Collectibles

Although there are many adventures to undertake in China, don't forget to explore the landscape and seek out all sorts of collectibles. There are many new collectibles to pick up in China and bring back to your home town that cannot be found anywhere else, so use these maps as guides for where to poke around. Remember, new collectibles spawn every morning, so if you did not spot a certain collectible you were looking for yesterday, check back today to see if it appears.

Dig Sites

China has several dig sites where you can root around and look for treasures and relics. Use this map of the various sites around China to see where your Sim can possibly excavate and hopefully dig up something valuable.

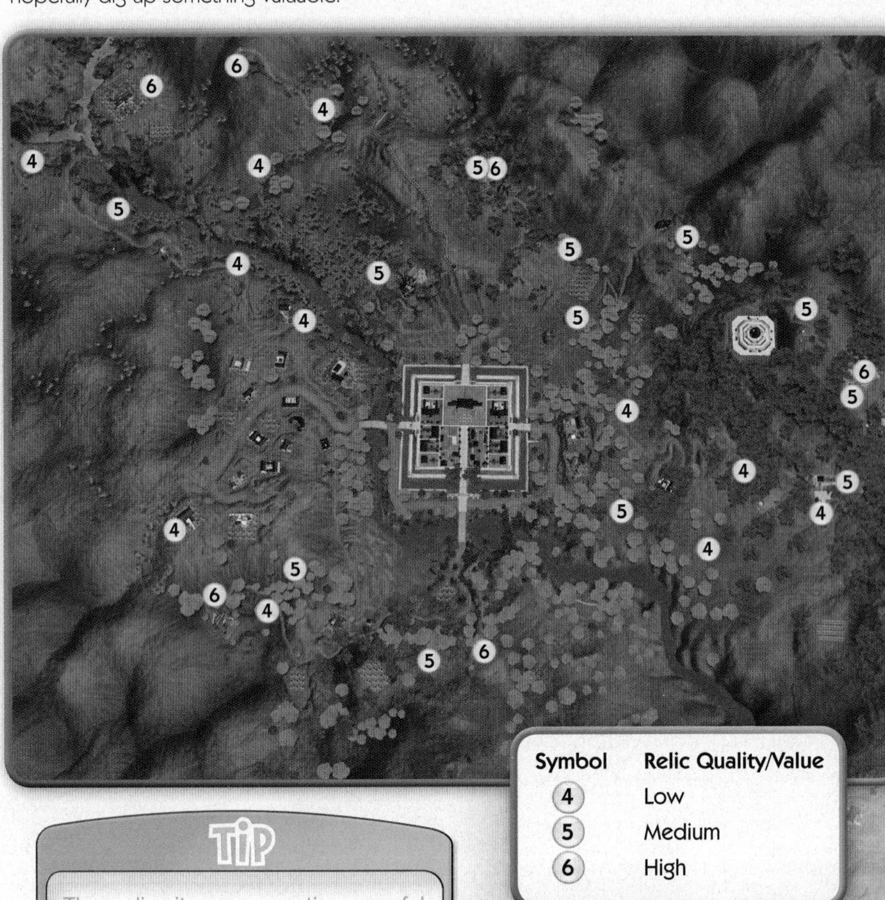

Symbol	Relic Quality/Value
4	Low
5	Medium
6	High

TIP

These dig sites are sometimes useful for uncovering relics and treasures that help with adventures.

Fishing Spots

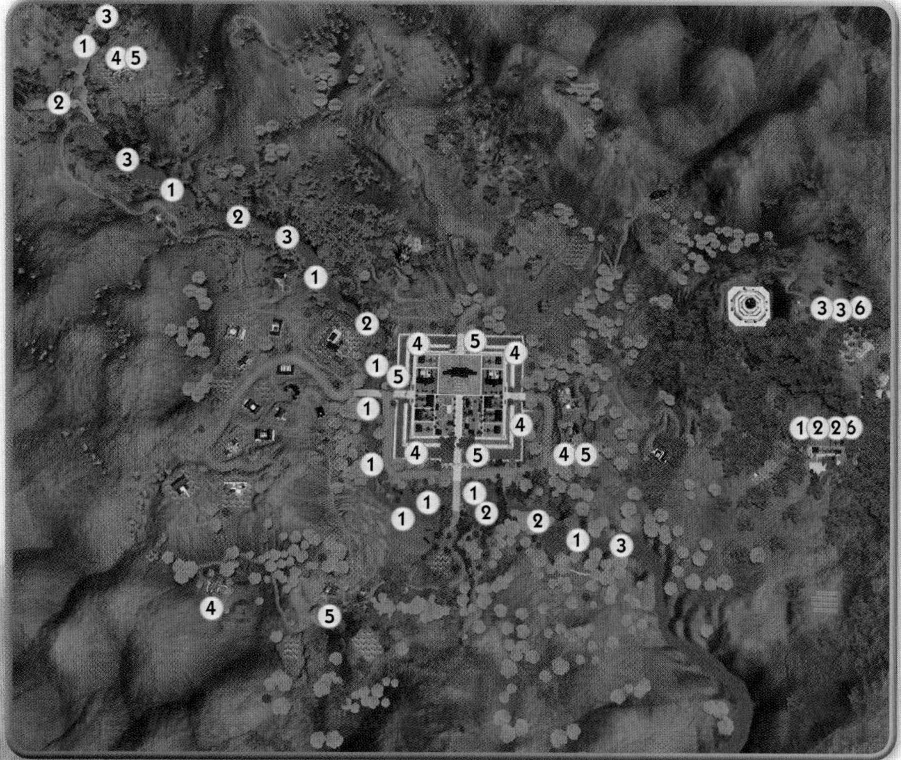

Symbol	Fish
① China, Common	Doitsu Koi, Goldfish, Red Herring, Kawarimono Koi, Angelfish
② China, Uncommon	Red Herring, Kawarimono Koi, Ochiba Koi, Black Goldfish, Angelfish
③ China, Rare	Red Herring, Kawarimono Koi, Ochiba Koi, Black Goldfish, Tancho Koi, Dragon Fish
④ China, Koi1	Goldfish, Kawarimono Koi, Tancho Koi
⑤ China, Koi2	Doitsu Koi, Ochiba Koi, Tancho Koi
⑥ China, Dragon Fish	Tancho Koi, Dragon Fish

There are many rivers in China that Sims may fish in, but there are also several tranquil fishing spots hidden in the mountains that would-be anglers owe themselves to try out. The two springs double as parks, making them ideal spots for just relaxing or perhaps running into locals or other tourists.

Dragon Springs

Hot Springs

Han's Orchard

NOTE

Han's Orchard contains several plants you can harvest, including tomatoes and potatoes.

China

Insects

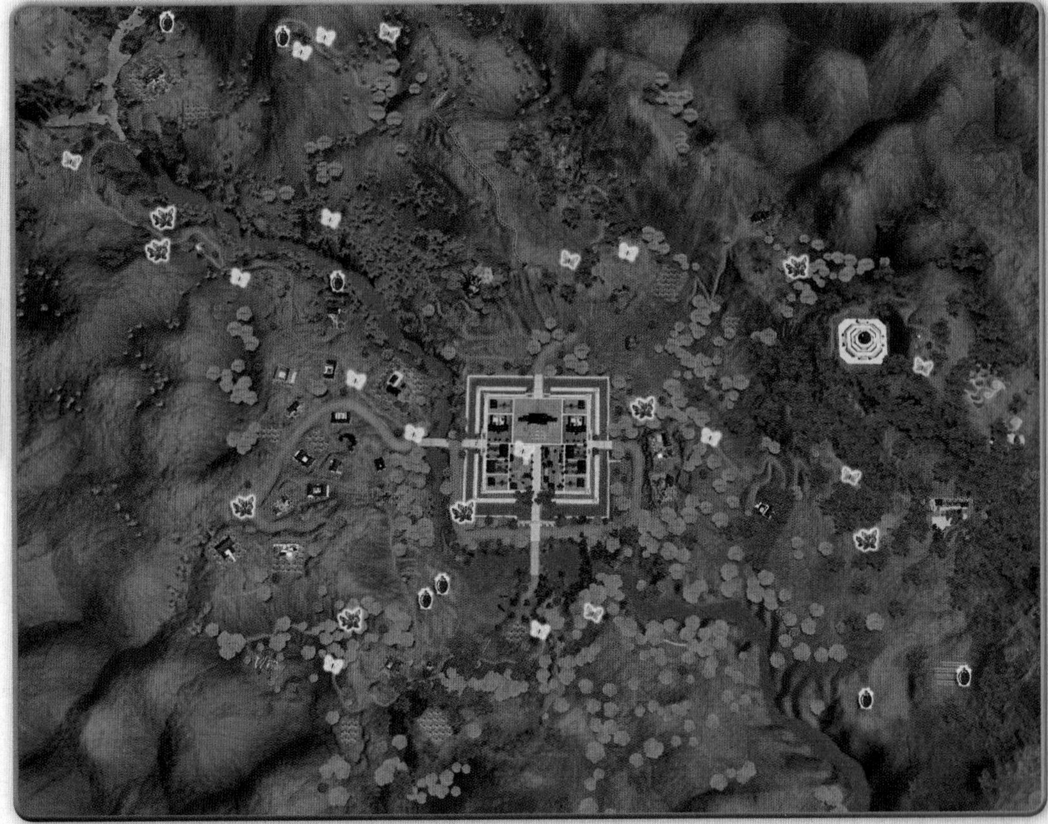

Beetles

 Red Assassin Bug, Water Beetle

Butterflys

 Bamboo

 Dart, Green

 Dart, Bamboo

Gems, Metals, and Meteorite

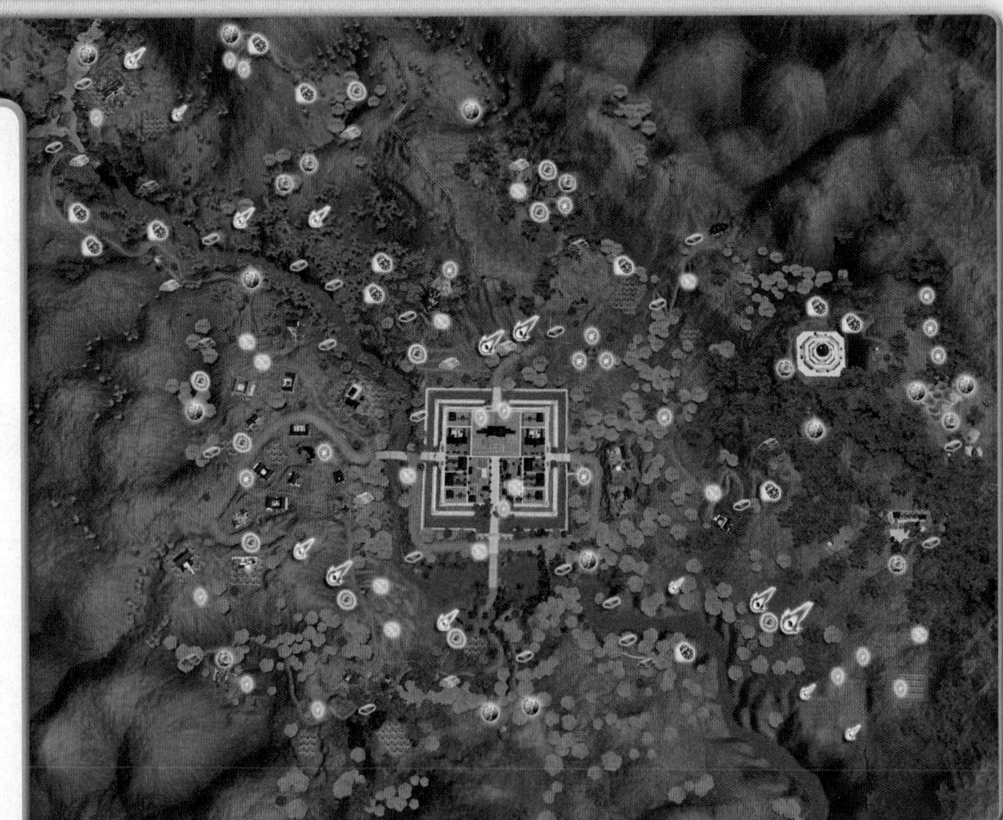

Gems

Lapis Lazuli, Emerald

Jade, Quartz, Crazy

Lapis Lazuli, Jade, Quartz, Yellow, Diamond

Quartz, Diamond, Rainbow

Metals

Copper, Silver, Platinum

Silver, Plutonium, Mercury

Copper, Silver, Gold, Palladium, Mercury, Platinum

Gold, Plutonium, Mercury, Platinum

Meteorites

 Small

 Small, Large

 Large

Huge

 Geode

Geode, Septarian

 Septarian

Adventure List

This is the full list of adventures you can undertake in China. Remember that the names of the locals who offers most adventures changes with each trip, so no two players see the same adventure over and over.

Adventure	Activity	How to Complete	Tomb?	Reward
		TREASURE HUNTER		
Seeking Adventure?	A local is looking for an adventurer to seek out a treasure. Are you able to answer the call?	Report in to the local offering the adventure.		Visa Points
Treasure Hunter	Retrieve a relic from the Hall of the Lost Army and return it to the local offering the adventure.		Hall of the Lost Army	Visa Points, Ancient Coins, Simoleons
		BUILDING A TOMB		
Constructing the Dragon Emperor Mini	The relic merchant offering this adventure desires to build a miniature tomb of the late Dragon Emperor.	Deliver two lapis lazuli to the local offering the adventure.		Visa Points
A Mini Mercurial Desire	The local now needs some mercury to continue building the miniature tomb.	Deliver two samples of mercury to the local offering the adventure.		Visa Points, Ancient Coins, Simoleons
The Mini Emperor's Honor Guard	No tomb would be complete without an honor guard. But what would be small enough to fit in this mini tomb?	Collect the requested number of red assassin bugs.		Visa Points, Ancient Coins, Simoleons
		SCHOLAR'S GARDEN		
The Fish of the Scholar	Can you catch some fish for the Scholar's Garden? There are four different types of koi fish that can be requested in this adventure: Doitsu Koi, Kawarimono Koi, Ochiba Koi, or Tancho Koi.	Catch a specified number of koi fish. Use the fishing map to zero in on the specific requested koi.		Visa Points, Ancient Coins, Simoleons
		BUILDING A TELESCOPE		
Telescopic Metal	This local wants to build a powerful telescope but needs your help. The first step in this multi-part adventure is to collect a set number of metal pieces.	Collect the requested number of metal samples. Any kind of metal will do, so use map view.		Visa Points, Ancient Coins, Simoleons
Pottery of Peculiar Properties	Now that the Sim has been able to fashion the telescope, they need to create a lens. They need just a few Common Relics to send to a glassmaker to be melted down.	Collect at least two Old Common Relics. Check tombs or dig sites.		Visa Points, Ancient Coins, Simoleons
Busted Parts	Oh no! The lens was broken in the mail. Can you possibly deliver it to a local who is able to fix it?	Deliver broken lens to repair person.		Visa Points
Repair Retrieval	Can you please retrieve the repaired lens for the local building the telescope?	Return fixed lens to collect reward.		Visa Points, Ancient Coins, Simoleons
Lights Out!	The telescope is complete, but the number of folks leaving their lights on affects being able to see stars at night. Can you convince three locals to turn their lights off?	Convince a specific number of locals to turn their lights out at night. Befriend them first and then use Convince. Then report in.		Visa Points
		A FINE WINE		
A Quality Bottle of Nectar	There is a Sim in China who would love to have some fine nectar, but can never make it out to France to retrieve a bottle for themselves. Can you do it for them?	Travel to France and either buy or create a bottle of nectar. Bring it back to China to collect the reward.		Visa Points, Ancient Coins, Simoleons
		LITERARY FRIEND		
The Worldly and Voracious Reader	There is a Sim in China who has read everything there is to read there, yet they want to consume more words. Perhaps you can help. Write them a new book and deliver it.	Bring a book your Sim has written to the requester.		Visa Points, Ancient Coins, Simoleons
		JADE ACQUISITION		
A Demand for Jade	A local does a pretty good side business as a jade merchant. Can you help restock supplies?	Bring the requested number of jade gems to the Sim requesting the stones.		Visa Points, Ancient Coins, Simoleons
		BRINGING MONK BACK		
The Lost Way	The Resolute Fist is missing one of its members. The Sim just stopped showing up to meetings or practice. Can you find that Sim (marked on your map) and ask them why they quit coming?	Talk to martial artists that left Resolute Fist. Befriend them first.		Visa Points
Lost Interest	The Sim tells you that their Martial Arts skills are just too beyond the Resolute Fist. Would you mind going back and expressing these regrets?	Report in to the original Sim.		Visa Points
A Convincing Story	Now you need to go back to the martial artist and tell them that there is more to know about the Resolute Fist and that they should give the order a second chance	Return to errant martial artist and convince them to return. Improve the relationship first.		Visa Points, Ancient Coins, Simoleons
A Wise Decision	The martial artist has a change of heart and will return to the Resolute Fist.	Report that the martial artist has agreed to come back.		Visa Points, Ancient Coins, Simoleons, Increased Relationship

China

Adventure	Activity	How to Complete	Tomb?	Reward
		DONG HUO TREASURE		
A Curious Note	A local has found an interesting note that hints of an incredible treasure. Can you help them decipher the note?	Report in.		Visa Points
The Concern of Illegible Handwriting	Take the note provided by the Sim to another Sim somewhere in the Forbidden City and ask them to decipher it.	Take note to merchant to have them decipher it.		Visa Points
Deep Within the Forbidden City	The translated note reveals that there is a special keystone required to enter the Treasure Trove.	Unlock the Market Caves by inspecting the hole behind the general store. Find the keystone in the Market Caves.	Market Caves	Visa Points, Ancient Coins, Increased Relationship
Haggling the Final Details	The Treasure Trove is actually on the property of another Sim. You must go and convince that merchant to let you poke around under his shop.	Convince the merchant to let you explore the tomb. Befriend them first.		Visa Points
Stealing the Warlord's Gold	Now that you have permission and the keystone, it is time to dive in Dong Huo's Treasure Trove.	Use the foot switch in the Shang Simla marketplace to unlock the Treasure Trove. Enter Dong Huo's Treasure Trove and find the treasure.	Dong Huo's Treasure Trove	Visa Points, Ancient Coins, Simoleons
		QIN SHAN HU WRITINGS		
Potent Signs of Potential	A local would like to invest in the Martial Arts training of a talented individual. One of pure heart, patient fists, and discipline.	Report into local offering adventure.		Visa Points
The Journey Begins	Before you can know the way of the Resolute Fist, you must first learn Martial Arts.	Visit academy and practice Martial Arts skill.		Visa Points, Increased Relationship
Learning from the Master's Palm	The local charging you with learning Martial Arts wants you to further your skill by sparring with an opponent.	Spar with designated opponent.		None
The Sparring Report	Your sparring was impressive. Now go tell the local offering the adventure just how impressive it was.	Report in on the sparring session.		Visa Points, Ancient Coins, Simoleons
Meditation Is the Key	Now it is time for you to learn the ancient art of meditation.	Meditate at Scholar's Garden until you have a vision. You need to be level 5 to Meditate.		Visa Points
The Writings of Qin Shan Hu	The vision points to the Ancient Monk Retreat. The sacred writings must be beneath the retreat.	Find the writings of Qin Shan Hu inside the Ancient Monk Retreat. Open the tomb with the floor switch at the base of the retreat. Report in when done.	Ancient Monk Retreat	Visa Points, Ancient Coins, Simoleons
		TEMPLE OF HEAVEN		
In the Aid of Monks	The Order of the Resolute Fist needs help.	Report in to accept adventure chain.		Visa Points
Monk Junk	The Order has learned of an ancient relic located inside the Temple of Heaven and needs your help finding it.	Enter the temple annex (located in the small building just outside the main temple). Inspect the holes in the walls of the annex to locate the special relic for the monks.	Annex of the Resolute Fist	Visa Points, Ancient Coins, Simoleons
Wait, Wait, There's More!	You must help the order create a new keystone to further explore the temple tombs.	Collect platinum and lapis lazuli for monks.		Visa Points, Ancient Coins, Simoleons
Baking the Keystone	The keystone will not be complete unless it cools in the air of the Scholar's Garden and the Martial Arts Academy.	Take the keystone to both locations and then return it to the monks.		Visa Points, Ancient Coins
Putting the Key to Use	The keystone is now complete. Take it back to the Temple of Heaven.	Return to the annex and use the keystone to unlock the rest of the tomb. Locate the treasure in the tomb.	Annex of the Resolute Fist	Visa Points, Ancient Coins, Simoleons
The Missing Piece	You've located the artifact, but some of it is missing. Perhaps a member of the order can help?	Report in with the artifact.		Visa Points
Here? The Entire Time?	It turns out that a local actually had the missing piece of the treasure the entire time... you must go to this local (marked on your map) and convince them to give you the piece.	Befriend the local with the rest of the treasure and convince them to part with it.		Visa Points
Homeward Bound	Delivering the treasure piece to the Sim marked on your map ends the chain of adventures and pays out a handsome reward.	Report in with the artifact.		Visa Points, Ancient Coins
		DRAGON EMPEROR		
Assisting an Elder	A local would like to deliver some old relics of Shang Simla to their grandfather, who lives on the other side of China.	Deliver Common Relics to local Sim.		Visa Points, Ancient Coins
Another Favor for an Elder	There is another relic that the local would like to deliver to the grandfather, but another Sim has it.	Speak to local on behalf of grandfather. Go to that local, befriend them, and then ask for the item.		Ancient Coins
No Late Fees?	The local wants the item returned as soon as possible.	Return the loaned item to the Sim to continue this adventure chain.		Visa Points, Ancient Coins, Simoleons
Descendants of the Guard	The grandfather is a direct descendant of the last Dragon Emperor's imperial guardsmen. He knows the history of the Dragon Emperors—their secrets and their treasures.	Explore the Tomb of the Dragon Emperor. The Tomb of the Dragon Emperor is located beneath the Terracotta Army. You will not be able to complete this exploration, though.	Tomb of the Dragon Emperor	Ancient Coins

Adventure	Activity	How to Complete	Tomb?	Reward
DRAGON EMPEROR, CONTINUED				
Stumped in the Tomb	You're stopped cold in the tomb without a keystone.	Report in about your progress.		Visa Points
A Monk's Approval is Key Pt. 1	The grandfather sent out a new keystone for the Tomb of the Dragon Emperor. But it needs a monk's incantation to work in the tomb.	Take keystone to monk for incantation.		None
A Monk's Approval is Key Pt. 2	Return with the activated keystone to discuss the final descent into the Tomb of the Dragon Emperor.	Report in with the keystone.		Visa Points, Simoleons
The Dragon Emperor's Secret Rooms	Now that you have the blessed keystone, you can dive back into the Tomb of the Dragon Emperor and quest for an ancient spear.	Explore Tomb of Dragon Emperor and retrieve artifact.	Tomb of the Dragon Emperor	Visa Points, Ancient Coins, Simoleons
THE AXE				
Confounded Boulder!	A local needs help with boulder removal. Are you up to the job?	Report in to Sim offering adventure.		Visa Points
Sign My Petition? Pt. 1	According to the Sim, there is a magical object that can shatter boulders. One of the locals knows where it is. But before that local pipes up with the location, you must convince a specified number of other local Sims to okay the excavation of the magical object.	Convince enough locals to talk about a magical treasure.		None
Sign My Petition? Pt. 2	The locals don't seem to have a problem with the boulder smashing now.	Report in to Sim offering adventure.		Visa Points, Ancient Coins, Simoleons
A Friendly Interview	You need speak directly to a local who knows the location of the boulder-smashing object.	Track down the local who knows about the object (marked on your map) and improve your relationship to the point you can successfully answer their questions.		Visa Points, Increased Relationship
Village Valuables	Before the Sim will tell you where to find the object that can smash boulders, you must do a favor for Shang Simla.	Track down lapis lazuli pieces to refill the city coffers. Return with required amount.		Visa Points, Ancient Coins, Simoleons
Pangu's Axe	The local gives you the Key of Pangu. Now you can quest for Pangu's Axe, the magical object that can shatter boulders. The Axe is at the Temple of Heaven.	Clear the rubble pile in the entrance to open the path to the keystone panel that accepts this new keystone.	Pangu's Haven	None
Return with Axe in Hand	You have found the magical Pangu's Axe!	Report in after finding Pangu's Axe.		Visa Points, Ancient Coins, Simoleons
Boulder Smash!	Rush to the temple above the Hot Springs and use Pangu's Axe to shatter the boulder blocking the path to the dive well. Jump into the dive well and follow the secret passage.	Use Pangu's Axe to open hidden tomb at Hot Springs and collect the relic. The levels of the tomb are connected by a series of dive wells.	Hot Springs	Visa Points, Ancient Coins, Simoleons
MAIN CHINA				
You There! Stranger!	This local Sim wants an outsider's help with a delicate matter, but promises a major reward. You are asked to explore the Temple of the Dragon, which is up by the Dragon's Maw carved in the mountains above Shang Simla. Inspect the panel in the maw to unlock the tomb.	Visit the Temple of the Dragon and explore as much as possible. You will soon be stopped by not having the needed keystone.	Temple of the Dragon	Visa Points, Ancient Coins
Explaining the Vision	Within the Temple of the Dragon, you experience a vision of a mummy and an adventurer fighting each other.	Explain the vision to the local.		Ancient Coins
Constructing the Vision Statue	It turns out that you are part of a vision about the Temple of the Dragon, You are destined to explore that tomb. But to start that process, you need to construct a meditation statue.	Collect requested amount of platinum to help construct a new keystone.		Visa Points, Ancient Coins, Simoleons
Statue Construction Continues	Now the statue needs some gems.	Collect the required number of lapis lazuli pieces and bring them back.		Visa Points, Ancient Coins, Simoleons
Final Touches on the Statue	The final step of creating the meditative statue is to gather up a Common Relic from a tomb or dig site. Once found, bring the relic back to the Sim to finish up the statue.	Collect a Common Relic and take it to Sim.		Visa Points, Ancient Coins, Simoleons
MAIN CHINA 2				
The Pilgrim's Walk Pts. 1, 2, and 3	The statue is complete. Now you must escort it to three different sites in China: Scholar's Garden, Temple of Heaven, and the Temple of the Dragon.	Take the statue to the sites.		None
A Good Walk Foiled	Within the Temple of the Dragon, you experienced a terrifying vision.	Return to the Sim who offered this set of adventures.		Visa Points, Ancient Coins, Simoleons
FRANCE				
Knowledge of the Past	A local Sim thinks he has a way to enter the Temple of the Dragon. In order to start this chain of adventures, report into this Sim and learn what you need to do to get closer to exploring the Temple of the Dragon.	Report in to start the adventure chain.		Visa Points
The, Uh, Potion… of Remembrance?	There is a potion that will help the local remember a useful fact about the Temple of the Dragon. But they cannot afford it right now.	Collect a designated number of platinum pieces and trade them with another Sim who has the potion.		Visa Points, Ancient Coins, Simoleons
Forget Me Not	Deliver the potion to the Sim marked on your map.	Deliver the potion.		Visa Points

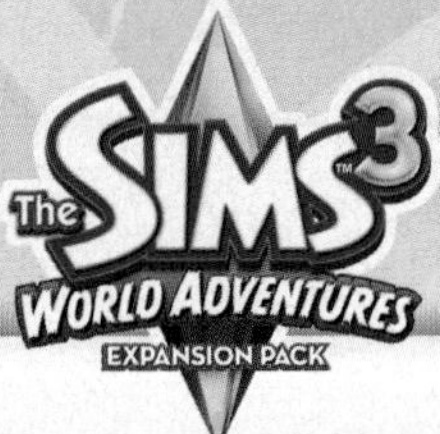

Adventure	Activity	How to Complete	Tomb?	Reward
FRANCE, CONTINUED				
Oh Sin Pah!	The potion jars loose a memory. There is a journal of an adventurer named James Vaughn that might know where the keystone for the for the Temple of the Dragon is located. A descendant of Sin Pah, Vaughn's assistant, is in Shang Simla. Talk to that assistant to collect the journal.	Locate the descendant of Sin Pah on your map. Go speak to the Sim and improve your relationship to the friend level so you can ask for the journal.		Visa Points
The Diary of Sin Pah	The Sim tells you that the keystone is actually not in China. It's in France. You must now travel to Champs Les Sims and speak to the Nectar Merchant to find the keystone.	Travel to France and speak to the merchant at the Nectary.		Ancient Coins
Speaking to the Groundskeeper	Apparently there is some bad blood between James Vaughan and the Landgraab household. A descendant of one of the groundskeepers knows more about the story.	Speak to the groundskeeper's descendant.		Visa Points, Ancient Coins, Simoleons
Quid Pro Keystone	The groundskeeper's descendant will help you find the missing keystone, but first you must hand over an opal.	Use map view to locate an opal and then return to the Sim with the gem. The opal is actually tucked under a giant boulder. Use Pangu's Axe to shatter the boulder and collect the gem.		Visa Points, Ancient Coins, Simoleons
Deep Within Landgraab Chateau	In return for the opal, the groundskeeper's descendant unlocks Landgraab Chateau. You must venture to the chateau and dive into the hidden vault to locate the keystone.	When you first approach the chateau, fire traps shoot flames into the air. Go around back and enter. Use the Landgraab Chateau tomb map to guide you.	Chateau du Landgraab	Visa Points, Ancient Coins, Simoleons
MAIN CHINA 3				
Why... That's the Keystone!	Now that you have collected the keystone for the Temple of the Dragon in France, return to China and deliver it to an old friend who has started this entire chain of adventures.	Deliver the keystone from France to the marked local in China.		Visa Points, Ancient Coins
Preparing for Battle	Before you go into the Temple of the Dragon, the local tells you that Dong Huo, a cursed warlord of the past, lurks there. You must be strong to face him. How strong? Level 10 of the Martial Arts skill.	Raise your Martial Arts skill to level 10 and then break a Space Rock board to prove yourself.		Visa Points, Ancient Coins
The Grand Master's Fight	So, it looks like you need to prove yourself even more. You must achieve the rank of Grand Master in the Martial Arts tournament to advance this chain of adventures. Accept all challenges. You are strong enough at level 10 to do this without breaking a sweat.	Win Grand Master Rank.		Visa Points, Ancient Coins
Crafting the Amulet of Protection	Now that you have proven yourself strong beyond measure, it is time to advance this adventure. You must collect a requested number of jade pieces and platinum ore in order to build an Amulet of Righteous Protection. This will guard you against Dong Huo, who is no longer mortal and quite a threat.	Retrieve requested number of pieces of jade and platinum to create amulet.		Visa Points, Ancient Coins, Simoleons
The Demise of Dong Huo Pt. 1	Now that you finally have the amulet, the keystone, and a fully developed Martial Arts skill, you are ready to report to the Temple of the Dragon and take on Dong Huo.	Quest to the lair of Dong Huo and defeat his spirit by completing a series of floor switches.	Temple of the Dragon	None
The Demise of Dong Huo Pt. 2	You have defeated Dong Huo! Return to the surface and tell of your victory!	Report back to end the adventure chain and collect the reward.		Visa Points, Ancient Coins, Simoleons

Tomb Maps

Ancient Monk Retreat

Basement Level 1

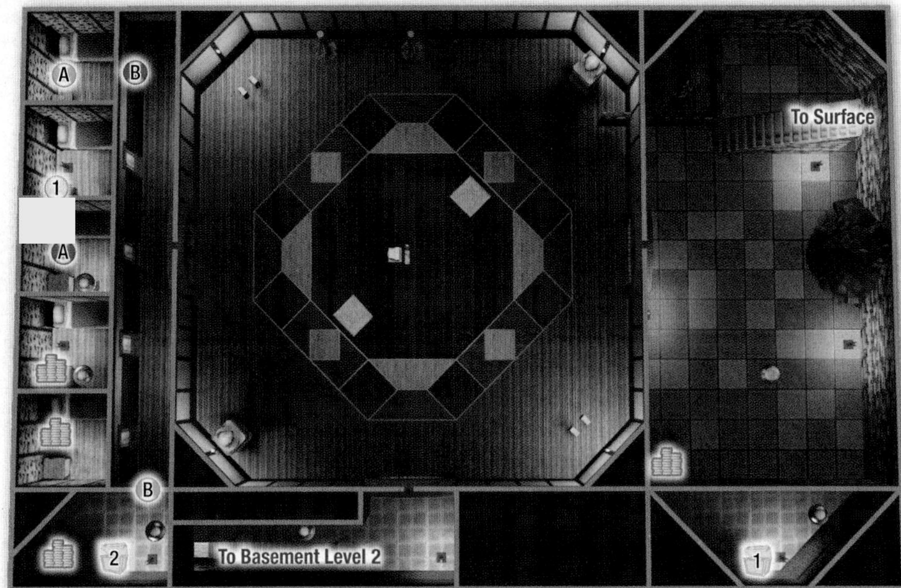

Tomb Features

Ancient Coins

A Hole opens Door 1
B Door 1
A Hole opens Door 2
B Door 2
1 Small Relic
1 Small Relic
2 Small Relic

Basement Level 2

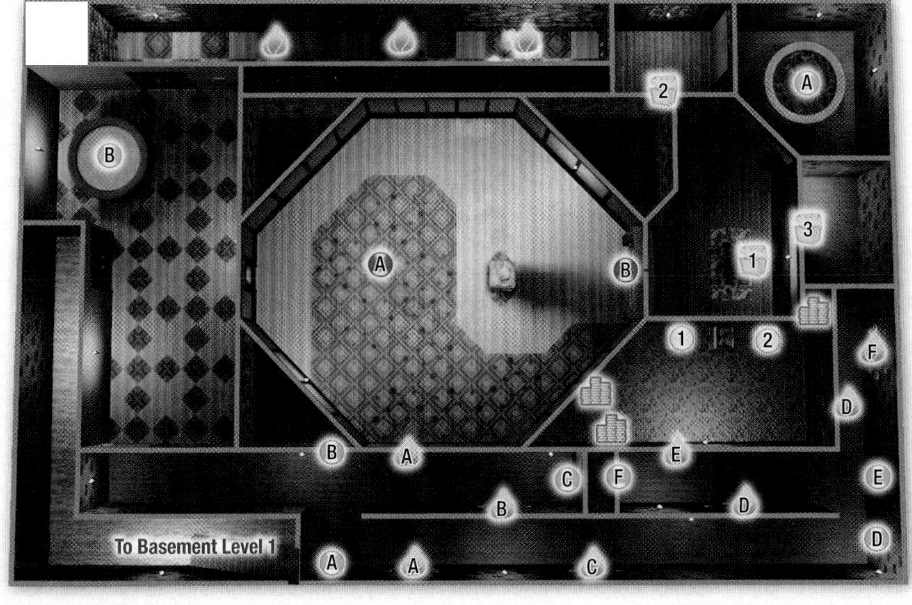

Traps

Fire Trap

Tomb Features

Ancient Coins

A Push Statue on Switch to open Door 1
B Door 1
A Hole shuts off Fire Trap A
B Hole shuts off Fire Trap B
C Hole shuts off Fire Trap C
D Hole shuts off Fire Trap D
E Hole shuts off Fire Trap E
F Hole shuts off Fire Trap F
A Dive Well leads to B
1 Small Relic
2 Small Relic
1 Large Relic
2 Medium Relic
3 Medium Relic

Dong Huo Treasure Trove—Market Caves

Treasure Trove Basement Level 1

Tomb Features

- Treasure Chest
- Ancient Coins

- (A) Dong Huo Keystone Panel
- (1) Small Relic

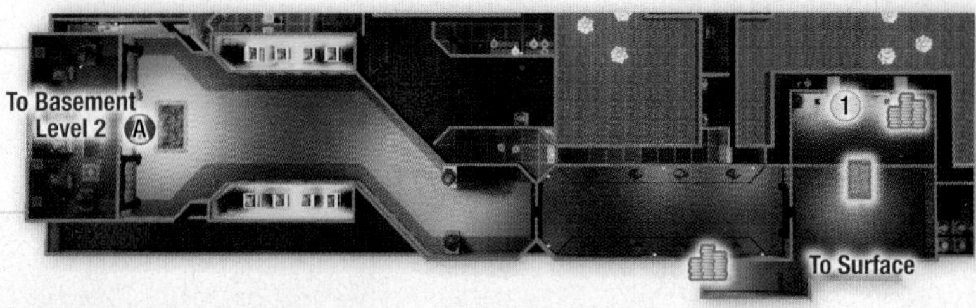

Treasure Trove Basement Level 2

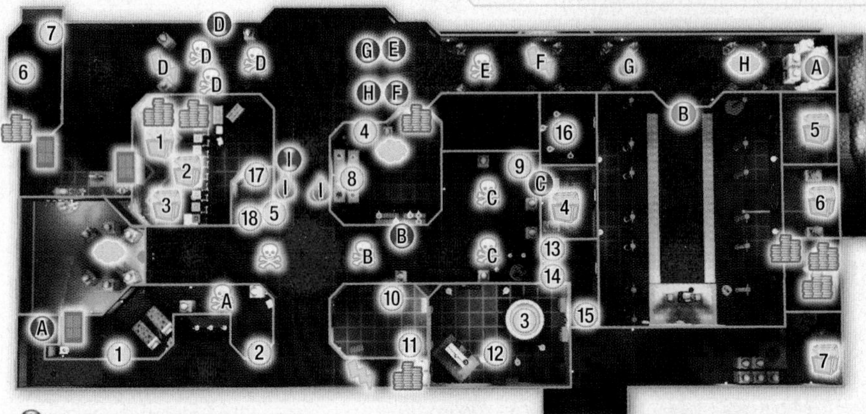

- (A) Floor Switch disables Poison Darts A
- (B) Hole disables Poison Darts B
- (C) Hole disables Poison Darts C
- (D) Hole disable all D Traps
- (E) Switch disables all E Traps
- (F) Switch disables all F Traps
- (G) Switch disables all G Traps
- (H) Switch disables all H Traps
- (I) Hole disables all I Traps

- (A) Floor Switch opens Door 1
- (B) Door 1
- (1) Crescent Keystone
- (2) Small Relic
- (3) Crescent Keystone
- (4) Crescent Keystone
- (5) Crescent Keystone
- (6) Mummy
- (7) §§§§§
- (8) Small Relic, MediumRelic
- (9) Medium Relic
- (10) Nectar Bottles
- (11) Nectar Bottles
- (12) Nectar Bottles
- (13) Fragments
- (14) Small Relic
- (15) Medium Relic
- (16) §§§
- (17) Small Relic
- (18) §

- 1 Small Relic
- 2 Large Relic
- 3 Medium Relic
- 4 Fragments
- 5 Large Relic
- 6 Adventure Goal (Family Treasure), §§§§
- 7 Large Relic

Traps

- Fire Trap
- Electric Trap
- Poison Darts
- Steam Jets

Tomb Features

- Hidden Door
- Treasure Chest
- Ancient Coins

Market Caves Basement Level 1

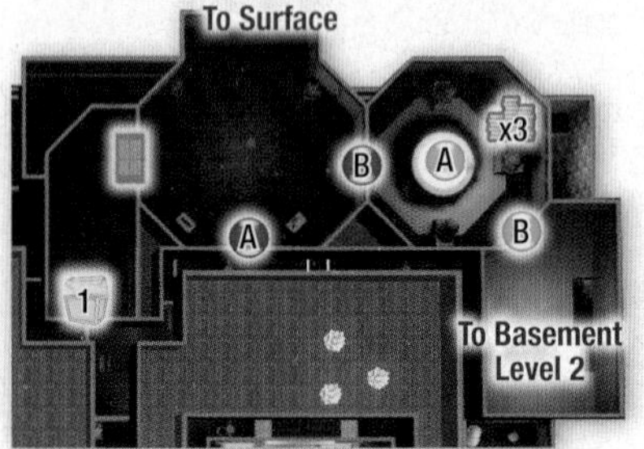

- (A) Sarcophagus opens Door 1
- (B) Door 1
- (A) Dive Well opens Door 2
- (B) Door 2
- 1 Medium Relic

Tomb Features

- Hidden Door
- Ancient Coins

Market Caves Basement Level 2

Market Caves Basement Level 3

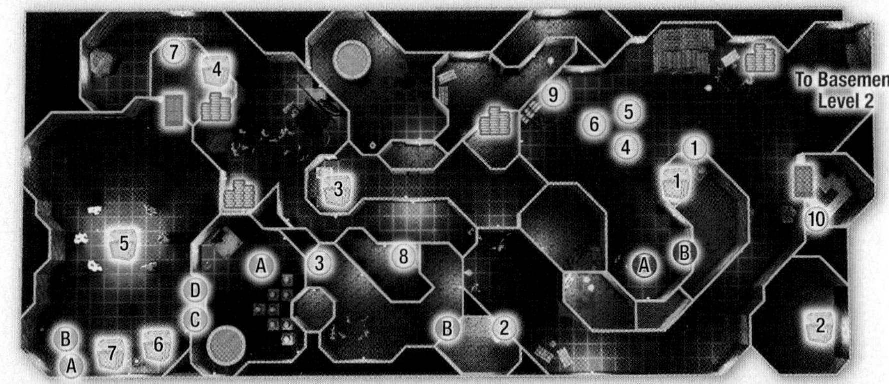

Tomb Features

- Hidden Door
- Treasure Chest
- Ancient Coins

- (A) Hole opens Door 1
- (B) Door 1
- (A) Floor Switch opens Door 2
- (B) Door 2
- (A) Mourn at Stone opens Hole
- (B) China Gem
- (C) Mourn at Stone opens Hole
- (D) Fragment

- (1) Dried Food
- (2) Crescent Keystone
- (3) Dried Food
- (4) §§§§§
- (5) Gem Expensive
- (6) Ancient Coins
- (7) China Gem
- (8) Small Relic
- (9) Small Relic
- (10) §§

- 1 Medium Relic
- 2 §§§
- 3 §§§§ or Metals China
- 4 §§§ or Collection
- 5 Dong Huo Keystone, Collection Relic, §§§
- 6 Small Relic
- 7 Ancient Coins

Temple of the Dragon

Basement Level 1

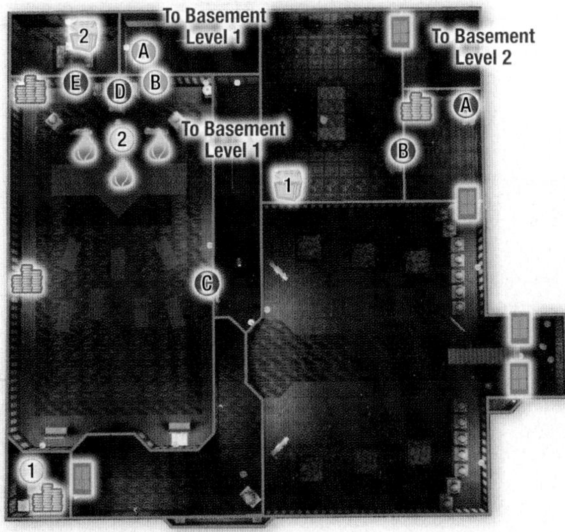

Traps

Fire Trap

Tomb Features

Hidden Door

Treasure Chest

Ancient Coins

- (A) Hole opens Door 1
- (B) Door 1
- (C) Keystone of the Dragon Panel
- (D) Switch opens Door 2
- (E) Door 2
- (A) Switch opens Door 3
- (B) Door 3

- (1) Fragments
- (2) Medium Relic
- 1 Medium Relic
- 2 Ancient Coins

Basement Level 2

To Basement Level 2
To Basement Level 1
To Basement Level 1
To Basement Level 1

Traps

Fire Trap

Tomb Features

Hidden Door

Treasure Chest

Ancient Coins

- (A) Switch opens Door 1
- (B) Door 1
- (A) Crescent Keystone Panel
- (B) Switch opens Door 2
- (C) Door 2
- (A) Remove Statue to reveal Hole that opens Door 2
- (B) Door 2
- (C) Clear Rubble to reveal Switch that turns off C Traps
- (D) Switch turns off D Traps
- (E) Switch turns off E Traps
- (F) Hole turns off F Traps
- (G) Floor Switch disables G traps

- (1) §§§§
- (2) Small Relic
- (3) Ancient Coins
- (4) Medium Relic
- (5) Dried Food
- (6) China Gem
- (7) §§§
- (8) Small Relic
- (9) Ancient Coins
- (10) Crescent Keystone
- 1 Ancient Coins

Basement Level 3

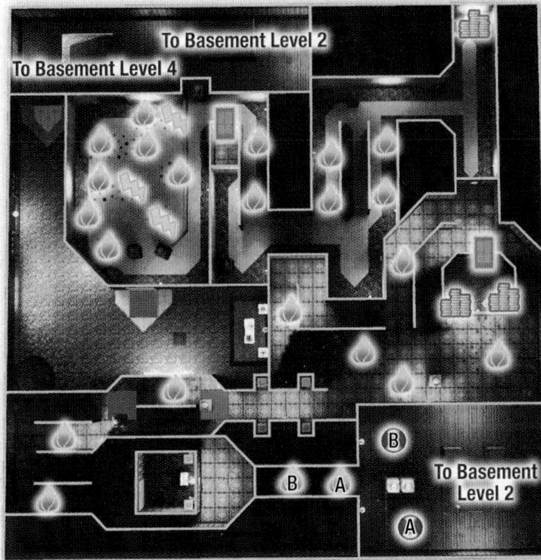

Traps

Fire Trap

Electric Trap

Tomb Features

Hidden Door

Ancient Coins

- (A) Switch turns off A Traps
- (B) Switch turns off B Traps

Basement Level 4

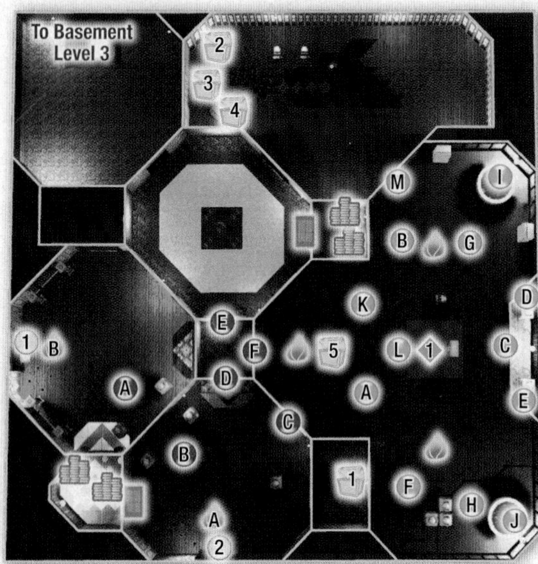

Traps

Fire Trap

Tomb Features

Hidden Door

Treasure Chest

Ancient Coins

- Ⓐ Turns off A Traps
- Ⓑ Turns off B Traps
- Ⓒ Crescent Keystone Panel unlocks Door 1
- Ⓓ Door 1
- Ⓔ Crescent Keystone Panel unlocks Door 2
- Ⓕ Door 2
- A Switch unlocks Switch B
- B Switch opens Door 3
- C Door 3
- D Switch turns on Fire Traps
- E Switch unlocks Switch F
- F Switch unlocks Switch G, releases Mummy near G
- G Switch unlocks Switch H
- H Switch unlocks Switch K, releases Mummy near B
- I To Dive Well at J
- J To Dive Well at I
- K Switch unlocks Switch L
- L Switch defeats Dong Huo and opens Door 4
- M Door 4
- 1 Crescent Keystone
- 2 Crescent Keystone
- 1 Collection
- 2 Large Relic
- 3 Fragments
- 4 Epic Relic
- 5 Epic Relic, §§§§§

Watch out for Mummies in this puzzle. Avoid them altogether or lead them into the fire traps.

Hot Springs Hidden Temple

Basement Level 1

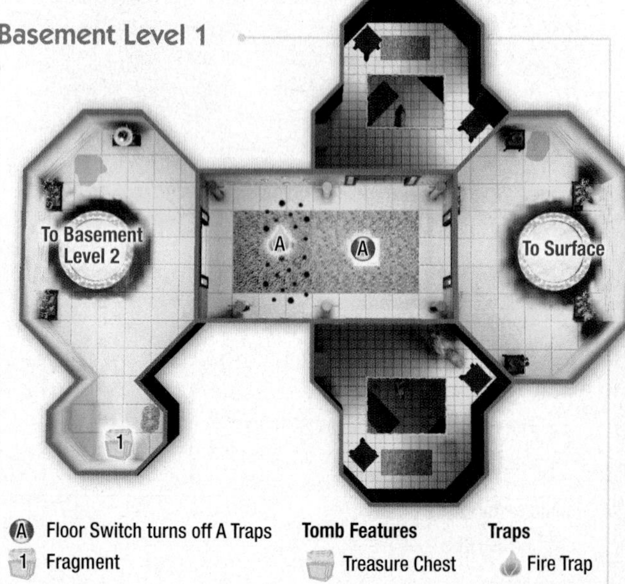

- Ⓐ Floor Switch turns off A Traps
- 1 Fragment

Tomb Features

Treasure Chest

Traps

Fire Trap

Basement Level 2

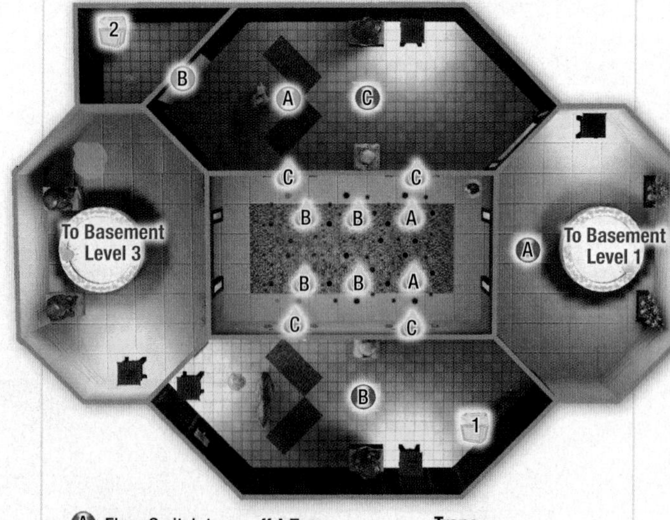

- Ⓐ Floor Switch turns off A Traps
- Ⓑ Floor Switch turns off B Traps, unlocks Hole (blue) A
- Ⓒ Floor Switch turns off C Traps
- A Hole unlocks Door 1
- B Door 1
- 1 §§§
- 2 Small Relic

Traps

Fire Trap

Tomb Features

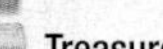
Hidden Door

Treasure Chest

Ancient Coins

Basement Level 3

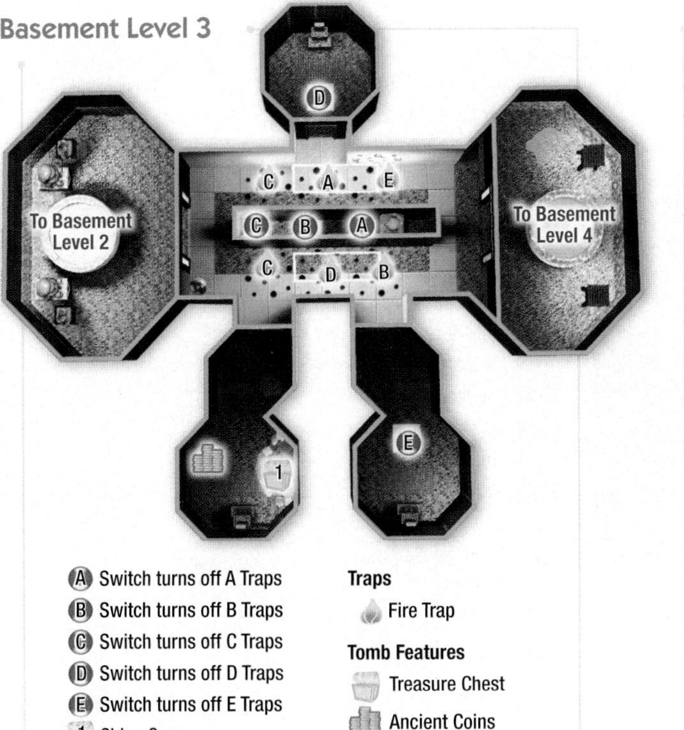

- (A) Switch turns off A Traps
- (B) Switch turns off B Traps
- (C) Switch turns off C Traps
- (D) Switch turns off D Traps
- (E) Switch turns off E Traps
- 1 China Gem

Traps

- Fire Trap

Tomb Features

- Treasure Chest
- Ancient Coins

Basement Level 4

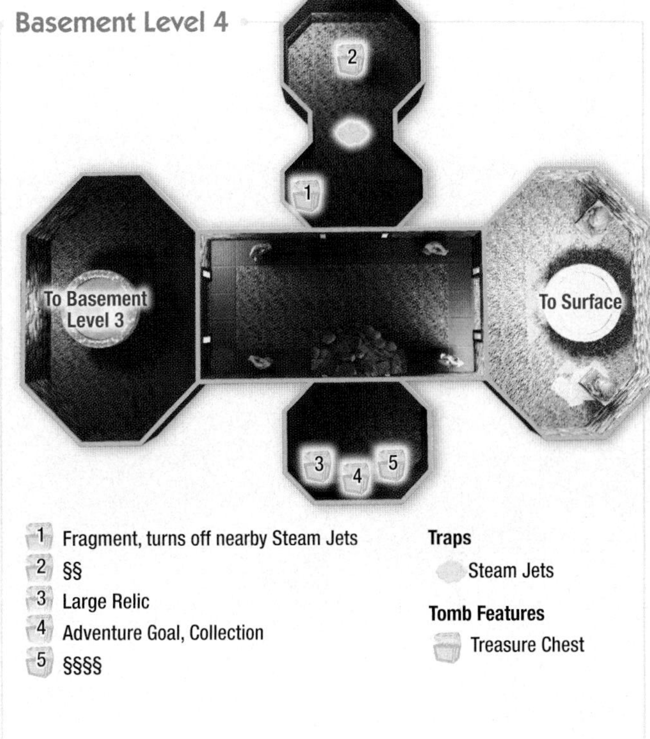

- 1 Fragment, turns off nearby Steam Jets
- 2 §§
- 3 Large Relic
- 4 Adventure Goal, Collection
- 5 §§§§

Traps

- Steam Jets

Tomb Features

- Treasure Chest

Tomb of the Dragon Emperor

Basement Level 1

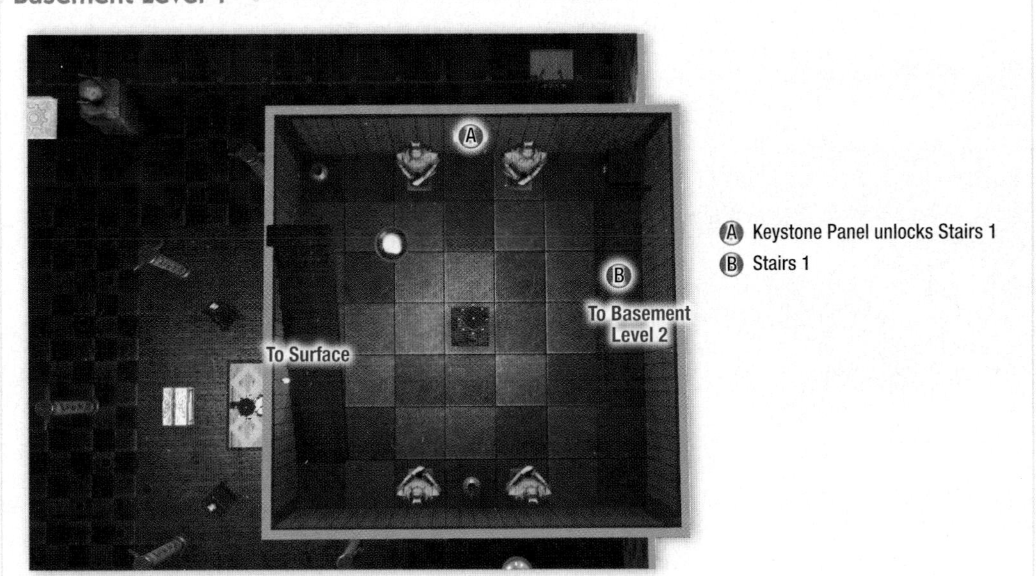

- (A) Keystone Panel unlocks Stairs 1
- (B) Stairs 1

China

Basement Level 2

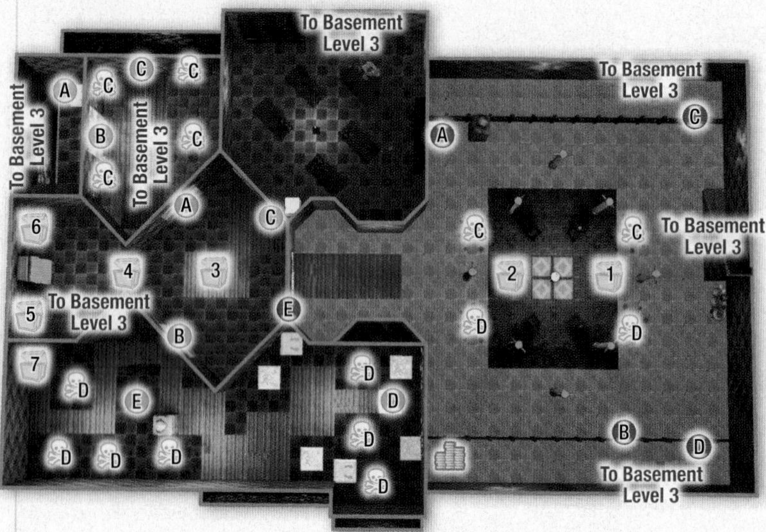

- A Switch unlocks Stairs 1
- B Stairs 1 (to B3)
- C Switch turns off C Traps
- D Switch turns off D Traps
- E Keystone Panel
- A Door 2
- B Door 3
- C Hole turns off Traps near Blue C and opens nearby Stairs
- D Switch turns off all Traps near Blue D and unlocks Stairs 2
- E Stairs 2
- A Switch unlocks Door 4, Stairs 3
- B Door 4, Stairs 3
- C Keystone Panel
- 1 Small Relic
- 2 Ancient Coins
- 3 Switch Door 2 and Door 3
- 4 Adventure Goal
- 5 Collection
- 6 Epic Relic
- 7 Star Keystone

Traps

- Poison Darts

Tomb Features

- Treasure Chest
- Ancient Coins

Basement Level 3

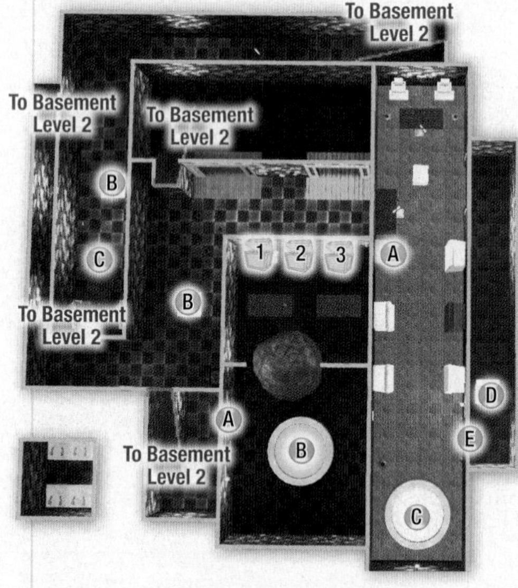

- A Switch makes Stairs 1 appear
- B Stairs 1
- C Switch makes Stairs 2 appear
- D Stairs 2
- A Star Keystone Panel
- B Dive Well 1 (connected to DW2)
- C Dive Well 2 (connected to DW1)
- D Switch opens Door 1
- E Door 1
- A Keystone for B2
- B Switch opens Stairs 3
- C Stairs 3
- 1 §§§§§
- 2 Large Relic
- 3 Ancient Coins

Tomb Features

- Treasure Chest

Temple of Heaven

Basement Level 1

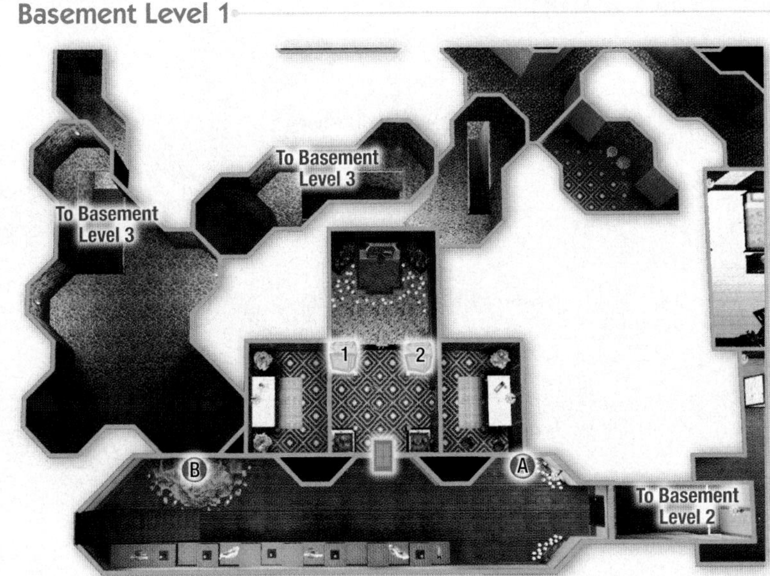

Tomb Features

- Hidden Door
- Treasure Chest

- (A) Temple of Heaven Keystone Panel
- (B) Clear Rubble Pile to access Entrance to Temple of the Axe
- 1 Ancient Coins
- 2 Small Relic

Temple of Heaven—Annex of the Resolute Fist

Basement Level 2

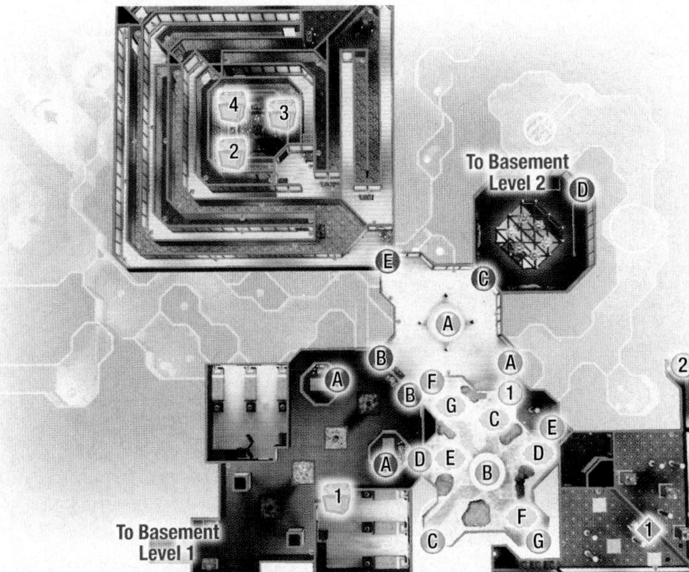

Traps

- Steam Jets

Tomb Features

- Treasure Chest

- (A) Hole unlocks Door 1
- (B) Door 1
- (C) Door 3
- (D) Hole makes Stairs to B2 appear
- (E) Door 4, opened by Floor Switches A on B2
- A Resolute Fist Annex Keystone Panel
- A Dive Well to B
- B Dive Well to A
- C Adventure Goal (Monk's Treasure), Hole disables Trap C
- D Hole disables Trap D
- E Hole disables Trap E
- F Hole disables Trap E
- G Hole disables Trap E
- 1 Fragments
- 2 Collection
- 1 Small Relic
- 2 Magic Gnome
- 3 Epic Relic
- 4 Adventure Goal (Monk Treasure), Symbol of the Resolute Fist

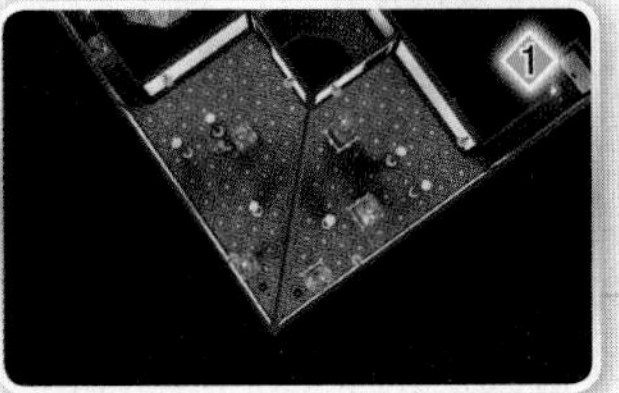

Replicate the positions of the statues on the other side of this mirror to unlock Door 3.

Temple of Heaven—Pangu's Haven

Basement Level 3

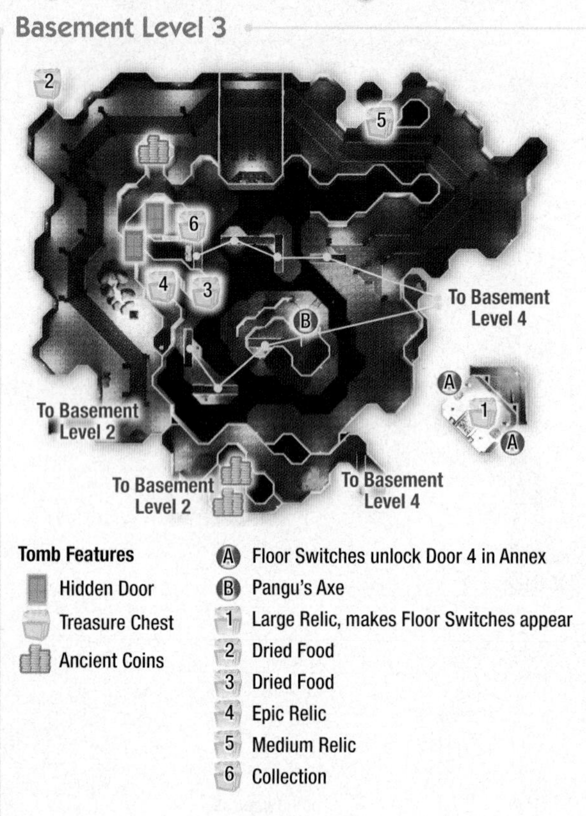

Tomb Features

- Hidden Door
- Treasure Chest
- Ancient Coins

- (A) Floor Switches unlock Door 4 in Annex
- (B) Pangu's Axe
- 1 Large Relic, makes Floor Switches appear
- 2 Dried Food
- 3 Dried Food
- 4 Epic Relic
- 5 Medium Relic
- 6 Collection

Basement Level 4

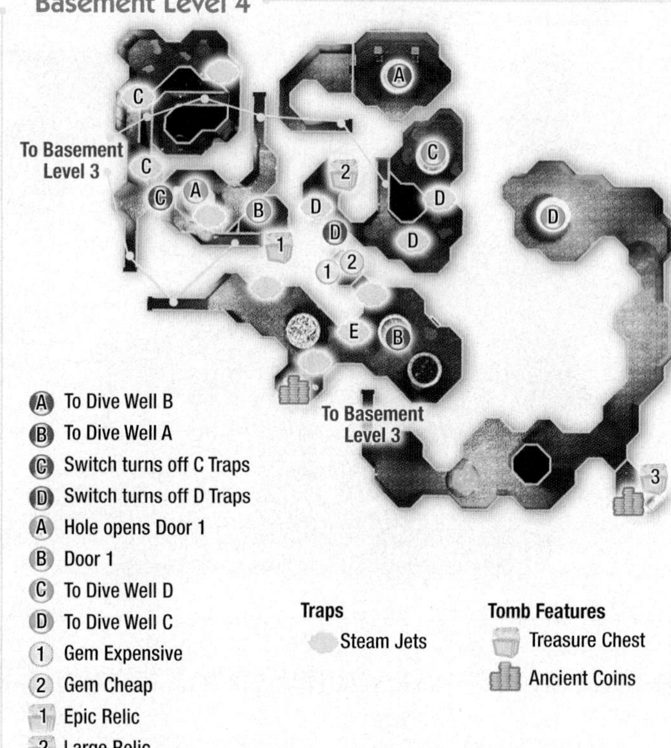

- (A) To Dive Well B
- (B) To Dive Well A
- (C) Switch turns off C Traps
- (D) Switch turns off D Traps
- A Hole opens Door 1
- B Door 1
- C To Dive Well D
- D To Dive Well C
- 1 Gem Expensive
- 2 Gem Cheap
- 1 Epic Relic
- 2 Large Relic
- 3 Large Relic

Traps

- Steam Jets

Tomb Features

- Treasure Chest
- Ancient Coins

Rice Paddy Hidden Temple

Floor 1

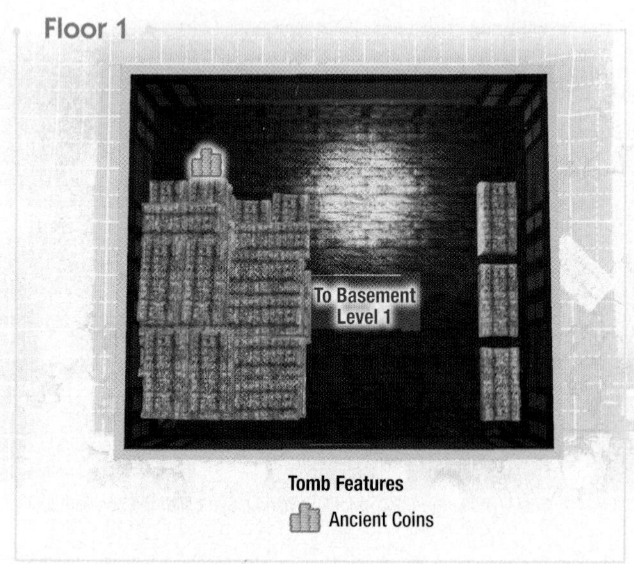

Tomb Features

- Ancient Coins

Basement Level 1

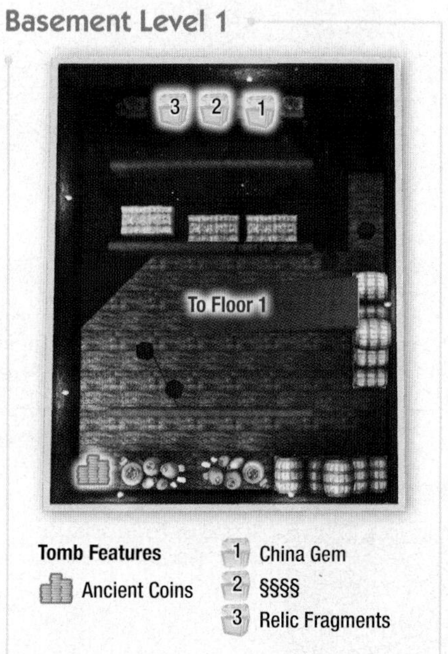

Tomb Features

- Ancient Coins

- 1 China Gem
- 2 §§§§
- 3 Relic Fragments

France

Welcome to France

Champs Les Sims was settled centuries ago, at the end of the medieval period. With firm roots in the past, this French hamlet has a finely developed sense of history. It is a place of good food and good culture, from the stunning works of art at the Gallerie d'Art to the fine nectars brewing at the Champs Les Sims Nectary. Sims who deserve a taste of nectar and the experience of a relaxed lifestyle should book a trip to France and soak up the majesty—and mystery—of Champs Les Sims.

Shopping & Skills

Though houses line both sides of the river and classic estates stretch toward the hills, Champs Les Sims' focus is its lovely downtown area. Here, you will see Sims leisurely strolling through the hamlet, doing a little shopping and socializing. Many of these Sims seem to be having the time of their lives, just soaking up the relaxed atmosphere of Champs Les Sims.

Town Square

Acquaint yourself with several small shops around the Champs Les Sims town square. The Circle of Knowledge is the bookstore. The Catania Cafe is where you can buy food. Essential gear is picked up at De Goncalves General Store. Relics are purchased at Alexis' Relics—check daily because inventory changes.

The Catania Cafe sells lots of fruit (including grapes) that you can use during your novice nectar making attempts.

GENERAL STORE

Item	Price (in Simoleons)
Low Quality Dried Food	5
Medium Quality Dried Food	20
High Quality Dried Food	40
Shower in a Can	120
Sim Scouts' Classic Camper	220
Colesim 2br Edition Tent	2,700
SnapTastic Flimsy-Cam	250
Little Boy Soldier Incense Holder	400
The Kenspa	650
Treasure Chest of Alouette	430

BOOKSTORE

Book	Genre/Skill Level Required	Price (in Simoleons)
GENERAL		
Flo and Her Kenspa	Fiction	109
Where's the Soup?	Humor	164
The White Flag of Victory	Historical	422
Avant-garde Literature for the Masses	Fiction	484
Mr. McKay's Photographics	Historical	487
Shadow of the Tower	Mystery	528
French Toast, French Fries, and French Kissing	Satire	569
Gibson's Delight	Non-Fiction	577
The Curator's Lost Museum	Mystery	663
Une Histoire de Champs Les Sims	Non-Fiction	725
Fashion Advice for Hermits	Humor	945
The Case of the Red Bicycle	Mystery	988
Film Noir or Just Black and White?	Non-Fiction	1,156
Parkour	Non-Fiction	1,333
Crepes et Cidres	Non-Fiction	1,350
Jimmy Sprocket and the Chalice of Nectar	Children's	1,376
Field of Sims	Fiction	1,663
Phillipe's Monuments	Historical	1,768
Le Velo de Tate	Fiction	1,968
For the Love of the Nectar	Non-Fiction	2,100
SKILLS		
L'amour de Nectar: An Introductory Reader	0	50
Nectar Making: The Culture, The Lifestyle	3	500
Advanced Nectarology	6	750
FISHING		
French Delicacies: Capturing Frogs, Snails, and Crawfish	0	100

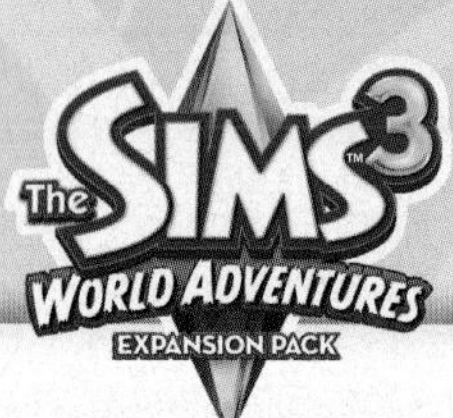

BOOKSTORE, CONTINUED

Book	Genre/Skill Level Required	Price (in Simoleons)
RECIPES		
Cheese Plate	1	100
Bouillabaisse	3	100
Crepes	8	540
Frogs Legs	3	900

NOTE

The items offered at the food store will change from one trip to the next.

SPECIAL MERCHANT

Item	Description	Cost (in Ancient Coins)	Required Visa Level
Pemmican	Special snack that sates hunger for longer and gives Carbed Up! moodlet.	10	1
Potion of Liquid Courage	Drink this to banish Fear and get an extra boost of courage.	40	1
Avornalino Grapes	Special grapes that make sweet nectar.	20	1
Skeleton Keystone	This special keystone fits any keystone panel except a tomb's unique keystone panel.	400	2
Escape Dust	Tired? Hungry? Just in a bad spot? Use this reward to instantly teleport back to base camp or an owned vacation home.	75	2
Meloire Grapes	Special grapes that make sweet nectar.	25	2
The Sultan's Tabernacle	This portable palace gives your Sim the Slept Like a King/Queen moodlet.	2,500	3
Certificate of Partnership with France	Allows bearer (and any traveling with) to stay at destination longer than possible with current visa.	1,000	3
Gralladina Fran Grapes	Special grapes that make sweet nectar.	40	3
Carnerlet Nuala Grapes	Special grapes that make sweet nectar.	50	3

Nectar Making Skill

While you should also work on the Photography skill in France, the native skill at this destination is Nectar Making. The fine art of dropping a bunch of fruit into a basket and then stomping the life out of it has been handed down through the generations. Now you can take part in the proud pastime of brewing up sweet nectar.

Champs Les Sims Nectary

This skill is best developed by just getting your feet covered in squished fruit, so head to the Champs Les Sims Nectary and use the free equipment there. Place the required amount of fruit in the basket next to one of the three Nectar Makers (two above ground, one underground in the nectar cellar). Then step in and start stomping.

Sight-Seeing

On your first visit to Champs Les Sims, the countryside may prove so intoxicating that you never wish to leave. You want to spend every day sitting out front of a little cafe, nibbling on a cheese plate while reading a fine book. But your visa says you only have three days in France before it's time to head home. Adventures will help you maximize that visa, but knowing where everything is and what most of the community buildings provide will help you get the most out of your visits.

Downstairs in the nectar cellar, you will meet other Sims interested in tasting nectars and talking about the skill. Share a glass with these folks. It's easy to make a new friend over a bottle of nectar.

Jump into the purple tank of nectar in the cellar and explore it like a dive well. You might bring up a relic.

NOTE

There is a hidden door in the cellar of the nectary. Check the back, just beyond the Nectar Maker. What adventure awaits you just beyond?

Marker	Lot
A	Base Camp
B	Town Square
C	Champs Les Sims Nectary
D	Chateau du Landgraab
E	Eastern Hills Cemetery
F	Eastern Watch
G	Forgotten Burial Mound
H	Le Gallerie d'Art
I	Little Woods
J	Rose Campground
K	Tulip Campground
L	Lake in the Hills

Community Locations

Champs Les Sims Base Camp

The Champs Les Sims base camp is a fully stocked place where your Sim can crash after a long day of adventuring, collecting, and making fine nectars. There are good-quality beds to sleep in for a solid night's rest, a kitchen to prepare meals, and good bathroom facilities for taking care of...business. This is always your first stop in France unless you have managed to procure one of this destination's many wondrous vacation homes.

Check the Adventure Board on your way into the town square—perhaps a bit of excitement is just waiting to be had?

Chateau du Landgraab

Chateau du Landgraab is the palatial estate of a very famous family. It is said to have an astounding library inside, but getting to it is not easy. It's not that the owners of the estate are unfriendly. No, "unfriendly" hardly describes somebody who would welcome guests with fire traps.

Eastern Hills Cemetery

Those who have passed in France are interred at the Eastern Hills Cemetery on the outskirts of Champs Les Sims. Pay your respects at this beautifully manicured graveyard, explore the catacombs for thrills, and just soak up the peaceful atmosphere. If your Sim loves the outdoors, this is a great place to just get away from it all for a few moments and recharge before going off on another adventure.

Sims who like art should view the statue at the heart of the cemetery for a mood bump.

Eastern Watch

The Eastern Watch is one of the surviving ruins of the people who lived in this valley centuries ago. Not much is known about the Eastern Watch, but perhaps on one of your adventures, you will learn more about this stone structure—such as how to even reach it. It's all the way over on an island.

There are dig sites on the Eastern Watch island to excavate for relics—and because it's hard to get out there, the chances of finding good treasures are greatly improved.

Forgotten Burial Mound

The stone circle near the mountains looks similar to SimHenge. Perhaps these ancient monoliths are somehow related? This peaceful site is a good place to visit and do some collecting during your downtime between adventures.

Stairs lead down to a burial chamber below the Forgotten Burial Mound. This looks like the start of an exciting adventure!

Le Gallerie d'Art

The museum in Champs Les Sims is enormous, full of beautiful works that only a Sim who hates art would be unable to appreciate. Tour the grounds of Le Gallerie d'Art to soak up some culture and get a mood boost. You may need it when it comes time to check out the catacombs just below the galleries.

TIP

The museum's Chinese collection features a Training Dummy and Board Breaker that you can use to develop the Martial Arts skill.

Little Woods

The Little Woods are a copse of trees outside of Champs Les Sims where you can just get away from it all. A collection of stones amid the trees deserves investigation, though.

The entrance to the Faerie Tomb is reached by smashing the giant boulders in the middle of the trees. You need Pangu's Axe to shatter the boulder and reveal the stairs down into the tomb. This tomb connects to another half of the tomb underneath the Eastern Watch. Be sure to explore this tomb. There are lots of cool treasures down there.

Camp Sites

There are two camp sites in France where your Sim can sleep overnight while on an adventure and without a tent. If the base camp is too far away, a simple night's rest at one of these campgrounds will keep you from getting too tired while out and about.

Rose Campground

Tulip Campground

Vacation Homes

Once you earn your level 3 visa for France, you can buy property. Check out these lavish vacation homes that could be yours if you save up enough Simoleons and complete enough adventures to max out that visa. You can also build on empty lots.

Marker	Lot	Marker	Lot
A	Abandoned Nectary	I	Le Tour Tower
B	Champs Les Sims Castle	J	Poinsettia House
C	Cowslip House	K	Rose House
D	Crocus House	L	Spruce House
E	Dogwood House	M	Pine House
F	Fir House	N	Thistle House
G	Ivy House		
H	Maple House		

France

Abandoned Nectary

Fir House

Rose House

Champs Les Sims Castle

Ivy House

Spruce House

Cowslip House

Maple House

Pine House

Crocus House

Le Tour Tower

Thistle House

Dogwood House

Poinsettia House

Collectibles

Much like your home town and the other destinations, France has no shortage of collectibles. There are new butterflies flitting about, new grapes to harvest for your nectars, and new gems to send off to be cut.

Dig Sites

Secrets do not remain buried forever in France. Use this map of dig sites around France to excavate ancient relics and (hopefully) valuable treasures. Digging up relics is a great way to make some side Simoleons and work on completing collections.

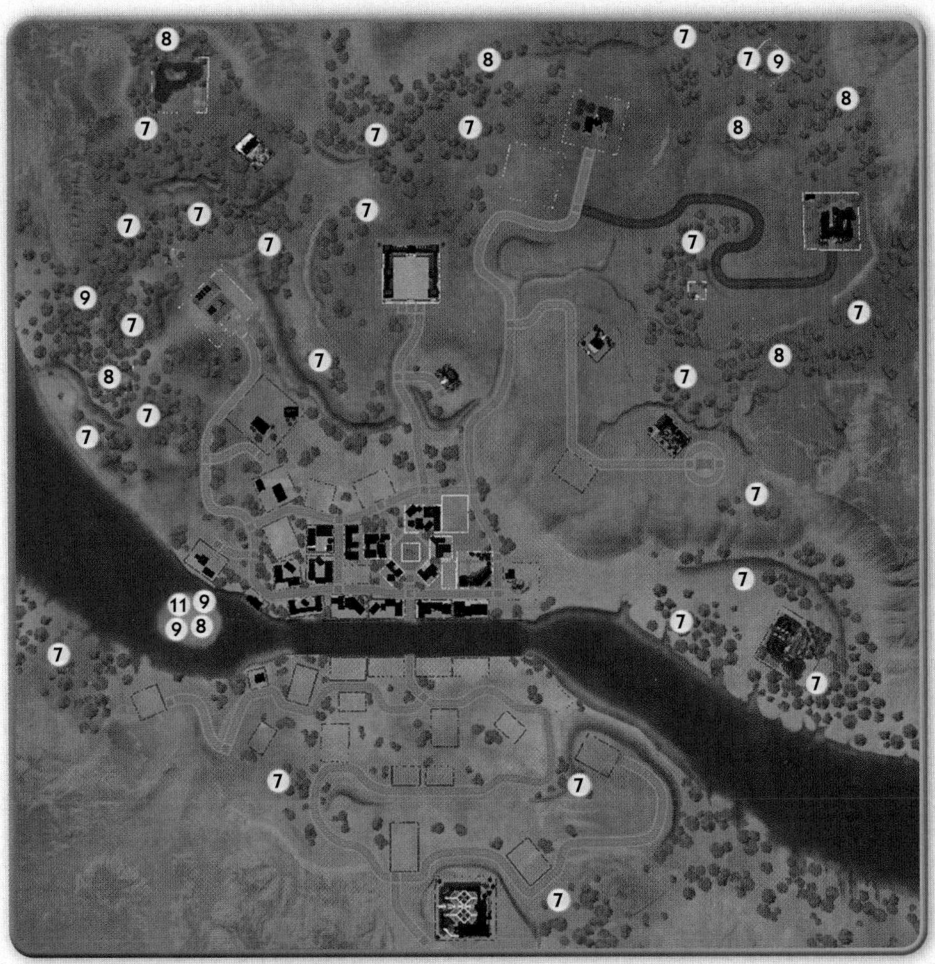

Symbol	Relic Quality/Value
7	Low
8	Medium
9	High
11	Fragments

Fishing Spots

A large river runs through the center of the Champs Les Sims city area, and it's a prime spot for fishing. However, travelers should also check out the Lake in the Hills for an additional fishing spot. The locals say the fish are almost always biting up there.

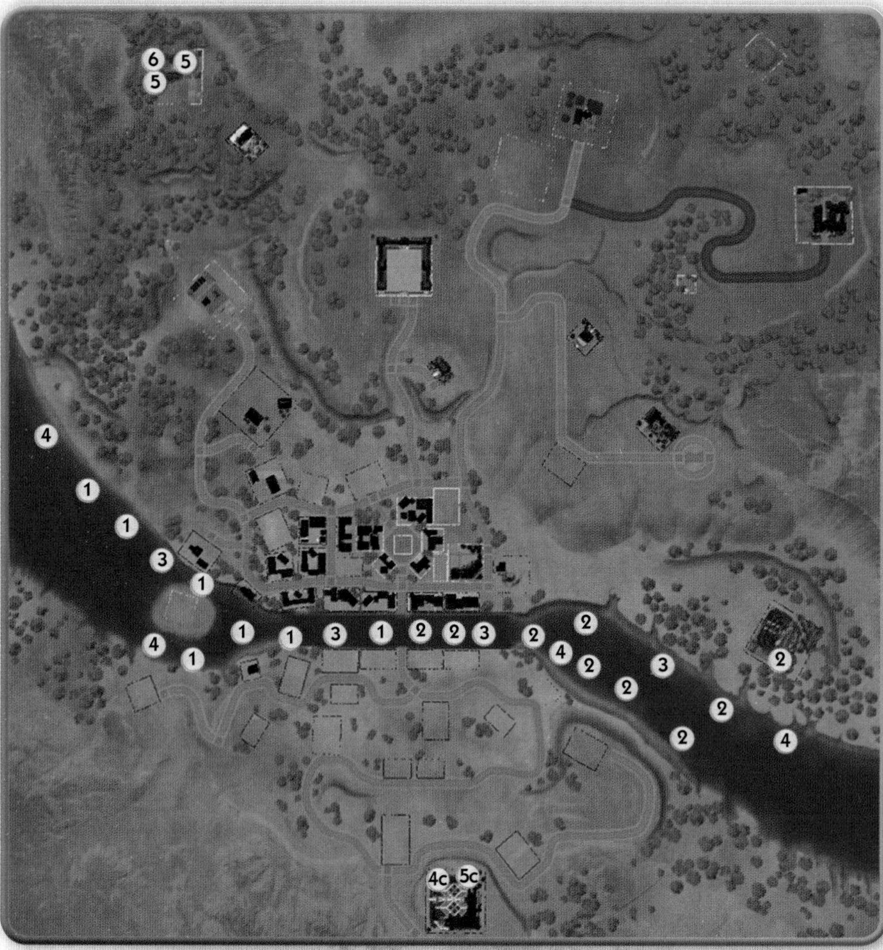

Lake in the Hills

Symbol		Fish
1	France, Common1	Frogs, Rainbow Trout, Red Herring, Snails, Crawfish
2	France, Common2	Frogs, Rainbow Trout, Red Herring, Snails, Crawfish
3	France, Uncommon	Frogs, Rainbow Trout, Red Herring, Snails, Crawfish, Black Goldfish
4	France, Rare	Frogs, Red Herring, Snails, Crawfish, Black Goldfish
5	France, FrogPond	Frogs, Minnow
4c	China, Koi1	Goldfish, Kawarimono Koi, Tancho Koi
5c	China, Koi2	Doitsu Koi, Ochiba Koi, Tancho Koi

Insects

Beetles

- Cerambyx, Light
- Ladybug
- Rainbow

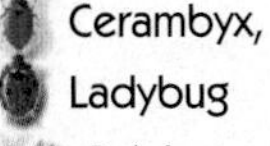

Butterflys

- Pasha, Gold
- Monarch, Gold, Green
- Gold, Blue, Silver
- Gold, Red, Purple, Silver, Zebra, Kite
- Pasha, Glowy

Gems, Metals, and Meteorites

Gems

- Amethyst, Citrine, Ruby
- Amethyst, Citrine, Yellow, Pink
- Amethyst, Opal
- Amethyst, Citrine, Opal
- Quartz, Diamond, Rainbow

Metals

- Titanium
- Iridium
- Silver, Gold, Titanium, Iridium
- Gold, Palladium, Titanium, Iridium

Meteorites

- Small
- 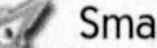 Small, Large
- Large
- Huge
- Geode
- Geode, Septarian
- Septarian

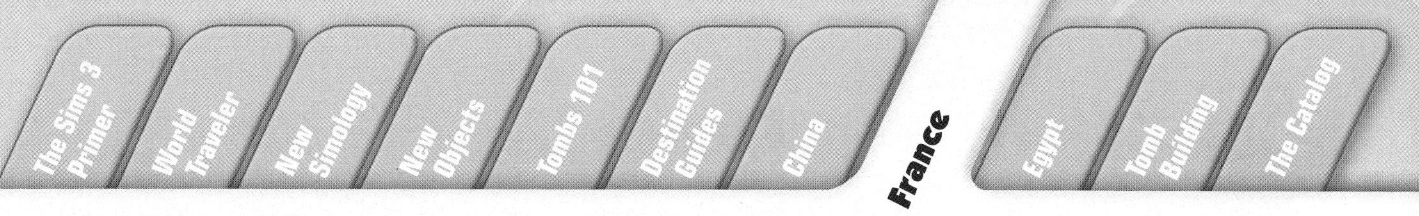

Adventure List

Use the following list to chart your way through adventures big and small in France.

Adventure	Activity	How to Complete	Tomb?	Reward
		A BETTER NECTAR		
An Endeavor for Flavor	The nectar maker in France has a request for you right away. Ten samples of Chermiola Bran grapes are required to make a fresh batch of nectar.	Go to the Catania Cafe in town and buy the grapes. Take them to the Nectary.		Visa Points
A Little Experimentation	The nectar merchant gives you a selection of fruits to make nectar. You need to create at least three bottles of Nice quality nectar from these new ingredients.	Place the fruits the merchant offers you into the Nectar Maker and run the machine.		Visa Points
Even Better!	The nectar merchant has one more task for you: make another set of bottles of Nice nectar. However, he does not offer any fruit.	Go to the food store and buy your own fruits or harvest from any available trees. Return to Nectary and make a Nice bottle of nectar.		Visa Points
		NECTAR A HISTORY		
The Search Begins	A local historian needs your help with a history paper on nectar. Can you assist by locating a Sim (named in the quest and marked on your map) and interviewing them?	Increase relationship with marked Sim and then ask about history. After that, report in.		Ancient Coins, Visa Points
The Lost Library of Landgraab	Explore lost library of Landgraab. You receive the keystone for the library at the Landgraab family's chateau. However, that place is boobytrapped, so you need to be careful.	The local says the library should be near the front of the home. Enter there and use keystone to reach the library.	Chateau du Landgraab	Visa Points, Ancient Coins
Code Breaker	The papers have been translated into an old code. Fortunately, there is a Sim in Champs Les Sims who can crack codes like this.	Take the papers to the new Sim marked on your map view and ask them to translate them.		Visa Points
Code Broken	It turns out that Champs Les Sims is the birthplace of nectar!	Return translated papers to historian.		Ancient Coins, Visa Points
		HISTORY OF LANDGRAAB		
Landgraab I... Kidnapper?	A local historian is digging into the disappearance of Anatasia Necteaux.	Report in to this local to start this chain of adventures.		Visa Points
The Groundskeeper's Journal	The groundskeeper may have kept a journal with information about the disappearance. Can you find it?	Look in basement of shack for the keystone to the shack's front door. The journal is in the treasure chest just inside.	Chateau du Landgraab Shack	Ancient Coins, Visa Points
The Key, Please	The groundskeeper's journal is locked. The historian believes another local might have a key that fits this journal.	Tell the local that opening the journal will be an act of service.		Visa Points
A New Ring Pts. 1 & 2	The local agrees to help—but before you can have the key, you must do them a favor. They need some gold to freshen up their jewelry collection.	Collect request number of gold pieces and amethyst for Sim.		Visa Points
Here's the Key	Now that you have helped the local create a nice new ring from gold and amethyst, you finally earn the key.	Return the key to the historian so the journal may be unlocked.		Visa Points, Ancient Coins
Chateau Crawl	The journal has been opened...and the mystery only deepens. There is a key inside the journal that will let you deeper into the chateau. Look around for more notes about the incident, but watch out for traps.	Enter the chateau through the side entrance. Turn on the stereo to make the floor switches appear in the first room. The notes are in a chest on the top floor of the chateau. Use foot switches in the chateau to unlock doors.	Chateau du Landgraab	Visa Points, Ancient Coins
		JEAN NECTEAUX		
Nectar Research Assistance Needed	A researcher requires an assistant. Can you offer the help?	Report in to the researcher.		Visa Points
In the Back of the Cellar	The researcher thinks there is a secret stash of old nectar in the cellar of the Nectary. Go find a really old bottle.	Head down into the Nectary, use the keystone on the locked door in the back of the cellar, and open the glowing chest. This unlocks a whole new section of the tomb.	Nectar Cellar	Visa Points
A Cellar Full of Clues	The researcher is intrigued by the new section of the Nectary Cellar that opened up. Go look for more secrets in the cellar.	Inspect the glowing hole on the back wall of the new section. This activates a switch and unlocks a riddle about three treasures.	Nectar Cellar	Visa Points
A Quick Follow-Up	Help the researcher decipher the riddle by speaking to a local historian.	Discuss the riddle with the historian marked on your map.		None
To Egypt!	The historian says you need to go speak to a friend in Egypt to discuss the riddle.	Collect the requested number of cerambryx beetles and then go to Egypt and find the friend marked on the map.		Visa Points
The Black Market	When Necteaux fled Egypt, he not only took the pharaoh's daughter, but also three mystical gems. These gems are part of the riddle.	Speak to the designated local to learn more about the gems.		Visa Points

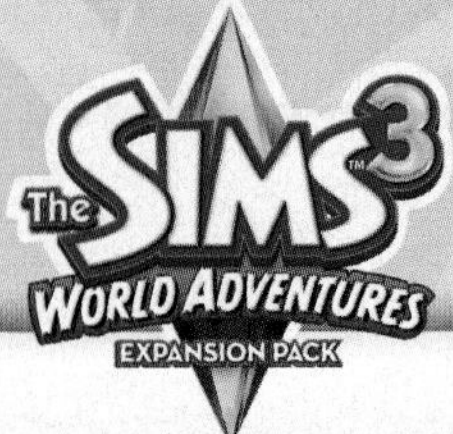

France

Adventure	Activity	How to Complete	Tomb?	Reward
JEAN NECTEAUX, CONTINUED				
The Sleazy Merchant	The gems are a ruby, emerald, and a sapphire. There is more the local knows, but a donation is required...	Deliver three relics worth a set number of Simoleons to learn where the ruby is. Check tombs and dig sites.		Visa Points
A Little Too Sleazy	While you were out gathering those relics, the merchant found the ruby you need. Now, how about some gratitude?	Buy the merchant a relic worth at least 500 Simoleons.		Visa Points
To France!	Now that you have the Ruby of Sakhara, return to France and discuss the location of a mythical sapphire with a local.	Return to France and visit with the local marked on your map.		Visa Points, Ancient Coins
Ruby-Colored Test Drive	The local is impressed with the ruby. Take it to the Nectar Cellars and inspect the three holes again.	Go back to the new section of the Nectar Cellar and inspect the glowing hole in the wall to open Isael's Tomb.	Nectar Cellar	None
The Way to Isael's Tomb	Locate the way into Isael's Tomb.	Inspect the hidden door to the right of the holes, between the statues. Use the floor switch to make the keystone appear back at the three holes.	Nectar Cellar	None
If the Key Fits...	Open the door to Isael's Tomb with the keystone.	Use the keystone on the door to the right of the three holes to unlock Isael's Tomb.	Nectar Cellar	None
At Last, the Sapphire	Now that the Tomb of Isael is open, explore it to find the Sapphire of the Crescent Moon.	Explore the Tomb of Isael. Use the heart keystone to unlock doors and disable traps until you reach the sapphire's chamber. Claim the sapphire and report in.	Tomb of Isael	Ancient Coins, Visa Points
Yes, But Does it Work?	You have the Sapphire of the Crescent Moon. See if it works just like the ruby.	Return to the Nectar Cellar and place the Sapphire in the glowing hole in the wall. Then report back.	Nectar Cellar	Visa Points
Have You Seen This Necklace?	The local recalls that there was once an emerald necklace worn by Anatasia Necteaux. Ask three locals about the auction where the necklace was once sold.	Befriend three local Sims and ask them about the emerald necklace.		Visa Points
Mmm, Nectar	A local bought the necklace. Talk to the new owners of the necklace.	Buy an Excellent quality bottle of nectar (if you did not find one in the Tomb of Isael) and visit the Sim marked on your map.		Visa Points
Success Is Sweet	The local gives you the emerald in return for the bottle of nectar and out of admiration that you are trying to help research the history of the city.	Report in to the researcher.		Ancient Coins, Visa Points
Opening the Tomb of Necteaux	The researcher thinks you can open the Tomb of Nectaux with the emerald.	Place the emerald in the middle hole of the Nectar Cellar to make the keystone for the Tomb of Necteaux appear.	Nectar Cellar	None
Inside the Tomb of Necteaux	You must find the Recipe of Necteaux inside the tomb.	Explore the Tomb of Necteaux. Locate the Recipe of Necteaux inside the tomb and report in to finish the adventure.	Tomb of Jean Necteaux	Visa Points, Ancient Coins, Nectar Bottles
SECRET GARDEN				
Surveying the Property	A local has discovered a secret area on their property. Can you help them figure out what it is?	Report in.		Visa Points
The Mystery Room	The locals offers a keystone for their basement, mentioning that the place is deep and emits mysterious noises.	Go to Sim's house, introduce self to family, and then explore baseent. Use keystone to open lock and then come up into the walled-off area.	Secret Garden	Simoleons, Visa Points, Increased Relationship
SECRET GARDEN 2				
More Like "Haunted Garden"	The Sim believes the secret garden on her lot is haunted. Can you communicate with the spirit?	Enter walled-off garden and mourn at the glowing gravestone.		None
Love in Bloom	The spirits laments that there are no pomegranates in the garden, which were a favorite of the ghost's beloved.	Bring 3 pomegranates to the garden. Pomegranates are native to Egypt. You can find them there.		Visa Points
Anything Else?	The family is just relieved the ghost is not angry. Does it need anything else?	Return to the garden and mourn again at the gravestone to communicate with the spirit.		None
Final Resting Place	The spirit wishes to have its remains buried next to its love's. The spirit offers its remains to you.	Take the remains back to the basement and open the secret chamber with the hole in the floor. Place remains inside the glowing chest.	Secret Garden	Visa Points
Laid to Rest	The family should be happy to know that the whole ghostly affair has ended.	Report the story of the restless ghost to the family.		Ancient Coins, Visa Points, Increated Relationship
A MUSEUM MYSTERY				
Trouble at the Museum	The curator of the museum needs a new security guard. Interested parties should apply immediately.	Report in to Sim offering adventure.		Visa Points
On Patrol	Security guard keep quitting their patrols at the museum. While the curator investigates, could you please patrol the Egyptian gallery?	Enter the museum and visit the Egyptian gallery on the second floor. Then report in.		Visa Points, Simoleons
Something in the Chinese Exhibit?	Nothing seemed strange in the Egyptian exhibit? There have also been rumors of noises in Chinese exhibit.	Return to the museum and visit the Chinese exhibit on the first floor. Use the hole in the wall to reveal a secret door. Then report in.		Visa Points, Simoleons

Adventure	Activity	How to Complete	Tomb?	Reward
		A MUSEUM MYSTERY, CONTINUED		
Strange Sounds	The curator thinks the strange noises are coming from behind the newly revealed door. Investigate the area.	Return to the museum and use the secret door near the hole in the wall. This leads to the museum basement. Explore to find the source of the noises, a grave at the bottom.	Museum Catacombs	Visa Points
The Curator's Final Exhibit	The previous curator met a sad fate inside a sarcophagus. Can you take his remains to the family plot at the cemetery?	Go the cemetery. Inspect the small hole in the ground next to the center crypt to unlock the door to the family plot. Place remains in the glowing chest and remove the heart keystone.		Visa Points
Success with the Haunting	The current curator will want to know all about this adventure.	Report in and explain the haunting.		Visa Points, Simoleons
		IT'S A SMALL WORLD		
To Egypt (On the Cheap)!	A French local would like to visit Egypt, but it's too expensive. Can you convince a local to let the Sim stay with them for free?	Travel to Egypt and befriend a local until you can successfully convince them to let the French local stay.		Visa Points, Simoleons
To China (On the Cheap)!	A French local would like to visit China, but it's too expensive. Can you convince a local to let the Sim stay with them for free?	Travel to China and befriend a local until you can successfully convince them to let the French local stay.		Visa Points, Simoleons
		HELP WITH BUSINESS		
Verbal Advertisement	The local shop is not doing too well. Can you convince locals to shop there?	Befriend three locals and convince them to shop at the store.		Visa Points, Simoleons
		FRANCE STARTER		
A Trivial Affair	A local needs little help with a minor matter. Can you assist?	Report in to the local.		Dried Food, Visa Points
Celtic Foray	The local needs some help retrieving something lost while exploring the Celtic Ruins. Can you help find it?	Explore the Celtic Ruins under the Forgotten Burial Mound to find the missing object.	Celtic Ruins	Ancient Coins, Visa Points
		PHOTOGRAPHY		
A New Photo in France	A local is preparing a pamphlet of photographs of France. Can you help with the project?	Take a new photo of anything in France.		Visa Points, Simoleons
Floral Photo	A local loves flower photographs. Can you take one for her?	Take a photo of flowers and deliver to Sim.		Visa Points, Simoleons
Headshot!	A local Sim is putting together a photo portfolio and needs a close-up of another Sim.	Take a photo of a Sim's face and deliver it.		Visa Points, Simoleons
		MATCHMAKER		
I Need a Date	A local Sim is too shy to ask their special someone out. Can you help?	Locate the Sim the local wants to date, befriend them, and then ask out on the local's behalf.		Visa Points, Simoleons, Increased Relationship
		GO RUNNING		
Fun Run	Fitness is not a priority in Champs Les Sims and a local wants to change that. Can you jog through the city and set an exmaple?	Jog through the city. You need to have a high enough Athletic skill to jog.		Visa Points, Simoleons
		COLLECTING OLD NECTAR		
Hankering for Old Nectar	A local would love to taste some quality, aged nectar.	Bring some Great quality nectar to the local. You can find some in the cellar under the Nectary.	Nectar Cellar	Ancient Coins, Visa Points
		NECTAR PARTS		
The New Nectar Machine	A local wants to improve their nectar making, but they need a new Nectar Maker.	Bring the requested number of platinum pieces to the Sim. Use map view to find them.		Visa Points, Simoleons
One More Component	The nectar maker now needs a special computer chip to finish the Nectar Maker.	Speak to the designated Sim (marked on your map) about the chip. However, you must befriend the Sim first.		Visa Points
Nectowhiz Delivery	Now that you have the computer chip, the nectar merchant can complete the Nectar Maker.	Return the chip to the nectar merchant.		Visa Points, Simoleons
		GOOD NECTAR		
Seeking a New Flavor	A local hasn't been enjoying any good nectar lately. Can you fix that?	Bring the Sim a bottle of nectar that is Nice quality or better.		Visa Points, Simoleons
Prove Me Wrong	A local desires a good bottle of nectar. Can you deliver one?	Bring the Sim a bottle of nectar that is Very Nice quality or better.		Visa Points, Simoleons
Flavortastic	A local wants to taste some quality nectar. Deliver them a worthy bottle?	Bring the Sim a bottle of nectar that is Great quality or better.		Visa Points, Simoleons
Nectar Me Crazy	A local has been too busy to track down some excellent nectar on their own time. Can you fetch an appropriate bottle?	Bring the Sim a bottle of Nectar that is Excellent quality or better.		Visa Points, Simoleons

France

Adventure	Activity	How to Complete	Tomb?	Reward
THE FEAST				
Frogs! And Make It Snappy	A local is holding a dinner party but is too busy planning to buy ingredients for Frog's Legs.	Catch three frogs and bring them back to the local.		Simoleons, Visa Points
Oops! Forgot the Meat	The Sim forgot about the appetizer. Could you purchase steak for them?	Go to the food store and buy the requested number of steaks, then report back.		Simoleons, Visa Points
Veggies...Now	Now the Sim needs some vegetables for the meal. Bring the Sim some veggies, please.	Bring the Sim the requested number of Very Nice quality vegetables. You may need to grow them if you cannot find or buy them outright.		Simoleons, Visa Points
A Vicious Delicacy	The Sim's latest dinner party will feature exotic meats: crocodile. Can you fetch this specialty?	Travel to Egypt and catch the requested number of crocodiles for the Sim. Report back with the crocodiles.		Simoleons, Visa Points
A Purple Delicacy	The Sim's latest feast will include a delicacy from China: plums. Provided you can provide the plums, of course.	Travel to China and bring back the requested number of Nice quality plums.		Simoleons, Visa Points
FROG FIND				
Frogs as Pets	A local Sim has finally gotten over the heartbreak of losing their pet frog and would like a new one.	Catch a frog from the waters of Champs Les Sims and deliver it back to the Sim.		Ancient Coins, Visa Points
EXOTIC FRUIT				
Global Nectar Making	A local wants to make a new type of nectar but needs some exotic ingredients. Can you travel abroad and bring some back?	Travel to the requested destination and bring back the desired fruits. (Example: pomengranates from Egypt.)		Simoleons, Visa Points
CAFE COOKING				
Café Quality Cooking	The café needs help since the chef is sick. Can you bring in some quality meals?	Prepare the requested number of dishes for the café manager.		Simoleons, Visa Points, Random Seed
FOOD AND NECTAR				
In Need of Nectar	The local is experimenting with food and nectar combinations, but has no time to get the nectar. Can you help?	Bring the local one bottle of Very Nice quality (or better) nectar. Look in tombs or develop skill and make your own.		Visa Points, Bottle of Nectar
In Need of Grub	The local loves the nectar. But now they need the food to go with it...	Bring the local one serving of any recipe. Use the kitchen at base camp to cook it up.		Visa Points, Bottle of Nectar

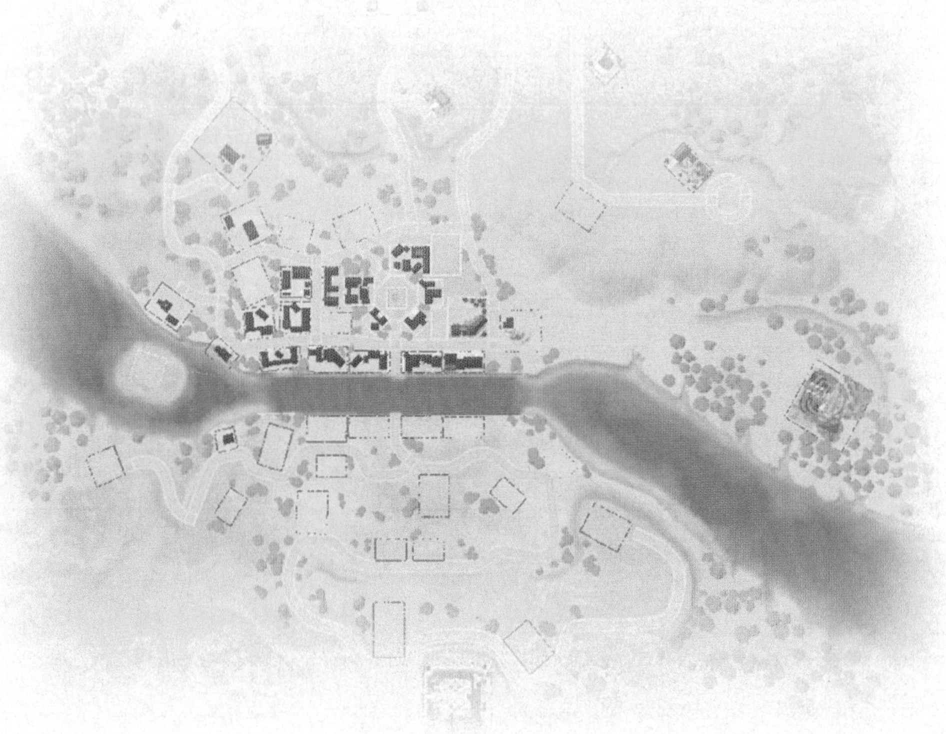

Tomb Maps

Celtic Burial Site

Basement Level 1

Traps
- Electric Trap

Tomb Features
- Hidden Door
- Treasure Chest
- Ancient Coins

- A Floor Switch opens Door1
- B Door 1
- C Unlocks Hole 1
- D Hole 1, unlocks Door 2
- E Door 2
- F Heart Keystone Panel
- G Switch opens Door 3
- H Door 3
- A Floor Switch makes Switch B appear
- B Switch B makes Switch C appear
- C Switch C makes nearby Stairs to B2 appear
- A Foot Switch opens Door 4
- B Door 4
- A Stairs into tomb, unlocked by Floor Switch on surface
- B Move Statues off Switch fires B traps
- C Heart Keystone Panel
- D Connected Dive Wells
- E Push Statues on Floor Switches to unlock Door 5
- F Door 5
- G Pull Switch to make Hole appear—Gem High inside
- H Heart Keystone Panel

- 2 §
- 3 Gem France
- 4 §, Small Relic
- 5 Heart Keystone
- 6 Small Relic
- 7 Heart Keystone
- 8 Heart Keystone
- 9 Small Relic
- 10 Large Relic
- 11 Medium Relic
- 1 Collection

An alternate entrance to the Celtic Burial Ground lies just outside the mound. Step on the floor switch to open some new stairs.

You need Pangu's Axe to smash the boulder covering the hole that opens these stairs.

Basement Level 2

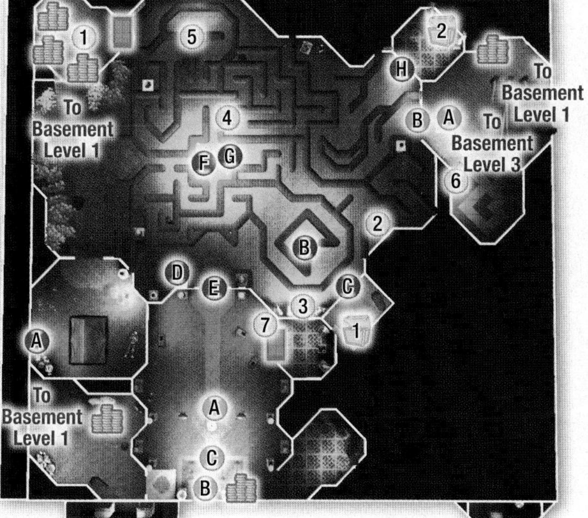

- A Dried Food
- B Switch opens Door 1
- C Door 1
- D Switch opens Door 2
- E Door 2
- F Mourn at Gravestone to make Hole 1 appear
- G Gem France
- H Heart Keystone Panel
- A Floor Switch opens Door 3
- B Door 3
- A Adventure Goal (Baseball)
- B Mourn at Gravestone to make Hole 2 appear
- C Hole 2—Medium Relic

- 1 Metals France
- 2 Ancient Coins
- 3 Small Relic
- 4 Gem Medium
- 5 Heart Keystone
- 6 §§
- 7 §§§
- 1 Medium Relic
- 2 Large Relic

Tomb Features
- Hidden Door
-  Treasure Chest
- Ancient Coins

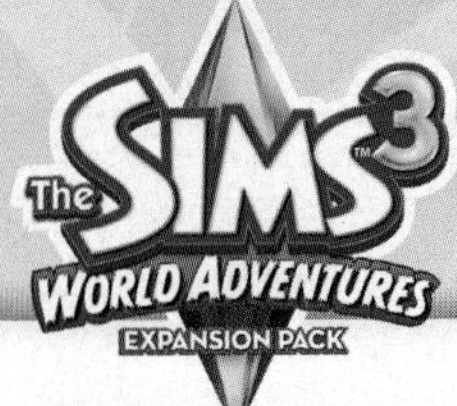

France

Basement Level 3

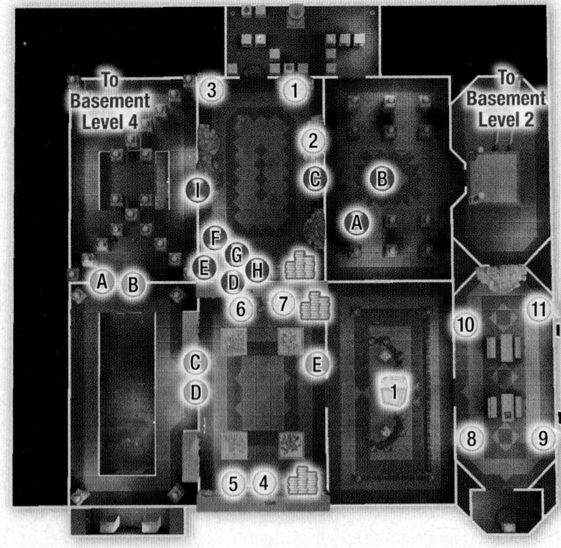

Tomb Features

- Treasure Chest
- Ancient Coins

- Ⓐ Move Statue to reveal Floor Switch B
- Ⓑ Step on Floor Switch to open Door 1
- Ⓒ Door 1
- Ⓓ Hole opens Hole 1
- Ⓔ Hole 1 opens Hole 2
- Ⓕ Hole 2 opens Hole 3
- Ⓖ Hole 3 opens Hole 4
- Ⓗ Hole 4 (Expensive Gem)
- Ⓘ Heart Keystone Panel
- A Heart Keystone Panel opens Door 2
- B Door 2
- C Heart Keystone Panel opens Door 3 and Door 1 (B4)
- D Door 3
- E Heart Keystone Panel

- 1 Heart Keystone
- 2 Gem France, §§§
- 3 Gem France
- 4 Heart Keystone
- 5 Relic Small
- 6 Relic Medium
- 7 France Metal
- 8 Dried Food
- 9 Fragments
- 10 §
- 11 Heart Keystone
- 1 Epic Relic

Basement Level 4

- 1 Fragments
- 2 2 Heart Keystones
- 3 Ancient Coins
- 4 Fragments
- Ⓐ Door 1 opened by Panel on B3

Traps

- Fire Trap
- Electric Trap
- Poison Darts
- Steam Jets

Chateau du Landgraab

Basement Level

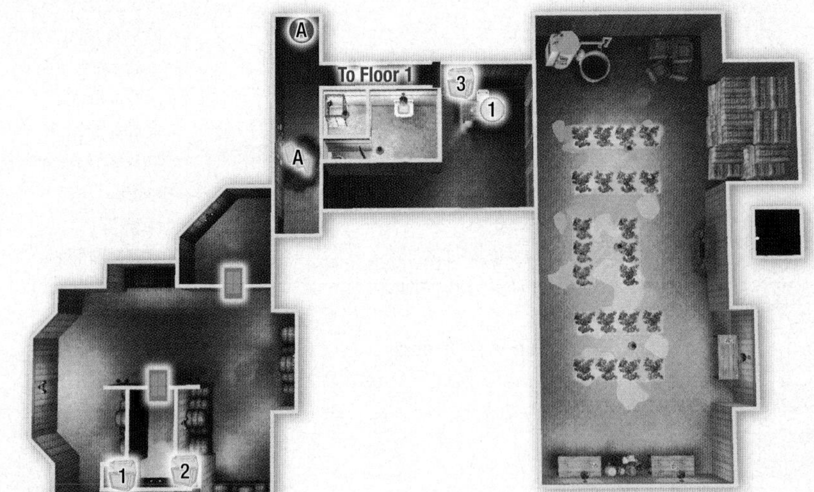

- Ⓐ Hole switches off A Traps
- 1 Charm Keystone
- 1 Gem High
- 2 Gem High
- 3 Epic Relic

Traps

- Electric Trap

Tomb Features

- Hidden Door
- Treasure Chest

Floor 1

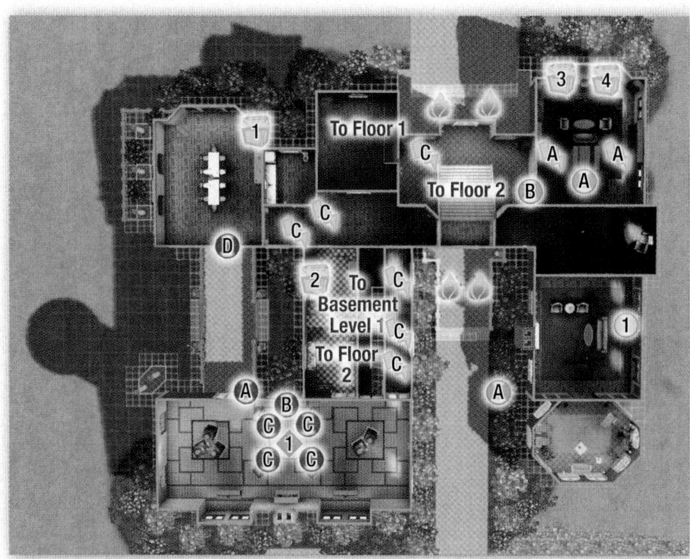

Traps

- Fire Trap
- Electric Trap

Tomb Features

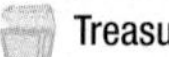

- Treasure Chest

- (A) Landgraab Ballroom Keystone Panel
- (B) Turn on Stereo to make C Floor Switches appear
- (C) Floor Switches turn off C Traps, open Door 1, and disable Electric Traps next to Stairs leading to F2
- (D) Door 1
- A Hole switches off Electric Traps near doors
- B Landgraab Library Keystone Panel
- A Turn on Stereo to disable nearby Electric Traps
- 1 Fragments
- 1 Large Relic
- 2 Dried Food
- 3 Ancient Coins
- 4 Adventure Goal (Paper), §

Turn on the stereo to make the Floor Switches appear. Push the statues on to the Floor Switches.

Floor 2

Traps

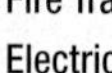

- Fire Trap
- Electric Trap

Tomb Features

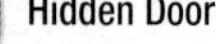

- Hidden Door
- Treasure Chest

- (A) Floor Switch unlocks Door 1
- (B) Door 1
- (C) Floor Switch unlocks Door 2
- (D) Door 2
- (E) Floor Switch unlocks Door 1 (3F) and disables Electric Trap (3F)
- A Use Toilet to disable A Traps
- 1 Small Relic
- 2 Gem France
- 1 §§§

Floor 3

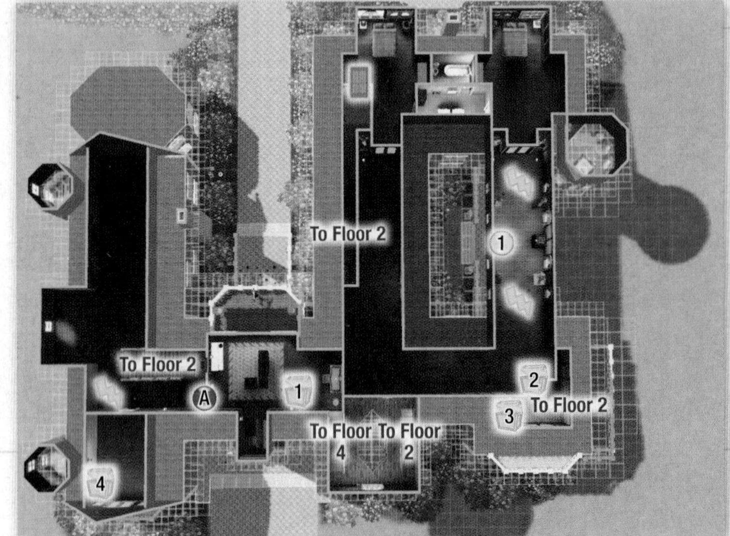

- (A) Door 1 (unlocked by Floor Switch on 2F)
- (1) Epic Relic
- 1 Adventure Goal (Documents), Ancient Coins
- 2 §§§§§
- 3 Ancient Coins
- 4 Medium Relic

Traps
- Electric Trap

Tomb Features
- Hidden Door
- Treasure Chest

Floor 4

- (A) Hole turns off A Traps
- 1 Epic Relic

Traps
- Electric Trap

Tomb Features
- Treasure Chest

Chateau du Landgraab—Groundskeeper's Shack

Groundskeeper Chateau

- (A) Heart Keystone
- (1) Small Relic

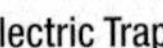

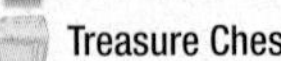

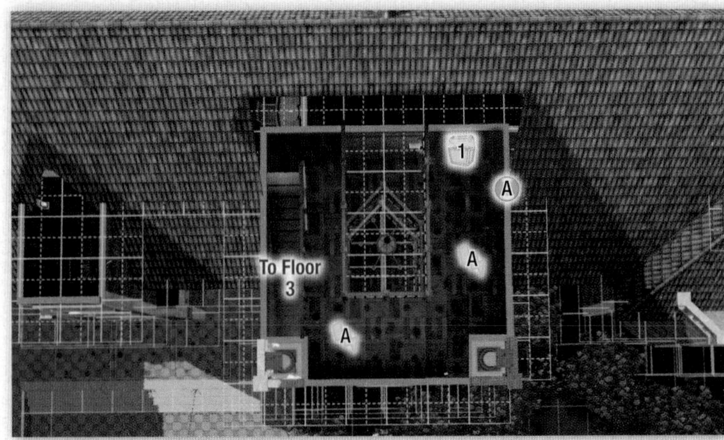

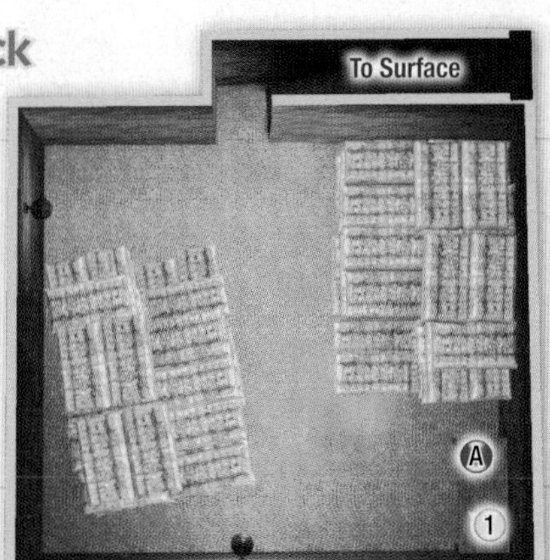

Faerie Tomb—Little Wood

Basement Level 1

Tomb Features

- Hidden Door
- Treasure Chest

Use Pangu's Axe to shatter the boulders and reveal the entry to the tomb.

- (A) Floor Switches open Door 1
- (B) Door 1
- (C) Floor Switch opens Door 2
- (D) Door 2
- (E) Switch opens Door 3
- (F) Switch unlocks Hole 1
- (G) Hole 1 opens Door 4 and Door 5
- (H) Door 4
- (I) Door 3
- (J) Door 5
- (1) Heart Keystone
- 1 Relic Large
- 2 Epic Relic
- 3 Ancient Coins, also unlocks Stairs to B2

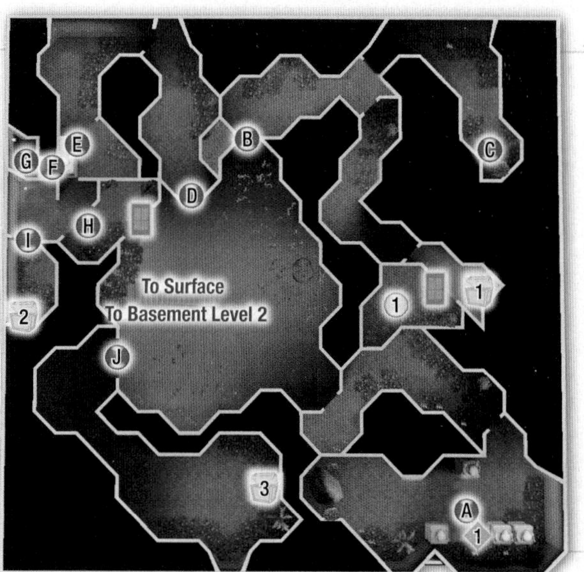

Basement Level 2

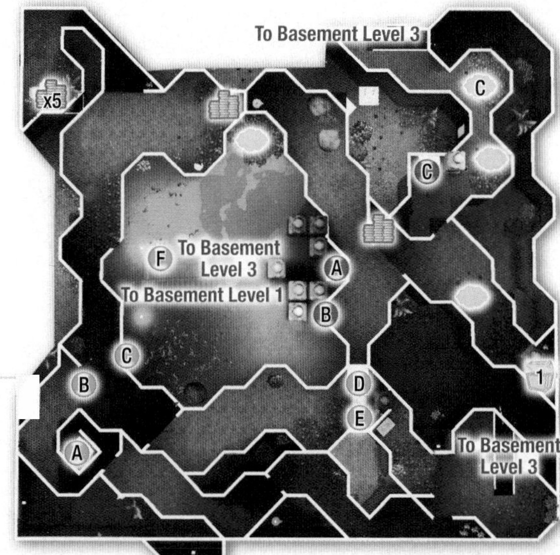

Traps

- Steam Jets

Tomb Features

- Treasure Chest
- Ancient Coins

- (A) Floor Switch opens Door 1
- (B) Door 1
- (C) Floor Switch shuts off C Trap
- A Floor Switch opens Door 2 and Door 3
- B Door 2
- C Door 3
- D Switch unlocks Floor Switch E
- E Floor Switch unlocks Stairs 1
- F Stairs 1 (to B3)
- 1 Relic Large

Basement Level 3

- (A) Switch turns off A Trap
- (B) Switch turns off B Trap
- (C) Switch turns off C Trap
- (D) Hole unlocks Door 1
- (E) Door 1
- A Dive Well to Faerie Tomb 2

Traps

- Poison Darts
- Steam Jets

Tomb Features

- Hidden Door

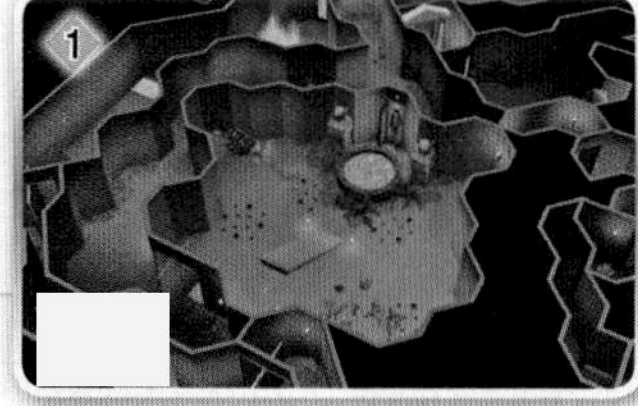

Use the hidden door near the dive well to bypass the traps and come at it from this side door.

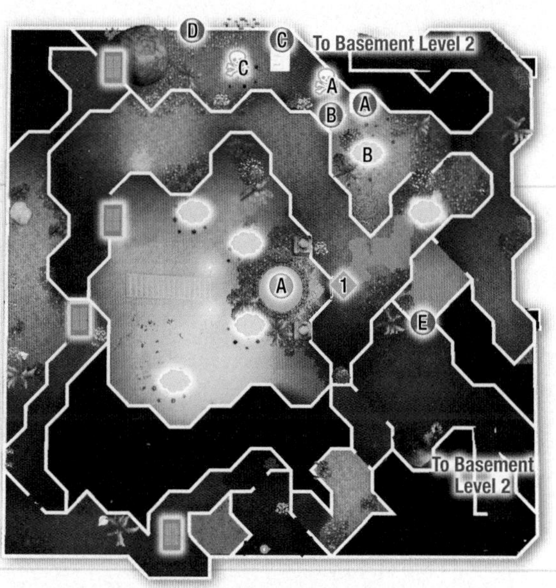

Faerie Tomb—Eastern Watch

Basement Level 1

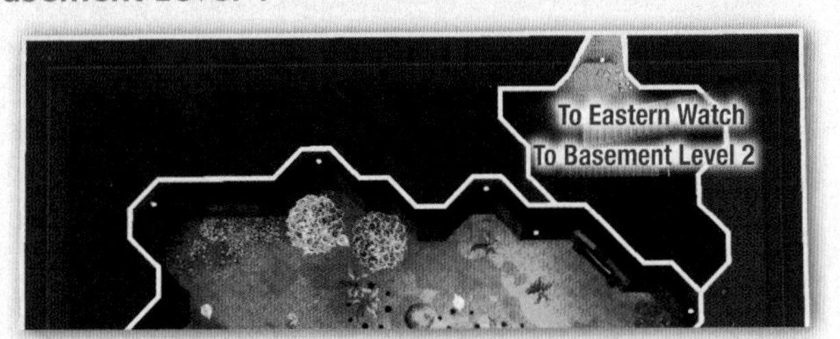

Basement Level 2

To Basement Level 2
To Basement Level 1

Basement Level 3

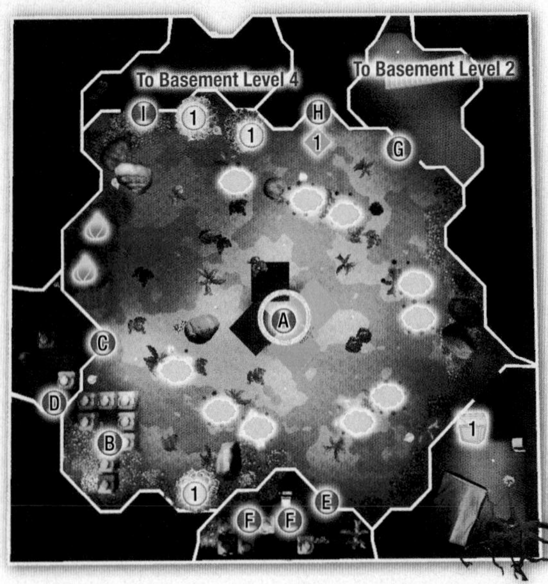

Traps

Fire Trap
Steam Jets

- A Dive Well to Faerie Tomb 1
- B Switch opens Door 1
- C Door 1
- D Switch opens Door 2
- E Door 2
- F Switches pressed together open Door 3
- G Door 3
- H Switch opens Door 4
- I Door 4
- 1 Money Tree
- 1 Dried Food

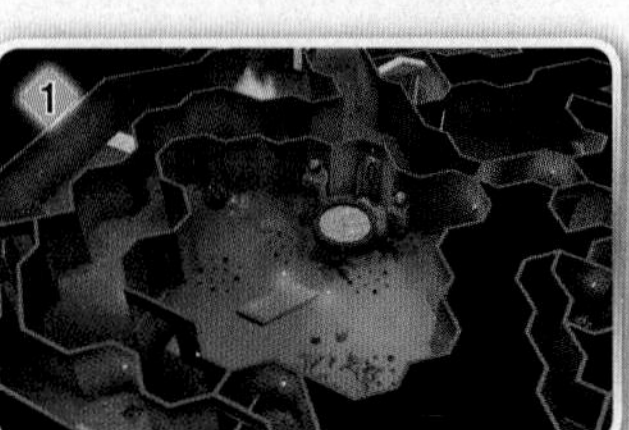

It's painted green to blend in, but there is a floor switch here!

Basement Level 4

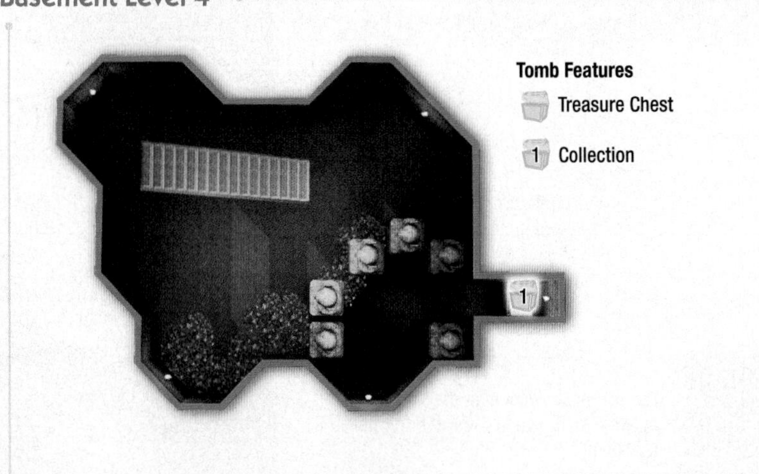

Tomb Features

Treasure Chest

1 Collection

Museum Catacombs

Basement Level 1

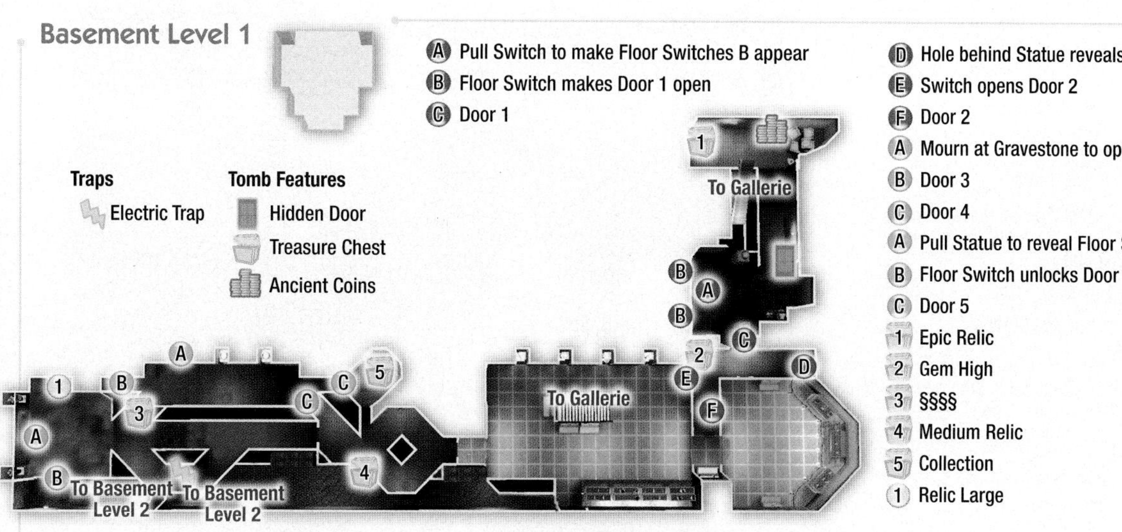

Traps

- Electric Trap

Tomb Features

- Hidden Door
- Treasure Chest
- Ancient Coins

- A Pull Switch to make Floor Switches B appear
- B Floor Switch makes Door 1 open
- C Door 1
- D Hole behind Statue reveals Floor Switch E
- E Switch opens Door 2
- F Door 2
- A Mourn at Gravestone to open Door 3 and Door 4
- B Door 3
- C Door 4
- A Pull Statue to reveal Floor Switch Green B
- B Floor Switch unlocks Door 5
- C Door 5
- 1 Epic Relic
- 2 Gem High
- 3 §§§§
- 4 Medium Relic
- 5 Collection
- 1 Relic Large

Basement Level 2

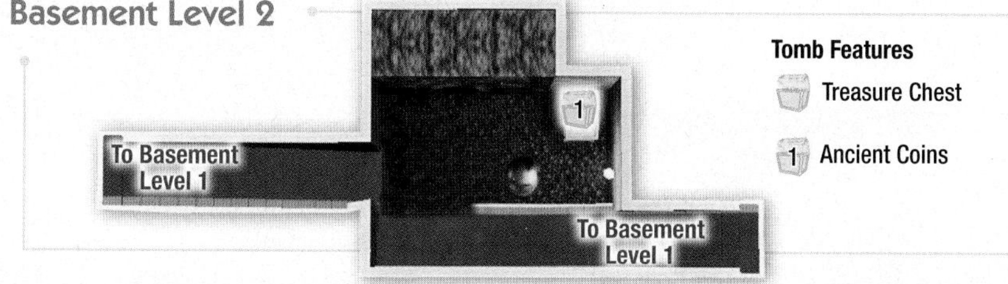

Tomb Features

- Treasure Chest
- 1 Ancient Coins

Tomb of Necteaux—Nectar Catacombs

Basement Level 1

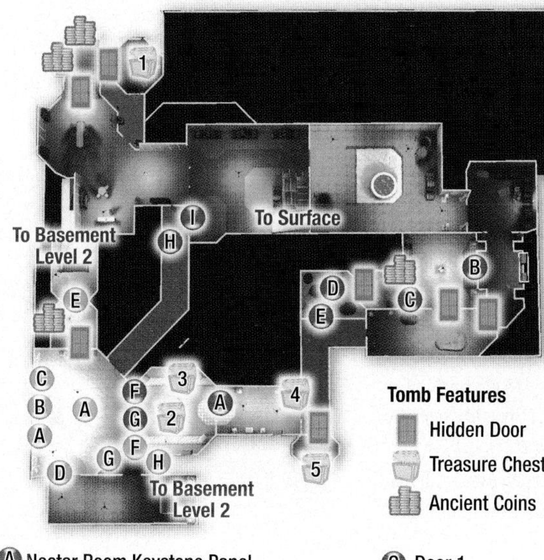

Tomb Features

- Hidden Door
- Treasure Chest
- Ancient Coins

- A Nectar Room Keystone Panel
- B Move Statue to open Door 1
- C Door 1
- D Hole opens Door 2
- E Door 2
- F Door 3
- G Door 4
- H Floor Switch opens Door 5
- I Door 5
- A Inspect Hole to trigger next adventure, Gem Hole (Ruby)
- B Gem Hole (Sapphire)
- C Gem Hole (Emerald)
- D Keystone to Jean Necteaux's Tomb Panel
- E Keystone to Isael's Tomb Panel
- F Large Relic
- G Dried Food
- H §§§
- A Keystones appear on this Pedestal, activated by Gem Holes
- 1 Gem France
- 2 Adventure Goal (Nectar Bottle), Nectar Bottle, opens Doors 3 & 4
- 3 Nectar Bottle
- 4 Nectar Bottle
- 5 Collection

Tomb of Necteaux—Tomb of Isael

Basement Level 2

Traps

Fire Trap

Electric Trap

Tomb Features

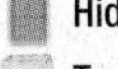
Hidden Door

Treasure Chest

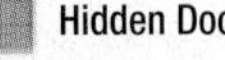
Ancient Coins

- A To Dive Well on B4
- B Heart Keystone Panel
- C Floor Switch activates C Traps
- 1 Heart Keystone
- 1 Adventure Goal (Sapphire of the Crescent Moon)
- 2 §§§§
- 3 Nectar Bottle
- 4 Fragments (shuts off nearby Fire Traps)

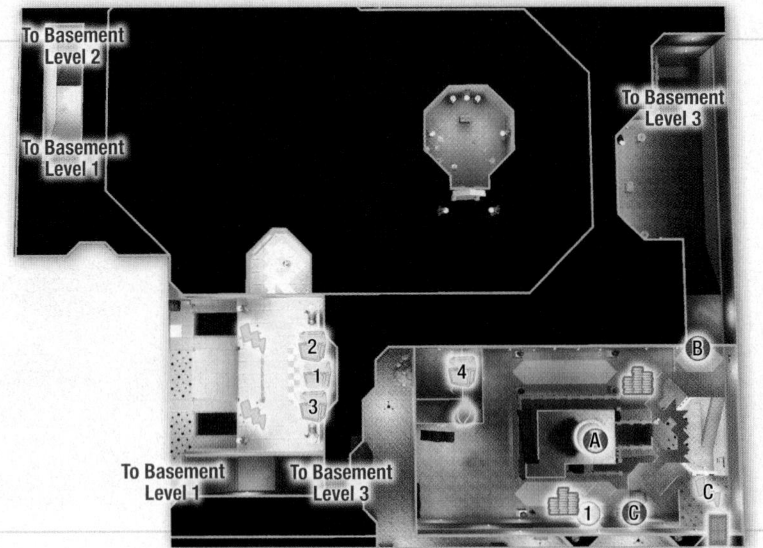

Basement Level 3

Traps

Fire Trap

Electric Trap

Tomb Features

Hidden Door

Treasure Chest

Ancient Coins

- A Use Toilet to unlock Door 1
- B Door 1
- C Hole unlocks Floor Switches D & E
- D Floor Switch unlocks Hole F
- E Floor Switch unlocks Floor Switch G
- F Heart Keystone
- G Floor Switch unlocks Doors directly below on B4
- A Dive Well unlocks Door 2
- B Door 2
- C Floor Switch unlocks Doors directly below on B4
- D Heart Keystone Panel shuts off Traps
- E Heart Keystone Panel shuts off Traps
- F Statue on Switch unlocks Switch G
- G Statue on Switch unlocks Doors 3 & 4
- H Door 3
- I Door 4
- J Place Item on Pedestal to unlock Door 5
- K Door 5
- A Heart Keystone Panel shuts off nearby Traps
- B Heart Keystone Panel
- C Floor Switches open Door 6
- D Door 6
- A Turns off Electric Traps below
- B Turns off B Traps

- 1 Nectar Bottle
- 2 Nectar Bottle, § (Beware: picking up bottle triggers a trap)
- 3 Gem France
- 4 Small Relic
- 5 Dried Food
- 6 Heart Keystone
- 7 Heart Keystone
- 8 Fragments
- 9 Fragments
- 10 Fragments
- 11 Epic Relic
- 12 Gem Cheap
- 13 Gem Cheap
- 1 Large Relic
- 2 Heart Keystone, Ancient Coins
- 3 Small Relic, §§
- 4 Dried Food, Medium Relic
- 5 Gem Cheap
- 6 Ancient Coins
- 7 §§§
- 8 Nectar Bottles
- 9 Dried Food

Tomb of Necteaux—Tomb of Jean Necteaux

Basement Level 4

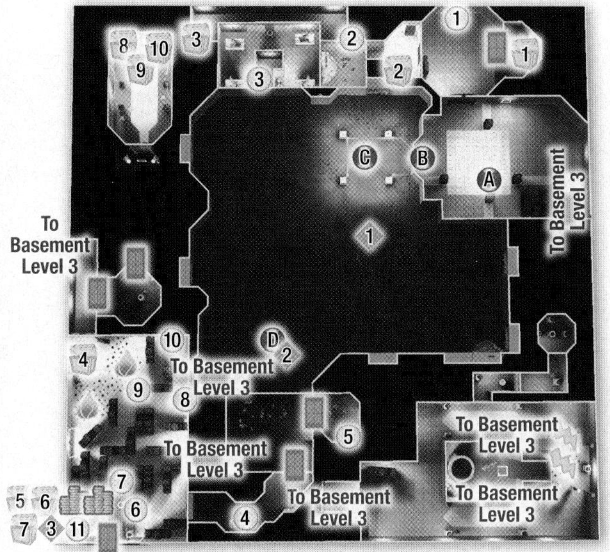

Traps

- Fire Trap
- Electric Trap

Tomb Features

- Hidden Door
- Treasure Chest
- Ancient Coins

- A Floor Switch unlocks Door 1
- B Door 1
- C Floor Switch activates Blue Lights
- D Floor Switch turns off all Traps
- 1 Nectar Bottle
- 2 Relic Medium
- 3 Gem France
- 4 Relic Large
- 5 Epic Relic
- 6 Metals France
- 7 Metals France
- 8 Ancient Coins
- 9 Relic Large
- 10 Dried Food
- 11 Adventure Goal (Recipe), turns off Fire Traps

- 1 Nectar Bottle
- 2 Nectar Bottle
- 3 Medium Relic
- 4 Epic Relic
- 5 §§§
- 6 Epic Relic
- 7 Small Relic
- 8 §§§§§
- 9 Fragments
- 10 Fragments

Follow the blue lights in this chamber to avoid traps.

The lights lead to this floor switch, which shuts off all traps in the room.

The hidden door here leads to a treasure trove.

Secret Garden

Basement Level

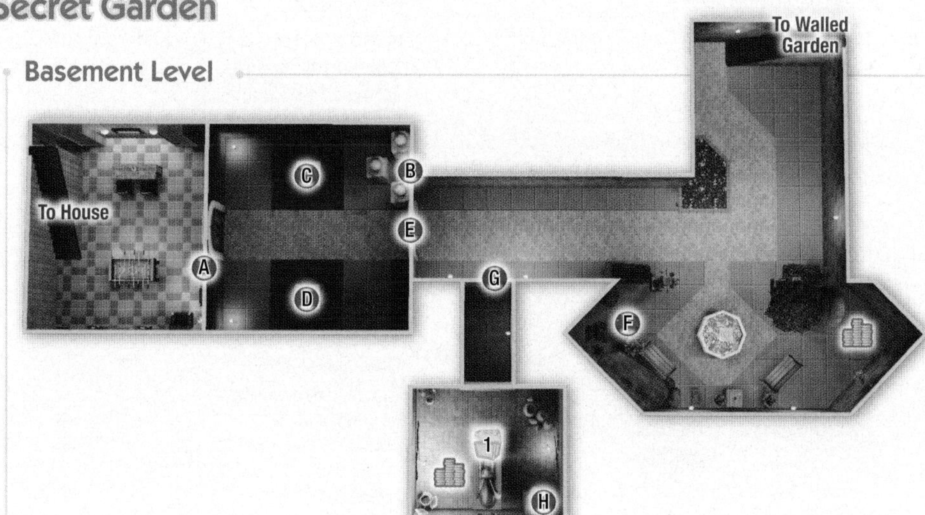

Tomb Features

- Treasure Chest
- Ancient Coins

- A Keystone Panel
- B Pull Switch to reveal Floor Switches
- C Place Statue on Switch
- D Place Statue on Switch
- E Door 1 opens when C and D are depressed
- F Hole unlocks Door 2
- G Door 2
- H France Gem
- 1 Empty (use in later adventure)

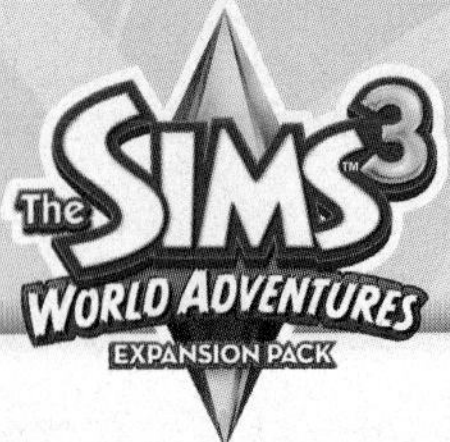

Welcome to Egypt

The city of Al Simhara is built on land that was once ruled by pharaohs. These pharaohs had awe-inspiring monuments built for them, such as the Great Pyramid and Great Sphinx. These towering masterpieces of ancient architecture—and the many crumbling ruins that were not so fortunate in the struggle against time—are all that is left of the ancients. Or are they? Have explorers really found all there is to find in the deserts around Al Simhara? Locals say that there are still treasures in the sands of Egypt, just waiting for an intrepid Sim to discover.

Shopping & Skills

Al Simhara Market

Like the marketplace in China, the Al Simhara market does not have defined store address on the map. Instead, travelers are encouraged to explore the market at their leisure, wandering in and out of the shops. Al Simhara has four individual shops: books, relics, food, and general store. You can buy all of the adventuring items you need at the general store, such as a Shower in a Can or a tent.

Shop for photography improvement books at the bookstore.

NOTE

The relic store's inventory changes daily, so check with the merchant often to see what's in stock.

GENERAL STORE

Item	Price (in Simoleons)
Low Quality Dried Food	5
Medium Quality Dried Food	20
High Quality Dried Food	40
Shower in a Can	120
Sim Scouts' Classic Camper	220
Colesim 2br Edition Tent	2,700
SnapTastic Flimsy-Cam	250
ChannonTec Outlaw SE	850
Hikon QX40di Gladiator	3,250
Snake Charming Basket	325
Mazzamesses II Incense Holder	500
Mummified Teddy Bear	50
The Kenspa	650
The Sultan's Keep-All	310

BOOKSTORE

Book	Genre/Skill Level Required	Price (in Simoleons)
GENERAL		
The Price of Treasure	Mystery	200
Ra! Ra! Ra!	Fiction	355

BOOKSTORE, CONTINUED

Book	Genre/Skill Level Required	Price (in Simoleons)
GENERAL, CONTINUED		
South of the Simhara	Non-Fiction	462
Are You My Mummy?	Humor	514
From Dead to Mummy: The History of Healing	Historical	567
The Keystone's Counterpart	Fiction	788
Do I Exist?	Satire	842
Thread Count	Non-Fiction	1,111
The Legend of Queen Nosylla and King Nayr	Drama	1,280
Advanced Facial Expressions	Non-Fiction	1,515
Tomb Raiding for Toddlers: What to Know	Non-Fiction	1,544
The Mummy in Love	Romance	1,816
The Sand Mirage	Non-Fiction	1,819
A Guide to Desert Stick Pokey	Non-Fiction	1,851
Photos from Dark Places	Historical	1,988
Jimmy Sprocket and the Mummy's Curse	Children's	2,002
Free Kicks, Hard Tackles, and Red Cards	Non-Fiction	2,210
That's a Wrap!: The True Life Story of the First Mummy Film Director	Non-Fiction	2,226
The River That Sustains Us	Non-Fiction	2,253
A Good Shawarma	Humor	2,275
SKILLS		
Photography Vol. 1: Taking Off the Lens Cap	0	50
FISHING		
Dead-ly Delights: Catching Crocodiles and Mummy Fish	2	750
RECIPES		
Shawarma	1	325
Falafel	5	475

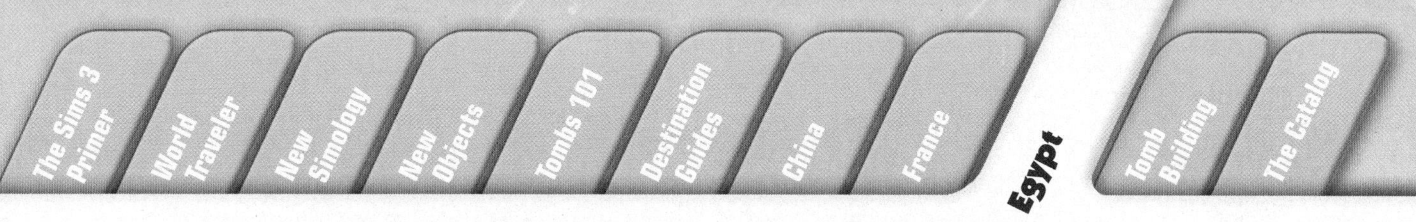

NOTE

The items offered at the food store will change from one trip to the next.

SPECIAL MERCHANT

Item	Description	Cost (in Ancient Coins)	Required Visa Level
Pemmican	Special snack that sates hunger for longer and gives Carbed Up! moodlet.	10	1
Potion of Liquid Courage	Drink this to banish Fear and get an extra boost of courage.	40	1
Mummy Snacks	Toss these snacks down to distract a mummy and make your escape.	100	1
Skeleton Keystone	This special keystone fits any keystone panel except a tomb's unique keystone panel.	400	2
Escape Dust	Tired? Hungry? Just in a bad spot? Use this reward to instantly teleport back to base camp or an owned vacation home.	75	2
Tear of Horus	This artifact makes relics and dig sites appear on your map.	1,600	2
The Sultan's Tabernacle	This portable palace gives your Sim the Slept Like a King/Queen moodlet.	2,500	3
Certificate of Partnership with Egypt	Allows bearer (and any traveling with) to stay at destination longer than possible with current visa.	1,200	3

Photography Skill

Egypt does not have a definitive skill like France or China. However, this is the only destination of the three where you can buy the top-tier cameras for developing the Photography skill as well as a Photography skill-building tome. So, consider Egypt the unofficial home of the Photography skill. While on your adventures, stop and take photos of everything to not only develop the skill, but also to fill some of the photo collections that result in Simoleons.

Snake Charming

Snake Charming is not a skill that you track like Martial Arts or Writing—it is more of a hidden skill. To start developing this skill, you need to buy the Snake Charmer's Basket from the general store in Al Simhara. Then, find a nice spot to sit down and practice. Your Sim uses a pungi to coax a snake out of the basket. Now, at first you are not going to be very good at this. But the longer you play for the snake, the better you get. Soon, you will be able to charm for tips, just as you can with the guitar.

Snake Charming is also one way to cure the Mummy's Curse moodlet given by a hardcore mummy attack. After charming for a long time, you may be able coax a cobra out of the basket and get the Snake Kiss! moodlet, which dispels the mummy's curse.

TIP

Take your Snake Charmer's Basket home and practice there. The locals back home will be amazed by your exotic hobby!

Egypt

Sight-Seeing

Sims who love to explore tombs will make Egypt one of their prime destinations. Just below the sands are labyrinths that have lain undisturbed for centuries upon centuries. Some tombs are hidden from sight and must be discovered before they can be combed. Others are easily accessed via many of these community locations, such as the pyramids.

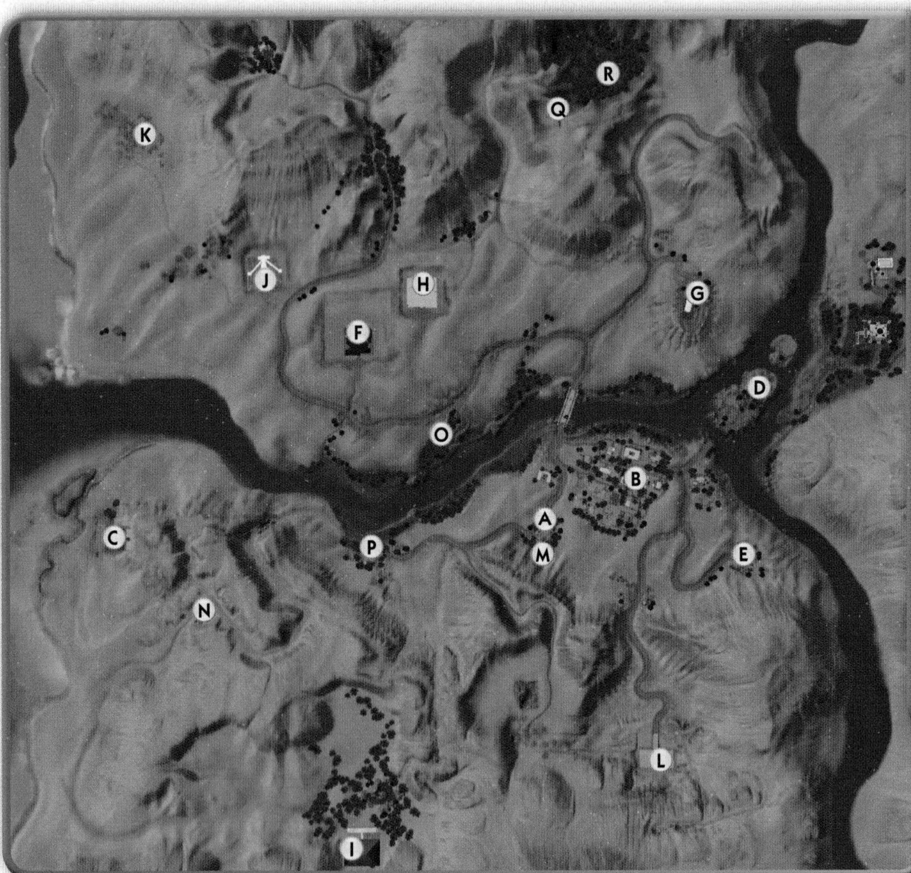

Marker	Lot
A	Base Camp
B	Al Simhara Market
C	Abu Simbel
D	Copper Quarry
E	Desert's End
F	Great Pyramid
G	Great Sphinx
H	Pyramid of the Burning Sands
I	Pyramid of the Sky
J	Pyramid of the Wind
K	Ruins of Karnak
L	Temple of Queen Hatshepsut
M	Tomb of Discovery
N	Camp Earth
O	Camp Moon
P	Camp Sun
Q	Ship's Oasis
R	Water in the Sand

Community Locations

Abu Simbel

The visages of the pharaohs were carved into the rock cliffs at Abu Simbel, preserving their memories for the millennia. Before bidding farewell to Egypt (but you will surely come back, yes?), be sure to bask in the wonder of this...well, wonder!

Al Simhara Base Camp

The facilities at Egypt's base camp are not as nice as those you find in France or China, but they do provide for all of your needs when first arriving in the desert paradise. There is a bathroom where you can attend to hygiene. You can grab a quick snack or prepare a meal at the small kitchen. Sleep, though, happens inside one of the provided tents—there are no nice beds here. If you want somewhere pleasant to sleep in Egypt, either pay out for a quality tent (perhaps the Sultan's Tabernacle) or buy a vacation home once you max out your Egypt visa.

Copper Quarry

The Copper Quarry on the small island near the Al Simhara marketplace is where the ancients pulled rich ore from the ground to create their amazing relics and treasures. Return to the site of ancient copperwork to explore for lost treasures and other valuables.

Desert's End

Although the pharaohs believed they could exist forever in the afterlife by being mummified (with their organs pulled from their bodies and placed in canopic jars), modern Sims don't quite go through all that trouble anymore. The Desert's End is a traditional cemetery site with a mausoleum to explore for fun. Take a stroll through the site to unwind and take in the beautiful views.

Great Pyramid

One of the wonders of the world, the Great Pyramid is a testament to the brilliance of ancient architects—and the will of the pharaohs. The Great Pyramid is an essential stop for any Sim visiting Egypt and the gateway to one of the destination's most dangerous tombs: the Tomb of Death. With a name like that, you just know there has to be something good down there. Why else would they give it such a scary name?

Great Sphinx

Though the ancients were dedicated to the exploration of math and early sciences, they were not without mysticism. The Great Sphinx that cuts a profile in the Al Simhara sky is a monument dedicated to a mythological creature said to possess incredible knowledge.

TIP

If you are ever afflicted by the Mummy's Curse moodlet, come and plead before the Sphinx to be cured.

To explore inside the Great Sphinx, inspect the door between its front paws.

Oh. Apparently the wisdom of the Sphinx requires a little ingenuity of your own.

Pyramid of the Burning Sands

The Pyramid of the Burning Sands may look small next to the Great Pyramid, but it's still deserving of wonder. The interior of the pyramid is home to the Tomb of Burning Sands, which is heated not by the blazing sun above, but a different heat source that grows naturally within its ancient chambers.

NOTE

This pyramid also contains the Tomb of the Rock, which you can explore whenever you like—even on your first visit. It's a good place to discover treasures when not on an adventure.

Pyramid of the Sky

The Pyramid of the Sky is set apart from the twins that rest in the gloating shadow of the Great Pyramid. This site deserves your attention, as you may find interesting relics just inside the pyramid's grand entrance. And after exploring, why not take a dip in the cool waters just outside the pyramid? A little swim is a great escape from the scorching sun.

Pyramid of the Wind

While thousands of years of wind have shorn some of the ornate stonework off this impressive pyramid, no earthly element has been able to bring it crashing down. The Pyramid of the Wind is near the Great Pyramid and the site of the Tomb of the Infinite Halls. Dare you brave this eerily named tomb?

Ruins of Karnak

The Ruins of Karnak hint at a site that once must have made jaws drop as Sims sailed in its shadow. The roof of the temple has long since collapsed, but many of the support pillars remain. They reach out of the sand like fingers, beckoning adventurers to investigate the ruins. This is the entrance to the Karnak Treasure Halls, a place you will surely want to explore while on an Egyptian adventure.

Temple of Queen Hatshepsut

This wide temple built into the dunes is impressive from first glance. But the name doesn't necessarily describe exactly what you will be exploring on this site. The real action below the sands is in the Servant's Quarters and Hatshepsut's Quarters. What secrets did these ancients keep? And can you survive the traps of the tombs to return them to the surface?

Tomb of Discovery

The Tomb of Discovery is usually the very first tomb explored in Egypt. The entrance to the tomb is in a small building just behind base camp. You are not the first person to explore this tomb, though, as you will discover when you take on the earliest adventure in Egypt.

Camp Sites

With so much adventuring to do in Egypt, you may not have time to make it back to base camp before your Sim gets exhausted. If you haven't bought a tent yet (understandable—travel is not cheap), use one of the three camp sites in Egypt to rest your weary bones after a long day of adventuring.

Camp Earth

Camp Moon

Camp Sun

Vacation Homes

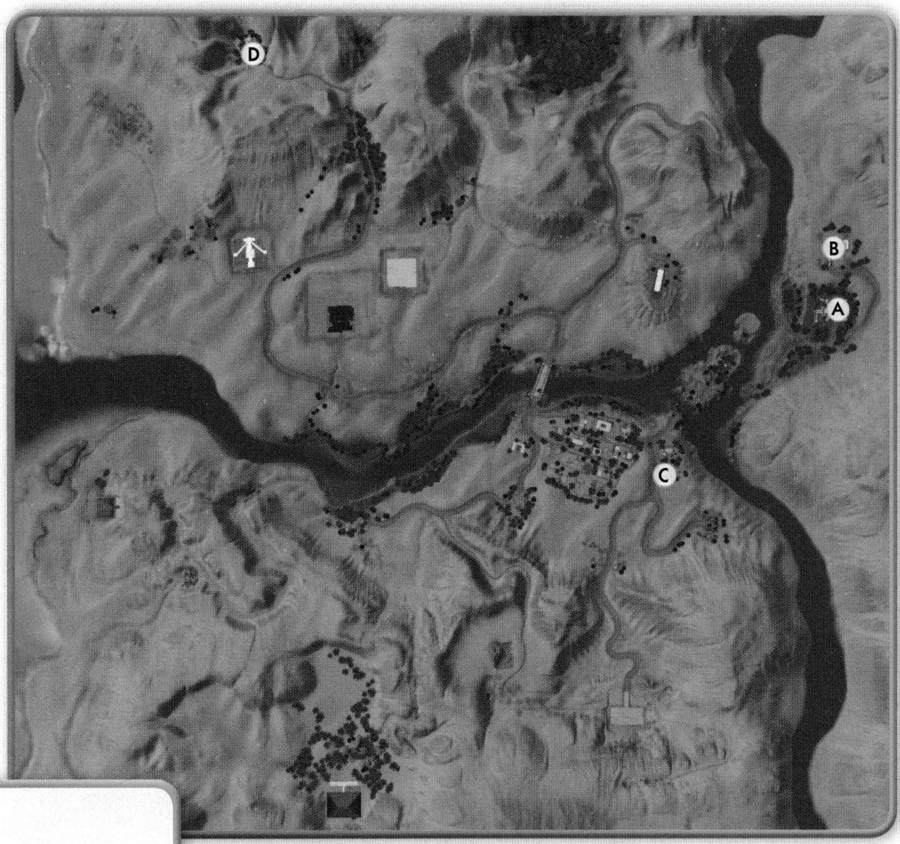

Marker	Lot
A	Acacia Palace
B	Almond Tree House
C	Pomegranate House
D	Lotus Oasis

There are many vacation homes you can purchase in Egypt, from a modest dwelling near the Al Simhara market to the incredible Acacia Palace estate along the edge of the river.

Acacia Palace

Pomegranate House

Almond Tree House

Lotus Oasis

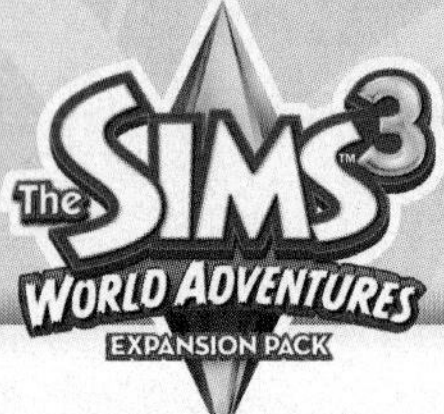

Collectibles

If you are into collecting, then Egypt is your destination—the sands give up wonderful treasures, from relics at dig sites to glistening gems. There are also many different bugs to collect in Egypt and bring home, not only to sell at the science facility, but also to display in terrariums around your house.

Dig Sites

Your Sim can pull treasures and relics out of the sand at Egypt's many dig sites. Use this map of the dig sites in Egypt so you can excavate without wasting any time just playing in a sandbox.

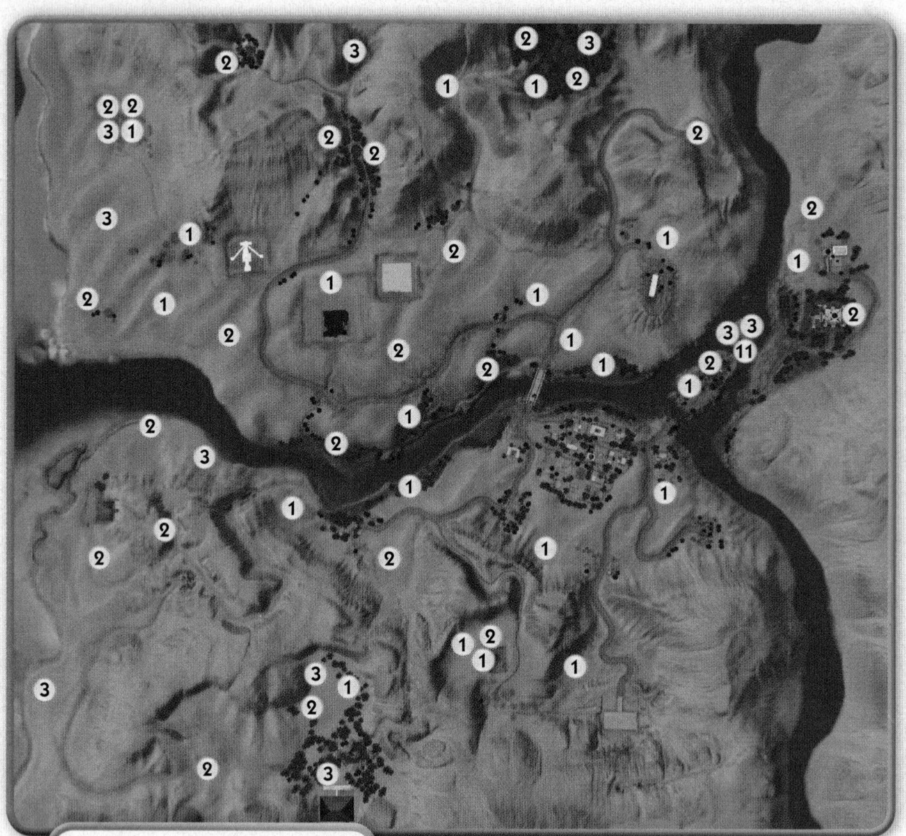

Symbol	Relic Quality/Value
1	Low
2	Medium
3	High
11	Fragments

Fishing Spots

It's easy to see why the ancients picked the site of Al Simhara—it's right on the shores of a life-giving river. Drop a line in the river to do a little fishing. However, be sure to stop by an oasis for a break from the burning sands. Not only are these great fishing spots, but they are beautiful spots just to relax and unwind. Just look at the Lotus Oasis. Who wouldn't want to read a book on the edge of those waters?

Lotus Oasis

Pharaoh's Oasis

Ship's Oasis

Water in the Sand

Symbol		Fish
1	Egypt, Oasis, Common	Frogs, Alley Catfish, Red Herring, Siamese Catfish, Crocodile
2	Egypt, Oasis, Rare	Frogs, Alley Catfish, Red Herring, Siamese Catfish, Crocodile
3	Egypt, River, Common	Alley Catfish, Red Herring, Siamese Catfish, Salmon, Crocodile
4	Egypt, River, Rare	Alley Catfish, Red Herring, Siamese Catfish, Salmon, Crocodile, Lobster
5	Egypt, Mummyfish	Mummy Fish
C4	China, Koi1	Goldfish, Kawarimono Koi, Tancho Koi
C5	China, Koi2	Doitsu Koi, Ochiba Koi, Tancho Koi

Egypt

Insects

Beetles

 Water Beetle

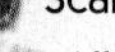 Scarab

 All

Butterflys

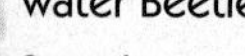 Crypt Moth

 Cleopatra

 Egypt Mix

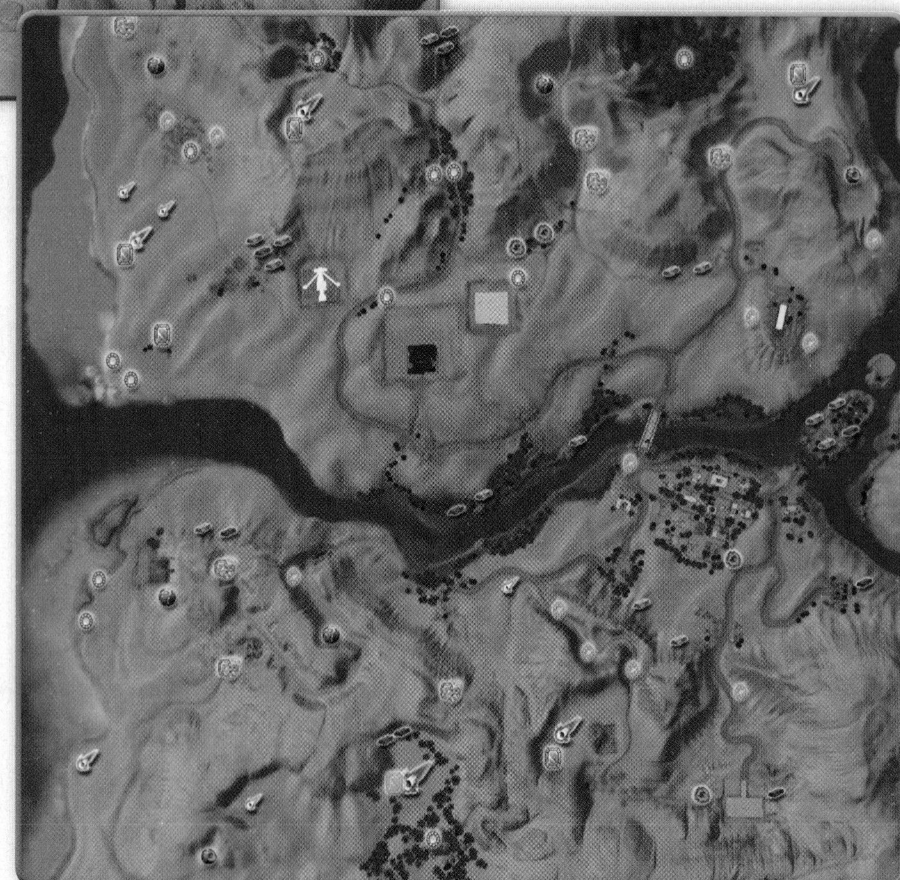

Gems, Metals, and Meteorites

Gems

Alabastar

Mix

 Tiberium High

 Tiberium

Turquoise

Metals

Copper

Mix High

Mix Low

Gold, Palladium, Titanium, Iridium

Meteorites

Small

Small, Large

Large

Huge

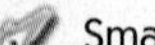 Geode

Geode, Septarian

Septarian

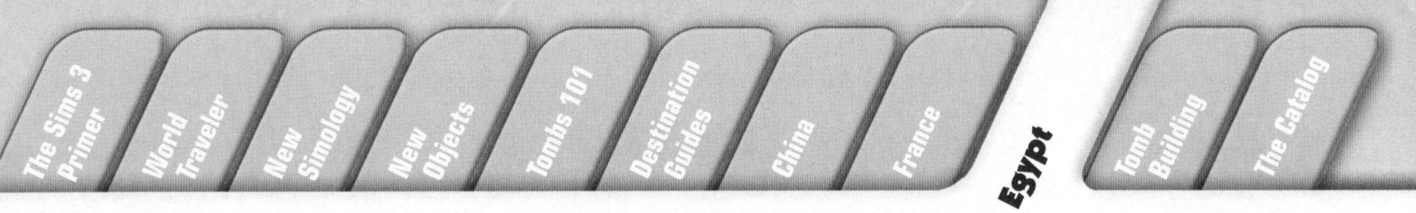

Adventure List

The following list of adventures will guide you through your travels in Egypt.

Adventure	Activity	How to Complete	Tomb?	Reward
PLUNDER OF EGYPT				
Business Abroad	MorcuCorp is working with the Egyptian government to locate three relics in Al Simhara. Any interested parties should report in.	Report in to the designated local to start this adventure chain.		Ancient Coins, Dried Food
An Introductory Test	The MorcuCorp representative left some papers in the Tomb of Discovery. Can you fetch them?	Explore to the bottom of the Tomb of Discovery by base camp. Find the papers and bring them back.	Tomb of Discovery	Visa Points, Dried Food
Agent of MorcuCorp	Bringing the papers back pleases the MorcuCorps representative. While they analyze the papers, report into a local lackey to get another adventure.	Report in to designated Sim.		Visa Points
Gems of the Sands	The lackey notes that the boss did not properly budget for the quarter. Can you help find enough turquoise to pay the locals?	Locate 4 pieces of turquoise. Use map view to quickly find the gems.		Simoleons
Local Intel	The lackey is concerned about the reputation of MorcuCorp with the locals. Can you survey a few and see what they think of MorcuCorp?	Befriend the designated number of locals and then ask them about MorcuCorps. The Al Simhara market is a good place to find several locals. Report back your findings.		Ancient Coins, Visa Points
Into the Fire	The lackey has a new job for you. Quest to the Pyramid of the Burning Sands and bring back a rare strain of Flame Fruits.	Explore the tombs and harvest the necessary number of Flame Fruits. Bring them back to collect your reward.	Tomb of the Burning Sands	Visa Points, Simoleons
Digging Deeper	The MorcuCorp representative admires your drive. Can you locate a local and inquire about a book that may have information about the desired relics?	Go to the designated local (use map view), befriend the local, and then ask about the book.		None
The Ancient Library	The local talks of an ancient library hidden inside a home in Al Simhara. Explore the library to find the book you need.	Go to the house marked on your map, befriend the family so you can enter, and then dive into the library to find the glowing chest.	Ancient Library	Visa Points, Ancient Coins
Race to Nowhere	The book describes the three powerful relics left by the ancient kings of Al Simhara. The relic merchant at the market knows where the first one, the Relic of the Sun, is located.	Go the the market and speak to the marked merchant. Befriend them and then ask about the relic.		None
Race to Copper	The merchant now realizes the value of the relic and wants some sort of payment.	Locate the requested number of copper pieces and then report back to the merchant. Hurry! Use map view.		None
On the Side of Good	The merchant hands over the relic and lets you know that the locals are aware something fishy is going on.	Take the relic back to the designated Sim on your map.		Ancient Coins, Visa Points
PLUNDER OF EGYPT—GOOD				
Preparing the Bribe	It turns out your MorcuCorps rep is really a double agent who wants to stop them. Can you help the Sim bribe 2 MorcuCorp guards?	Use map view to collect two pieces of Mummitomium and bring them back.		Ancient Coins, Simoleons, Visa Points
HQ Infiltration	Now that you have the rare element, it must be delivered to the MorcuCorp Headquarters—but real quiet-like!	Befriend family at HQ (marked on map) and then slip into the shack. Use hole in wall to unlock stairs into tomb. Locate the glowing chest and deposit the bribe.	MorcuCorp HQ	Visa Points
Hacker!	Nice work placing the bribe. Now you need to hack the computer at MorcuCorp HQ.	Locate the computer inside MorcuCorp HQ (it's in a room by itself) and hack it.	MorcuCorp HQ	Visa Points
The Second Relic	The hack worked. The second relic is in the Tomb of the Desert Ocean: the Relic of Life. Explore the tomb and bring the relic back.	Go to the Pyramid of the Sky. Inspect the front door. Explore the Tomb of of the Desert Ocean to find the Relic of Life.	Tomb of the Desert Ocean	Ancient Coins, Visa Points
Trading Shawarma for Information	You have retrieved the Relic of Life. Now it is time to close in on the third relic. Get information from the relic merchant.	Befriend the relic merchant and then ask for information.		Visa Points
Egyptian Cuisine	The merchant will share the information with you if you give them a free meal.	Bring the relic merchant a plate of Shawarma. Go to the food store first.		Visa Points, Simoleons
The Third Relic	The merchant tells you that the third relic—Relic of Eternity—is in the Great Pyramid.	Explore the Tomb of Death and locate the Relic of Eternity.	Tomb of Death	Visa Points, Ancient Coins
PLUNDER OF EGYPT—BAD				
Nefarious Intentions	MorcuCorps is looking for hardened adventurers for a few operations here in Egypt. Report in to the agent designated on your map.	Use map view to find the person you must speak with, and report in.		Visa Points
Preparing the Bribe	You have signed up with MorcuCorp! The company needs to buy off some local officials with copper. Can you find some?	Deliver the requested number of copper samples.		Ancient Coins, Simoleons
Delivering the Bribe	You must now deliver the bribe of copper to one of the merchants in Al Simhara's market. In return, you learn the location of MorcuCorp's opposition.	Deliver bribe to merchant marked on map.		Ancient Coins. Visa Points
Black Bag Job	As a result of the bribe, you learn the location of a secret base where they plot against MorcuCorp. Infiltrate the base.	Enter the Secret Base (marked on your map) and find the computers.	Secret Base	Ancient Coins
Spreading "Information"	Now that you have the information, you must spread it amongst the locals and convince them how bad the resistance is.	Befriend the specified number of locals and tell them about the resistance.		Ancient Coins

Egypt

Adventure	Activity	How to Complete	Tomb?	Reward
PLUNDER OF EGYPT—BAD, CONTINUED				
The Contract, Part 1	Your information campaign has been a success. But not everybody has been convinced…	Go to the designated local and talk about a contract with MorcuCorp.		Visa Points
The Contract, Part 2	The local is not quite ready to accept the contract. Some turquoise might change their attitude.	Deliver the requested number of turquoise gems to the local.		Simoleons
The Contract, Part 3	Your "offering" has been accepted (and appreciated). The contract has been accepted.	Report in your success.		Visa Points, Ancient Coins
METAL TRADE				
The Age of Copper	The relic merchant needs copper to make imitation pieces that fool tourists. Can you help?	Bring back the requested number of copper pieces (use map view).		Simoleons, Ancient Coins, Visa Points
A Longing for Gold	A local Sim noticed that the price of gold has spiked. Can you bring them gold ore?	Bring back the requested number of gold pieces (use map view).		Simoleons, Ancient Coins, Visa Points
Finding Mummitomium	A local has just heard about Mummitomium. Can you bring them some samples of it?	Bring back the requested number of Mummitomium pieces (use map view).		Simoleons, Ancient Coins, Visa Points
A Bit More Copper	The copper you brought back to the merchant was great—now more is needed to keep up with demand!	Bring back the requested number of copper pieces (use map view).		Simoleons, Ancient Coins, Visa Points
Heaps of Gold	Remember that local who was into gold? Now they want even more to sell on the markets.	Bring back the requested number of gold pieces (use map view).		Simoleons, Ancient Coins, Visa Points
Mounds of Mummitomium	The local that wanted Mummitomium now needs even more to sell. The local will pay handsomely for the delivery.	Bring back the requested number of Mummitomium pieces (use map view).		Simoleons, Ancient Coins, Visa Points
TRAPPED AT HOME				
Trapped at Home	A local family would love to use their basement, but it turns out it's an ancient tomb that's loaded with traps. They will pay a Sim who can disarm the traps.	Befriend family first so you can enter home. Then use stairs to enter basement. Soak in dive well to thwart fire traps and inspect wall holes to disarm others.	Trap Nexus	Visa Points, Ancient Coins, Simoleons
TOMB TOURS				
Tomb Tours	The Al Simhara Cartographers Union (Local #458) is in search of an aspiring adventurer to explore the local tombs. Please visit the Great Pyramid, Sphinx, the Temple of Karnak, the Temple of Queen Hatshepsut, and Pyramid of the Wind.	Follow the order of the sites in the listing and check into the tombs. You only need to breach the entrances. Report back at the end to earn the cash rewards. The Visa points are doled out with each tomb visit.		Visa Points, Simoleons, Ancient Coins
TOURIST BROCHURE				
Al Simhara Tomb Tourist Brochure	The Al Simhara Board of Tourism and Falafel needs someone to photograph tomb devices for use in an upcoming tourist brochure.	Enter a tomb and take a photo of a trap. Then report in to claim reward.		Visa Points, Simoleons, Ancient Coins
Al Simhara Tomb Tourist Brochure	The Al Simhara Board of Tourism and Falafel needs someone to photograph tomb devices for use in an upcoming tourist brochure.	Enter a tomb and take a photo of a pushable statue. Then report in to claim reward.		Visa Points, Simoleons, Ancient Coins
Al Simhara Tomb Tourist Brochure	The Al Simhara Board of Tourism and Falafel needs someone to photograph tomb devices for use in an upcoming tourist brochure.	Enter a tomb and take a photo of a pile of Ancient Coins. Then report in to claim reward.		Visa Points, Simoleons, Ancient Coins
Al Simhara Tomb Tourist Brochure	The Al Simhara Board of Tourism and Falafel needs someone to photograph tomb devices for use in an upcoming tourist brochure.	Enter a tomb and take a photo of a floor switch. Then report in to claim reward.		Visa Points, Simoleons, Ancient Coins
Al Simhara Tomb Tourist Brochure	The Al Simhara Board of Tourism and Falafel needs someone to photograph tomb devices for use in an upcoming tourist brochure.	Enter a tomb and take a photo of a rubble pile. Then report in to claim reward.		Visa Points, Simoleons, Ancient Coins
Al Simhara Tomb Tourist Brochure	The Al Simhara Board of Tourism and Falafel needs someone to photograph tomb devices for use in an upcoming tourist brochure.	Enter a tomb and take a photo of a treasure chest. Then report in to claim reward.		Visa Points, Simoleons, Ancient Coins
Al Simhara Tomb Tourist Brochure	The Al Simhara Board of Tourism and Falafel needs someone to photograph tomb devices for use in an upcoming tourist brochure.	Enter a tomb and take a photo of a giant boulder. Then report in to claim reward.		Visa Points, Simoleons, Ancient Coins
BUG HUNT				
Icky Egyptian Entomology	Scientists at the Landgraab Industries Science Facility are dying to study the indigenous bug species of Egypt and are willing to pay top dollar for specimen. Can you catch some scarab beetles?	Locate and collect the requested number of scarab beetles, then report in.		Simoleons, Visa Points
THE CURSE OF THE MUMMY				
Cursed!	You have befallen the curse of the mummy. A local knows of a way to dispel the curse. Prove your interest by delivering an artifact to them.	Bring a relic worth a specified number of Simoleons to the local on your map.		None
Journey to the Sphinx	Your dedication has been proven. Now you must go to the Sphinx and beg it to help, then follow the path the Sphinx reveals.	Go to Sphix and use "Plead" interaction to unlock front door of Sphinx.		None
Into the Sphinx	Now that the interior of the Sphinx has been opened, seek the Soulpeace statue to cleanse the curse.	Explore the tomb until you find the Soulpeace statue and then use the "Cleanse" interaction.	Soulpeace Chambers	Mummy's Curse Lifted

Adventure	Activity	How to Complete	Tomb?	Reward
		ANCIENT LOVE AFFAIR		
In Search of Love	A local is in need of romantic advice.	Report in to Sim for next step.		Visa Points
A Few Words with a Friend	The local actually needs you to now go speak with another friend about an ancestor and the Hatshepsut.	Report in to Sim for next step.		Visa Points
Woo Them with Jewels	This friend needs help proving that an ancestor was a consort to Queen Hatshepsut. But right now, they have an idea to help the romantically challenged friend.	Collect requested number of alabaster samples.		Visa Points, Simoleons
Teach Him to Cook	The friend's next idea is to teach the unromantic Sim how to cook.	Read the book you are given and then talk to first local in adventure chain.		Visa Points
The Key to Her Heart	Apparently, one of Queen Hatshepsut's secret lairs is below this city. Go look for clues inside of it.	Go to the house on the map, inspect the hole in the ground behind it, and explore the tomb.	The Queen's Hideaway	None
Love in the Servant's Quarters	The key located in the Queen's Hideaway should unlock the Servant's Quarters at the Temple of Queen Hatshepsut. Explore for clues.	Travel to Temple of Queen Hatshepsut and use keystone. Explore the Servant's Quarters. The door is under the stairs.	Temple of Queen Hatshepsut	Visa Points, Ancient Coins, Simoleons
Promoting Anwar	The friend still needs some romantic help. While the local inspects the relic you brough back, talk to other Egyptians about the friend.	Befriend the requested number of locals and talk about friend.		Visa Points, Ancient Coins
Love Is Bazaar	The relic you brought back from the Servant's Quarters has a keystone in it. Use it in the Bazaar Tombs.	Explore the Bazaar Tomb, starting with the new keystone Panel and locate the Queen's chambers.	Bazaar Tomb	Visa Points, Ancient Coins
Online Dating	The relic reveals that more trysts took place in another secret spot. But for now, let's help the friend start online dating...with a profile picture.	Take a photo of the friend.		Visa Points, Simoleons
Love Laid to Rest	The relic had another keystone in it! This keystone opens the queen's personal chambers at Queen Hatshepsut's temple.	Travel to bottom of the quarters and locate the glowing chest next to the queen's bed.	Temple of Queen Hatshepsut	Visa Points, Ancient Coins
		BAD EXPLORER		
Oh Where is My Lost Treasure?	A local has misplaced a treasure found in a tomb. Can you help them recover it?	Go to the Al Simhara marketplace and use the stairs in the small building behind the general store to enter the Bazaar Tombs. Locate the relic in the glowing chest.	Bazaar Tomb	Visa Points, Simoleons
The Society's Lost and... Found?	The Al Simhara Historical Society lost an ancient relic during a tomb expedition.Can you help them recover it?	Go to the Copper Quarry and seek the glowing treasure chest on the bottom level of the tomb.	Copper Quarry	Visa Points, Simoleons
In Search of My Sought Treasure	Another adventurer has lost a relic in a tomb exploration. Can you recover it?	Go to the Pyramid of the Burning Sands and locate the glowing chest in the tomb.	Tomb of the Burning Sands	Visa Points, Simoleons
Missing Relic Believed to be Lost	Another explorer has misplaced a relic in a tomb. They will reward the adventurer who can recover it.	Go to the Tomb of Discovery and locate the glowing treasure chest.	Tomb of Discovery	Visa Points, Simoleons
ISO: Relic	While an explorer was fleeing a tomb, they dropped a relic they found. Dare you go back to that tomb and recover it for them?	Go to the Copper Quarry and use the keystone to open the door leading downstairs to the glowing chest.	Copper Quarry	Visa Points, Simoleons
		MUMMIFICATION		
Proof of Mummification, Part 1	A local needs a photo of a mummy to win a bet with another Sim. Can you help out?	Take a clear photo of a mummy from a tomb with a mummy (such as Tomb of the Burning Sands), and report in.		Simoleons, Visa Points, Ancient Coins
Proof of Mummification, Part 2	The Al Simhara Historical Society needs proof of the existence of mummies in order to win a grant from the government.	Take a clear photo of a mummy from a tomb with a mummy (such as Tomb of the Burning Sands), and report in.		Simoleons, Visa Points, Ancient Coins
		NATIVE FRIEND		
A Friend to the Natives	A local in the food business wants your help with making friends. If you befriend people, you will hopefully lead to more friend-making among the local Sims. That in turn may lead to more parties. Mores means more food. More food means more business...	Befriend the requested number of locals and report in.		Simoleons, Visa Points
		POMEGRANATE FARMER		
Pomegranate Farmer	A local is having trouble with their pomegranate crop and would like see if you can do beter.	Deliver the requested number of pomegranates of Nice or higher quality. If you cannot harvest from natural plants, you may need to grow your own via the Gardening skill.		Simoleons, Visa Points
Oh Please! More Pomegranates!	The previous pomegranates you grew were a hit. Can you grow more? And better ones, please?	Deliver the requested number of Great or higher quality pomegranates to the local.		Simoleons, Visa Points
		TOMB DISASTERS		
Tombs: When Not to Raid	The Al Simhara Council for Safe and Fun Tomb Exploration is working on a pamphlet about dangers in tomb. They need help from Sims willing to be Torched, Soaked, and Cursed.	After accepting the adventure, go into a tomb and get either Torched, Soaked, or Mummy's Curse moodlet. Then report in.		Visa Points, Simoleons

Tomb Maps

Ancient Library

Basement Level 1

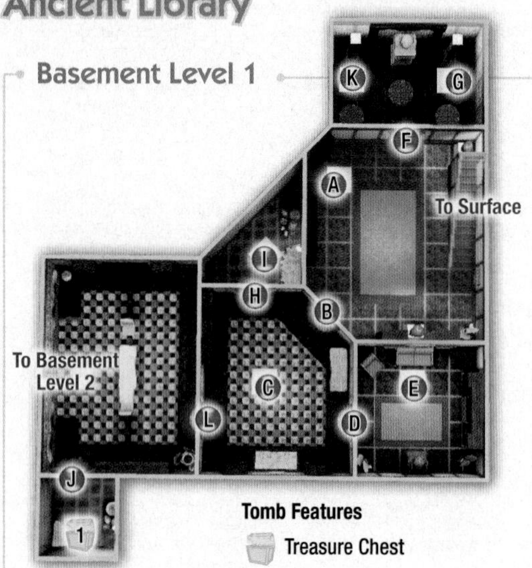

A Switch opens Door 1
B Door 1
C Switch opens Door 2
D Door 2
E Switch opens Door 3
F Door 3
G Switch opens Door 4
H Door 4
I Switch opens Door 5
J Door 5
K Switch opens Door 6 and Stairs to B2
L Door 6
1 Medium Relic

Tomb Features

Treasure Chest

Basement Level 2

Tomb Features

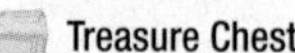

Treasure Chest

1 Collection
2 Adventure Goal (Saga of Three Relics), Fragments

Bazaar Tomb

Basement Level 1

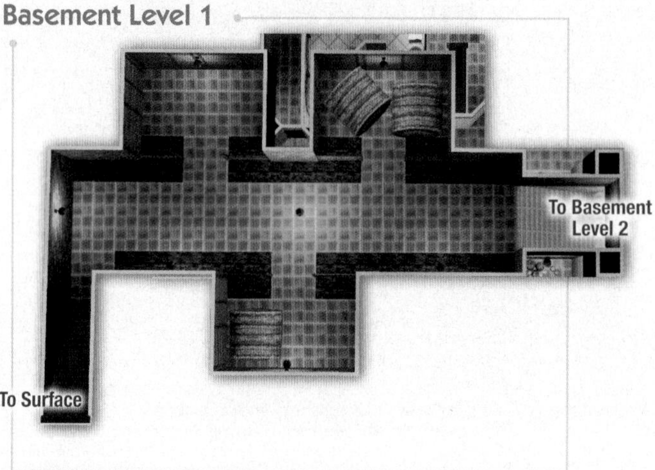

Basement Level 2

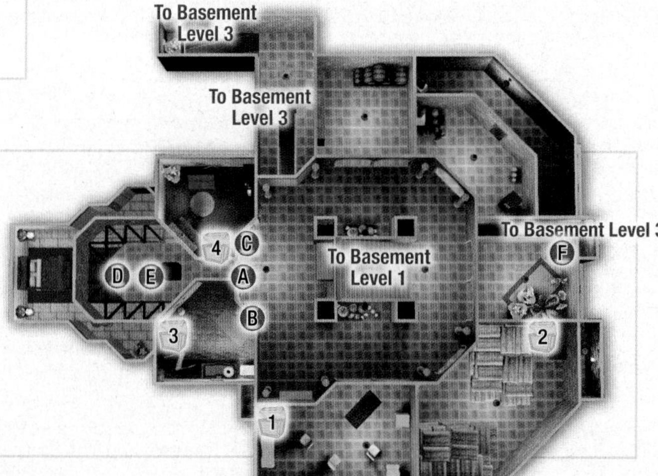

Tomb Features

Treasure Chest

A Marketplace Storage #4 Keystone Panel
B Moonstone Keystone Panel
C Marketplace Storage #5 Keystone Panel
D Hole makes Floor Switch E appear
E Floor Switch unlocks Door 1
F Door 1

1 §§§
2 Moonstone Keystone
3 Relic Medium
4 Magic Gnome, §§§§

Basement Level 3

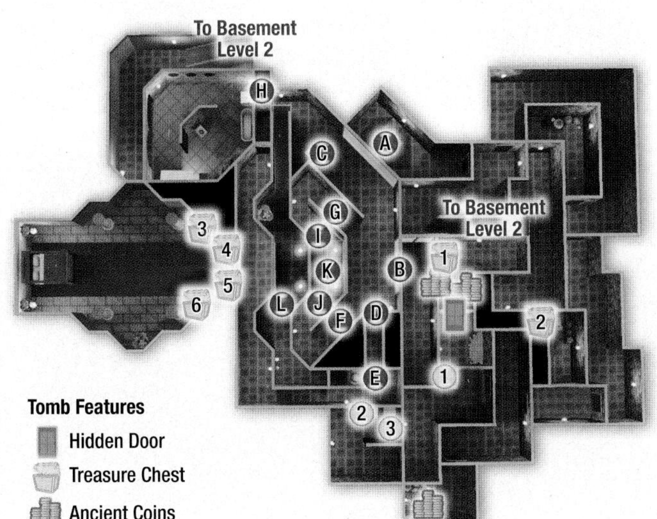

- (A) Floor Switch opens Door 1
- (B) Door 1
- (C) Floor Switch opens Door 2
- (D) Door 2
- (E) Floor Switch opens Door 3 & Door 4
- (F) Door 3
- (G) Door 4
- (H) Floor Switch opens Door 5 & Door 6
- (I) Door 7
- (J) Door 6
- (K) Hole opens Door 7
- (L) Door 7

- (1) Epic Relic
- (2) Metal Egypt
- (3) Misc. Gem
- [1] Large Relic
- [2] Dried Food
- [3] §§§§§
- [4] Epic Relic
- [5] Adventure Goal (Inscribed Relic), Ancient Coins
- [6] Ancient Coins

Copper Quarry

Basement Level 1

Tomb Features

Ancient Coins

- (A) Copper Quarry Keystone Panel
- (B) Inspect to open Door 1
- (C) Door 1
- (1) Gem Cheap
- (2) Metal Egypt
- (3) Metal Egypt
- (4) Metal Egypt
- (5) Random Metal
- (6) Metal Egypt
- (7) Random Metal
- (8) Small Relic
- (9) Gem Egypt
- (10) Random Metal

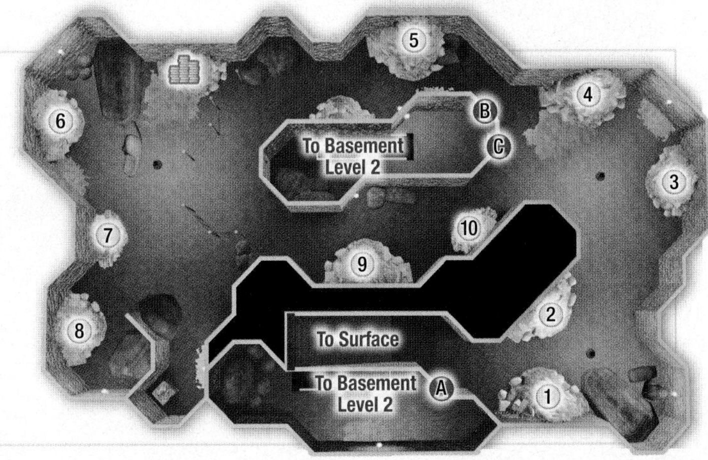

Basement Level 2

- (1) Random Metals
- (2) Metal Egypt
- (3) Metal Egypt
- (4) Random Metals
- (5) Copper Quarry Keystone
- (6) Metal Egypt
- (7) Metal Egypt

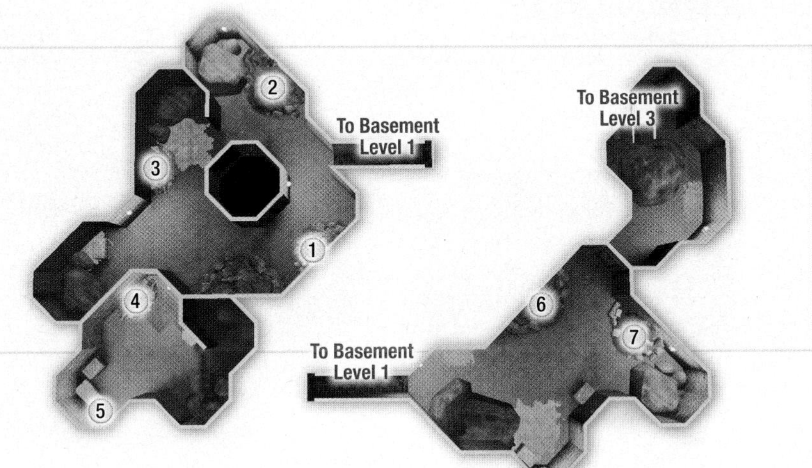

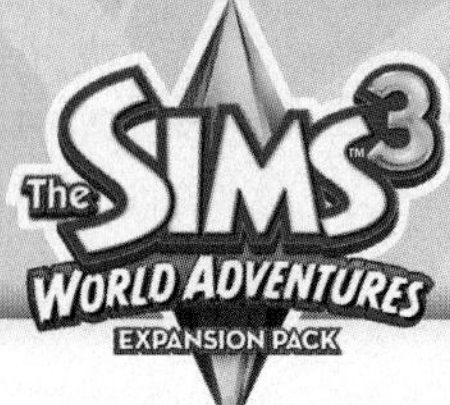

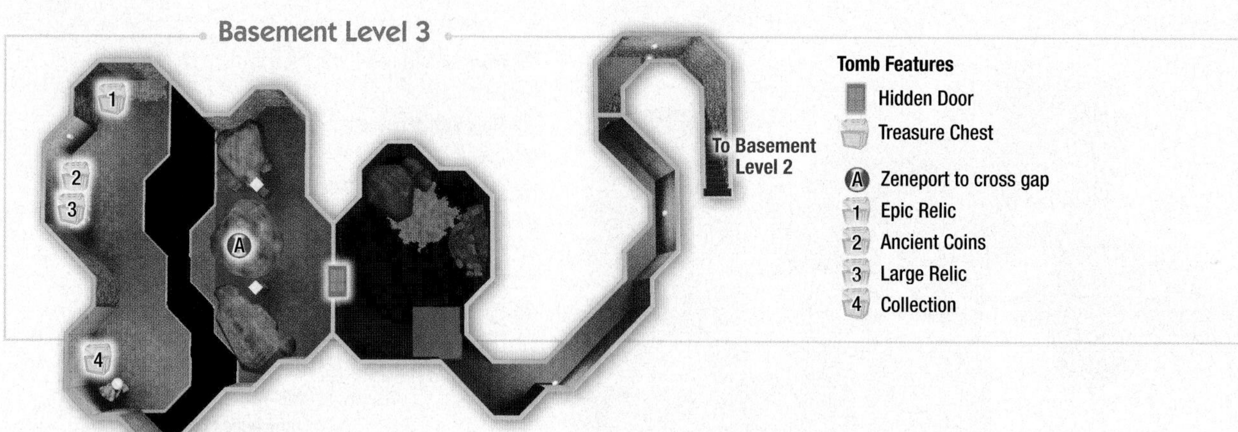

Hatshepsut's Getaway

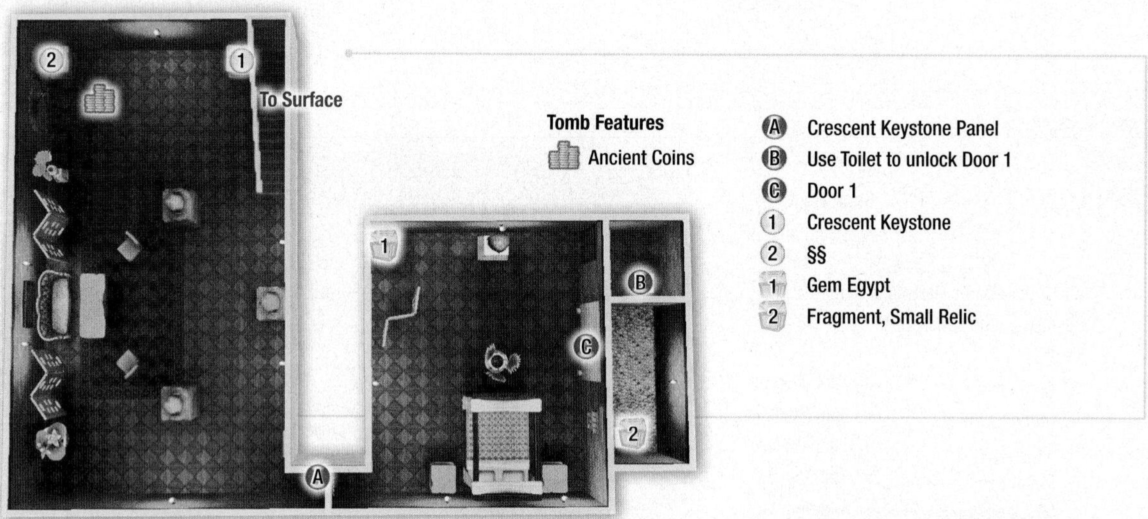

James Vaughn's Command Center

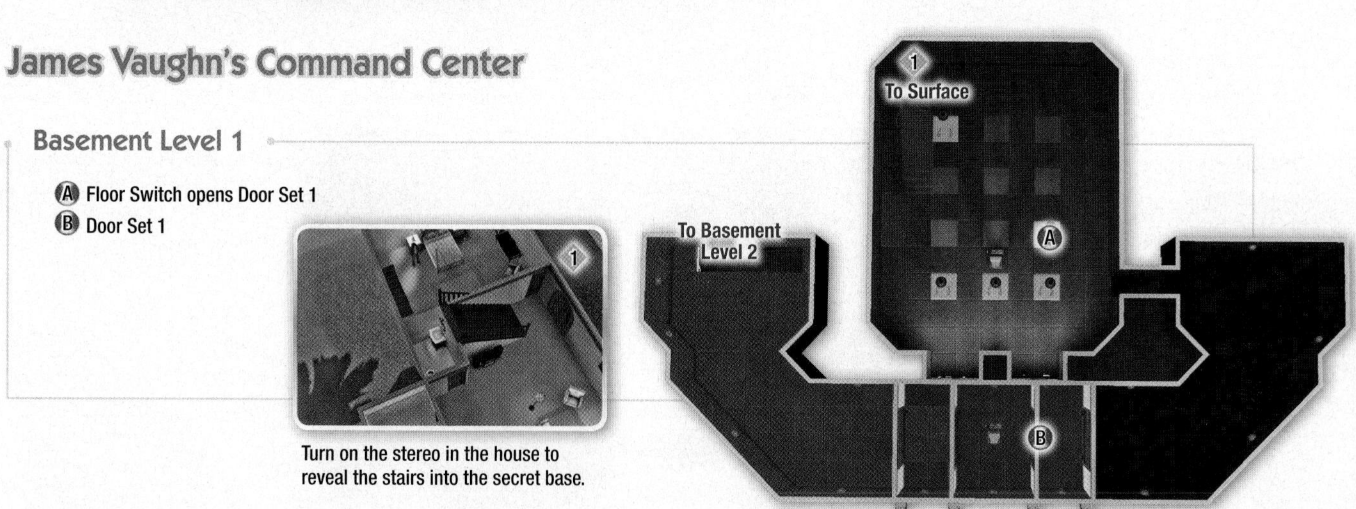

Turn on the stereo in the house to reveal the stairs into the secret base.

Basement Level 2

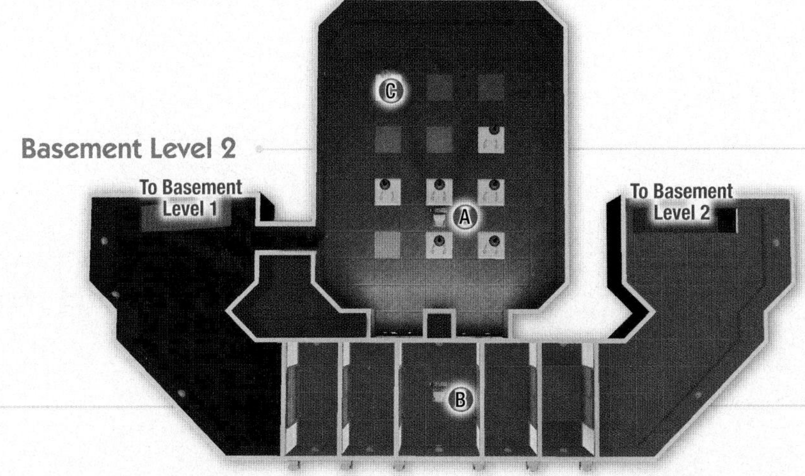

- (A) Floor Switches open Door Set 2
- (B) Door Set 2
- (C) Reset Switches

Basement Level 3

- (A) Floor Switches open Door Set 3
- (B) Door Set 3
- (C) Reset Switches

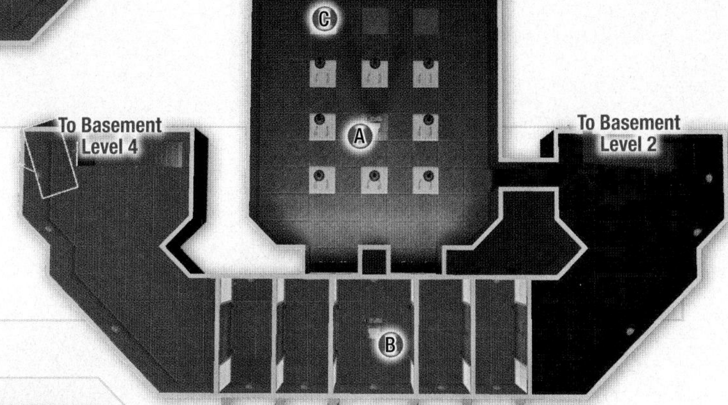

Basement Level 4

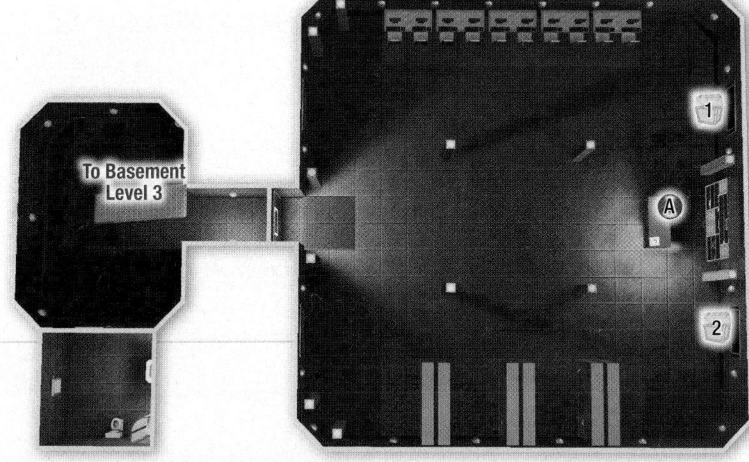

Tomb Features

Treasure Chest

- (A) Adventure Goal (Hack Computer)
- 1 §§§§§
- 2 Collection

Karnak Treasure Hall

Tomb Features

Treasure Chest

- (1) Gem Egypt
- 1 Fragments

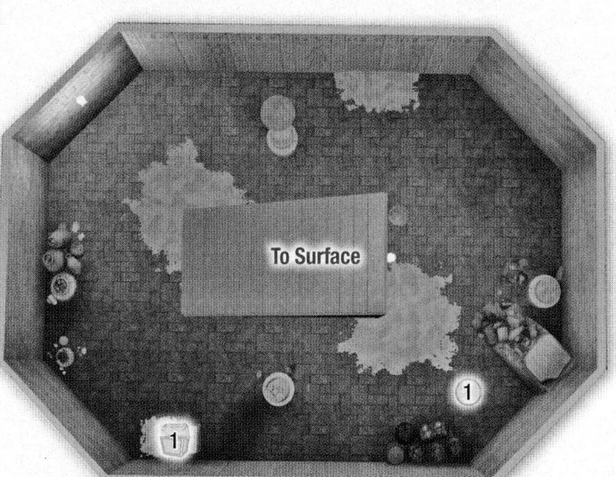

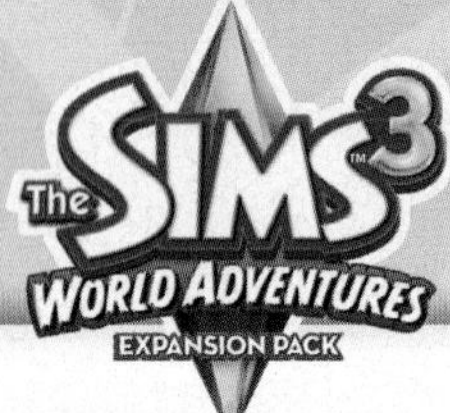

Egypt

MorcuCorp HQ

Floor 1

(A) Reveals Stairs to B1

Basement Level 1

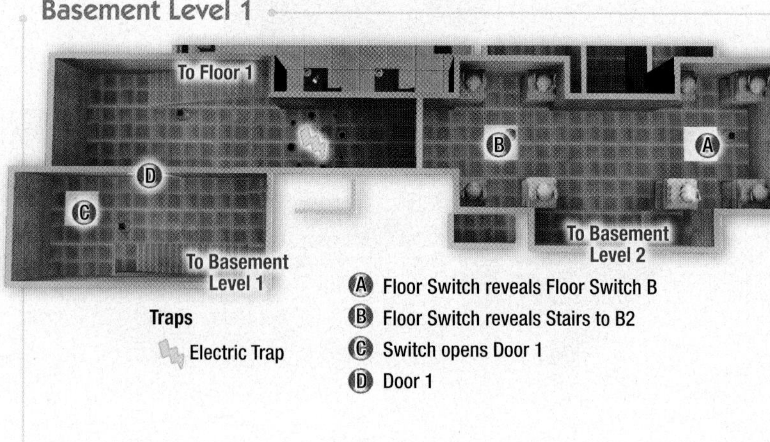

Traps

Electric Trap

(A) Floor Switch reveals Floor Switch B

(B) Floor Switch reveals Stairs to B2

(C) Switch opens Door 1

(D) Door 1

Basement Level 2

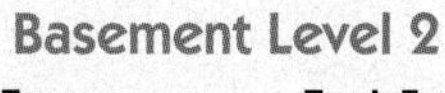

Traps

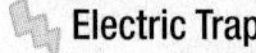

Electric Trap

Tomb Features

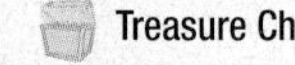

Treasure Chest

(A) Crescent Keystone Panel reveals Floor Switch B

(B) Floor Switch opens Door 1

(C) Door 1

1 Ancient Coins

2 Crescent Keystone

3 §§§

4 Nectar Bottle

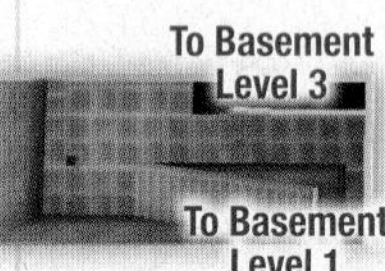

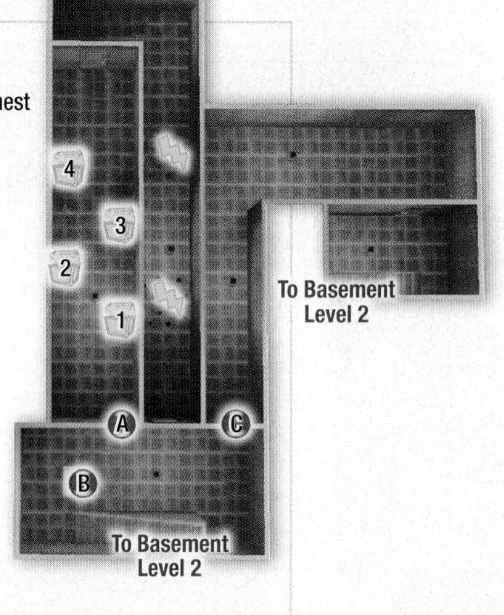

Basement Level 3

Tomb Features

Treasure Chest

(A) Floor Switch opens Door 1

(B) Door 1

(C) Floor Switch opens Door 2

(D) Door 2

(E) Adventure Goal (computer)

1 Collection

2 Adventure Goal (place package here), §§§§§

3 §§§§

Hack this computer to complete the adventure.

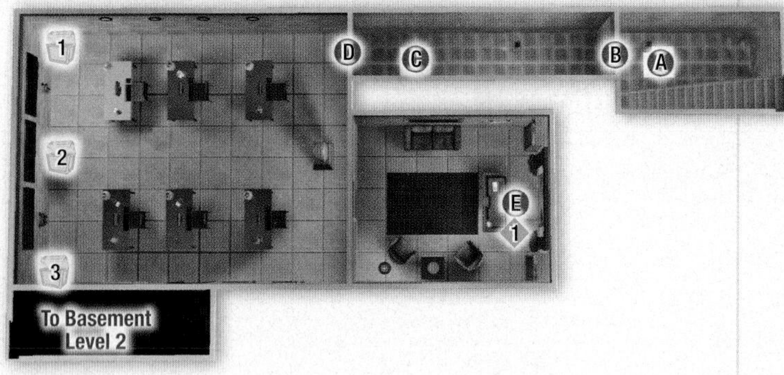

Temple of Queen Hatshepshut — Servant's Quarters / Queen's Quarters

Basement Level 1

Tomb Features

- Hidden Door
- Treasure Chest
- Ancient Coins

- (A) Floor Switch unlocks Door 1
- (B) Door 1
- (C) Floor Switch unlocks door 2
- (D) Door 2
- (E) Floor Switch opens Stairs 1
- (F) Stairs 1 (to B2)
- (G) Floor Switch opens Door 3
- (H) Door 3
- 1 Seeds

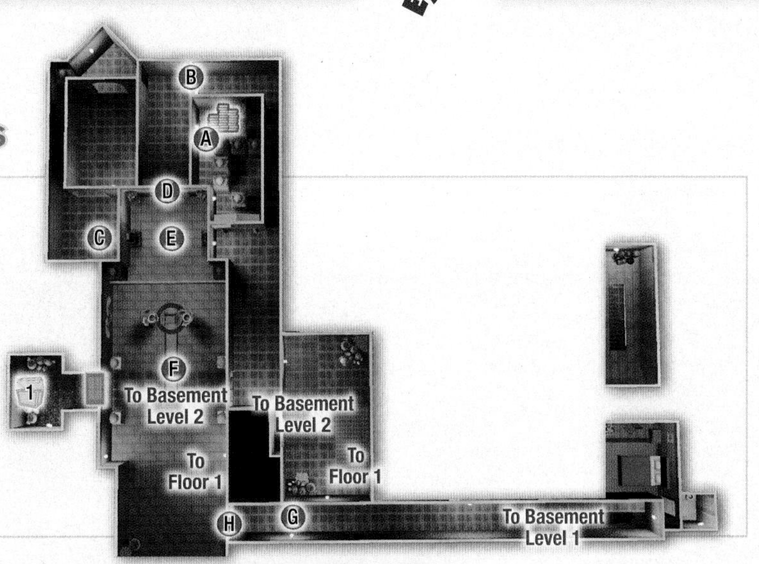

Basement Level 2

Tomb Features

- Hidden Door
- Treasure Chest

- (A) Floor Switch makes Floor Switch B appear
- (B) Floor Switch unlocks Door 1
- (C) Door 1
- (D) Floor Switch makes Floor Switch E appear
- (E) Floor Switch makes Stairs 1 appear
- (F) Stairs 1 (to B3)
- 1 Ancient Coins
- 2 Gem Egypt, Dried Food
- 3 Adventure Goal (Queen's Diary), Nectar Bottle
- 4 Collection, Ancient Coins

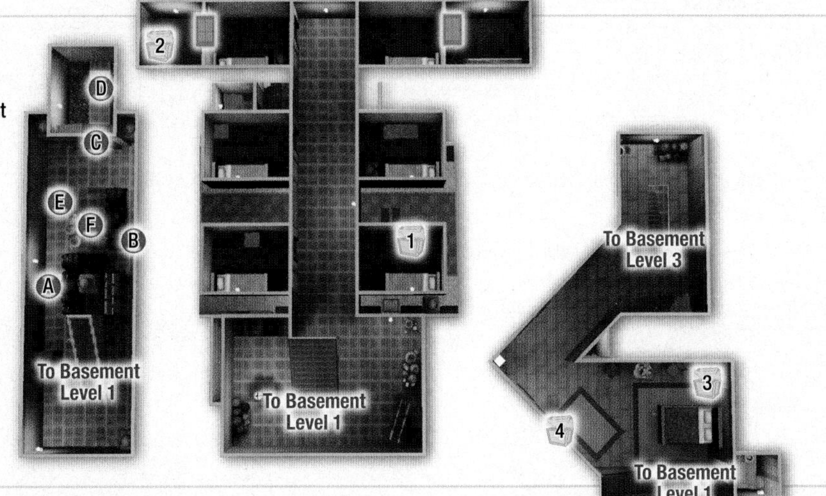

Basement Level 3

- (A) Floor Switch unlocks Door 1
- (B) Door 1
- (C) Crescent Keystone Panel
- (D) Queen's Personal Chambers Keystone Panel
- (1) Queen's Personal Chambers Keystone
- 1 Dried Food, §§§§
- 2 Reveals Floor Switch A, Crescent Keystone, Ancient Coins
- 3 Marketplace Storage Key #5, Medium Relic

Tomb Features

- Hidden Door
- Treasure Chest

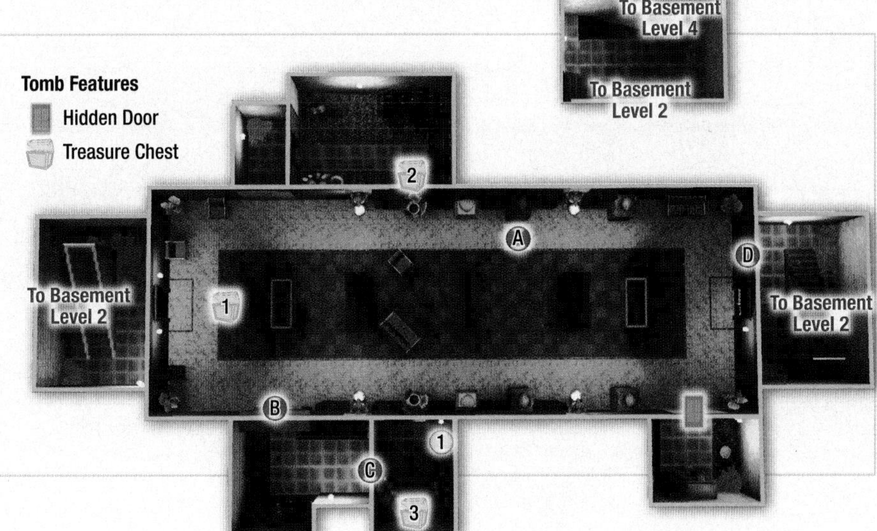

Basement Level 4

Tomb Features

Treasure Chest

1 Adventure Goal (Enscribed Relic), Nectar Bottle

Floor 1

Ⓐ Insert Servants' Quarters Keystone to make Stairs 1 appear

Ⓑ Stairs 1 (to B1)

Ⓒ Insert Keystone of Queen Hatshepsut to make Stairs 2 appear

Ⓓ Stairs 2 (to B1)

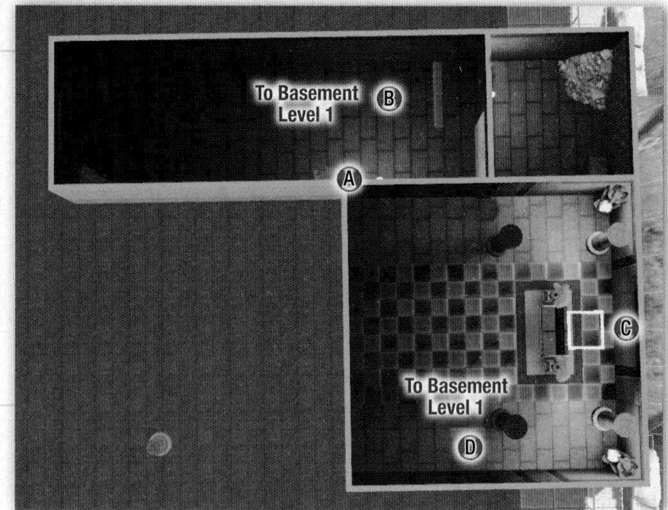

Soulpeace Chambers—Sphinx

Floor 1

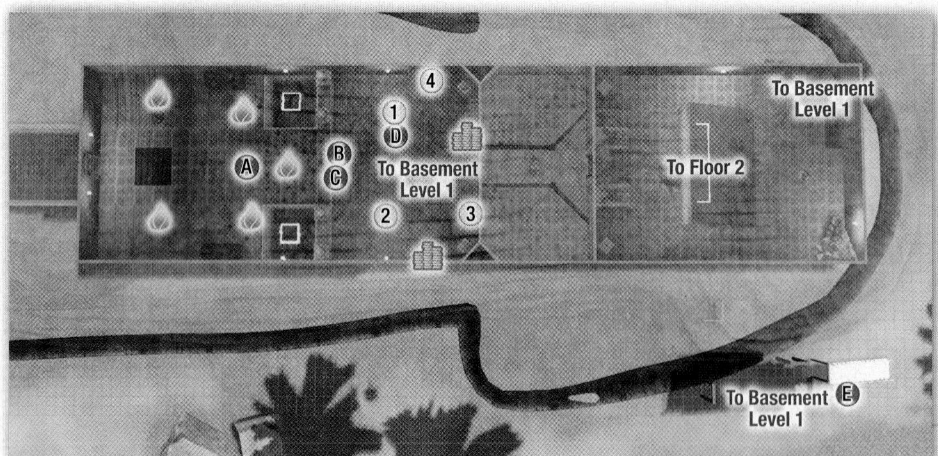

Traps

Fire Trap

Tomb Features

Ancient Coins

Ⓐ Floor Switch shuts off nearby Fire Traps

Ⓑ Switch reveals 1

Ⓒ Switch reveals 2

Ⓓ Inspect both Holes to reveal Stairs to B1

Ⓔ Floor Switch unlocks Stairs to B1

1 Dried Food

2 §§§

3 Gem Medium

4 Gem Medium

Floor 2

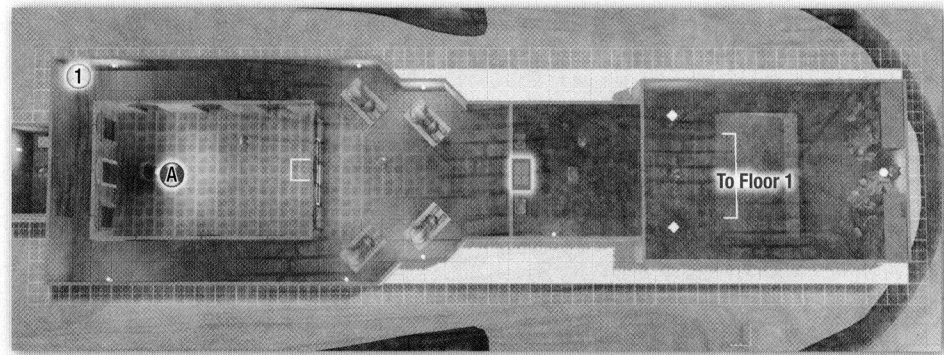

Tomb Features

- Hidden Door

- Ⓐ Soulpeace Statue
- ① Soulpeace Gem

Basement Level 1

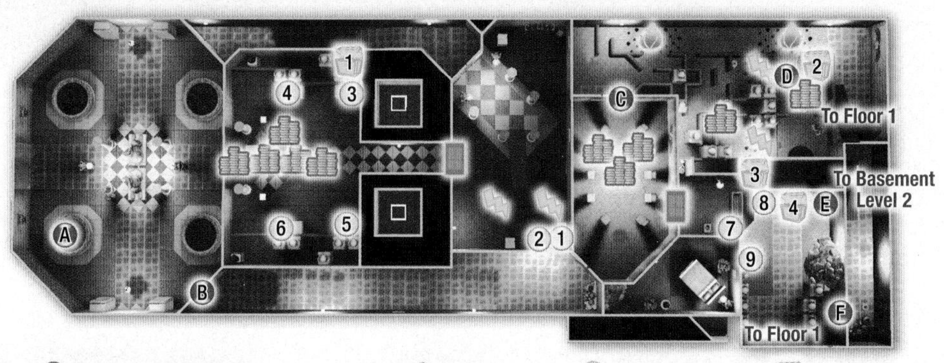

Traps

- Fire Trap
- Electric Trap

Tomb Features

- Hidden Door
- Treasure Chest
- Ancient Coins

- Ⓐ Dive Well unlocks Door 1
- Ⓑ Door 1
- Ⓒ Star Keystone Panel
- Ⓓ Floor Switch shuts off nearby Fire Traps
- Ⓔ Floor Switch opens Door 2
- Ⓕ Door 2

- ① Gem Egypt
- ② Gem Cheap
- ③ Aqua
- ④ Metal Egypt
- ⑤ Metal Egypt
- ⑥ Gem High
- ⑦ Star Keystone
- ⑧ Metal Egypt
- ⑨ Dried Food

Treasure Chests:

- 1 Emerald
- 2 Epic Relic
- 3 Gem Egypt
- 4 Large Relic

Basement Level 2

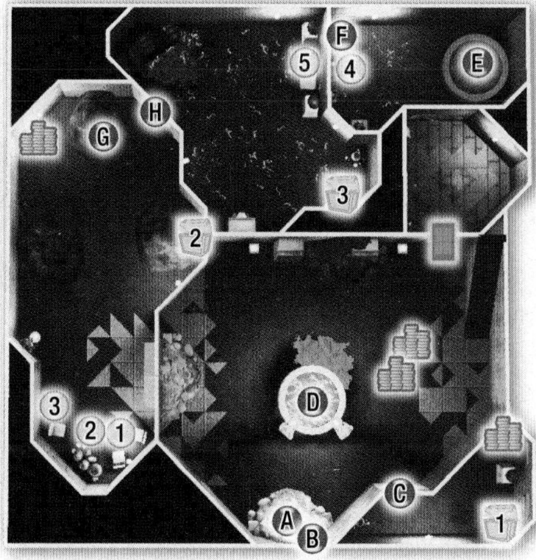

Tomb Features

- Hidden Door
- Treasure Chest
- Ancient Coins

- Ⓐ Floor Switch makes Hole B appear
- Ⓑ Inspect Hole to make Door 1 appear
- Ⓒ Door 1
- Ⓓ Dive Well to E
- Ⓔ Dive Well to D
- Ⓕ Mourn at Gravestone to make 4 appear
- Ⓖ Smash boulder to reveal Floor Switch that opens Door 2
- Ⓗ Door 2

- ① §§
- ② §
- ③ §
- ④ Fragment
- ⑤ Small Relic, Medium Relic

Treasure Chests:

- 1 §§§
- 2 Fragment
- 3 Dried Food

Tomb of Burning Sands—Pyramid of Burning Sands

Floor 1

Traps

Fire Trap

- (A) Keystone of Burning Sands Panel
- (B) Floor Switch opens Door 1
- (C) Door 1
- (D) Dive Well unlocks Door 2
- (E) Door 2
- (F) Floor Switch shuts off Fire Trap and opens Door 3
- (G) Door 3
- (H) Hole unlocks Stairs 1 (to B1)
- (I) Stairs 1
- A Floor Switch opens Door 4
- B Door 4
- C Floor Switch opens Door 5
- D Door 5
- 1 Egypt Gem
- 2 Crescent Keystone
- 1 Medium Relic

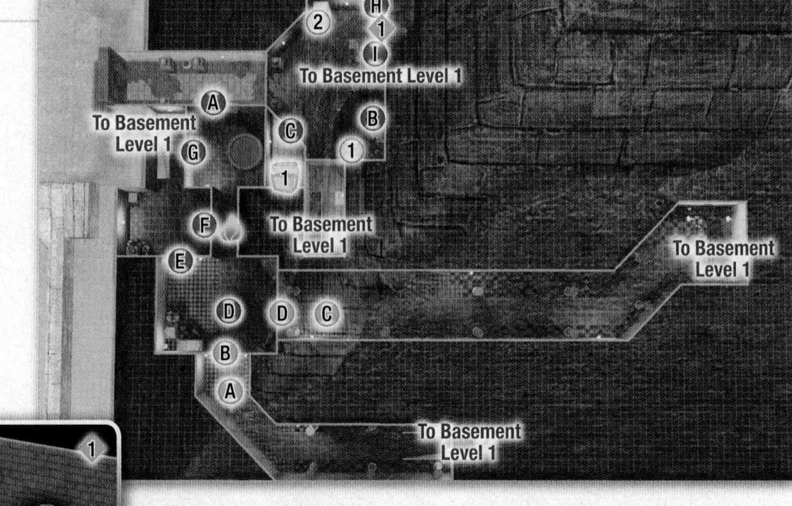

There are two tombs in this pyramid. To access the Tomb of the Rock, clear the rubble in this corner and inspect the hole to reveal stairs. This tomb is entirely optional, but fun!

Basement Level 1

Traps

Fire Trap

Tomb Features

- Hidden Door
- Treasure Chest
- Ancient Coins

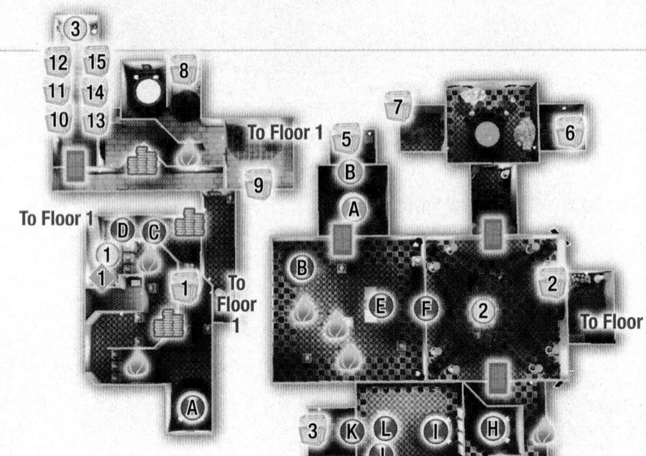

Harvest the Flame Fruits to complete this adventure. But why not explore the rest of the tomb before leaving?

- (A) To Dive Well B
- (B) To Dive Well A
- (C) Floor Switch opens Door 1
- (D) Door 1
- (E) Floor Switches open Door 2
- (F) Door 2
- (G) Hole shuts off nearby Fire Traps
- (H) Dive Well to I
- (I) Dive Well to H
- (J) Floor Switch opens Door 3
- (K) Door 3
- (L) Floor Switches unlock Door 5
- (M) Door 5

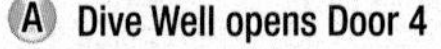

- A Dive Well opens Door 4
- B Door 4
- 1 Flame Fruits
- 2 Flame Fruits
- 3 Mummy

- 1 Fragments
- 2 Collection
- 3 Crescent Keystone, Unlocks Floor Switch Red L
- 4 Gem High
- 5 Fragments
- 6 Small Relic
- 7 Epic Relic
- 8 Fragments
- 9 Crescent Keystone
- 10 Fragments
- 11 Gem Medium
- 12 Gem Egypt
- 13 §
- 14 Ancient Coins
- 15 Collection

Tomb of Death—Great Pyramid

Floor 1

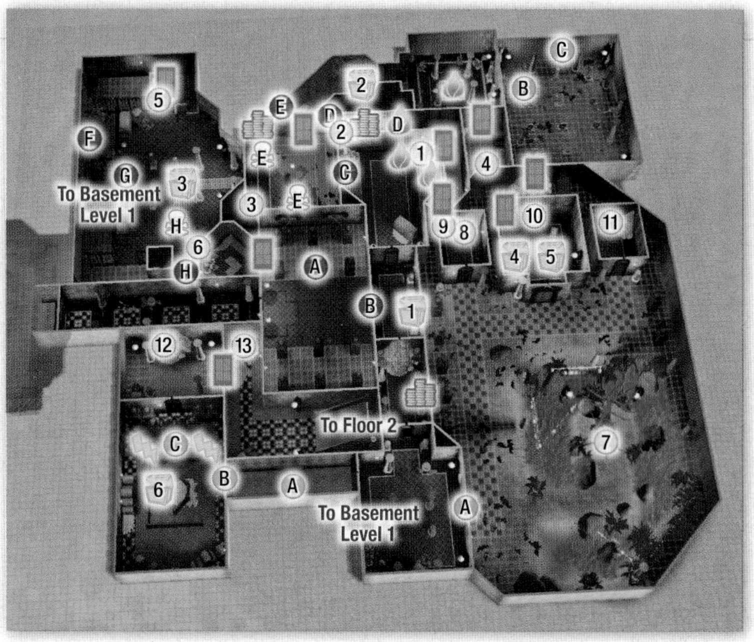

Traps

- Fire Trap
- Electric Trap
- Poison Darts

Tomb Features

- Hidden Door
- Treasure Chest
- Ancient Coins

- A Move Statue to unlock Door 1
- B Door 1
- C Star Keystone Panel
- D Inspect Hole to shut off D Traps
- E Inspect Hole to shut off E Traps
- F Floor Switch unlocks Stairs 1
- G Stairs 1 (to B1)
- H Inspect Hole to shut off H Traps
- A Lodestone Keystone Panel
- B Mourn at Gravestone to reveal Hole 1
- C Hole contains Nectar Bottle
- A Floor Switch (under Giant Boulder) unlocks Door 2
- B Door 2
- C Floor Switches turn off nearby Traps

- 1 Star Keystone
- 2 Star Keystone
- 3 Large Relic
- 4 Epic Relic
- 5 §§§
- 6 Fragments, §§§
- 7 Death Tomb Depths Keystone
- 8 Small Relic
- 9 §§
- 10 Epic Relic
- 11 Small Relic
- 12 Medium Relic
- 13 §§§§

Treasure Chests:

- 1 Dried Food
- 2 Small Relic
- 3 Small Relic
- 4 Ancient Coins
- 5 Large Relic
- 6 Large Relic

Floor 2

Traps

- Fire Trap

Tomb Features

- Treasure Chest

- A Hole unlocks Door 1
- B Door 1
- 1 Mummy, Fragments

Treasure Chests:

- 1 Fragments, §§
- 2 Epic Relic, §§§§
- 3 Gem Expensive

Watch out for a mummy to pop out of the sarcophagus when you open the treasure chest.

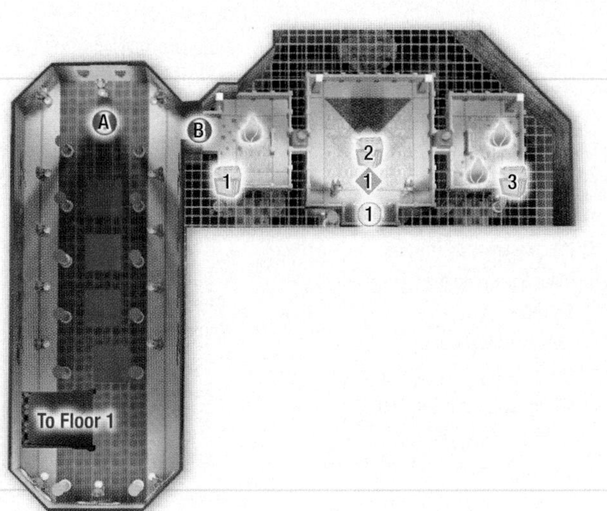

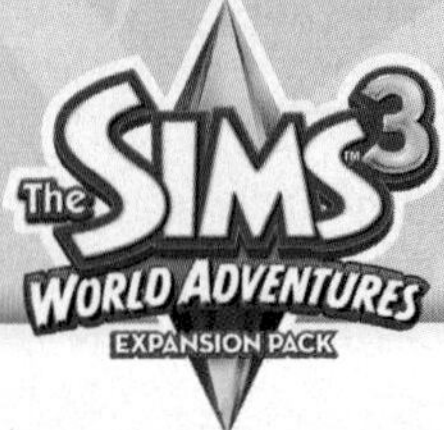

Egypt

Basement Level 1

Traps
- Fire Trap
- Poison Darts

Tomb Features
- Hidden Door
- Ancient Coins

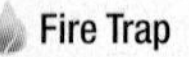

- Ⓐ Inspect Hole to shut off A Traps and unlock Door 1
- Ⓑ Door 1
- Ⓒ Floor Switch reveals Floor Switch D
- Ⓓ Floor Switch reveals Floor Switch E
- Ⓔ Floor Switch unlocks Door 2
- Ⓕ Door 2
- Ⓖ Star Keystone Panel opens Door 3
- Ⓗ Door 3
- Ⓘ Floor Switch opens Door 4, enables I Traps
- Ⓙ Door 4
- Ⓚ Floor Switch opens Door 5 and Door 6
- Ⓛ Door 5
- Ⓜ Door 6

1. Ancient Coins
2. Star Keystone
3. §§§§§
4. Small Relic

Use the green lights as a hint. Only inspect this hole to shut off the traps in this room.

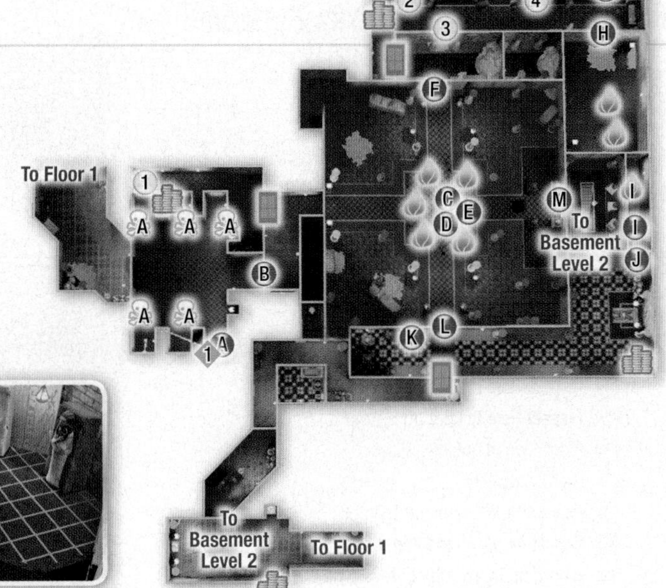

Basement Level 2

Traps
- Fire Trap
- Electric Trap

Tomb Features
- Hidden Door
- Treasure Chest
- Ancient Coins

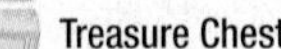

- Ⓐ Hole unlocks Doors 1 and 2
- Ⓑ Door 1
- Ⓒ Door 2
- Ⓓ Earthstone Keystone Panel
- Ⓔ Switch unlocks Door 3
- Ⓕ Door 3
- Ⓖ Earthstone Keystone Panel
- Ⓗ Death Tomb Depths Keystone Panel
- Ⓘ Switch unlocks Door 4
- Ⓙ Door 4
- A Hole unlocks Hole B
- B Hole disables all B Traps
- C Floor Switch unlocks Door 5
- D Door 5
- E Hole unlocks Door 6
- F Door 6
- G Mourn at Gravestone to reveal Hole containing §§§§§§
- H Floor Switch activates H Traps

1. Dried Food
2. §§§§
3. Medium Relic
4. Gem Egypt
5. Earthcore Keystone, Dried Food
6. Lodestone Keystone
7. Medium Relic
8. Egypt Gem
9. Small Relic
10. §§
11. Small Relic
12. §§
13. Medium Relic
14. Mummy, Epic Relic
15. Mummy, Dried Food
16. Fragments
17. §§
18. Medium Relic

Treasure Chests:

1. Collection
2. Fragments
3. Ancient Coins
4. Adventure Goal (Relic of Eternity), Fragment, §§§
5. Epic Relic
6. Fragments
7. Gem Egypt

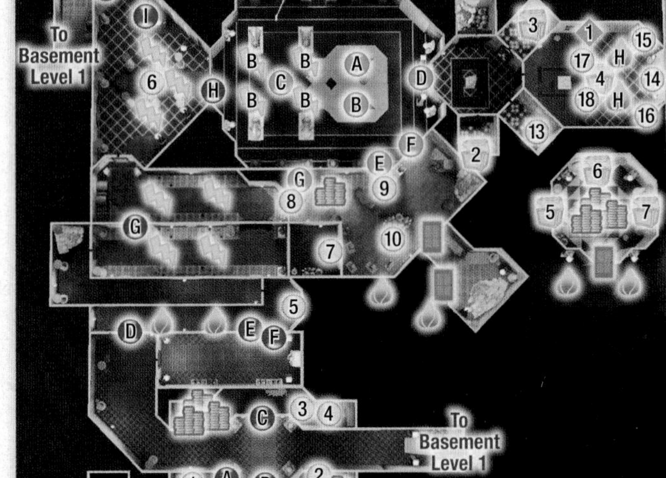

Beware of mummies in this room! They may step out when you try to grab the Relic of Eternity.

Tomb of Discovery

Basement Level 1

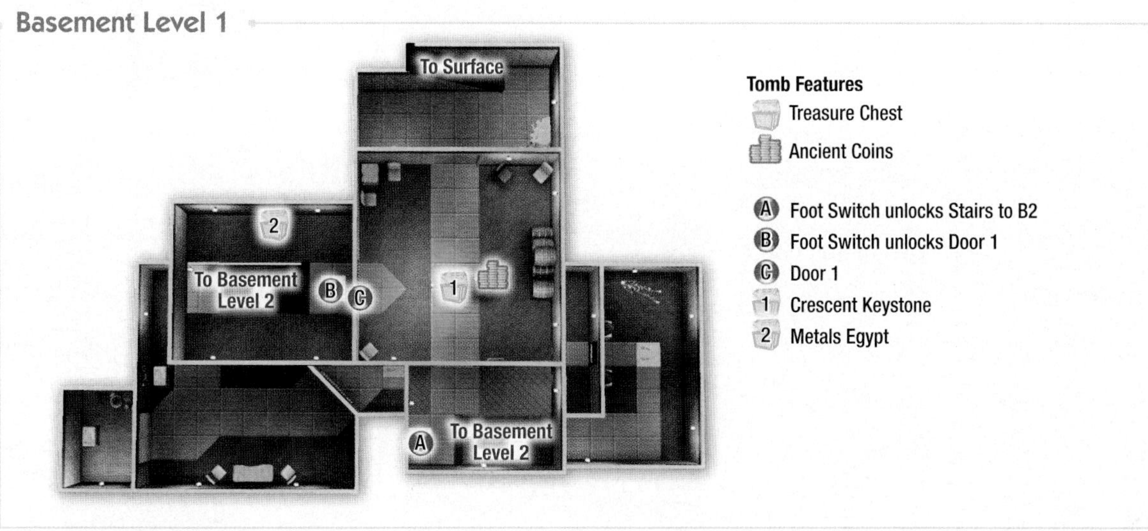

Tomb Features

- Treasure Chest
- Ancient Coins

- (A) Foot Switch unlocks Stairs to B2
- (B) Foot Switch unlocks Door 1
- (C) Door 1
- 1 Crescent Keystone
- 2 Metals Egypt

Basement Level 2

Tomb Features

- Hidden Door
- Treasure Chest
- Ancient Coins

- (A) Floor Switch unlocks Door 1
- (B) Door 1
- (C) Floor Switch unlocks Door 2
- (D) Door 2
- (E) Floor Switch unlocks Door 3
- (F) Floor Switch unlocks Door 3
- (G) Door 3
- 1 Adventure Goal (papers)
- 2 Collection

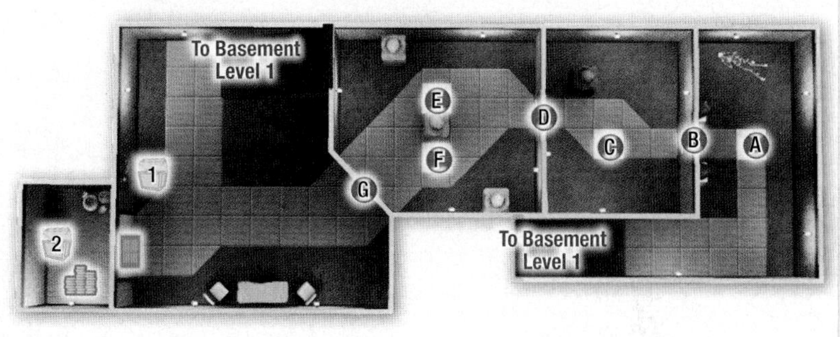

Tomb of Infinite Halls—Pyramid of the Wind

Floor 1

Tomb Features

- Treasure Chest

- (A) Hole unlocks Stairs 1
- (B) Stairs 1 (to B1)
- 1 Egypt Metals

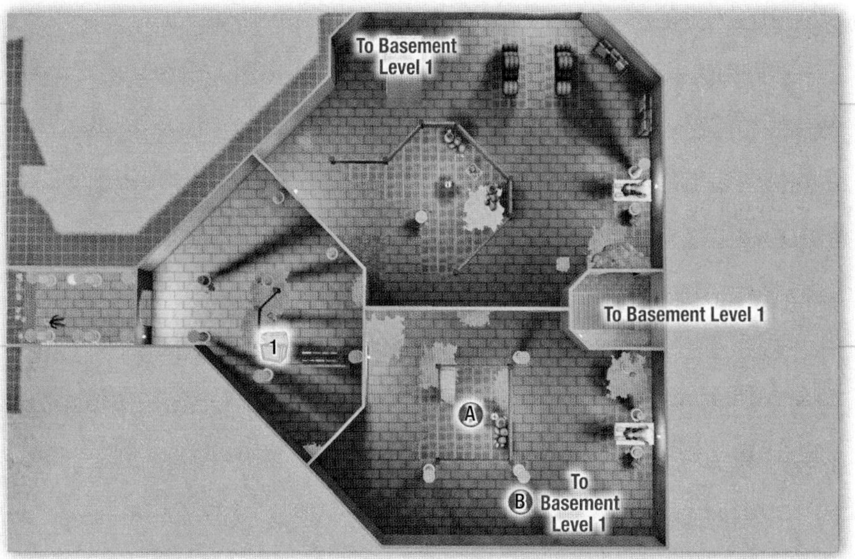

Egypt

Basement Level 1

Tomb Features
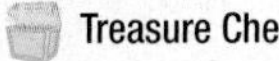
Treasure Chest
Ancient Coins

1. Crescent Keystone
2. Gem Egypt
3. Fragments
4. Mummy, Small Relic

Chest 1 Dried Food
Chest 2 Small Relic
Chest 3 Fragments

Trap Nexus

Basement Level 1

Traps
Fire Trap
Electric Trap
Poison Darts

Tomb Features
Hidden Door
Treasure Chest
Ancient Coins

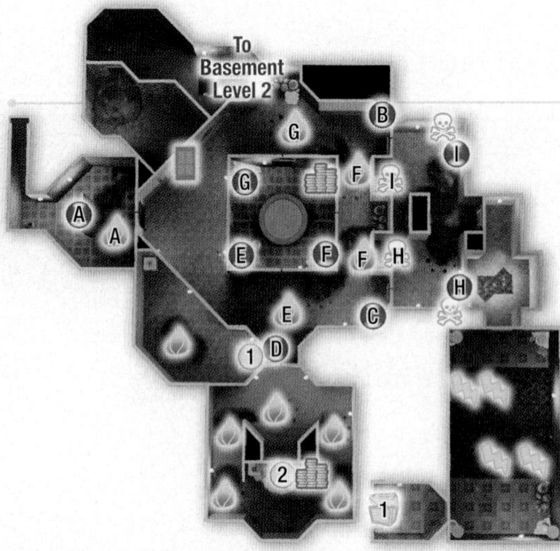

- (A) Hole disables A Traps
- (B) Lodestone Keystone Panel
- (C) Lodestone Keystone Panel
- (D) Star Keystone Panel
- (E) Hole disables E Traps
- (F) Hole disables F Traps
- (G) Hole disables G Traps
- (H) Hole disables H Traps
- (I) Hole disables I Traps
- 1 Star Keystone
- 2 Lodestone Keystone
- Chest 1 Fragments, Adventure Goal (disables all remaining traps)

Basement Level 2

Tomb Features
Treasure Chest

1. Mummy, Large Relic
2. Mummy, Large Relic

Chest 1 Epic Relic

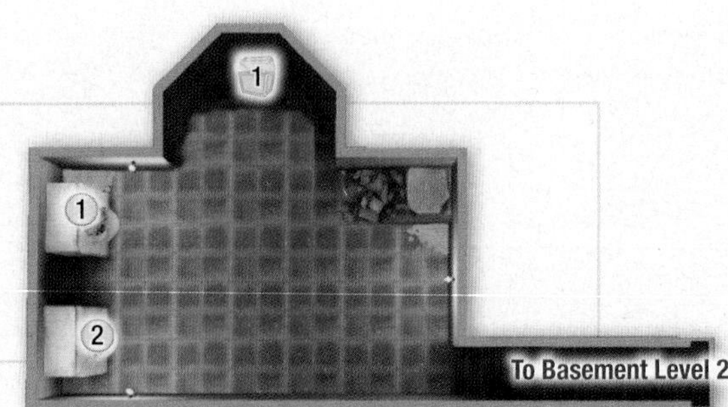

Abu Simbel

Floor 1

- (A) Tomb Entrance requires 2 offerings: Ancient Relic and Small Rock
- (B) Dive Well to C
- (C) Dive Well to B
- (D) Floor Switch unlocks Door 1
- (E) Door 1
- (F) Star Keystone Panel
- (1) Star Keystone
- 1 Fragments
- 2 Epic Relic

Tomb Features

- Hidden Door
- Treasure Chest

Basement Level 1

- (A) Floor Switch lights Lamp
- (B) Floor Switch lights Lamp
- (C) Floor Switch lights Lamp
- (D) Floor Switch lights Lamp
- (E) Door 1 unlocked when four Lamps are lit
- (F) Place Gold Figure on Pedestal to disable F Traps
- (G) Floor Switch unlocks Door 2
- (H) Door 2
- (I) Place any donation to disable Fire Traps
- (A) Floor Switch opens Door 3
- (B) Door 3
- (C) Floor Switch opens Door 4
- (D) Door 4
- (E) Floor Switch opens Door 5
- (F) Door 5
- (G) Floor Switch opens Door 6
- (H) Door 6
- (I) Floor Switch opens Doors 3-6 but enables Traps near Blue I
- (A) Left Eye of Horus
- (B) Right Eye of Horus
- (C) Floor Switch opens Door 7
- (D) Door 7
- (E) Inspect Hole to reveal Wall Switch, pull this Switch first to reveal Floor Switch at F, step on this Floor Switch first
- (F) Inspect Hole to reveal Wall Switch, pull this Switch second to reveal Floor Switch at E, step on this Floor Switch second
- (A) Place Right Eye of Horus on Pedestal to unlock Treasure Chest 7
- (B) Place Left Eye of Horus on Pedestal to unlock Treasure Chest 6
- (1) Large Relic (Mummy if you try to open without donation or steal other nearby relics)
- (2) Epic Relic, Mummy

Traps

- Fire Trap

Tomb Features

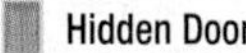

- Hidden Door
- Treasure Chest

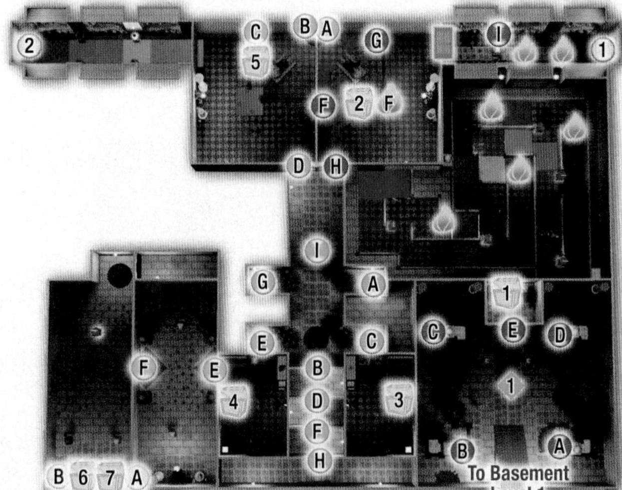

- 1 Epic Relic
- 2 Gold Figurine
- 3 Epic Relic
- 4 Epic Relic
- 5 Gold Figurine
- 6 Gold Figurine
- 7 Gold Figurine

Step only on the marked floor switches in this room to unlock the door. The unmarked switches just arm fire traps.

Egypt

Tomb of the Desert Ocean—Pyramid of the Sky

Floor 1

- Ⓐ Star Keystone Panel
- Ⓑ Floor Switch turns off B Traps
- Ⓒ Floor Switch turns off C Traps
- Ⓓ Hole turns off D Traps
- Ⓔ Floor Switch opens Door 1
- Ⓕ Door 1
- Ⓖ Star Keystone Panel
- Ⓗ Hole unlocks Door 2
- Ⓘ Door 2
- Ⓙ Reveals 3
- A To Dive Well B
- B To Dive Well A
- C Floor Switch unlocks Door 3
- D Door 3
- E Floor Switch reveals Floor Switch F
- F Floor Switch unlocks Stairs to B1
- G Foot Switch opens Door 4
- H Door 4
- A Heart of the Water Temple Keystone Panel
- B Floor Switch opens Door 5
- C Door 5

Traps

- Fire Trap
- Electric Trap
- Poison Darts
- Steam Jets

Tomb Features

- Hidden Door
- Treasure Chest
- Ancient Coins

- 1 Star Keystone
- 2 Star Keystone
- 3 §§
- 4 Money Tree
- 5 Money Tree
- 6 Fragments

- 1 Dried Food
- 2 §§§§
- 3 Fragments
- 4 Large Relic
- 5 Medium Relic
- 6 Ancient Coins
- 7 Collection, Fragments
- 8 Adventure Goal (Relic of Life), Fragments
- 9 Aqua
- 10 Small Relic
- 11 Large Relic, §§§§§
- 12 Large Relic

You must explore the right half of this tomb and the two lower floors to locate the Heart of the Water Temple Keystone.

Basement Level 1

Tomb Features

- Hidden Door
- Treasure Chest

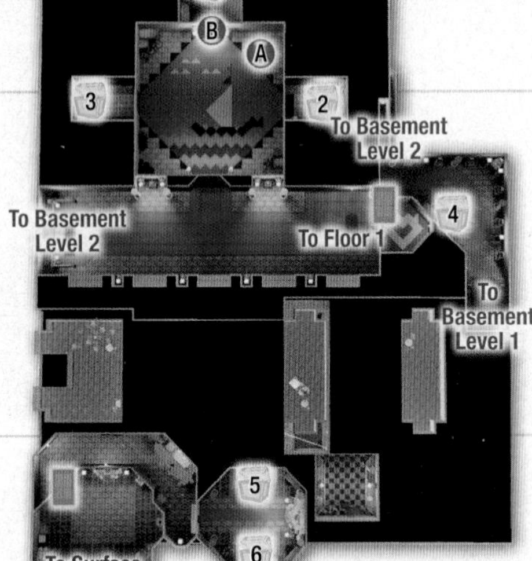

- Ⓐ Floor Switch opens Door 1
- Ⓑ Door 1
- 1 Gem Egypt
- 2 Ancient Coins
- 3 Epic Relic
- 4 Small Relic
- 5 Fragments
- 6 Gem Cheap

Basement Level 2

- Ⓐ Hole unlocks Door 1
- Ⓑ Door 1
- Ⓒ Push Statue to reveal Floor Switch
- Ⓓ Push Statue to reveal Floor Switch
- Ⓔ Push Statue to reveal Floor Switch
- Ⓕ Traps disabled when C, D, and E are activated
- Ⓖ Hole reveals nearby Traps and Hole H
- Ⓗ Inspect Hole to shut off H Traps
- Ⓘ Door 2
- 1 §§§
- 2 §§§
- 1 Medium Relic
- 2 Large Relic
- 3 Heart of Water Temple Keystone, unlocks Door 2

Traps

- Fire Trap
- Electric Trap

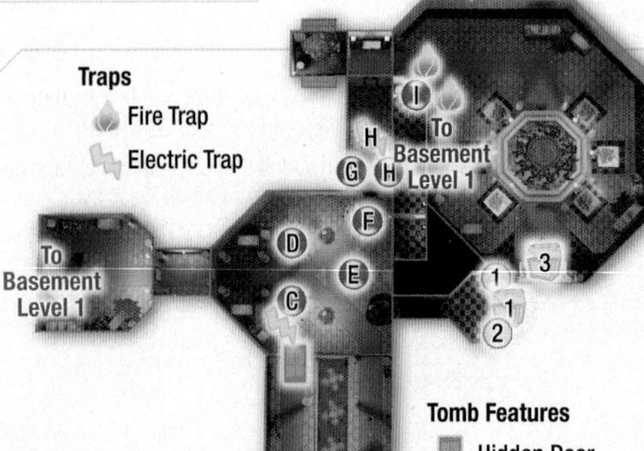

Tomb Features

- Hidden Door
- Treasure Chest

Tomb Building

Do-It-Yourself Tombs

You've had fun exploring the tombs below the sands of Egypt or in the grand homes of France. Wouldn't it be great if you could make your very own trap-laden tombs? Well, you can—you just need to sneak in through a back door in *World Adventures* to do so.

Getting Started

You can build tombs on your own lots through Build and Buy Mode. Although you are not required to build underground for a tomb, you may want to start by installing a basement under your house via the new Basement tool in Build Mode. Once you have constructed a basement, make sure you have stairs leading down to it so Sims can access the would-be tomb.

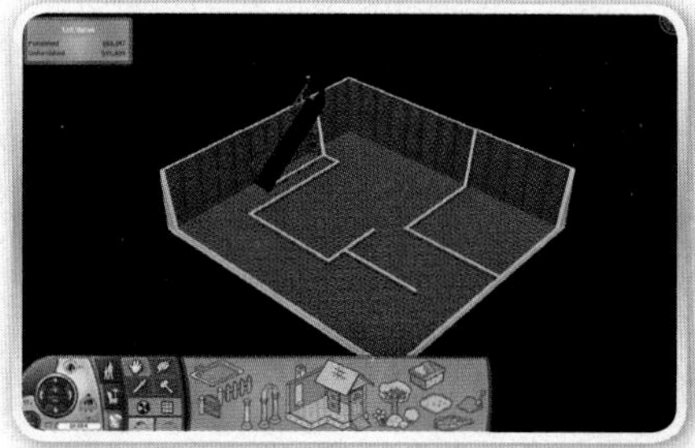

Basements make great tombs, but you could set up traps in a bedroom if you really wanted to.

To build a tomb, you have to open the Cheat menu and input a command to access a special collection of Buy Mode objects. To access this Cheat menu, press [Shift] + [Control] + [C]. In the blue line that drops from the top of the screen, type: buydebug. This unlocks a new category in Buy Mode: Special Items.

Once you have activated the special Buy Mode collection of tomb items, you can enter Buy Mode and start placing the very same traps, triggers, and tomb objects you have seen in your travels. The tomb objects are located in the new Debug collection, viewable if you choose to sort the objects by function.

Here is a full catalog of the tomb objects you can purchase in this special tomb-building Buy Mode:

TOMB OBJECTS

Tomb Object	Price (in Simoleons)
Ancient Coin Pile	0
Corner Rubble Pile	0
Dive Well	0
Escape Dust	0
Floor Skeleton	0
Giant Boulder	0
Hidden Trigger Panel	0
Large Rubble Pile	0
Keystone Panel	0
Left Eye of Horus	0
Right Eye of Horus	0
Pangu's Axe	0
Processor	0
Puddle/Burnt Tile Marker	0
Sands of Understanding	0
Small Hole - Floor	0
Small Hole - Wall	0
Soulpeace Statue	0
Tomb Room Marker	0
Torch Lever	0
Trap - Floor	0
Trap - Wall	0
Treasure Spawn Point	0
Sarcophagus	1
Floor Switch	3
Keystone	3
Inscription Plaque	10
Pushable Statue	10
Tomb Passage from TombTech	80
Tomb Passage Deluxe from Tomb Tech	125
Elegant Double Doors	400
The Sultan's Keep-All	310
Treasure Chest of Alouette	430
Jiangzhou's Chest	475

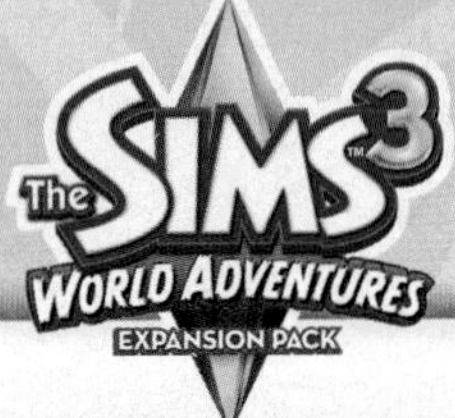

NOTE

You can find all of these objects by sorting objects in Buy Mode by function and then selecting the Debug sort. Then, click on the Tomb Objects tab. If you click on the Misc. Objects tab, you will find a bunch of objects you can use to give the tomb some ambiance.

NOTE

Many—but not all—tomb objects are completely free of charge.

Of course, just placing traps and switches in your basement does not automatically make it a tomb. You must set up triggers and behaviors so the tomb also works as more than just a gallery. The first thing you need to do is go back into the Cheat console. Then, input: "testingcheatsenabled true" (no quotation marks). This allows you to then start assigning triggers and behaviors. To add triggers to objects, left-click on them while holding down Shift + Control.

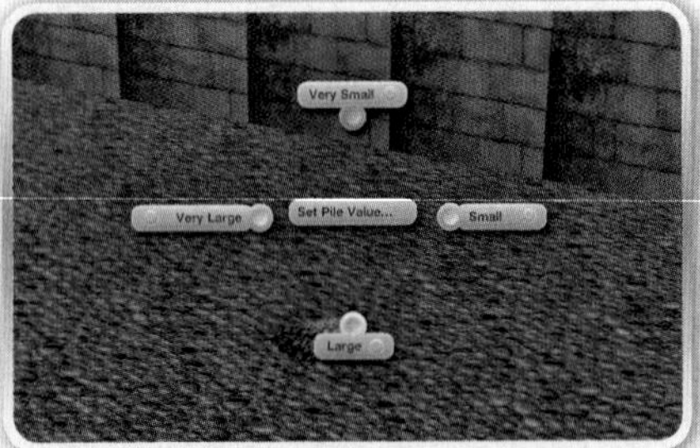

For treasures, such as a pile of Ancient Coins, you must set up a value. You can place objects in chests or use the treasure spawner to place treasures out in the open.

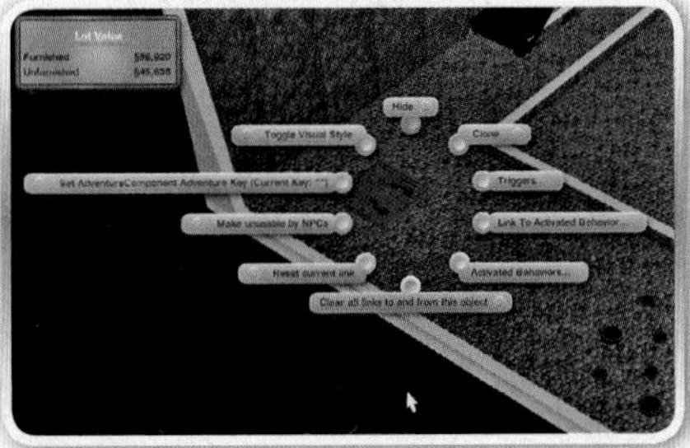

For switches, the trigger menu lets you select a behavior, such as shutting off the nearby trap.

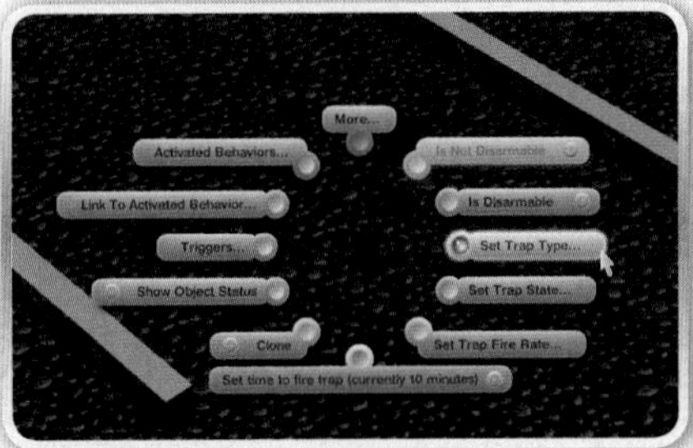

To select what kind of trap you are setting, click on the placed trap and then choose "Set Trap Type." You can then choose how the trap functions with "Set Trap State" and make the trap invisible, disarmable, dormant, and more.

NOTE

We offer a couple of examples of setting up tomb behaviors at the end of this chapter.

By now, you recognize many of the tomb objects such as traps, rubble piles, and floor switches. But there are a few objects in the catalog that you need to understand how to use to improve your tombs:

Tomb Room Marker: This silver orb is actually the fog that casts a room in darkness until a Sim enters it. This lets you create a real atmosphere of mystery (or dread) in your tomb. Install these in rooms so the player will not see everything in the tomb right away.

Inscription Plaque: Leave notes and hints on the walls for Sims to read. This is a good way to add personality to your tomb.

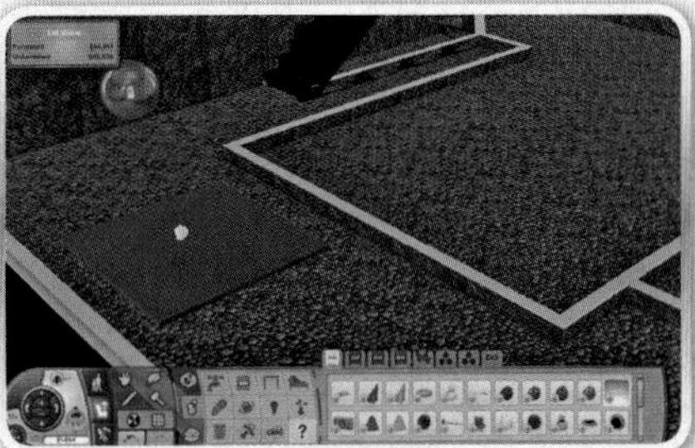

Hidden Trigger Panel: You know how sometimes traps started firing when you walked into a certain area of a room? The hidden trigger panel controls those. Place these in your tombs and associate them with traps and such to make the tomb interactive and full of surprises.

Triggers and Activated Behaviors

This is the most important part of building a tomb, because assigning triggers and behaviors is what makes the tomb function properly. Just setting a few traps and floor switches won't cut it. You need to instruct these objects to interact and be triggered by each other.

TIP

Switch to Live Mode and test your tomb often.

To see how your triggers are working, hold the cursor over the object. The lines show which objects are triggered by the current object. The purple arrow line indicates the object that is being affected by the object your cursor is positioned over. The green arrow lines indicate that the object is being affected by whatever the line is pointing to.

Here is a series of examples for creating tomb objects, triggers, and interactions:

Floor Switch to Unlock Door

1. Place the door.
2. Place the floor switch.
3. Lock the door using Buy Mode Interactions.
4. Use the "Link Triggers...Step On" interaction on the floor switch. The trigger is Step On.
5. Use the "Link to Activated Behavior... Unlock" interaction on the door. The Activated Behavior for the last trigger is to Unlock.

Keystone Panel to Unlock a Door

1. Place the door.
2. Place the keystone panel on the wall near the door.
3. Place a keystone in the room.
4. Use the "Set Shape" interaction on the keystone and keystone Panel so they match.
5. Lock the door.
6. Use the "Link Triggers...Insert Keystone" interaction on the keystone panel.
7. Use the "Add the Ability to Add Triggers and Activated Behaviors" interaction on the door.
8. Use the "Link to Activated Behavior... Unlock" interaction on the door.

Pushable Statue on Floor Switch Makes a Small Hole Appear and Unlock Door

1. Place pushable statue.
2. Place a floor switch.
3. Use the "Toggle Visual Style" interaction on the floor switch. This makes the switch appear as a gear—this is the visual state that represents a switch that requires a pushable statue.
4. Place a small hole - floor.
5. Place door.
6. Lock the door.
7. Use the "Hide" interaction on the small hole - floor.
8. Use the "Make Visibly Movable - (Currently: None)" interaction on the pushable statue.
9. Use the "Link Triggers...Step On" interaction on the floor switch.
10. Use the "Link to Activated Behaviors...Appear" interaction on the small hole - floor.
11. Use the "Link Triggers...Step Off" interaction on the floor switch.
12. Use the "Link to Activated Behaviors...Disappear" interaction on the small hole - floor.
13. Use the "Link Triggers...Hidden Switch" interaction on the small hole - floor.
14. Use the "Add the Ability to Add Triggers and Activated Behaviors" interaction on the door.
15. Use the "Link to Activated Behaviors...Unlock" interaction on the door.

Tip

You can use the "Treasure Component" interaction to place treasure inside a small hole, even when it is already being used to unlock a door.

Travel Between Two Dive Wells

1. Place two dive wells on the same lot.
2. Use the "Make this a warp well" interaction on both dive wells.
3. Sims can now use the "Explore" interaction on either dive well and travel to the other one.

Tip

In a normal dive well, the Sim will always choose the closest dive well to travel to that is designated as a warp well. To specifically designate which dive well the Sim travels to, name the destination dive well with the "Change this Well's Name" interaction, and then use the "Make this an uber warp well" interaction on the initial dive well, and enter the name of the destination.

Add Treasure to a Treasure Chest

1. Place a treasure chest.
2. Use the "Treasure Component" interaction.
3. Use the "Set One Time Treasure Info" interaction to determine what loot is given the first time the treasure chest is opened.
4. Use the "Set Regular Treasure Info" interaction to determine what loot is given any subsequent time the treasure chest is opened.

Tip

Many items can hold treasure, such as dive wells, small holes, sarcophagi, and the treasure spawn point.

Cause Trap to Trigger

1. Place a floor trap.
2. Place a hidden trigger panel.
3. Use the "Set Trap Type...Fire" interaction on the floor trap.
4. Use the "Set Trap State...Dormant and Hidden" interaction on the floor trap.
5. Use the "Link Triggers...Hidden Switch" interaction on the hidden trigger panel.
6. Use the "Link to Activated Behaviors...Set to Fire" interaction on the floor trap.
7. Return to Live Mode, and have your Sim walk over the area where the hidden trigger panel was placed, and the invisible trap will go off!

Note

Want more information on tomb building? Check the Community Forums at *www.thesims3.com*.

The Catalog

Welcome to the grand catalog of objects and socials—all pertinent information about these important day-to-day features of a Sim's life are found here. This catalog features objects and socials from *The Sims 3,* while Lifetime Wishes and careers from *The Sims 3* are featured in *The Sims 3* Primer chapter.

NOTE

All new objects, socials, and wishes from *World Adventures* are detailed in the New Simology and New Objects chapters.

Objects

Object	Price (in Simoleons)	Daily Depreciation	Fully Deprec. Value	Environment	Hygiene	Hunger	Bladder	Energy	Fun	Logic	Charisma	Cooking	Athletic	Painting	Guitar	Handiness	Gardening	Writing	Fishing	Stress Relief	Group Activity	Comfort
SOFAS & LOVESEATS																						
The Cuddler Loveseat	225	22.5	90																			1
Big Sky County Couch	335	33.5	134																			1
Power of Loveseat	350	35	140																			2
The Prim and Proper	400	40	160																			2
Super Sunshine Happy Sofa	450	45	180																			2
The Plutonic Loveseat	695	69.5	278																			2
El Sol Sofa by Gunter	750	75	300	2																		2
The Matchmaker	795	79.5	318	2																		3
Sofa LE	895	89.5	358																			2
Catharti-Couch	900	90	360																			2
Patata del Sofa	915	91.5	366																			2
The Suitable Sofa	925	92.5	370																			2
Sofa Souffle	985	98.5	394	3																		3
Sofa Sonata	1,100	110	440	3																		2
The Dromedary	1,200	120	480	3																		3
LIVING ROOM CHAIRS																						
The Savannah	115	11.5	46																			1
Lazy Lounger	225	22.5	90																			2
The Avant	375	37.5	150	2																		2
Swank Living Room Chair	450	45	180	2																		2
Passable Mission Chair	660	66	264	2																		3
The Olafian	695	69.5	278	2																		3
Bracken Living Room Chair	900	90	360	2																		3
Pete's Living Room Chair	1,000	100	400	2																		3
ALARMS																						
Panic Rouser Fire Alarm	100	10	40																			
Thief-Tech's Gotcha! Burglar Alarm	250	25	100																			
TVS																						
Old Timey Tele	200	20	80						3				x								x	
Channel Trowler 27" Deluxe TV	500	50	200						4			x	x								x	

Object	Price (in Simoleons)	Daily Depreciation	Fully Deprec. Value	Environment	Hygiene	Hunger	Bladder	Energy	Fun	Logic	Charisma	Cooking	Athletic	Painting	Guitar	Handiness	Gardening	Writing	Fishing	Stress Relief	Group Activity	Comfort
UberVision Panoramic from Landgraab Industries	1,200	120	480						5				x				x		x			
36" HiFi Plasmondo TV from Landgraab Industries	3,500	350	1,400						6			x	x				x		x			
WallVuu Standard TV	8,000	800	3,200						8													
VIDEO GAMES																						
Maxoid Game Simulator 2 1/2	750	75	300						7													
SimLife Goggles	9,500	950	3,800						10													
COFFEE TABLES																						
Two-Ton Table	90	9	36																			
Old Timer's Coffee Table	125	12.5	50																			
The Mission Coffee Table by Lulu Designs	150	15	60																			
Roman Coffee Table	185	18.5	74	1																		
The Larger Mission Coffee Table by Lulu Designs	245	24.5	98	1																		
Isometric Table	265	26.5	106	1																		
Case Closed Coffee Table	285	28.5	114	2																		
Literal Coffee Table	300	30	120	1																		
Decaf Coffee Table	325	32.5	130	1																		
AUDIO																						
Audio Lite by LoFi Audio	150	15	60						3				x								x	
18 Disc Stereo System from Albacore Audio	475	47.5	190						3				x								x	
85g Audio Explosion from Landgraab Industries	1,800	180	720						3				x								x	
RUGS																						
Poor Man's Half-Round Rug	30	3	12	2																		
The Saxony	35	3.5	14	2																		
L7 Rug	50	5	20	2																		
Modern Oval Rug	50	5	20	2																		
Welcome, Matt	65	6.5	26	2																		
Aristocratic First Oval Rug	80	8	32	3																		
Purrrfect Rug	95	9.5	38	3																		
Flying Carpet	100	10	40	3																		
RocketRug from Randy Homson	140	14	56	3																		
Marathon Carpet Runner	165	16.5	66	4																		
Dated, Faded Floral Rug	315	31.5	126	4																		
Chandelier Rug	400	40	160	4																		
REFRIDGERATORS																						
Chillgood Fridge	375	37.5	150			5																
2-Door Galore Refrigerator	650	65	260			6																
Icebox Drawer	1,200	120	480			7																
The Fresher Refrigerator	1,800	180	720	1		8																
STOVES																						
SimmerChar Dual-State Stove	400	40	160			4						x										
Cowpoke Stove	550	55	220			5						x										
Tri-Forge Stove	800	80	320			7						x										

Object	Price (in Simoleons)	Daily Depreciation	Fully Deprec. Value	Environment	Hygiene	Hunger	Bladder	Energy	Fun	Logic	Charisma	Cooking	Athletic	Painting	Guitar	Handiness	Gardening	Writing	Fishing	Stress Relief	Group Activity	Comfort
Festus 44	1,000	100	400			9						x										
SINKS																						
Plain Basin	120	12	48		2																	
Squatter's Sink	150	15	60		2																	
Pepper Pot Sink	215	21.5	86		3																	
The Unsinkable Sink	240	24	96		3																	
Rinky Dinky Kitchen Sinky	290	29	116		3																	
Volcanor Sulphorous Sink	315	31.5	126		4																	
Fontainebleu Fountain Sink	390	39	156	2	4																	
Sink in Despair	500	50	200	3	5																	
COUNTERS																						
Country Fried Counter	140	14	56																			
Country Fried Counter Island	145	14.5	58																			
Counter Culture Counter	215	21.5	86	1																		
Counter Culture Counter Island	220	22	88	1																		
The Impossible Mission Counter	475	47.5	190	1																		
The Impossible Mission Counter Island	480	48	192	1																		
The Immemorial Counter	625	62.5	250	2																		
Immemorial Counter Island	630	63	252	2																		
Real Flat Counter	800	80	320	2																		
Real Flat Counter Island	805	80.5	322	2																		
CABINETS																						
Country Fried Overhead Cabinet	100	10	40	1																		
Country Fried Overhead China	105	10.5	42	1																		
Counter Culture Overhead Cabinet	130	13	52	1																		
Counter Culture Overhead Cabinet (Double-Sided)	135	13.5	54	1																		
Hanging Pot Rack	150	15	60	1																		
Immemorial Overhead Cabinet	165	16.5	66	1																		
Immemorial Overhead Cabinet (Double-Sided)	170	17	68	1																		
The Impossible Mission Overhead Cabinet	230	23	92	1																		
The Impossible Mission Overhead Cabinet (Double-Sided)	235	23.5	94	1																		
Real Flat Overhead Cabinet	310	31	124	2																		
Real Flat Overhead Cabinet (Double-Sided)	315	31.5	126	2																		
DISPOSALS																						
Open Arms and Feelings Trashcan	25	2.5	10																			
Mirage Garbage	50	5	20																			
Crazy Grady's Trash Compactor	400	40	160																			
SMALL APPLIANCES																						
Steak & Prank Microwave	240	24	96									x										
Ingredient Eviscerator 235X	280	28	112									x										
The Nanowaver	300	30	120									x										
Excellent Anson Hot Beverage Maker	1,100	110	440					3														

Object	Price (in Simoleons)	Daily Depreciation	Fully Deprec. Value	Environment	Hygiene	Hunger	Bladder	Energy	Fun	Logic	Charisma	Cooking	Athletic	Painting	Guitar	Handiness	Gardening	Writing	Fishing	Stress Relief	Group Activity	Comfort
DISHWASHERS																						
Swish Dishwasher	300	30	120																			
Primo Delux Dishwasher	700	70	280	2																		
DINING TABLES																						
Table-Licious	60	6	24																			
Knack Outdoor Tables	85	8.5	34																			
Table de Bistro by Bourgeois Creations	195	19.5	78																			
Another Era Dining Table	200	20	80																			
Sunup Breakfast Table	225	22.5	90	1																		
Rendezvous Picnic Table	235	23.5	94																			
Style Town Dining Table	250	25	100	1																		
The Upscale Dining Table	285	28.5	114	1																		
Great Eats' Recycled Consumables Buffet Table	300	30	120			4																
Phobic Dining Table	450	45	180	2																		
Missionaire Dining Table	650	65	260	2																		
Xtra Long Dining Table	900	90	360	2																		
DINING CHAIRS																						
The Exquisite Bistro Chair by Bourgeois Creations	40	4	16																			1
Simmer Down Chair	75	7.5	30																			1
Rafkin's Dining Chair	80	8	32																			1
Mount of Comfort Dining Chair	90	9	36																			1
The Cozinator 450	100	10	40																			1
Final Contribution Dining Chair from Mike's Garage	115	11.5	46																			1
The Elsinore	120	12	48																			2
Sit-Up Straight Dining Chair	150	15	60																			2
Yankee Doodle Dining Chair	225	22.5	90																			2
The Muga Sitzer	325	32.5	130	2																		2
Old Sam's Dining Chair	900	90	360	2																		3
UV by Uwe	50	5	20																			1
Wellness Dining Chair	165	16.5	66																			2
Overworked Office Chair	195	19.5	78																			2
BARS																						
Class E Juice Bar	640	64	256	1					6													
Juice Station	725	72.5	290	1					6													
Bar de Mish	975	97.5	390	1					6													
Family Time Bar	1,500	150	600	1					6													
BARSTOOLS																						
Parlor Perch Barstool	185	18.5	74																			1
Sturdy Stool	215	21.5	86																			2
Barstool de Mish	285	28.5	114																			2
Bab's Towering Barstool	435	43.5	174																			2
Old Sam's Barstool	520	52	208																			2
Parlor Perch Barstool	185	18.5	74																			1

Object	Price (in Simoleons)	Daily Depreciation	Fully Deprec. Value	Environment	Hygiene	Hunger	Bladder	Energy	Fun	Logic	Charisma	Cooking	Athletic	Painting	Guitar	Handiness	Gardening	Writing	Fishing	Stress Relief	Group Activity	Comfort
Sturdy Stool	215	21.5	86																			2
Barstool de Mish	285	28.5	114																			2
Bab's Towering Barstool	435	43.5	174																			2
Old Sam's Barstool	520	52	208																			2
CURTAINS & BLINDS																						
Cortinas Festivas!	50	5	20	2																		
Traditional Curtains	68	6.8	27.2	2																		
Eyes Aside Curtains by Fancy Drapes	80	8	32	2																		
Vickleberry County Curtains	95	9.5	38	2																		
Tangle-Free Blinds	105	10.5	42	2																		
Shout Out Shutters	130	13	52	2																		
Lofty Curtains	155	15.5	62	3																		
Shy Shutters	160	16	64	3																		
Cute Lil' Curtain	170	17	68	3																		
Simple Shade	185	18.5	74	3																		
Flattery Curtains	195	19.5	78	3																		
Antique Curtains by Respectable Rags	215	21.5	86	3																		
Hygieni-Curtains	230	23	92	3																		
Static Blinds	260	26	104	3																		
Curtains de Mish	285	28.5	114	3																		
Three Bean Bay Curtain	315	31.5	126	3																		
Wide, Lofty Curtains	325	32.5	130	3																		
The Window Protector	400	40	160	3																		
MISC. DECOR																						
Wish-You Tissues	4	0.4	1.6	1																		
Stack o'Mags	7	0.7	2.8	1																		
Plain Pad & Pen Set	12	1.2	4.8	1																		
Beauty Box	15	1.5	6	1																		
Rooster Utensil Holder	18	1.8	7.2	1																		
Super-Absorbent Super Towels	20	2	8	1																		
Decorative Fire Tools	25	2.5	10	1																		
Stink Mask Perfume	35	3.5	14	1																		
Crocks O' Stuff	45	4.5	18	1																		
Life Preserver	55	5.5	22	1																		
His/Hers Trophy Shelf	62	6.2	24.8	1																		
Magazine Restraint System	65	6.5	26	1																		
Mood-Lite Candle	65	6.5	26	1																		
The MediCabi	75	7.5	30	1																		
The Shrinkomatic Fishbowl	80	8	32																			
Main Attraction Puzzle Shelf	85	8.5	34	1																		
Wall-Mounted Fish	85	8.5	34	1																		
Already Retro CD Display Shelving	120	12	48	1																		
Mission Partition	180	18	72	4																		
Globe Sculpture	195	19.5	78	4																		
Bathroom Junk Holder	225	22.5	90	4																		

Object	Price (in Simoleons)	Daily Depreciation	Fully Deprec. Value	Environment	Hygiene	Hunger	Bladder	Energy	Fun	Logic	Charisma	Cooking	Athletic	Painting	Guitar	Handiness	Gardening	Writing	Fishing	Stress Relief	Group Activity	Comfort
Peekaboo! Partition	410	41	164	5																		
Cow Plant	475	47.5	190	6																		
Sun Disk	1,500	150	600	7																		
Medusa Victim	1,650	165	660	7																		
Nearly-Perfect Pedestal	2,000	200	800	5																		
Immoderate Water Fountain	2,150	215	860	8																		
Ambiguity Itself	12,225	1,222.5	4,890	10																		
BEDS																						
The Single Post Bed from McKraken Industries	300	30	120					4												3		
Small Brass Bed	425	42.5	170					4												3		
B.R.A.S.S. Double Bed	450	45	180					4												3		
The Slumber Saddle of Sleepnir by Dulac Industries	560	56	224					4												3		
The Four Post Bed from McKraken Industries	650	65	260					4												3		
The Emoti-Cot	700	70	280					4												3		
The Lullaby Bed	950	95	380	2				5												3		
The Legendary Bedscalibur by Dulac Industries	1,100	110	440					5												3		
Single Sophisticate Bed	1,450	145	580	4				8												3		
Double Sleep Raft	1,500	150	600	2				6												3		
LuxurLove Sleepset from Lothario Designs	2,200	220	880	2				8												3		
The Lexington	2,800	280	1,120	3				8												3		
Sleep-Slave Double Bed	3,500	350	1,400	4				10												3		
DRESSERS																						
The Evrityme Dresser	450	45	180																			
Werkbunnst Stonewood Dresser	515	51.5	206																			
Homestead Dresser from McKraken Industries	600	60	240	2																		
Drawers of Dismissal Dresser	650	65	260	2																		
Smooth Slides Luxury Dresser	725	72.5	290	2																		
DeForester Dresser by William DeForester	850	85	340	2																		
END TABLES																						
Syntactic End Table	45	4.5	18																			
Trails End Table	50	5	20																			
LuLu's Artisan End Table	75	7.5	30																			
Double-Delux End Table	125	12.5	50																			
Virtual End Table	165	16.5	66	1																		
Meta Table	195	19.5	78	1																		
Tabla Del Extremo	245	24.5	98	1																		
Chaible	255	25.5	102	1																		
Gibson Butter Table from Gibson Dairy and Furnishings	285	28.5	114	1																		
Royal Francois End Table from XIV Antiquities	315	31.5	126	2																		

Object	Price (in Simoleons)	Daily Depreciation	Fully Deprec. Value	Environment	Hygiene	Hunger	Bladder	Energy	Fun	Logic	Charisma	Cooking	Athletic	Painting	Guitar	Handiness	Gardening	Writing	Fishing	Stress Relief	Group Activity	Comfort
MIRRORS																						
Mirror of Variance	50	5	20	2					3		x											
The Reflektor	80	8	32	2					3		x											
The Outhouse Mirror	100	10	40	2					3		x											
Functional Eloquence Mirror	175	17.5	70	2					3		x											
Feel Good Mirror	200	20	80	3					3		x											
Stock Mirror	250	25	100	3					3		x											
Reflection V	275	27.5	110	3					3		x											
Hi-Def Mirror	300	30	120	3					3		x											
Rustic Glass	320	32	128	4					3		x											
The Reflectinator	350	35	140	4					3		x											
Clearer Mirror	400	40	160	4					3		x											
Looking Glass Supreme	500	50	200	4					3		x											
Fabulous, Darling Mirror	950	95	380	3					3		x											
CLOCKS																						
Quick Tick Wall Clock	40	4	16																			
No Snooze! Alarm Clock	60	6	24																			
4258g Alarm Clock from Landgraab Industries	150	15	60																			
TUBS																						
JustaTub	500	50	200		3															4		
Schmidt's Clawed Tub	1,000	100	400		5															6		
Bath Today from Plumbrite	1,400	140	560		6															7		
Shower of Power	1,600	160	640	1	9															9		
Tub Nouveau	2,100	210	840	4	7															9		
SHOWERS																						
Simple Shower	425	42.5	170		7																	
Exhilarating X-Foliator Shower	925	92.5	370		9																	
Shower of Power	1,600	160	640	1	9															9		
ACCENTS																						
Three-Ply Tushy Tissue from Plumbrite	2	0.2	0.8	1																		
NeveRust Towel Ring	30	3	12	1																		
The Rack by DecorCorp	35	3.5	14	1																		
TOILETS																						
First Step Potty Chair	70	7	28																			
Bargain John	250	25	100				10															
Odor-Free Toilet	575	57.5	230				10															
Toilet Stall	700	70	280				10															
The Thru-Flush Toilet	800	80	320				10															
The Porcelain Throne	1,800	180	720	2			10															
BOOKSHELVES																						
Classically Tasteful Literature Shelving	175	17.5	70						2	x		x				x						
Back2SChool Bookshelf	250	25	100						2	x		x				x						
21st Century Library Bookshelf	325	32.5	130						3	x		x				x						
Shelves de Libro	350	35	140						3	x		x				x						

Object	Price (in Simoleons)	Daily Depreciation	Fully Deprec. Value	Environment	Hygiene	Hunger	Bladder	Energy	Fun	Logic	Charisma	Cooking	Athletic	Painting	Guitar	Handiness	Gardening	Writing	Fishing	Stress Relief	Group Activity	Comfort
The Book Corral	430	43	172	1					3	x		x				x						
Bookshelf Revisited	545	54.5	218	1					3	x		x				x						
Penningway Bookshelf	650	65	260	1					4	x		x				x						
The Constitutional Bookshelf	750	75	300	2					5	x		x				x						
Sturdy Shelf	895	89.5	358	2					5	x		x				x						
COMPUTERS																						
Easy Machine from Fred's PC Hut	800	80	320						3													
oTron 200 Thinking Computer from Landgraab Industries	3,000	300	1,200						3													
XS 4258p Laptop from Landgraab Industries	4,000	400	1,600						7													
DESKS																						
Drawltop Worksurface	150	15	60																			
Workspace de Mish	300	30	120																			
Desk Moderne from Gorog Designs	325	32.5	130	1																		
The Rollin' Secretary from McKraken Industries	450	45	180																			
Desk Historia from XIV Antiquities	900	90	360	1																		
INDOOR ACTIVITIES																						
Shut-in Treadmill	900	90	360										x							5		
The Exercise Queen	1,500	150	600										x							5		
Mad Llama Foosball Table	6,250	625	2,500						9												x	
HOBBIES & SKILLS																						
Artsy Easel	300	30	120						2					x								
Epic 10th Anniversary Chess Set	450	45	180						4	x												
Astral Playground Telescope	600	60	240						2	x												
Sonaflux Guitar	600	60	240						2						x							
TOYS																						
Baby Brainiac Peg Toy Box	30	3	12						5													
Rip Co. Xylophone	40	4	16						5													
Wugglesworth Schnuggles Bear	50	5	20						6													
Infinitoy Imagination Station	55	5.5	22						5													
Toy Pirate Chest	60	6	24						5													
Roy Rock's Toy Box	75	7.5	30						5													
Rip Co. Little Baker Oven	100	10	40						3													
Genesis Building Blocks	200	20	80						4													
Sunnybrook Home Dollhouse	650	65	260						7													
KIDS FURNITURE																						
Yummer's High Chair	60	6	24																			
Kinder Kontainer	275	27.5	110					4														
Rock-a-Baby Crib	425	42.5	170					5														
KIDS DECOR																						
Space Mobile	70	7	28	1																		
Elevated Train Set	185	18.5	74	2																		
Real Pretty Butterflies	265	26.5	106	2																		

Object	Price (in Simoleons)	Daily Depreciation	Fully Deprec. Value	Environment	Hygiene	Hunger	Bladder	Energy	Fun	Logic	Charisma	Cooking	Athletic	Painting	Guitar	Handiness	Gardening	Writing	Fishing	Stress Relief	Group Activity	Comfort
PAINTINGS & POSTERS																						
Anabolic Champ	9	0.9	3.6	2																		
Bethany and Miranda	15	1.5	6	2																		
Edgy, Edgy Bill	25	2.5	10	2																		
Forest-Fresh Corkboard	25	2.5	10	1																		
Detention Hall Poster	30	3	12	7																		
Heinrich Stubbman and the Gypsies	45	4.5	18	2																		
Diva Doll Poster	55	5.5	22	2																		
Giraffe Family Portrait	80	8	32	3																		
Dancing Bunny	100	10	40	3																		
My Little House	110	11	44	4																		
Obscure Film Poster	160	16	64	4																		
Speedinator Marketing Poster	175	17.5	70	4																		
Village No. 7	250	25	100	5																		
Fishing Scene	300	30	120	5																		
Photo Series: Hipster Edition	400	40	160	6																		
Bouquet in Repose	500	50	200	6																		
Saturday Morning Fun Kids!	620	62	248	6																		
Insouciance No. 12	750	75	300	6																		
McBob Landscape	800	80	320	6																		
Still-Life Harvest	930	93	372	6																		
Smooth Jam in Three Parts	1,100	110	440	7																		
Capital City Skyline	2,300	230	920	7																		
Mission at Noon, Lance Ng	3,900	390	1,560	8																		
Puck's Soliloquy	7,300	730	2,920	10																		
PHONES																						
998 Table Top Topia Phone	35	3.5	14																			
Immobile Phone	50	5	20																			
LIGHTS																						
Light Freshner	65	6.5	26																			
Werffelhousen Sconce	75	7.5	30																			
Wall-eyed Wall Lamp	80	8	32																			
Far Out Wall Sconce	95	9.5	38																			
Funshine Wall Lamp	115	11.5	46																			
Modern Sconce	125	12.5	50																			
The Candle Cradler	125	12.5	50																			
"The Snake Lamp"	130	13	52																			
Feisty Fiesta Wall Lantern	145	14.5	58	1																		
Photophile Wall Light	150	15	60	1																		
Old's Kool Lighting	165	16.5	66	1																		
Bawdy Candle	65	6.5	26																			
Blushing Torchiere	120	12	48																			
Omnidirection Lightcaster	165	16.5	66	1																		
Flora's Funky Floor Lamp	225	22.5	90																			
Bunker Hill Floor Lights	300	30	120	2																		

Object	Price (in Simoleons)	Daily Depreciation	Fully Deprec. Value	Environment	Hygiene	Hunger	Bladder	Energy	Fun	Logic	Charisma	Cooking	Athletic	Painting	Guitar	Handiness	Gardening	Writing	Fishing	Stress Relief	Group Activity	Comfort
Delux Lux	365	36.5	146	2																		
Moderne-Torchiere Floor Lamp	385	38.5	154	2																		
Goldon Glow Floor Lamp	415	41.5	166	2																		
Lodge Lights	45	4.5	18																			
Lucid Light	95	9.5	38	1																		
The Swinging Light	115	11.5	46																			
Luz del Sol	180	18	72	1																		
Greaves' Ceiling Lights	225	22.5	90																			
The Revita-Lite	350	35	140	2																		
Sawed-off Lightcaster	45	4.5	18																			
The Bloomington Lamp	50	5	20																			
Lamp Revere	65	6.5	26																			
Hurricane Candle	70	7	28																			
Lodge Lamp	75	7.5	30																			
Homespun Table Lamp	85	8.5	34																			
Luz Lenta	285	28.5	114	2																		
The Baronian Table Lamp	300	30	120	2																		
The Photon-Master 3000 Tabletop Edition	325	32.5	130	2																		
PLANTS																						
Small Ivy	5	0.5	2	2																		
Hanging Fern	15	1.5	6	2																		
Fern Keeper Deluxe!	25	2.5	10	1																		
Sphere of Ivy	35	3.5	14	2																		
Narcissus Vase	40	4	16	1																		
Potted Perennials	40	4	16	2																		
Ring-O-Posies Commercial Planter	42	4.2	16.8	2																		
Fern	45	4.5	18	2																		
Calla Lillies	48	4.8	19.2	2																		
Hanging Basket	50	5	20	2																		
Mixed Flowers Planter by BowerFlox	65	6.5	26	2																		
Blossoming Sunflower Vase	70	7	28	1																		
The Perma-Palm	70	7	28	1																		
Orchid Vase	90	9	36	1																		
Philodendron	95	9.5	38	1																		
Tigervine Plant	135	13.5	54	2																		
Ficus Tree Shrub	230	23	92	2																		
The Modern Orchid	435	43.5	174	5																		
OUTDOOR COOKING																						
Birthday Inferno Birthday Cake	30	3	12			2																
Fuzzy-Logic Picnic Basket	150	15	60			4															x	
Portable Fire Pit	295	29.5	118			2			4												x	
Carnivore XL	300	30	120			2						x										
Barbe-Cute	600	60	240			4						x										
Deluxe Agile Grill	1,200	120	480			5						x										

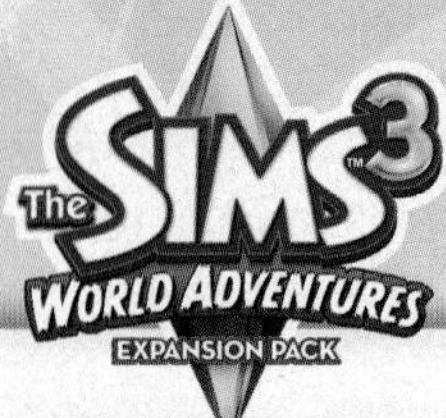

Object	Price (in Simoleons)	Daily Depreciation	Fully Deprec. Value	Environment	Hygiene	Hunger	Bladder	Energy	Fun	Logic	Charisma	Cooking	Athletic	Painting	Guitar	Handiness	Gardening	Writing	Fishing	Stress Relief	Group Activity	Comfort
OUTDOOR SEATING																						
Community Bench	85	8.5	34																			
Comtempto Outdoor Living Lounge	200	20	80																			1
The Breckenridge	325	32.5	130																			2
Herkimer Loveseat	400	40	160																			2
The Dawdler Lounge Chair	515	51.5	206	2																		2
Sticky Bench	650	65	260																			2
Tomorrow Lounger	750	75	300	2																		2
OUTDOOR ACTIVITIES																						
Baseball	65	6.5	26						5				x									
Foot-and-hand-ball	85	8.5	34						6				x									
Schuper Schprinkler from Schprinkler Tech	90	9	36						5													
The Waxbottom Slide	335	33.5	134						8													
Outdoor Chess Table	350	35	140						4	x												
Skyscreamer Swings	400	40	160						3												x	
The Juungal Jungle Gym	550	55	220						8													
POOL ITEMS																						
Pool Rules Sign	13	1.3	5	1																		
Sea Underwater Pool Lights from Landgraab Industries	35	3.5	14																			
Mesmerizing Mosaic	212	21.2	85																			
Aquatic Ascent Ladder	315	31.5	126																			
OUTDOOR LIGHTS																						
Limelights	30	3	12																			
Patio Party Lamp	30	3	12																			
The Aftergloe II	35	3.5	14																			
The Little Lamp That Could	35	3.5	14																			
Volcano Table Torch	35	3.5	14																			
Cobblestone Fence Light	40	4	16																			
Burb-Light	45	4.5	18																			
Mason Lamp	50	5	20																			
Path Glow Garden Lighting	50	5	20																			
Simple Porch Light	70	7	28																			
Step Lights	75	7.5	30																			
Stoic Bollard	100	10	40																			
Pele's Postlight from Nothing Atoll	125	12.5	50																			
Ankle-Height Light by GamGleam Industries	175	17.5	70																			
Apology Streetlight	200	20	80																			
Clean-Wave Streetlight	245	24.5	98	2																		
Seramorson Streetlamp	335	33.5	134	2																		
The Streetbrite	340	34	136	2																		
Hard Knocks Streetlight	500	50	200	2																		
The Champ	565	56.5	226																			
Multifunction Searchlight Device	4,500	450	1,800	1																		

Object	Price (in Simoleons)	Daily Depreciation	Fully Deprec. Value	Environment	Hygiene	Hunger	Bladder	Energy	Fun	Logic	Charisma	Cooking	Athletic	Painting	Guitar	Handiness	Gardening	Writing	Fishing	Stress Relief	Group Activity	Comfort
LAWN ORNAMENTS																						
Shocking Pink Flamingo - 2nd Edition	5	0.5	2	1					2													
Party Balloons	15	1.5	6	1																		
Sleeping Gnome McMulty	35	3.5	14	1					2													
Square Hay Bale	4	0.4	1.6																			
Round Hay Bale	65	6.5	26																			
Obelisk Vine	145	14.5	58	2																		
Fire Hydrant	150	15	60																			
Beach Sign	201	20.1	80.4																			
Traditional Sign	223	22.3	89.2																			
Modern Sign	242	24.2	96.8																			
Mission Sign	270	27	108																			
Country Sign	318	31.8	127.2																			
Contemporary Sign	322	32.2	128.8																			
Stacked Hay Bales	350	35	140																			
Cemetery Sign	365	36.5	146																			
Commercial Dumpster	659	65.9	263.6																			
Town Clock	1,200	120	480																			
Farm Windmill	2,130	213	852																			
Outdoor School Bell	2,500	250	1,000																			
Military Guard Tower	6,475	647.5	2,590																			
The Plaza Gusher	50,000	5,000	20,000	9																		
Landgraab Industries Science Facility Fountain	60,000	6,000	24,000	10																		
F-Class Hunter-Killer	75,000	7,500	30,000	10																		
TRANSPORTATION																						
Vertistation Bike Rack (Speed: 0)	35	3.5	14																			
Car-Spot Parking Space (Speed: 0)	150	15	60																			
Bi-Trike for Kids (Speed: 1)	250	25	100																			
NostalgiCycle (Speed: 2)	250	25	100																			
Closure Garage Door (Speed: 0)	600	60	240																			
Sloppy Jalopy (Speed: 3)	950	95	380																			
Big Lemon (Speed: 3)	1,200	120	480																			
Vorn P328 (Speed: 4)	3,700	370	1,480																			
Wornado Triage (Speed: 4)	4,500	450	1,800																			
4-Everything Van (Speed: 4)	6,100	610	2,440																			
Yomoshoto Evasion (Speed: 5)	9,800	980	3,920																			
Tofunda Wagon (Speed: 5)	19,600	1,960	7,840																			
VFN Kompensator (Speed: 6)	36,000	3,600	14,400																			
Bwan Speedster YL (Speed: 8)	85,000	8,500	34,000																			
Margaret Vaguester (Speed: 10)	105,000	10,500	42,000																			
TREES																						
Small Bamboo Tree	65	6.5	26																			
Small Aspen Tree	95	9.5	38																			
Buckhorn Tree	100	10	40																			

Object	Price (in Simoleons)	Daily Depreciation	Fully Deprec. Value	Environment	Hygiene	Hunger	Bladder	Energy	Fun	Logic	Charisma	Cooking	Athletic	Painting	Guitar	Handiness	Gardening	Writing	Fishing	Stress Relief	Group Activity	Comfort
Bamboo Tree	115	11.5	46																			
Aspen Tree	125	12.5	50																			
Small Pear Tree	130	13	52																			
Small Spruce Tree	140	14	56	2																		
Small Black Gum Tree	150	15	60	2																		
Small Cherry Tree	155	15.5	62																			
Pear Tree	165	16.5	66																			
Small Fir Tree	180	18	72																			
Spruce Tree	190	19	76																			
Black Gum Tree	200	20	80	3																		
Tall Fir Tree	210	21	84	3																		
Small Juniper Tree	245	24.5	98	3																		
Cherry Tree	250	25	100																			
Small Purple Tree	260	26	104																			
Small Cypress Tree	265	26.5	106																			
Large Juniper Tree	270	27	108																			
Fan Leaf Palm Tree	275	27.5	110																			
Tall Cypress Tree	300	30	120																			
Small Western Cypress Tree	315	31.5	126																			
Oak Tree	320	32	128																			
Purple Tree	325	32.5	130																			
Classic Palm Tree	335	33.5	134																			
Large Western Cypress Tree	340	34	136																			
Willlow Tree	350	35	140																			
Creepy Tree	400	40	160																			
SHRUBS																						
Brambles	5	0.5	2																			
Waterlillies	8	0.8	3.2																			
Cattail	9	0.9	3.6																			
Pampas Grass	12	1.2	4.8																			
Cattails	10	1	4																			
Coleus	15	1.5	6																			
Boston Fern	35	3.5	14	2																		
Buckhorn	40	4	16	2																		
Boxwood	50	5	20																			
Banana Leaf	60	6	24																			
Round Hedge	70	7	28																			
Evergreen	80	8	32																			
Hedge	85	8.5	34	3																		
Topiary Plant	95	9.5	38	3																		
FLOWERS																						
Hydrangea	1	0.1	0.4																			
Dandelions	2	0.2	0.8																			
Popular Pansies	8	0.8	3.2																			
Clover	10	1	4																			

Object	Price (in Simoleons)	Daily Depreciation	Fully Deprec. Value	Environment	Hygiene	Hunger	Bladder	Energy	Fun	Logic	Charisma	Cooking	Athletic	Painting	Guitar	Handiness	Gardening	Writing	Fishing	Stress Relief	Group Activity	Comfort
Clover w/Diagonal Corners	10	1	4																			
Clover w/Rounded Corners	10	1	4																			
Daisies of our Lives	10	1	4	2																		
Ice Plant	10	1	4	2																		
Ice Plant w/Diagonal Corners	10	1	4																			
Ice Plant w/Rounded Corners	10	1	4																			
Lithodoroa	10	1	4																			
Lithodoroa w/Diagonal Corners	10	1	4																			
Lithodoroa w/Rounded Corners	10	1	4	3																		
Moss Rose	10	1	4	3																		
Moss Rose w/Diagnonal Corners	10	1	4	3																		
Moss Rose w/Rounded Corners	10	1	4																			
Phlox	10	1	4																			
Phlox w/Diagonal Corners	10	1	4																			
Phlox w/Rounded Corners	10	1	4																			
Plot of Daisies w/Diagonal Corners	10	1	4																			
Plot of Daisies w/Rounded Corners	10	1	4																			
Perennial Pansies	11	1.1	4.4																			
Agapanthus	12	1.2	4.8																			
Dianthus	14	1.4	5.6																			
Marigold	16	1.6	6.4																			
Solo Sunflower	17	1.7	6.8																			
Sunflowers	19	1.9	7.6																			
Heather	20	2	8																			
Azaleas	22	2.2	8.8																			
Classic Daisies	23	2.3	9.2																			
Laizy Daises	24	2.4	9.6																			
Vivid Roses	25	2.5	10																			
Pink Roses	35	3.5	14																			
Wild Rosey Roses	40	4	16																			
Semi Roses	42	4.2	16.8																			
Rosey Roses	45	4.5	18																			
ROCKS																						
Landscaping Rock - Small Round	5	0.5	2																			
Landscaping Rock - Horizontal	6	0.6	2.4																			
Landscaping Rock - Medium Round	15	1.5	6																			
Landscaping Rock - Square	18	1.8	7.2																			
Landscaping Rock - Vertical	30	3	12																			
Ancient Rock	35	3.5	14																			

Socials

The follow chart details all of the Actor-Target socials you can perform in a conversation. Use this chart to judge the effect of a social before using it by looking at the commodity and cross-referencing that with which commodities affect which STCs. Here is how the chart is broken down:

- **Social:** Name of social as seen in the conversation menu
- **Commodity:** Commodity associated with the social
- **Actor/Target Age:** Ages in which the social is applicable
  - C=Child
  - T=Teen
  - Y=Young Adult
  - A=Adult
  - E=Elder
- **Social Available When?:** What prompts the use of the social
- **Required Trait:** Social is only available when Actor has this trait
- **Social Encouraged by Trait?:** Social is potentially more "powerful" due to Actor's trait
- **Social Prevented by Trait?:** Actor's trait prevents them from using this social
- **# of Uses Before Boring:** Number of uses in a conversation before the social is Dull. Default is two. Exceptions are specified.
- **# of Uses if Recharged:** Number of times the social can be used if another social interrupts the re-use of the social

SOCIAL MASTER LIST

Social	Commodity	Actor Age	Target Age	Social Available When?	Required Trait	Social Encouraged By Trait?	Social Prevented By Trait?	# of Uses Before Boring	# of Uses if Recharged
Accuse of Being a Crybaby	Insulting	T, Y, A, E	T, Y, A, E	Actor knows the Target is a Loser		Mean-Spirited	Good		
Accuse of Being a Workaholic	Insulting	T, Y, A, E	T, Y, A, E	Actor knows the Target is a Workaholic		Family Oriented			
Accuse of Being Boring	Insulting	T, Y, A, E	T, Y, A, E	Actor knows the Target has No Sense of Humor		Mean-Spirited	Good		
Accuse of Being Childish	Insulting	T, Y, A, E	T, Y, A, E	Actor knows the Target is Childish		Dislikes Children, Mean-Spirited	Good		
Accuse of Being Evil	Insulting	T, Y, A, E	T, Y, A, E	Actor knows the Target is Evil		Good			
Accuse of Being Insane	Insulting	T, Y, A, E	T, Y, A, E	Actor knows the Target is Insane		Mean-Spirited	Good		
Accuse of Being Unflirty	Insulting	T, Y, A, E	T, Y, A, E	Actor knows the Target is Unflirty		Flirty	Unflirty		
Accuse of Cheating	Insulting	Y, A, E	Y, A, E	Actor has had Jealousy triggered on Target		Neurotic, Hopeless Romantic		1	1
Accuse of Mean-Spiritedness	Insulting	T, Y, A, E	T, Y, A, E	Actor knows the Target is Mean-Spirited		Good, Friendly			
Admire	Friendly	C, T, Y, A, E	C, T, Y, A, E	Sims are in the Very Friendly STC and are Friends or above or on the romantic relationship		Easily Impressed, Schmoozer, Charismatic			
Amorous Hug	Amorous	T, Y, A, E	T, Y, A, E	Sims are in the Seductive STC or Flirty STC, if not Acquaintances		Hopeless Romantic		1	
Announce Birthday	Friendly	C, T, Y, A, E	C, T, Y, A, E	It is the Actor's birthday		Excitable			
Announce Engagement	Friendly	Y, A, E	C, T, Y, A, E	Actor has become engaged		Family Oriented, Hopeless Romantic, Excitable			
Announce Pregnancy	Friendly	Y, A, E	C, T, Y, A, E	Actor has become pregnant		Family Oriented, Excitable			

Social	Commodity	Actor Age	Target Age	Social Available When?	Required Trait	Social Encouraged By Trait?	Social Prevented By Trait?	# of Uses Before Boring	# of Uses if Recharged
Announce Promotion	Friendly	T, Y, A, E	C, T, Y, A, E	Actor has gotten a promotion		Snob, Workaholic, Excitable			
Apologize	Neutral	C, T, Y, A, E	C, T, Y, A, E	Sims are in a negative STC		Friendly, Schmoozer		1	1
Applaud Hard Work	Friendly	T, Y, A, E	T, Y, A, E	Actor knows the Target is a Workaholic		Workaholic, Schmoozer			
Applaud Vegetarianism	Friendly	T, Y, A, E	T, Y, A, E	Actor knows the Target is a Vegetarian		Vegetarian, Schmoozer			
Argue	Insulting	C, T, Y, A, E	C, T, Y, A, E	Actor thinks the Target is being impolite or unforgivably rude or Sims are in Insulting STC		Hot-Headed, Mean-Spirited, Grumpy, Insane		4	
Ask About Antisocial Action	Insulting	T, Y, A, E	T, Y, A, E	Target has performed an antisocial action		Good			
Ask About Bath	Friendly	T, Y, A, E	T, Y, A, E	Actor and Target are in a committed relationship and Target has had a bath					
Ask About Day	Friendly	C, T, Y, A, E	C, T, Y, A, E	Always available		Friendly, Good, Charismatic, Schmoozer		1	1
Ask About Game	Friendly	T, Y, A, E	T, Y, A, E	Target has played a game					
Ask About Missing Work	Friendly	T, Y, A, E	T, Y, A, E	Target has the Missing Work buff		Workaholic, Neurotic			
Ask About News	Friendly	T, Y, A, E	T, Y, A, E	Target has read the newspaper		Genius			
Ask About Occupation	Friendly	T, Y, A, E	T, Y, A, E	Actor does not know the Target's career		Workaholic, Schmoozer, Ambitious			
Ask About Partner	Amorous	T, Y, A, E	T, Y, A, E	Actor does not know the Target's relationship status		Family Oriented, Flirty, Hopeless Romantic			
Ask About School	Friendly	C, T, Y, A, E	C, T, Y, A, E	Actor learns the Target goes to school		Workaholic, Family Oriented, Ambitious			
Ask About Sleep	Friendly	T, Y, A, E	T, Y, A, E	Target has slept		Heavy Sleeper, Light Sleeper			
Ask About Work	Friendly	C, T, Y, A, E	T, Y, A, E	Always available		Workaholic, Ambitious, Schmoozer			
Ask Are You OK	Friendly	T, Y, A, E	T, Y, A, E	Target has the Too Many People, Horrified, Singed, Lonely, Afraid of the Dark, or Humiliated buff		Good, Friendly	Evil, Mean-Spirited		
Ask for a Promotion	Friendly	T, Y, A, E	T, Y, A, E	Target is Actor's Boss (and it's been 3 days since the Boss was last asked)		Ambitious		1	
Ask for a Raise	Friendly	T, Y, A, E	T, Y, A, E	Target is Actor's Boss (and it's been 5 days since the Boss was last asked)		Ambitious		1	
Ask Good Book	Friendly	T, Y, A, E	T, Y, A, E	Target has read a book		Bookworm			
Ask for Campaign Donation	Friendly	Y, A, E	Y, A, E	Can ask for campaign donations		Schmoozer		1	3
Ask Service Sim to Stay Over	Friendly	C, T, Y, A, E	C, T, Y, A, E	Target is visiting the Actor at home				1	

Social	Commodity	Actor Age	Target Age	Social Available When?	Required Trait	Social Encouraged By Trait?	Social Prevented By Trait?	# of Uses Before Boring	# of Uses if Recharged
Ask Service Sim to Stay Over Romantically	Amorous	Y, A, E	Y, A, E	Target is visiting the Actor at home		Flirty		1	1
Ask to Behave	Neutral	T, Y, A, E	C, T, Y, A, E	When in the Very Friendly STC and the Sims have at least 60 LTR		Good			
Ask to Break Up With	Insulting	T, Y, A, E	T, Y, A, E	Wedding Canceled				1	1
Ask to Go Inside	Friendly	C, T, Y, A, E	C, T, Y, A, E	Actor requests Target follow them inside				1	
Ask to Hang Out	Friendly	C, T, Y, A, E	C, T, Y, A, E	Target is a Service Sim on the job				1	
Ask to Leave	Neutral	T, Y, A, E	C, T, Y, A, E	Sim asks Target to leave lot					
Ask Everyone to Leave	Neutral	C, T, Y, A, E	C, T, Y, A, E	Sim asks all Targets to leave lot		Loner			
Ask to Move In	Friendly	Y, A, E	Y, A, E	Sims are in the Very Friendly STC and are Friends or above or on the romantic relationship				1	3
Ask to Stay Over	Friendly	C, T, Y, A, E	C, T, Y, A, E	Actor is visiting the Target at home				1	
Ask to Stay Over Romantically	Amorous	Y, A, E	Y, A, E	Actor is visiting the Target at home		Flirty		1	1
Ask: Good show?	Friendly	T, Y, A, E	T, Y, A, E	Target has watched TV		Couch Potato	Technophobe		
AskAboutFish	Friendly	T, Y, A, E	T, Y, A, E	Target has fished or Actor is Insane		Angler, Loves the Outdoors, Insane			
Baby Play With	Friendly	T, Y, A, E	T, Y, A, E	Target is a baby		Family Oriented			
Baby Toddler Snuggle	Friendly	T, Y, A, E	T, Y, A, E	Target is a baby		Family Oriented			
Beg for Job Back	Friendly	T, Y, A, E	T, Y, A, E	Target is Actor's Boss and Actor quit work		Workaholic, Loser		1	1
Best Friends Forever	Friendly	T	T	Sims are teens, Best Friends, or Old Friends, and in the Very Friendly STC				1	
Birthday Congratulations	Friendly	C, T, Y, A, E	C, T, Y, A, E	It is the Target's birthday		Family Oriented, Friendly, Schmoozer			
Boast About Athleticism	Friendly	T, Y, A, E	T, Y, A, E	Actor acquired Athletic skill		Athletic, Snob		1	
Boast About Bicycle	Friendly	T, Y, A, E	T, Y, A, E	Actor is a Snob who owns a bicycle	Snob	Snob		1	
Boast About Car	Friendly	T, Y, A, E	T, Y, A, E	Actor is a Snob who owns a car	Snob	Snob		1	
Boast About Computer	Friendly	T, Y, A, E	T, Y, A, E	Actor is a Computer Whiz who improved their computer	Computer Whiz	Computer Whiz, Snob		1	
Boast About Culinary Prowess	Friendly	T, Y, A, E	T, Y, A, E	Actor acquired Cooking skill		Natural Cook, Snob		1	
Boast About Dancing	Friendly	T, Y, A, E	T, Y, A, E	Actor is dancing		Party Animal, Snob		1	
Boast About Finally Winning Something!	Friendly	T, Y, A, E	T, Y, A, E	Actor is a Loser who won	Loser	Loser		1	
Boast About Fishing Feats	Friendly	C, T, Y, A, E	C, T, Y, A, E	Actor acquired Fishing skill		Angler, Snob		1	
Boast About Gardening Glory	Friendly	T, Y, A, E	T, Y, A, E	Actor acquired Gardening skill		Green Thumb, Snob		1	
Boast About Party	Friendly	T, Y, A, E	T, Y, A, E	Actor threw a party		Party Animal, Snob		1	
Boast About Pool	Friendly	T, Y, A, E	T, Y, A, E	Actor is a Snob who has a pool	Snob	Snob		1	

Social	Commodity	Actor Age	Target Age	Social Available When?	Required Trait	Social Encouraged By Trait?	Social Prevented By Trait?	# of Uses Before Boring	# of Uses if Recharged
Boast About Reviving Plant	Friendly	T, Y, A, E	T, Y, A, E	Actor revived a plant		Green Thumb, Snob		1	
Bore to Death	Friendly	C, T, Y, A, E	C, T, Y, A, E	Actor has No Sense of Humor or Target thinks the Actor is being very boring		No Sense of Humor		1	
Brag About Being a Doctor	Friendly	Y, A, E	Y, A, E	Actor is in the Medical career		Ambitious, Snob		1	
Break Up	Insulting	T, Y, A, E	T, Y, A, E	Actor and Target are in a committed relationship but not married		Commitment Issues			
Brighten Day	Friendly	T, Y, A, E	T, Y, A, E	Actor is Good	Good	Good			
Calm Down	Friendly	C, T, Y, A, E	C, T, Y, A, E	Target has the Betrayed, Can't Stand Art, Offended, Rude Awakening, Rude Guest, or Stuff Taken buff		Good, Friendly, Charismatic	Mean-Spirited, Evil		
Cancel Wedding	Insulting	Y, A, E	Y, A, E	Available on engaged Sim		Commitment Issues			
Charming Introduction	Friendly	T, Y, A, E	T, Y, A, E	Actor has Charisma skill		Charismatic, Schmoozer			
Chat	Friendly	C, T, Y, A, E	C, T, Y, A, E	Always available		Schmoozer, Charismatic		4	6
Cheer Up	Friendly	C, T, Y, A, E	C, T, Y, A, E	Target has the Heart Broken, Mourning, or Rejected buff		Good, Friendly		3	
Complain About All the People	Friendly	T, Y, A, E	T, Y, A, E	Actor had the Too Many People buff or is a Loner	Loner	Loner, Grumpy		1	
Complain About Art	Friendly	T, Y, A, E	T, Y, A, E	Actor Can't Stand Art, knows the Target is Artistic or recently visited an Art Gallery		Can't Stand Art, Grumpy		1	
Complain About Baby	Friendly	T, Y, A, E	T, Y, A, E	Actor has the Crying Baby buff		Dislikes Children, Grumpy	Family Oriented	1	
Complain About Being a Loser	Friendly	T, Y, A, E	T, Y, A, E	Actor is a Loser who lost	Loser	Loser, Grumpy		1	
Complain About Being a Slob	Insulting	T, Y, A, E	T, Y, A, E	Actor knows the Target is a Slob		Neat, Perfectionist, Snob, Grumpy		1	
Complain About Children	Friendly	T, Y, A, E	T, Y, A, E	Actor Dislikes Children	Dislikes Children	Dislikes Children, Grumpy		1	
Complain About Darkness	Friendly	T, Y, A, E	T, Y, A, E	Actor is Scared of the Dark	Coward	Coward, Grumpy		1	
Complain About Exercise	Friendly	T, Y, A, E	T, Y, A, E	Actor recently visited the gym or is a Couch Potato and recently exercised	Couch Potato	Couch Potato, Grumpy		1	
Complain About Foolish Joke	Friendly	T, Y, A, E	T, Y, A, E	Actor has No Sense of Humor and humor was attempted	No Sense of Humor	No Sense of Humor, Grumpy		1	
Complain About Good People	Insulting	T, Y, A, E	T, Y, A, E	Actor knows the Target is Good		Evil, Mean-Spirited, Grumpy	Good	1	
Complain About Inappropriateness	Insulting	T, Y, A, E	T, Y, A, E	Actor knows the Target is Inappropriate		Good, Grumpy	Inappropriate	1	
Complain About Laziness	Insulting	T, Y, A, E	T, Y, A, E	Actor knows the Target is a Couch Potato		Athletic, Grumpy	Couch Potato	1	
Complain About Meat	Friendly	T, Y, A, E	T, Y, A, E	Actor is disgusted by meat	Vegetarian	Vegetarian, Grumpy		1	
Complain About Mess	Friendly	T, Y, A, E	T, Y, A, E	Actor is disgusted by mess	Neat	Neat, Grumpy		1	

Social	Commodity	Actor Age	Target Age	Social Available When?	Required Trait	Social Encouraged By Trait?	Social Prevented By Trait?	# of Uses Before Boring	# of Uses if Recharged
Complain About Other	Friendly	T, Y, A, E	T, Y, A, E	Actor is annoyed with a third party		Inappropriate, Mean-Spirited, Grumpy		1	
Complain About Other's Stench	Friendly	C, T, Y, A, E	C, T, Y, A, E	Target has the Stinky buff		Neat, Perfectionist, Snob, Grumpy	Slob	1	
Complain About Being Woken Up	Friendly	C, T, Y, A, E	C, T, Y, A, E	Actor was woken up		Heavy Sleeper, Light Sleeper, Grumpy		1	
Complain About Broken Bathtub	Friendly	C, T, Y, A, E	C, T, Y, A, E	Broken bathtub		Neat, Perfectionist, Grumpy		1	
Complain About Broken Toilet	Friendly	C, T, Y, A, E	C, T, Y, A, E	Broken toilet		Neat, Perfectionist, Grumpy		1	
Complain About Dirty Bathtub	Friendly	C, T, Y, A, E	C, T, Y, A, E	Dirty bathtub		Neat, Perfectionist, Snob, Grumpy		1	
Complain About Dirty Dishes	Friendly	C, T, Y, A, E	C, T, Y, A, E	Dirty dishes		Neat, Perfectionist, Snob, Grumpy		1	
Complain About Dirty Toilet	Friendly	C, T, Y, A, E	C, T, Y, A, E	Dirty toilet		Neat, Perfectionist, Snob, Grumpy		1	
Complain About Feeling Sore	Friendly	C, T, Y, A, E	C, T, Y, A, E	Actor has the Sore buff		Couch Potato, Grumpy		1	
Complain About Outdoors	Friendly	T, Y, A, E	T, Y, A, E	Actor has the Hates Outdoors trait and is outdoors	Hates the Outdoors	Hates the Outdoors, Grumpy		1	
Complain About Party	Friendly	C, T, Y, A, E	C, T, Y, A, E	Actor is preparing for or recently had a party		Loner, Grumpy	Party Animal	1	
Complain About Politicians	Insulting	T, Y, A, E	T, Y, A, E	Actor learns the Target is in the Political career		Insane, Grumpy		1	
Complain About School	Friendly	C, T, Y, A, E	C, T, Y, A, E	Actor can complain about school		Couch Potato, Party Animal, Grumpy		1	
Complain About the Police	Insulting	T, Y, A, E	T, Y, A, E	Actor learns the Target is in the Law Enforcement career		Evil, Inappropriate, Grumpy		1	
Complain About TV	Friendly	C, T, Y, A, E	C, T, Y, A, E	Actor is Technophobe and the TV is on	Technophobe	Technophobe, Grumpy		1	
Complain About TV Being Turned Off	Friendly	C, T, Y, A, E	C, T, Y, A, E	Actor is not Technophobe and the TV was turned off		Couch Potato, Grumpy	Technophobe	1	
Complain About Work	Friendly	T, Y, A, E	T, Y, A, E	Actor has the Fired or Overworked buff, just got home from work, or can complain about work		Grumpy	Workaholic	1	
Compliment	Friendly	C, T, Y, A, E	C, T, Y, A, E	Sims are in the Very Friendly STC and are below Friends		Charismatic, Schmoozer, Easily Impressed			3
Compliment Appearance	Amorous	T, Y, A, E	T, Y, A, E	Romance is available and Target's outfit changed or Sims are not in the Seductive or Hot STC		Charismatic, Schmoozer, Easily Impressed, Flirty			3
Compliment Athleticism	Amorous	T, Y, A, E	T, Y, A, E	Target did something athletic		Athletic, Schmoozer, Easily Impressed, Flirty			3
Compliment Braveness	Friendly	T, Y, A, E	T, Y, A, E	Target did something brave		Coward, Schmoozer, Easily Impressed			3

Social	Commodity	Actor Age	Target Age	Social Available When?	Required Trait	Social Encouraged By Trait?	Social Prevented By Trait?	# of Uses Before Boring	# of Uses if Recharged
Compliment Cleverness	Friendly	T, Y, A, E	T, Y, A, E	Actor knows the Target is a Genius		Genius, Schmoozer, Easily Impressed			3
Compliment Cooking	Friendly	C, T, Y, A, E	C, T, Y, A, E	Target has made food		Natural Cook, Family Oriented, Schmoozer, Easily Impressed			3
Compliment Dancing	Friendly	C, T, Y, A, E	C, T, Y, A, E	Target is dancing		Party Animal, Schmoozer, Easily Impressed			3
Compliment Garden	Friendly	T, Y, A, E	T, Y, A, E	Actor can compliment garden		Green Thumb, Schmoozer, Easily Impressed	Hates the Outdoors		3
Compliment Handiness	Friendly	T, Y, A, E	T, Y, A, E	Target has repaired something		Handy, Schmoozer, Easily Impressed			3
Compliment Home	Friendly	C, T, Y, A, E	C, T, Y, A, E	Actor is visiting the Target at home		Schmoozer, Easily Impressed			3
Compliment Music	Friendly	T, Y, A, E	T, Y, A, E	Target has performed music		Virtuoso, Schmoozer, Easily Impressed			3
Compliment Party	Friendly	C, T, Y, A, E	C, T, Y, A, E	Actor is attending or recently attended a party		Party Animal, Schmoozer, Easily Impressed			3
Compliment Personality	Amorous	T, Y, A, E	T, Y, A, E	Romance is available, Sims are not in the Seductive or Hot STC and don't dislike each other or aren't currently engaged/married		Schmoozer, Easily Impressed, Flirty			3
Confess Cheating	Neutral	T, Y, A, E	T, Y, A, E	Target has had Jealousy triggered on Actor		Good, Family Oriented			
Confess Attraction	Amorous	T, Y, A, E	T, Y, A, E	Romance is available, Sims are not in the Seductive or Hot STC and don't dislike each other or already romantic		Hopeless Romantic, Flirty		1	1
Confess Attraction for Another	Friendly	T, Y, A, E	T, Y, A, E	Actor is attracted to a third party		Hopeless Romantic			
Confess to Being Fired	Friendly	T, Y, A, E	T, Y, A, E	Actor has the Fired buff					
Console	Friendly	C, T, Y, A, E	C, T, Y, A, E	Target is having a bad day, or has the Scared, Heart Broken, Mourning, or Rejected buff		Good, Family Oriented, Friendly	Mean-Spirited		
Coo Over Children	Friendly	T, Y, A, E	C, T, Y, A, E	Actor is Family Oriented	Family Oriented	Family Oriented			
Criticize His Family	Insulting	T, Y, A, E	T, Y, A, E	Actor is Mean-Spirited or Inappropriate or is being Insulting to the Target who is in a committed relationship with them	Mean-Spirited, Inappropriate	Mean-Spirited, Inappropriate		1	
Criticize Lousy Book	Friendly	C, T, Y, A, E	C, T, Y, A, E	Sims are responding to a book		Bookworm, Perfectionist, Snob, Grumpy		1	
Cry on Shoulder	Friendly	T, Y, A, E	T, Y, A, E	Actor has the Heart Broken, Mourning, or Rejected buff		Over Emotional			
Cuddle	Amorous	T, Y, A, E	T, Y, A, E	Can try on Sim		Hopeless Romantic		1	1
Debate Politics	Friendly	T, Y, A, E	T, Y, A, E	Actor or Target is in the Political career		Schmoozer, Charismatic		3	

Social	Commodity	Actor Age	Target Age	Social Available When?	Required Trait	Social Encouraged By Trait?	Social Prevented By Trait?	# of Uses Before Boring	# of Uses if Recharged
Declare Nemesis	Steamed	T, Y, A, E	T, Y, A, E	Sims are in the Steamed STC		Evil, Mean-Spirited, Hot-Headed			
Deep Conversation	Friendly	T, Y, A, E	T, Y, A, E	Sims are in the Very Friendly STC and are Good Friends or above or in a committed relationship		Genius		3	4
Deliver Opportunity	Friendly	T, Y, A, E	T, Y, A, E	An opportunity needs to be delivered					
Determine Gender of Baby	Friendly	C, T, Y, A, E	C, T, Y, A, E	Target is pregnant					
Disapprove of Criminals	Insulting	T, Y, A, E	T, Y, A, E	Actor learns the Target is in the Criminal career		Good	Evil	1	
Discuss Favorite TV Shows	Friendly	C, T, Y, A, E	C, T, Y, A, E	TV is on		Couch Potato, Charismatic	Technophobe	3	
Discuss Fine Cuisine	Friendly	C, T, Y, A, E	C, T, Y, A, E	Respond to the Hunger buff		Natural Cook, Snob		3	
Discuss Work	Friendly	T, Y, A, E	T, Y, A, E	Actor is a Workaholic or is talking to a co-worker		Workaholic, Ambitious			
Dismiss	Neutral	T, Y, A, E	T, Y, A, E	Target is a Service Sim on the job					
Dismiss Rudely	Insulting	T, Y, A, E	T, Y, A, E	Target is a Service Sim on the job		Mean-Spirited	Good		
Divorce	Insulting	Y, A, E	Y, A, E	Actor and Target are married		Commitment Issues			
Embrace	Amorous	Y, A, E	Y, A, E	Sims are in the Hot STC or Seductive STC if the Sims are in a romantic relationship or are exes		Hopeless Romantic, Flirty		1	1
End Service	Neutral	T, Y, A, E	T, Y, A, E	Target is a Service Sim on the job and the Sims are Friends or higher		Frugal			
Enthuse About Business	Friendly	T, Y, A, E	T, Y, A, E	Actor learns the Target is in the Business career		Excitable			
Enthuse About Cooking	Friendly	T, Y, A, E	T, Y, A, E	Actor learns the Target is in the Culinary career		Natural Cook, Excitable			
Enthuse About Exercise	Friendly	T, Y, A, E	T, Y, A, E	Actor recently visited the gym or is Athletic and recently exercised or knows the Target is Athletic		Athletic, Excitable	Couch Potato		
Enthuse About Fishing	Friendly	T, Y, A, E	T, Y, A, E	Actor is an Angler or knows the Target is an Angler		Angler, Excitable			
Enthuse About Journalism	Friendly	T, Y, A, E	T, Y, A, E	Actor learns the Target is in the Journalism career		Excitable			
Enthuse About Law Enforcement	Friendly	T, Y, A, E	T, Y, A, E	Actor learns the Target is in the Law Enforcement career		Excitable			
Enthuse About Music	Friendly	T, Y, A, E	T, Y, A, E	Actor is a Virtuoso or learns the Target is in the Music career		Virtuoso, Excitable			
Enthuse About New House	Friendly	C, T, Y, A, E	C, T, Y, A, E	Actor or Target has a new house		Excitable			
Enthuse About Outdoors	Friendly	T, Y, A, E	T, Y, A, E	Actor Loves the Outdoors		Loves the Outdoors, Excitable	Hates the Outdoors		
Enthuse About Party	Friendly	T, Y, A, E	T, Y, A, E	Actor is preparing for a party		Party Animal, Excitable			
Enthuse About Politics	Friendly	T, Y, A, E	T, Y, A, E	Actor learns the Target is in the Political career		Excitable			
Enthuse About Science	Friendly	T, Y, A, E	T, Y, A, E	Actor learns the Target is in the Science career		Excitable			
Enthuse About the Military	Friendly	T, Y, A, E	T, Y, A, E	Actor learns the Target is in the Military career		Excitable			

Social	Commodity	Actor Age	Target Age	Social Available When?	Required Trait	Social Encouraged By Trait?	Social Prevented By Trait?	# of Uses Before Boring	# of Uses if Recharged
Enthuse About Wedding	Friendly	T, Y, A, E	T, Y, A, E	Actor is at their wedding party		Hopeless Romantic, Family Oriented, Excitable	Commitment Issues		
Enthuse About Work	Friendly	T, Y, A, E	T, Y, A, E	Actor has gotten home from work		Workaholic, Excitable			
Express Condolences	Friendly	C, T, Y, A, E	C, T, Y, A, E	Actor is at a Funeral		Good, Friendly			
Express Condolences to Victim	Friendly	C, T, Y, A, E	C, T, Y, A, E	Actor knows Target has been cheated on		Family Oriented, Hopeless Romantic			
Express Embarrassment	Friendly	C, T, Y, A, E	C, T, Y, A, E	Actor has the Embarrassed buff or a conversation has turned Awkward				1	
Express Fear of Graveyards	Friendly	T, Y, A, E	T, Y, A, E	Actor has the Creepy Graveyard buff		Coward, Neurotic	Brave	1	
Express Fear of Swimming	Friendly	T, Y, A, E	T, Y, A, E	Actor is Hydrophobic	Hydrophobic	Hydrophobic		1	
Express Fear of the Dark	Friendly	T, Y, A, E	T, Y, A, E	Actor has the Afraid of the Dark buff		Coward, Neurotic	Brave	1	
Express Fondness	Friendly	T, Y, A, E	T, Y, A, E	Sims are in the Very Friendly STC and are Friends or above or in a romantic relationship		Friendly			
Express Humiliation	Friendly	T, Y, A, E	T, Y, A, E	Actor has the Humiliated buff				1	
Express Need for Exercise	Friendly	T, Y, A, E	T, Y, A, E	Actor is Athletic		Athletic		1	
Express Sympathy for Victim	Neutral	C, T, Y, A, E	C, T, Y, A, E	Actor knows a third party has been cheated on		Family Oriented, Hopeless Romantic			
Family Hug	Friendly	C, T, Y, A, E	C, T, Y, A, E	Actor is Family Oriented		Family Oriented			
Feel Tummy	Friendly	C, T, Y, A, E	T, Y, A, E	Target is pregnant		Family Oriented			1
Fight!	Steamed	T, Y, A, E	T, Y, A, E	Actor has the Betrayed, Can't Stand Art, Offended, Rude Awakening, Rude Guest, or Stuff Taken buff, or Sims are in the Steamed STC		Mean-Spirited, Hot-Headed, Evil	Good		
Fire	Insulting	T, Y, A, E	T, Y, A, E	Target is a Service Sim on the job and the Sims are not Friends or higher		Mean-Spirited			
First Kiss	Amorous	T, Y, A, E	T, Y, A, E	Sims are in the Seductive or Hot context and have not kissed		Great Kisser		1	
Flatter	Friendly	C, T, Y, A, E	C, T, Y, A, E	Actor is a Schmoozer	Schmoozer	Schmoozer			3
Flirt	Amorous	T, Y, A, E	T, Y, A, E	Romance is available		Flirty, Hopeless Romantic	Unflirty		3
Flirty Joke	Amorous	T, Y, A, E	T, Y, A, E	Romance is available but not too hot		Good Sense of Humor, Flirty	Unflirty		3
Fret Over Commitment	Friendly	Y, A, E	Y, A, E	Actor has made a commitment	Commitment Issues	Commitment Issues			
Friendly Hug	Friendly	C, T, Y, A, E	C, T, Y, A, E	Sims are Friends or above		Friendly			
Gaze Into Eyes	Amorous	T, Y, A, E	T, Y, A, E	Sims are in the Seductive STC and Actor is a Hopeless Romantic	Hopeless Romantic	Hopeless Romantic			
Get Married	Amorous	Y, A, E	Y, A, E	Actor is at their wedding party		Hopeless Romantic, Family Oriented		1	3

Social	Commodity	Actor Age	Target Age	Social Available When?	Required Trait	Social Encouraged By Trait?	Social Prevented By Trait?	# of Uses Before Boring	# of Uses if Recharged
Give Inspirational Speech	Friendly	T, Y, A, E	T, Y, A, E	Actor can give an inspirational speech		Charismatic			
Give Medical Advice	Friendly	Y, A, E	Y, A, E	Target is pregnant		Genius			
Goodbye	Neutral	C, T, Y, A, E	C, T, Y, A, E	Always available to end conversation					
Goodbye Hug	Friendly	C, T, Y, A, E	C, T, Y, A, E	End conversation with friendly commodity					
Goodbye Kiss	Amorous	T, Y, A, E	T, Y, A, E	End conversation with amorous commodity					
Goodbye Rude	Insulting	C, T, Y, A, E	C, T, Y, A, E	End conversation with insulting commodity		Mean-Spirited	Good		
Goof Around	Funny	C, T, Y, A, E	C, T, Y, A, E	Sims are in the Funny or Hilarious STC		Childish, Good Sense of Humor	No Sense of Humor		
Gossip	Friendly	C, T, Y, A, E	C, T, Y, A, E	Always available		Snob			
Gossip About Other	Friendly	T, Y, A, E	T, Y, A, E	Actor can talk about third party		Mean-Spirited, Snob			
Greet	Friendly	C, T, Y, A, E	C, T, Y, A, E	Always available		Friendly			
Greet Amusing	Funny	T, Y, A, E	T, Y, A, E	Actor has Charisma Level 2–5		Good Sense of Humor, Charismatic			
Greet Flirty	Amorous	T, Y, A, E	T, Y, A, E	Actor has Charisma Level 4–7		Flirty, Charismatic			
Greet Friendly	Friendly	C, T, Y, A, E	C, T, Y, A, E	Always available		Friendly, Charismatic			
Greet Funny	Funny	T, Y, A, E	T, Y, A, E	Actor has Charisma Level 6–7		Good Sense of Humor, Charismatic			
Greet Hilarious	Funny	T, Y, A, E	T, Y, A, E	Actor has Charisma Level 8–10		Good Sense of Humor, Charismatic			
Greet Hot	Amorous	Y, A, E	Y, A, E	Actor has Charisma Level 10		Flirty, Charismatic			
Greet Insulting	Insulting	C, T, Y, A, E	C, T, Y, A, E	Start conversation with insulting commodity		Mean-Spirited	Good		
Greet Seductive	Amorous	Y, A, E	Y, A, E	Actor has Charisma Level 8–9		Flirty, Charismatic			
Guitar Serenade	Amorous	T, Y, A, E	T, Y, A, E	Actor has guitar skill		Charismatic, Flirty		1	1
Have Private Wedding	Amorous	Y, A, E	Y, A, E	Sims are engaged		Family Oriented, Hopeless Romantic		1	1
Hello Rude	Insulting	C, T, Y, A, E	C, T, Y, A, E	Start conversation with insulting commodity		Mean-Spirited	Good		
Hold Hands	Amorous	T, Y, A, E	T, Y, A, E	Romance is available but not too hot		Hopeless Romantic			
Impersonate Celebrity	Funny	C, T, Y, A, E	C, T, Y, A, E	Sims are in the Hilarious STC		Snob, Good Sense of Humor	No Sense of Humor		
Imply Mother is a Llama	Insulting	T, Y, A	T, Y, A, E	Actor is being insulting or unforgivably rude		Inappropriate, Mean-Spirited, Hot-Headed	Good	1	
I Named A Star After You	Friendly	C, T, Y, A, E	C, T, Y, A, E	Actor named a star after Target					
Insult	Insulting	Y, A, E	T, Y, A, E	Wedding Canceled, Target is being creepy or frightening, or Actor is not being insulting or unforgivably rude		Mean-Spirited	Good		
Insult Bookworms	Insulting	T, Y, A, E	T, Y, A, E	Actor knows Target is a Bookworm		Mean-Spirited	Good		
Insult Home	Insulting	T, Y, A, E	T, Y, A, E	Actor is visiting the Target at home		Mean-Spirited, Inappropriate	Good		
Interview	Friendly	T, Y, A, E	T, Y, A, E	Actor is in the Journalism career					

Social	Commodity	Actor Age	Target Age	Social Available When?	Required Trait	Social Encouraged By Trait?	Social Prevented By Trait?	# of Uses Before Boring	# of Uses if Recharged
Invite In	Friendly	C, T, Y, A, E	C, T, Y, A, E	Actor has Sims on front lawn of lot					
Invite Everyone In	Friendly	C, T, Y, A, E	C, T, Y, A, E	Actor has Sims on front lawn of lot					
Invite Over	Friendly	C, T, Y, A, E	C, T, Y, A, E	Actor is not on their home lot				1	
Joke About Children	Funny	T, Y, A, E	T, Y, A, E	Target is the Baby-sitter		Dislikes Children			
Joke About Cooking	Funny	T, Y, A, E	T, Y, A, E	Actor learns the Target is in the Culinary career		Natural Cook, Good Sense of Humor			
Joke About Criminals	Funny	T, Y, A, E	T, Y, A, E	Actor learns the Target is in the Criminal career		Inappropriate, Evil, Good Sense of Humor			
Joke About In-Laws	Funny	Y, A, E	Y, A, E	Sims are engaged or married and are in the Hilarious STC		Good Sense of Humor			
Joke About Old Times	Funny	Y, A, E	Y, A, E	Sims are engaged, married or Good Friends or higher and are in the Hilarious STC		Good Sense of Humor			3
Joke About the Police	Funny	T, Y, A, E	T, Y, A, E	Actor learns the Target is in the Law Enforcement career		Inappropriate, Evil, Good Sense of Humor			
Joke About Work	Funny	T, Y, A, E	T, Y, A, E	Actor is talking to a co-worker		Good Sense of Humor			
Joke That He Can't Cook	Funny	T, Y, A, E	T, Y, A, E	Target has made food		Mean-Spirited, Good Sense of Humor			
Kiss	Amorous	T, Y, A, E	T, Y, A, E	Actor is Inappropriate or Sims have kissed		Inappropriate, Great Kisser		1	
Kiss on Cheek	Amorous	T, Y, A, E	T, Y, A, E	Sims have kissed and STC is not too hot		Hopeless Romantic		1	3
Leap Into Arms	Amorous	Y, A, E	Y, A, E	Sims are in the Hot STC		Hopeless Romantic, Flirty		1	1
Lecture Teen	Steamed	Y, A, E	T, Y, A, E	Target is a teen caught after curfew		Family Oriented			
Let's Just Be Friends	Insulting	T, Y, A, E	T, Y, A, E	Sims are Romantic Interests, Exes, or Ex Spouses					
Listen to Tummy	Friendly	T, Y, A, E	T, Y, A, E	Target is pregnant		Family Oriented			1
Make Fun Of	Insulting	T, Y, A, E	T, Y, A, E	Actor is Inappropriate	Inappropriate	Inappropriate			
Make Out	Amorous	T, Y, A, E	T, Y, A, E	Sims are in the Hot STC or Seductive STC if the Sims are in a committed relationship		Great Kisser		1	1
Make Silly Face	Funny	C, T, Y, A, E	C, T, Y, A, E	Always available		Childish, Good Sense of Humor	No Sense of Humor		
Massage	Amorous	T, Y, A, E	T, Y, A, E	Actor is responding to the Sore buff or Sims are in the Seductive STC		Flirty		1	1
Mastermind Plot	Friendly	C, T, Y, A, E	C, T, Y, A, E	Actor is Evil	Evil	Evil			
Mock	Insulting	C, T, Y, A, E	C, T, Y, A, E	Target is being odd		Mean-Spirited	Good	1	
Mock Ambition	Insulting	T, Y, A, E	T, Y, A, E	Actor knows the Target is Ambitious		Mean-Spirited	Ambitious, Good	1	
Mock Appearance	Insulting	T, Y, A, E	T, Y, A, E	Target's outfit changed		Inappropriate, Mean-Spirited	Good	1	
Mock Cleverness	Insulting	T, Y, A, E	T, Y, A, E	Actor knows the Target is a Genius		Mean-Spirited	Genius, Good	1	

Social	Commodity	Actor Age	Target Age	Social Available When?	Required Trait	Social Encouraged By Trait?	Social Prevented By Trait?	# of Uses Before Boring	# of Uses if Recharged
Mock Dancing	Insulting	T, Y, A, E	T, Y, A, E	Target is dancing		Inappropriate, Mean-Spirited	Good	1	
Mock Grumpiness	Insulting	T, Y, A, E	T, Y, A, E	Actor knows the Target is Grumpy		Mean-Spirited	Grumpy, Good	1	
Mock Hydrophobia	Insulting	T, Y, A, E	T, Y, A, E	Actor knows the Target is Hydrophobic		Inappropriate, Mean-Spirited	Hydrophobic, Good	1	
Mock Misfortune	Insulting	T, Y, A, E	T, Y, A, E	Actor is responding to misfortune		Evil, Inappropriate, Mean-Spirited	Good	1	
Mock Musicians	Insulting	T, Y, A, E	T, Y, A, E	Actor learns the Target is in the Music career		Mean-Spirited	Virtuoso, Good	1	
Mock Party	Insulting	T, Y, A, E	T, Y, A, E	Actor is attending or recently attended a party		Inappropriate, Mean-Spirited	Good	1	
Mock Scientific Pretension	Insulting	T, Y, A, E	T, Y, A, E	Actor learns the Target is in the Science career		Mean-Spirited	Genius, Good	1	
Mock Snobbishness	Insulting	T, Y, A, E	T, Y, A, E	Actor knows the Target is a Snob		Mean-Spirited	Snob, Good	1	
Mock Vegetarianism	Insulting	T, Y, A, E	T, Y, A, E	Actor knows the Target is a Vegetarian		Inappropriate, Mean-Spirited	Vegetarian, Good	1	
Mooch Food	Friendly	C, T, Y, A, E	C, T, Y, A, E	Actor is a Mooch	Mooch	Mooch		1	
Mooch Money (Small)	Friendly	C, T, Y, A, E	C, T, Y, A, E	Actor is a Mooch	Mooch	Mooch		1	
Mooch Money (Large)	Friendly	C, T, Y, A, E	C, T, Y, A, E	Actor is a Mooch	Mooch	Mooch		1	
Patronize	Insulting	T, Y, A, E	C	Target is a Child and Sims are not in the Unforgivably Rude STC		Dislikes Children, Mean-Spirited	Good		
Persuade to Change Body Shape	Friendly	C, T, Y, A, E	C, T, Y, A, E	Actor suggests to Target to get healthier				1	
Petty Jab	Insulting	T, Y, A, E	T, Y, A, E	Sims are in the Insulting or Unforgivably Rude STC		Mean-Spirited	Good	1	
Pick Up Line	Amorous	T, Y, A, E	T, Y, A, E	Sims are Acquaintances and not in the Seductive or Hot STC		Charismatic, Flirty	Unflirty	1	3
Play Catch	Friendly	C, T, Y, A, E	C, T, Y, A, E	Actor is Childish		Athletic, Loves the Outdoors, Childish			
Play Tag	Friendly	C, T, Y, A, E	C, T, Y, A, E	Actor is Childish or Play topic is active		Loves the Outdoors, Childish			
Policeman Talk to Sim	Neutral	Y, A, E	Y, A, E	Actor is a Policeman who needs to talk to the Target					
Policeman Lecture Sim	Insulting	Y, A, E	Y, A, E	Actor is a Policeman who needs to lecture to the Target					
Policeman Express Disappointment	Neutral	Y, A, E	Y, A, E	Actor is a Policeman who needs to express disappointment to the Target					
Policeman Arrest Burglar	Insulting	Y, A, E	Y, A, E	Actor is a Policeman who needs to arrest the Target burglar					
Point Out Flaws	Insulting	T, Y, A, E	T, Y, A, E	Actor is being insulting or unforgivably rude		Perfectionist, Inappropriate, Mean-Spirited	Good	1	
Praise	Friendly	C, T, Y, A, E	C, T, Y, A, E	Target is praiseworthy or Actor is a Schmoozer		Schmoozer, Family Oriented			3
Praise Fantastic Book	Friendly	C, T, Y, A, E	C, T, Y, A, E	Sims are responding to a book		Bookworm, Artistic, Easily Impressed			

Social	Commodity	Actor Age	Target Age	Social Available When?	Required Trait	Social Encouraged By Trait?	Social Prevented By Trait?	# of Uses Before Boring	# of Uses if Recharged
Praise Written Book	Friendly	T, Y, A, E	C, T, Y, A, E	Target has written a book		Bookworm, Artistic, Easily Impressed			
Propose Going Steady	Amorous	T, Y, A, E	T, Y, A, E	Sims are Romantic Interests and in the Hot STC		Hopeless Romantic		1	1
Propose Marriage	Amorous	Y, A, E	Y, A, E	Actor is Inappropriate or Insane or Sims are Partners and in the Hot STC		Inappropriate, Family Oriented, Hopeless Romantic		1	1
Propose Truce	Neutral	T, Y, A, E	T, Y, A, E	Sims are Enemies or Old Enemies and are in the Friendly or Very Friendly STC		Good, Friendly			
Question	Friendly	T, Y, A, E	T, Y, A, E	Actor is in the Law Enforcement career					
Quit Job	Neutral	T, Y, A, E	T, Y, A, E	Target is Actor's Boss		Commitment Issues			
Ramble Aimlessly	Friendly	C, T, Y, A, E	C, T, Y, A, E	Actor is being boring		No Sense of Humor		1	
Refuse Entrance	Insulting	Y, A, E	T, Y, A, E	Actor wants to deny entry to Sims		Mean-Spirited	Good		
Regret Commitment	Friendly	T, Y, A, E	T, Y, A, E	Actor needs to turn down invitation		Commitment Issues		1	
Reminisce	Friendly	Y, A, E	Y, A, E	Sims are BFFs, Old Friends, or Spouses and are in the Friendly or Very Friendly STC					
Request Ask for Food	Neutral	C, T, Y, A, E	C, T, Y, A, E	Actor has the Hunger buff or is pregnant					
Request Clean Up	Neutral	C, T, Y, A, E	C, T, Y, A, E	Dirty bathtub, dishes, or toilet		Neat			
Request Do Your Homework	Neutral	C, T, Y, A, E	C, T, Y, A, E	Adult to child		Family Oriented			
Request Feel My Tummy	Friendly	Y, A, E	C, T, Y, A, E	Actor is pregnant		Family Oriented		1	3
Request Go to Bed	Neutral	C, T, Y, A, E	C, T, Y, A, E	Target has the Tired buff		Family Oriented			
Request Go to School	Neutral	C, T, Y, A, E	C, T, Y, A, E	Adult to child		Family Oriented			
Request Practice Your Skills	Neutral	C, T, Y, A, E	C, T, Y, A, E	Adult to child		Family Oriented			
Request Take Out the Trash	Neutral	C, T, Y, A, E	C, T, Y, A, E	Available on Sim when trash is full		Neat			
Return Stolen Object	Friendly	C, T, Y, A, E	C, T, Y, A, E	Available on Sim you stole object from	Kleptomaniac	Good			
Reveal Secret	Friendly	C, T, Y, A, E	C, T, Y, A, E	Sims are Best Friends or BFFs and are in the Friendly or Very Friendly STC					4
Salute	Friendly	C, T, Y, A, E	C, T, Y, A, E	Greeting for military career					
Say Good Job	Friendly	T, Y, A, E	T, Y, A, E	Target has done homework		Family Oriented, Genius			
Say You Look Scared	Friendly	T, Y, A, E	T, Y, A, E	Target has the Creepy Graveyard buff		Good, Friendly			
Say You Look Upset	Friendly	T, Y, A, E	T, Y, A, E	Target has the Upset buff		Good, Friendly			
Set Burglar Free	Friendly	Y, A, E	Y, A, E	Target is a burglar		Evil			
Share Interests	Friendly	C, T, Y, A, E	C, T, Y, A, E	Sims are Acquaintances		Charismatic, Friendly			6
Share Trivia	Friendly	C, T, Y, A, E	C, T, Y, A, E	Actor has No Sense of Humor	No Sense of Humor	No Sense of Humor		3	3
Share Worries	Friendly	T, Y, A, E	T, Y, A, E	Actor is Neurotic		Neurotic		1	
Shoo	Neutral	C, T, Y, A, E	C, T, Y, A, E	Actor needs to send Sims home					
Sign Autograph	Friendly	C, T, Y, A, E	C, T, Y, A, E	Special interaction from autograph section					

Social	Commodity	Actor Age	Target Age	Social Available When?	Required Trait	Social Encouraged By Trait?	Social Prevented By Trait?	# of Uses Before Boring	# of Uses if Recharged
Slap	Steamed	T, Y, A, E	T, Y, A, E	Actor has had Jealousy triggered on Target or Sims are in the Steamed STC		Mean-Spirited, Hot-Headed, Evil	Good		
Smooth Recovery	Neutral	T, Y, A, E	T, Y, A, E	Actor has level 5 Charisma		Charismatic, Schmoozer			
Social Worker Yell At	Insulting	T, Y, A, E	T, Y, A, E	Actor wants to be angry with Social Worker Service Sim					
Speak Highly of Other	Friendly	C, T, Y, A, E	C, T, Y, A, E	Actor is at a Funeral		Good, Friendly			
Speak Madness	Friendly	T, Y, A, E	T, Y, A, E	Actor is Insane or is being creepy or frightening		Insane		1	1
Speak Poorly of Other	Friendly	C, T, Y, A, E	C, T, Y, A, E	Actor is at a Funeral or has had Jealousy triggered on a third party		Mean-Spirited, Inappropriate	Good	1	
Stroke Cheek	Amorous	T, Y, A, E	T, Y, A, E	Sims are in the Hot STC or Seductive STC if the Sims are in a romantic relationship or are exes		Hopeless Romantic		1	
Talk About Burglary	Friendly	T, Y, A, E	T, Y, A, E	Actor can talk about burglary					3
Talk About Fire	Friendly	C, T, Y, A, E	C, T, Y, A, E	Actor can talk about fire					3
Talk About Medicine	Friendly	T, Y, A, E	T, Y, A, E	Actor learns the Target is in the Medical career					3
Talk About Art	Friendly	T, Y, A, E	T, Y, A, E	Actor is Artistic, knows the Target is Artistic or recently visited an art gallery		Artistic			3
Talk About Books	Friendly	T, Y, A, E	T, Y, A, E	Actor is a Bookworm, knows the Target is a Bookworm or is visiting the library		Bookworm			3
Talk About Celestial Object	Friendly	C, T, Y, A, E	C, T, Y, A, E	Actor has Logic skill					3
Talk About Computers	Friendly	T, Y, A, E	T, Y, A, E	Actor is a Computer Whiz, knows the Target is a Computer Whiz or recently used a computer		Computer Whiz			3
Talk About Conspiracies	Friendly	T, Y, A, E	T, Y, A, E	Actor is Neurotic or Insane		Insane, Neurotic			3
Talk About Cooking	Friendly	T, Y, A, E	T, Y, A, E	Actor or Target has cooked		Natural Cook			3
Talk About Family	Friendly	C, T, Y, A, E	C, T, Y, A, E	Actor is Family Oriented		Family Oriented			3
Talk About Gardening	Friendly	T, Y, A, E	T, Y, A, E	Actor is a Green Thumb, knows the Target is a Green Thumb or acquired Gardening skill		Green Thumb			3
Talk About Great Outdoors	Friendly	C, T, Y, A, E	C, T, Y, A, E	Actor is visiting park, graveyard, or pool, or responding to a park visit		Loves the Outdoors	Hates the Outdoors		3
Talk About Movies	Friendly	C, T, Y, A, E	C, T, Y, A, E	TV is on or Actor is visiting the theatre		Couch Potato			3
Talk About My Possessions	Friendly	T, Y, A, E	T, Y, A, E	Actor is a Snob	Snob	Snob			3
Talk About New Job	Friendly	T, Y, A, E	T, Y, A, E	Actor has a new job		Workaholic, Ambitious			3
Talk About Self	Friendly	T, Y, A, E	T, Y, A, E	Actor is a Snob	Snob	Snob			3
Talk About Sim in Room	Insulting	T, Y, A, E	T, Y, A, E	Actor is Inappropriate	Inappropriate	Inappropriate			
Talk About the Bookstore	Friendly	T, Y, A, E	T, Y, A, E	Actor is visiting a bookstore or responding to a book		Bookworm			3
Talk About Weather	Friendly	T, Y, A, E	T, Y, A, E	Actor is outdoors		Loves the Outdoors			3
Talk to Tummy	Friendly	T, Y, A, E	T, Y, A, E	Target is pregnant		Family Oriented			1

Social	Commodity	Actor Age	Target Age	Social Available When?	Required Trait	Social Encouraged By Trait?	Social Prevented By Trait?	# of Uses Before Boring	# of Uses if Recharged
Tell Dirty Joke	Funny	T, Y, A, E	T, Y, A, E	Sims are in the Hilarious STC and are Friends or above or in a romantic relationship		Inappropriate, Flirty, Good Sense of Humor			
Tell Dramatic Story	Friendly	T, Y, A, E	T, Y, A, E	Sims are in the Very Friendly STC or Friendly STC, if Friends or above or in a romantic relationship		Charismatic, Schmoozer			
Tell Funny Story	Funny	C, T, Y, A, E	C, T, Y, A, E	STC is not too funny		Charismatic, Good Sense of Humor			
Tell Ghost Story	Friendly	C, T, Y, A, E	C, T, Y, A, E	Actor is Insane, can tell a ghost story, or is visiting a graveyard		Insane, Childish			
Tell Inside Joke	Funny	C, T, Y, A, E	C, T, Y, A, E	Sims are Good Friends or better		Good Sense of Humor		3	3
Tell Intriguing News Story	Friendly	T, Y, A, E	T, Y, A, E	Actor is in the Journalism career					
Tell Joke	Funny	C, T, Y, A, E	C, T, Y, A, E	Sims are in Dull, Drab, Funny or Hilarious STC		Charismatic, Good Sense of Humor		4	6
Tell Story	Friendly	C, T, Y, A, E	C, T, Y, A, E	Before Tell Dramatic Story, but not until Friendly if Acquaintances		Charismatic			
Teen Insult	Insulting	T	T, Y, A, E	Always for teen		Mean-Spirited	Good		
Thank	Friendly	C, T, Y, A, E	C, T, Y, A, E	General thank		Good			1
Thank for Cleaning	Friendly	C, T, Y, A, E	C, T, Y, A, E	Thank for cleaning		Good, Neat			1
Thank for Cooking	Friendly	C, T, Y, A, E	T, Y, A, E	Thank for cooking		Good, Natural Cook			1
Thank for Promotion	Friendly	C, T, Y, A, E	T, Y, A, E	Thank for promotion		Good, Snob, Workaholic			1
Thank for Tutoring	Friendly	C, T, Y, A, E	C, T, Y, A, E	Thank for tutoring		Good, Genius, Workaholic			1
Toddler Chat	Friendly	T, Y, A, E	T, Y, A, E	Target is a toddler		Family Oriented			
Toddler Tickle	Friendly	T, Y, A, E	T, Y, A, E	Target is a toddler		Family Oriented			
Toddler Toss In Air	Friendly	T, Y, A, E	T, Y, A, E	Target is a toddler		Family Oriented			
Trade Kitchen Secrets	Friendly	T, Y, A, E	T, Y, A, E	Actor or Target has cooked, Actor has available recipes to learn and Target has Cooking skill (and it's been 1 day since the Target was last asked)		Natural Cook		1	3
Train Sim	Friendly	T, Y, A, E	T, Y, A, E	Train Sim		Athletic			
Try for Baby	Amorous	Y, A, E	Y, A, E	Sims are romantic and are in the Hot STC		Family Oriented			
Tutor Sim	Friendly	T, Y, A, E	C, T	Actor has Logic skill		Family Oriented		1	0
Tutor Sim in Skill	Friendly	C, T, Y, A, E	C, T, Y, A, E	Actor wants to teach Target skill					
Wedding Congratulations	Friendly	C, T, Y, A, E	C, T, Y, A, E	Target had a wedding		Family Oriented, Friendly, Schmoozer			
Watch This	Friendly	T, Y, A, E	T, Y, A, E	Actor is a Daredevil	Daredevil	Daredevil			
Whine About Broken Computer	Friendly	T, Y, A, E	T, Y, A, E	Computer is broken		Computer Whiz	Technophobe	3	3
Whine About Broken TV	Friendly	T, Y, A, E	T, Y, A, E	TV is broken		Couch Potato	Technophobe	1	
Whine About Plant Dying	Friendly	T, Y, A, E	T, Y, A, E	Plant died		Green Thumb		1	

Social	Commodity	Actor Age	Target Age	Social Available When?	Required Trait	Social Encouraged By Trait?	Social Prevented By Trait?	# of Uses Before Boring	# of Uses if Recharged
Whine About Swimming	Friendly	T, Y, A, E	T, Y, A, E	Actor is Hydrophobic or a Couch Potato and has just been swimming	Hydrophobic, Couch Potato	Hydrophobic, Couch Potato		1	
Whisper in Ear	Amorous	Y, A, E	Y, A, E	Sims are in the Hot STC		Flirty, Hopeless Romantic		1	
Wooo!	Friendly	T, Y, A, E	T, Y, A, E	Party happening	Party Animal	Party Animal		1	3
WooHoo	Amorous	Y, A, E	Y, A, E	Sims are romantic and are in the Hot STC					
Worry About Grades	Friendly	T, Y, A, E	T, Y, A, E	Can worry about grades		Workaholic, Neurotic		1	1
Worry About Money	Friendly	T, Y, A, E	T, Y, A, E	Can worry about money		Frugal, Neurotic		1	
Worry About Relationship	Friendly	T, Y, A, E	T, Y, A, E	Can worry about relationship		Hopeless Romantic, Neurotic		1	
Worry About Work	Friendly	T, Y, A, E	T, Y, A, E	Can complain about work		Workaholic, Neurotic		1	
Worship	Friendly	C, T, Y, A, E	C, T, Y, A, E	Target is in the Music or Athletic career		Easily Impressed		1	
Yell At	Steamed	T, Y, A, E	T, Y, A, E	Actor has the Betrayed, Can't Stand Art, Offended, Rude Awakening, Rude Guest, or Stuff Taken buff, or Sims are in the Steamed STC		Mean-Spirited, Hot-Headed	Good	5	